AMERICAN REDEMPTION EXTENDED EDITION

A GOVERNMENT OF THE PEOPLE, BY THE PEOPLE, FOR THE PEOPLE NOW WITH READER'S GUIDES

AMERICAN RENEWAL
BOOK 3

JIM VINCENT

American Redemption: A Government of the People, by the People, for the People

© 2025 Jim Vincent

All rights reserved.

No part of this publication may be reproduced, stored in a retrieval system, or transmitted in any form or by any means—electronic, mechanical, photocopy, recording, or otherwise—without the prior written permission of the publisher, except for brief quotations used in reviews, articles, or scholarly analysis.

This is a work of nonfiction. Every effort has been made to ensure accuracy. Any errors are the responsibility of the author. The author is not a lawyer, and nothing in this book should be construed as legal advice. Opinions expressed are the author's own and do not represent any organization or institution.

Cover design by Jim Vincent.

Published by Vincent Press

Printed in the United States and other countries through authorized print-on-demand services.

First Edition VP 1.0 2025

ISBN 978-1-7641693-4-9 (Paperback)

ISBN 978-1-7641693-9-4 (eBook)

For more information, visit https://jimvincent.us

"Democracy is not just the right to vote. It is the right to live in dignity."
  — Naomi Klein

CONTENTS

Preface ix
Preface to the Extended Edition xi
Introduction xiii

Prologue 1
1. The Conditions for Redemption 3
2. Part I: A Nation That Cares For Its Own 7
3. Universal Health Care — Public Good, Not Private Gain 13
4. The Health of a Nation 23
5. Shelter and the Soul of a Democracy 39
6. A Home for All 47
7. The Floor Beneath Every Life 55
8. The Floor We Build Together 65
9. Security in the Long Run — Rebuilding Retirement for All 77
10. The Architecture of Care 87
11. Fair Taxation and Wealth Reform 93
12. Restore the Power to Tax 103
13. The Nation That Lasts 109
14. Part II. A Nation That Educates and Elevates 113
15. The Collapse of Public Education 119
16. The Restoration of Public Education 127
17. The System That Took Their Future 135
18. Dignity Without Debt 141
19. The Collapse of Worker Power 147
20. Full Employment and National Contribution 153
21. What We Choose to Build Together 159
22. Part III. A Nation That Is Safe, Just, and Free 163
23. To Serve and Protect 169
24. Justice That Heals 175
25. The Weaponization of a Nation 181
26. A Future Without Fear 187

27. Cybersecurity and Infrastructure Protection	193
28. The Cybersecurity Redemption Plan	199
29. Defending Democracy from Foreign Interference	205
30. The Defense We Still Need	211
31. The Collapse of Criminal Justice	219
32. A Justice That Holds	225
33. Part IV. A Nation That Belongs to Everyone	231
34. Immigration and Citizenship: The Collapse of a Just System	237
35. Immigration and Citizenship: The Restoration Agenda	243
36. The Collapse of Online Safety and Trust	249
37. The Restoration of Online Safety and Trust	255
38. Environmental Injustice and a Broken Climate Policy	261
39. A Nation That Belongs to Everyone	267
40. The Belonging We Build	273
41. Part V: A Nation That Prepares for the Future	279
42. Digital Maturity and Democratic Survival	285
43. Taking Back the Future	289
44. Public Service and Civic Reengagement	295
45. The Future We Choose	301
46. American Redemption	305
47. American Reinstitution	311
How to Use the Reader's Guides	321
Reader's Guide: Part I. A Nation That Cares For Its Own	323
Reader's Guide: Part II. A Nation That Educates and Elevates	381
Reader's Guide: Part III. A Nation That Is Safe, Just, and Free	415
Reader's Guide: Part IV. Reader's Guide: A Nation That Belongs to Everyone	465
Reader's Guide: Part V. A Nation That Prepares for the Future	501
Reader's Guide: American Redemption	531
Reader's Guide: American Reinstitution	537
Afterword: The Redemption Architecture	543

Epilogue: The Circle We Complete	547
Appendix A: American Redemption – Fixing What No Longer Works	549
Also by Jim Vincent	555
About the Author	557
Colophon	559

PREFACE

"We are not what we were. We are what we choose to become."
— adapted from Octavia Butler

This book is called *American Redemption*. But it is not about salvation. It is not religious. It does not promise deliverance, and it does not rest its hope in a redeemer. Redemption here means something different—something democratic. It means to recover what was lost. To restore the worth of what was broken. To fulfill the promises of a republic that was never perfect, but not yet finished. This is not a return to the past. It is a reckoning with what the past failed to do—and what only we can do now.

From the beginning, this project has followed five phases. *American Renewal* named the crisis: a democracy hijacked by minority rule and an economy captured by oligarchs. *American Restoration* laid out the structural reforms needed to rebuild the constitutional and institutional foundations of self-government. This volume turns to the promises. Not what must be defended. Not what must be rebuilt. But what must be made real—at last.

Redemption, in this context, means to keep faith with the people who were told they belonged to a democracy, but were never truly included in it. It means to turn the power of government toward care, dignity, safety, and trust. It means to stop asking whether a country this divided can survive—and start asking whether it deserves to. Because survival is not enough. A democracy must do more than persist. It must deliver.

These reforms are not symbolic. They are specific. Health care. Housing. Food. Child care. Climate action. Retirement security. Digital protection. Fair taxation. Immigration with dignity. A nation that cares for its people and makes room for all. These are not partisan preferences. They are democratic obligations. And they are what this final volume sets out to define.

The title of this book is not a metaphor. It is a demand. Not for comfort or nostalgia—but for moral clarity and constitutional courage. Redemption is not a passive process. It requires design. It requires power. And above all, it requires choice.

We cannot rebuild everything. But we can build what matters. We can decide what this country becomes—not just through elections, but through the structure and outcomes of public life. That is the purpose of this book. Not to predict the future. But to shape it.

Redemption is not a passive process. It requires design. It requires power. And above all, it requires choice.

The future will not arrive on its own. It must be made—by us.

PREFACE TO THE EXTENDED EDITION

———✦———

This Expanded Edition was created for readers who don't just want to understand what must change—but who want to lead that change.

The core text of *American Redemption* remains unchanged: a blueprint for what a functioning democracy must deliver in order to last. Health care. Housing. Food. Work with dignity. Safety in the digital and physical world. Climate action. Public trust. A republic that keeps its word. These are not future luxuries. They are democratic necessities.

But what we've added here is more than volume. It is support. For every chapter, you'll find a Reader's Guide—written not to summarize, but to extend. Each guide asks what the chapter demands of us as individuals, as citizens, and as a democratic movement. These are not academic questions. They are practical tools for classroom dialogue, community workshops, civic groups, and every reader who wants to connect personal action to public purpose.

We know these reforms will be resisted. We know the habits of obstruction run deep. That is why this edition goes further: not just naming what must be built, but helping readers equip themselves to build it.

This is the third volume in the American Renewal series—but it is also the first built not just for reading, but for organizing. It belongs to those who are ready to turn democratic power into democratic results.

The chapters that follow lay out what must be done. The Reader's Guides are here to help you do it.

INTRODUCTION
A GOVERNMENT THAT SERVES THE PEOPLE—
AND LASTS

American Redemption: A Government of the People, by the People, for the People

On May 25, 1961, President John F. Kennedy stood before Congress and committed the United States to do what no nation had done: send a man to the moon and return him safely to Earth before the decade was out. He had no plan. He had no blueprint. He had no working rocket, no navigational system, no tested reentry shield, no engine that could fire on the lunar surface and lift off again. The scientists and engineers did not need to tell him it was impossible. They were already saying it publicly—citing gravity, fuel mass, computing limitations, and the overwhelming number of unproven systems needed to succeed.

Kennedy didn't argue with them. He reframed the entire proposition. "We choose to go to the moon," he later declared, "not because it is easy, but because it is hard." He understood that the impossible was not a verdict—it was a challenge. Problems without solutions were simply problems not yet solved. The moonshot was not a boast. It was a bet on the future: that human ingenuity, given purpose, could overcome what fear and doubt had written off.

This book is a moonshot. Not for space, but for democracy. Not to plant a flag on distant rock, but to build a nation that fulfills the promises it has already made. Not to prove our strength, but to prove we still deserve to lead ourselves. *American Redemption* is not a wish list. It is a blueprint for a country that keeps faith with its own people. A country that guarantees care, dignity, education, safety, and belonging—not as charity, but as civic birthright. Every one of these reforms will be called unrealistic. Too ambitious. Too expensive. Too disruptive. But so was the idea of walking on the moon.

We are not naïve. We know these reforms cannot be achieved by legislation alone. They require systems we have not yet built, alliances we have not yet forged, and moral clarity we have not practiced in generations. There is no guaranteed path from here to there. But there is a direction. There is a promise. And there is a choice to be made—now, while we still can—about what kind of nation we intend to become.

The United States is not failing because it is incapable. It is failing because it no longer chooses to aim high. The market is efficient. The courts are captured. The rich are safe. But democracy was never meant to serve the strong alone. It was built on the premise that ordinary people, given real freedom and the means to exercise it, could govern themselves. That idea has been ridiculed, weakened, hollowed out by cynicism and sabotage. Yet it remains the most powerful organizing principle in the history of self-government.

American Redemption is the third and final volume in this series. It is not a map of what was lost, but a vision of what could still be made real. Volume I—*American Renewal*—defined the problem: a broken democracy and a captured economy. Volume II—*American Restoration*—outlined what must be rebuilt. This volume turns to the future. It is not about reclaiming the old. It is about designing what comes next.

These chapters are organized by democratic obligation, not bureaucratic department. Each reform begins with the premise that democracy is not the right to vote every four years. It is the right to live in dignity every day. Health care, housing, food security, education, labor rights, digital access—none are luxuries. They are prerequisites to freedom. Each reform is presented with historical context, international comparison, and a path forward. Some will take five years. Some, a generation. But the clock is running. Delay is itself a decision.

We do not offer these reforms because we believe America is ready. We offer them because readiness is not the condition for action—it is its result. The path forward will not be easy. But as Kennedy understood, easy is not the measure. The measure is worth. The measure is need. The measure is whether a people who still claim to believe in liberty will rise to defend not just its form, but its substance.

It is time to aim again. Not higher. But deeper. Into the soil of democracy itself—into its unkept promises and its yet-unrealized power. The future will not build itself. But it remains ours to reach.

PROLOGUE
WRITING WHILE THE COUNTRY FELL APART

This book was always part of the plan.

When I began writing *American Renewal*, I wasn't just responding to collapse—I was charting a way out. From the first line, there were five phases. First, defense: protect what remains. Second, resistance: expose the damage and delay the descent. Third, restoration: rebuild what was broken. Fourth, redemption: fulfill the promises the republic was meant to keep. And finally, reinstitution: ensure it cannot fall again. These were not slogans. They were a strategy—conceived in the wreckage of Trump's return, but aimed far beyond him.

American Renewal was about survival. *American Restoration* was about repair. *American Redemption* is about fulfillment.

This is the fourth phase—not just what we must defend or restore, but what we must finally realize. A government that serves. A democracy that functions. A republic that keeps its word. Not permanent rule for any faction, but permanent fairness in the frame. Not a system bent toward wealth and power, but one grounded in dignity and trust. These eighteen reforms are not partisan—they are democratic. They define what a working democracy must do to last.

Because after all the marches, the votes, the setbacks and victories, the cruelty and courage—this is the point. Not merely to stop tyranny. Not merely to fix what's broken. But to build something worthy of belief.

The reforms in this book are not preferences. They are prerequisites. Together, they answer a single question: What should democracy deliver? Health without ruin. Work with dignity. Education without lifelong debt. Housing that anchors, not extracts. A digital sphere that informs, not deceives. Public safety that protects. Climate action that preserves life. And a civic culture that includes all of us. These are not ideals for later. They are the conditions for democracy now.

We are not building back to what was. We are building forward to what was promised.

I didn't write this because the crisis was over. I wrote it because the opportunity has arrived—and we cannot waste it. After years of erosion, obstruction, and near collapse, we have reclaimed the presidency. We have retaken Congress. We have restored enough of the system to make it work. But now comes the question that every democracy must face when the dust settles: What do we do with power once we have it?

American Redemption is the next step in that journey—not a chance to seize power, but to use it. To turn the hard-won victories of 2028 into enduring progress—not with purity, but with purpose. We have reclaimed a functioning democracy. Now we must prove it can still serve its people.

Let's begin.

1

THE CONDITIONS FOR REDEMPTION
WHAT THIS BOOK ASSUMES—AND WHAT IT HOPES TO PROVE

"The future doesn't happen all at once. It happens when people are ready —and when they refuse to wait any longer."
— Unknown organizer's saying

This book begins after three turning points. The first was survival: that the American people endured the most dangerous presidency in their history—twice. That despite all attempts to rig, delay, or derail the process, the 2026 midterms proceeded. That turnout was high, gerrymanders were overcome, and Democrats retook both the House and the Senate. That the damage inflicted on democratic institutions during Trump's second term was immense—but not fatal. This we call *American Renewal*—not as a slogan, but as a description of what had to be held until it could be repaired.

The second was reversal. In 2028, Americans once again rejected authoritarian rule. The presidential election was free, fair, and decisive. A new Democratic President was elected. Congress remained in Democratic control, with a reform-driven majority in the Senate and a veto-proof House. This was the breakthrough. It created the conditions necessary to enact the full agenda laid out in *American Restoration*: eighteen structural reforms to rebuild the constitutional, institutional, and civic infrastructure of self-government.

Only after those two turning points could the third begin: Redemption. This book assumes that we now have a working democracy—flawed, fragile, but real. That elections are free. That the courts function. That the agencies are staffed. That we have the tools to govern—and the will to use them. On that foundation, this book asks a different question. Not how to restore democracy. But what a just, democratic republic should now deliver.

Each part of this book addresses one of five domains where democracy must be made real: care, education, justice, belonging, and the future. Within those five parts are eighteen major reforms—each a critical function that a democratic republic must fulfill to survive. For every reform, we offer two chapters: the first to diagnose the failure, the second to design a remedy. These are not policy white papers. They are civic arguments. Each chapter offers historical context, legal grounding, comparative examples, and a proposed reform—designed not to punish a broken system, but to replace it with something better.

The first chapter in each pair begins with collapse. These chapters trace the breakdown of constitutional purpose and public function over time—through legal erosion, institutional sabotage, captured systems, and the long Republican effort to turn government against its own people. They identify the actors, name the profiteers, expose the failures, and show how the for-profit model has undermined public trust. Each is grounded in law, history, and structure—not scandal or sentiment. Together, they build a case for why reform is not optional, but required.

The second chapter in each pair turns from failure to design. These chapters follow a consistent arc: first, showing why regulation alone has failed—piecemeal, reversible, and often captured by those it was meant to restrain. Then, explaining how the for-profit system —dominant in nearly every sector—has treated citizens as markets and left millions without access, trust, or fairness. From there, we propose a different kind of solution: not more control, but more capacity. Not to eliminate the private sector, but to offer a powerful public alternative—one good enough to draw people in, not force them across. These are reforms that attract, not coerce. The goal is not oversight, but replacement. When the public system works, it resets the incentives, reshapes the market, and rebuilds the baseline of freedom. This is how we move from failed regulation to durable transformation. We build something better—and let it prove itself.

We do not present these eighteen reforms as the final word. Some may be too much. Others may be missing. The details will change. The legislation will evolve. But the democratic obligations they speak to—health, housing, truth, justice, voice—do not go away just because the proposals are imperfect. If these are blueprints, they are drafts: provisional, incomplete, and open to challenge. They are not specifications. They are starting points—for thinking, for arguing, for legislating, and for building something better than what we inherited.

This is the condition of redemption. Not the return to what was, but the design of what must be. Not purity, but progress. Not ideology, but responsibility. Democracy does not defend itself. And once it is reclaimed, it must prove itself again—by what it delivers, by whom it serves, and by whether it lasts.

This is where the work begins.

2

PART I: A NATION THAT CARES FOR ITS OWN

NO DEMOCRACY SURVIVES WITHOUT CARE

"The test of our progress is not whether we add more to the abundance of those who have much, but whether we provide enough for those who have too little."
— Franklin D. Roosevelt

No democracy survives without care—not as charity, but as infrastructure. A republic that abandons its people to hunger, illness, or eviction has already failed its purpose. For decades, America has subsidized capital while extracting labor, protected wealth while dismantling public care. It is a nation with billionaires and child hunger. A nation where private equity owns homes and hospitals—both of which are now collapsing. What has failed is not only compassion, but design.

The U.S. Constitution begins with a promise: to 'promote the general welfare.' (*Article I, Section 8*) That phrase was not a flourish.

It was a foundation. The framers understood that liberty, while essential, was insufficient. A republic that left its citizens destitute, diseased, or homeless was no republic at all. The idea that government might support human well-being was not radical in 1787. It was elemental. Yet no explicit right to health care, housing, food, or income was ever written into the Constitution. That omission has haunted us since.

The Fourteenth Amendment, adopted after the Civil War, offered a second chance. Its equal protection clause laid the groundwork for a more inclusive vision of care *U.S. Constitution, Amendment XIV; see also Goldberg v. Kelly (1970), which established due process rights in public assistance.*—one that recognized the state's duty to ensure not just legal equality, but meaningful access to survival. During Reconstruction, that vision briefly stirred: land reform, public institutions, basic services. But it was swiftly dismantled. The promise of a nation that cares was deferred again.

Only in the twentieth century did care return to the national project. The New Deal established Social Security, unemployment insurance, and the rudiments of a welfare state. The Great Society added Medicare, Medicaid, and food assistance. These were not acts of charity. They were structural recognitions that democracy cannot function when vast swaths of its people are too poor, too hungry, or too sick to participate.

Even then, the system was riddled with exclusions. Domestic workers and farm laborers were left out of early Social Security *Social Security Act of 1935 initially excluded domestic and agricultural workers, disproportionately affecting Black and Latino laborers..* Medicaid was fragmented by state lines. Housing programs were laced with racial redlining. Yet for a time, the arc bent toward dignity. The federal government accepted partial responsibility for ensuring that Americans could survive and contribute.

That consensus began to unravel in the 1970s and collapsed in the 1980s.

Inflation, oil shocks, and urban unrest gave rise to backlash. A new ideology emerged—one that saw public assistance not as a democratic stabilizer but as a threat to personal virtue. Care became conditional. Welfare a slur. Reagan's ascendance sealed it. The "welfare queen" caricature gave moral cover to deep cuts in aid. Government, Reagan declared, was not the solution. It was the problem. The safety net was slashed in the name of freedom. Markets were worshipped. Poverty became a moral failing, not a policy outcome.

By the 1990s, the attack on care was bipartisan. Bill Clinton's "welfare reform" ended the federal guarantee of income support for poor families. Housing assistance stagnated. Mental health care was deinstitutionalized without replacement. Public systems hollowed out. By the early 2000s, conservatives had succeeded in decoupling care from democracy. The market would provide. If it didn't, you were on your own.

Then came Trump.

In 2016, he ran on a promise to repeal the Affordable Care Act and replace it with "something terrific." He claimed, again and again, that a better plan would arrive "in two weeks." It never did. Instead, his administration dismantled core ACA protections: eliminating the individual mandate, slashing outreach budgets, encouraging junk plans. Millions lost coverage. Medicaid expansion stalled. The sick paid the price.

The cruelty went further. Trump officials proposed rent increases for low-income tenants, cut food stamps, imposed harsh work requirements, and sought to block access for immigrants and refugees. Programs like CHIP and Head Start faced repeated threats. During the pandemic, relief became a tool of political favoritism. States that praised Trump got aid quickly; others faced delays. Unemployment systems buckled. Eviction moratoriums faltered. Hunger surged. None of it was accidental.

In his second term, the destruction became policy. In early 2025, Trump introduced what he called his 'Big Beautiful Bill'—a sweeping budget that slashed Medicaid, shrank Medicare, and narrowed Social Security eligibility under the guise of efficiency. There was no replacement. The point was elimination. ery—but no one is left uncovered.mass firings of civil servants. Agency leadership was purged. Block grants were weaponized.

Under this same "beautiful" bill, housing vouchers were capped. SNAP (food assistance) benefits restricted. Tax breaks for the ultra-rich expanded and made permanent. At the same time, the IRS faced renewed staffing cuts, making tax enforcement nearly impossible. Across every sector, the message was clear: if you need care, the state will not help. It may even hurt you.

Other democracies show another way. In Canada, health care is a right, not a product. In Finland, housing is infrastructure, not investment. Germany offers universal child care with professional standards. New Zealand budgets for national well-being. France provides subsidized food and housing as civic stabilizer *See OECD Health Statistics, and EU Childcare and Early Education Report (2023)*s. No system is perfect. But all outperform the United States in delivering baseline dignity.

What must be done is not mysterious. Health care must be universal and public. Housing must be affordable, accessible, and shielded from speculation. No one should go hungry or bankrupt due to job loss, illness, age, or military service. Child care must be treated as essential infrastructure. Retirement must be secured through a stronger, broader Social Security system—one that honors labor, disability, and loss. Veterans must receive not just praise, but care: timely health services, guaranteed housing, income support, and long-term dignity. Taxes must be fair—levied not just on earnings, but on extraction. These reforms are not in competition; they are interdependent. They form a web of care, not a menu. None can stand alone.

The harder part is how we get there. Entrenched interests will fight every inch—with money, disinformation, threats, and influence. Institutions built on suffering do not yield easily. But we have direction. We have models. We have public support. What we have lacked is courage. And clarity. And the refusal to accept a politics of despair. These reforms will come only through organizing, legislation, implementation, and relentless pressure. They may take years. So did the moonshot.

What stands in the way is not complexity, but courage. Every reform in this book depends on three things. First, leaders who are willing to try—who will face the fury of donors, lobbyists, and industries built on exploitation, and still act. Second, a public that will not waver—one that pressures, protests, organizes, and votes until change is not only possible, but unavoidable. And third, a working plan—not just what to fix, but how to fix it, in what order, and with what fallback when sabotage comes.

This is the architecture of real reform. Without courageous leaders, the ideas never reach law. Without sustained public pressure, the law is watered down or reversed. Without a real plan, the victory collapses under complexity or neglect. These reforms are not merely goals. They are tests. They will reveal whether our democracy still functions—whether it can face the profiteers and say: not here, not anymore.

We begin here—because care is the test. Care is the measure of whether democracy means anything beyond procedure and profit. Care is more than the right to vote. A citizen must be able to live. With dignity. With safety. With hope. A nation that abandons its people forfeits its freedom. A nation that chooses care chooses to begin again.

3

UNIVERSAL HEALTH CARE — PUBLIC GOOD, NOT PRIVATE GAIN

DEMOCRACY COLLAPSES WHEN HEALTH IS A PRIVILEGE—AND PROFIT COMES BEFORE LIFE.

"Of all the forms of inequality, injustice in health is the most shocking and inhuman."
— Martin Luther King Jr.

Health care in the United States is not a right. While the U.S. Constitution does not guarantee health care, international treaties like the Universal Declaration of Human Rights (Article 25) define it as a basic human right. It is a transaction—rationed by wealth, brokered by intermediaries, and governed by profit. Its price is not set by need, but by leverage. Its denial is not seen as a failure of government, but as the natural order of a market system. That fact alone places the United States in defiance of its constitutional promise: to promote the general welfare. A nation that allows people to sicken or die for lack of money is not a republic. It is a sorting machine—designed to reward the healthy and discard the poor.

The Constitution does not mention health care. But it also does not mention police, highways, or public schools. What it provides is a mandate—to establish justice, ensure domestic tranquility, secure liberty, and promote the general welfare. None of that is possible without access to health. And yet, in every nation that claims to be just, access to health is treated as foundational—not because of enumerated rights, but because of human need. A citizen wracked by untreated pain cannot participate, cannot consent, cannot be free. A child denied insulin has no liberty. A parent choosing between chemotherapy and eviction is not self-governing. Health is not a privilege. It is the precondition of freedom.

The framers understood this. Benjamin Franklin co-founded America's first public hospital. Jefferson saw civic obligation in the care of others. Hamilton argued that national strength rested in public capacity. They lived in a pre-industrial world, but their vision was clear: freedom without health is a shell. They did not imagine a future where hedge funds would own hospitals, or where a cancer diagnosis would lead to bankruptcy. The crisis we face today is not due to constitutional silence. It is due to the betrayal of its spirit.

The American health system was not planned. It emerged through tax incentives, wartime improvisation, and corporate opportunism. In the 1940s, employers began offering insurance to attract workers during wage freezes. This accidental model hardened into a national structure. Today, more than 150 million Americans rely on job-tied insurance—non-portable, fragile, and profit-driven. No other wealthy democracy binds care to employment. OECD data confirms that among high-income nations, the U.S. is unique in tying primary health coverage to employment. Most use tax-based or nonprofit insurance models. We didn't build this system because it worked. We kept it because it paid.

In 1965, Medicare and Medicaid were created—not as universal care, but as emergency lifelines for the elderly and the very poor. Even then, they were riddled with exclusions. Southern Democrats ensured that many Black Americans, domestic workers, and farm laborers were left out. The 1965 Medicaid and Medicare laws excluded many due to compromises with segregationist lawmakers. Domestic and agricultural workers were also excluded from earlier Social Security coverage. Medicaid became fragmented by state lines. Medicare was partially privatized from the beginning. What should have been a step toward national care became instead a patchwork of segmented, unequal coverage—structurally divided by race, geography, and income.

Every attempt at universal coverage has been blocked. Truman's 1945 proposal was defeated by the American Medical Association and conservative politicians branding it "socialized medicine." Truman's national health insurance plan faced aggressive opposition from the American Medical Association and conservatives, labeling it "socialized medicine." Nixon favored HMOs over national insurance. Clinton's 1993 plan was buried under an avalanche of industry-funded propaganda. Even the Affordable Care Act passed only after dropping the public option and empowering private insurers. It helped millions—but left millions more behind. And from the start, Republicans vowed to dismantle it.

No party has done more to sabotage care than the modern GOP. From Reagan's warnings of "tyranny" under Medicare, In 1961, Ronald Reagan released a recording warning that Medicare would lead to government tyranny and loss of freedom, part of the AMA's opposition campaign. to Gingrich's bid to privatize it, to McConnell's crusade to repeal the ACA, Republican leaders have treated health care not as a duty—but as a danger to the market order. They opposed not just programs, but the principle that government should care for its people. "Freedom," in their language, meant the freedom of insurers to deny coverage, the freedom of corporations to charge what they like, and the freedom of government to abandon the sick.

But Democrats enabled the drift. They expanded Medicare Advantage—inviting private plans into public care. They pushed managed care models that rewarded denials and delays. They accepted lobbying dollars from insurers, drug companies, and hospital chains. Many Democratic leaders still speak of health care as a cost center, not a nation-defining institution. They trimmed reforms to fit the budgetary frame of Congress rather than the moral frame of the Constitution.

Meanwhile, the profiteers grew. Insurance companies restricted networks and raised premiums while posting record profits. Pharmaceutical giants set prices ten times higher than abroad. Private equity firms acquired hospitals, nursing homes, and hospices—then cut staff, hiked fees, and collapsed safety standards. Pharmacy benefit managers obscured who pays what, and for what reason. These entities do not provide care. They extract it—and sell it back, piecemeal, overpriced, and delayed.

The results are devastating. The United States spends nearly 18% of its GDP on health care According to the Centers for Medicare & Medicaid Services (CMS), U.S. health spending reached 17.3% of GDP in 2022 and is projected to exceed 18% by 2025.—more than any other country on Earth. Yet it ranks behind dozens of nations in life expectancy, maternal and infant mortality, and chronic disease outcomes. When care is commodified, prevention is ignored, outcomes worsen, and cruelty becomes operational policy.

Medical debt now burdens over 100 million Americans. A 2022 investigation by KFF Health News and NPR found that more than 100 million people in the U.S. carry medical debt. One in five households carries bills they cannot pay. Even those with insurance are underinsured—facing deductibles, denials, and exclusions. Families turn to GoFundMe to survive. Diabetics ration insulin. Cancer patients delay treatment. Ambulance rides trigger financial collapse. In the wealthiest country on Earth, falling ill can mean falling into poverty. This is not a glitch. It is the design.

Racial and geographic inequities expose the rot. Black women die in childbirth at three times the rate of white women. Data from the CDC shows that Black women in the U.S. face a maternal mortality rate nearly three times higher than white women, even after controlling for income and education.The 2025 budget proposal introduced by the Trump administration—marketed under the slogan "Big Beautiful Bill"—included cuts to Medicaid and Medicare and revived Schedule F to purge federal agencies. Indigenous communities face epidemic levels of diabetes, addiction, and suicide. Latino workers endure occupational hazards with little coverage. Rural hospitals are closing. Poor white communities face rising mortality from preventable conditions. This is not incidental. It is what happens when health is governed by market logic.

Trump made it worse. In his first term, he sabotaged the ACA, eliminated outreach funding, expanded junk insurance plans, and encouraged states to impose work requirements on Medicaid recipients. During the COVID pandemic, he politicized health guidance, downplayed risk, and delayed aid to states that opposed him. Public trust collapsed. Deaths surged. All the while, he promised a "terrific" replacement—coming, he said, in two weeks. The weeks passed. The plan never came.

Trump's second term escalated the assault. The "Big Beautiful Bill" of 2025 gutted Medicaid, narrowed Medicare eligibility, and attacked Social Security through work requirements and fraud-based restrictions. Schedule F returned. The 2025 budget proposal introduced by the Trump administration—marketed under the slogan "Big Beautiful Bill"—included cuts to Medicaid and Medicare and revived Schedule F to purge federal agencies., purging civil servants across health agencies. Robert F. Kennedy Jr., appointed Secretary of Health and Human Services In January 2025, President Trump appointed Robert F. Kennedy Jr. to head HHS. Kennedy's tenure began with the dismissal of CDC vaccine advisory staff and suspension of NIH funding lines., dismissed the entire CDC vaccine advisory committee and replaced them with conspiracy-aligned appointees. NIH funding was slashed. Cancer, AIDS, and pediatric research were suspended. The CDC's Morbidity and Mortality Weekly Report was paused The MMWR, a vital epidemiological resource, was reportedly suspended in early 2025, per coverage in *Science* and *STAT News*. Critics cited political interference.—cutting off the nation's key source of death data. Scientific leadership was replaced with loyalists. Public health became a target of ideology and revenge. The consequences are already visible: outbreaks unchecked, programs dismantled, trust erased.

These actions collectively signified a profound shift in federal policy—from public health guided by science to public health subordinated to ideology. But the assault did not stop at research institutions or federal agencies. It extended to the borders of care itself. Immigrants were deliberately excluded. DHS rewrote eligibility rules to block mixed-status families. Health waivers were revoked. Safety net access was tied to loyalty and status. State Medicaid programs were turned into block grants ripe for misappropriation. The goal was not reform—it was expulsion.

And still, Americans are told that care must be earned. That health is a matter of responsibility, not justice. That public systems are inefficient, and private ones are virtuous. These are lies. Other nations show what is possible. Germany covers everyone through nonprofit insurers. France provides comprehensive care with modest copays. Canada guarantees hospital treatment without billing. Australia blends public and private delivery—but no one is left uncovered. Health systems in Germany, France, Canada, Australia, and New Zealand offer universal coverage through public or nonprofit systems. OECD and WHO reports confirm the lower cost and higher health outcomes of these models.

They differ in structure, but not in principle: care comes first. People come first. Profit is secondary—or prohibited. No one loses coverage with a job change. No one bankrupts themselves for treatment. No one dies waiting for a plan to be approved. Their systems work not because they are perfect, but because they are governed by public interest—not financial extraction. These outcomes are no accident. They are the result of deliberate national commitments made decades ago. After World War II, most industrial democracies treated health care as a shared obligation. The U.S. treated it as a market opportunity.

In these countries, even foreign visitors are treated with dignity. A tourist in the U.K. who breaks a bone is treated across multiple hospitals without a bill. In New Zealand, a foreigner needing hospitalization and ambulance transfer pays only a few dollars for medication. In Australia, inpatient emergency care is delivered with no cost at all. These governments do not ask for proof of citizenship before acting. Case studies and official government policy from the UK, New Zealand, and Australia confirm that emergency care is provided to noncitizens at low or no cost, with minimal administrative burden.. They do not bill illness as a commodity. They respond as societies should: with care.

By contrast, in much of the United States, a visitor without insurance may be denied emergency treatment or discharged with tens of thousands in debt. The country that sells itself as a beacon to the world cannot meet the most basic standard of global decency.

In a profit-driven system, wellness is not rewarded—it is discouraged. Every illness becomes a revenue stream. Every prevented crisis, a missed billing opportunity. Insurers resist paying for preventive care; hospitals profit from readmissions, not from routine checkups. But in public systems, wellness is the goal. Routine screenings are free. Gym memberships and smoking cessation programs are subsidized. Addiction support is anonymous and accessible. Acupuncture, chiropractic care, physical therapy, and mental health services are encouraged—not as luxuries, but as cost-saving necessities. The logic is simple: when you stay healthy, the system saves money. A recovered patient frees a bed. A managed condition avoids a crisis. Health is not just an outcome. It is the infrastructure of a sustainable society.

And the benefits go far beyond cost. A healthy person is more likely to keep a job, survive financial stress, and recover quickly when illness does strike. Chronic pain doesn't just disappear—it gives people back their work, their marriages, their sports, their children, their joy. Skiing and biking need not be reserved for the young. Playing with your kids shouldn't be a luxury. In a system that invests in wellness, health is not just survival. It is a return to life.

America is capable of such a system. We already have the tools. Medicare proves it. The VA proves it. Public health departments across the country prove it—underfunded, overworked, but faithful to their mission. We know how to deliver care that heals, prevents, and sustains. What we lack is not knowledge. What we lack is power —power in the hands of the public, not the profiteers. We do not lack models. We lack leaders willing to confront the industries that treat sickness as an asset and wellness as a threat.

The way forward is not mysterious. Every person must have guaranteed access to essential health services—without financial ruin, without delay, without discrimination. That is the goal. It can be achieved through a public plan, through state expansion, through phased rollout, or through national law. But it cannot be achieved by patchwork. It must be built on principle.

It must also be built to last. That means naming the opposition: insurance lobbies, drug companies, hospital monopolies, and politicians funded to preserve the status quo. It means public organizing, strategic legislxation, federal standards, and enforcement mechanisms. It means courage.

We begin here—because care is still the test. It is not enough to say the word democracy. We must ask what democracy means when people are left to die for lack of money.

A nation that ends it does not just fix its health system. It reclaims its soul—and begins again.

4

THE HEALTH OF A NATION

A NATIONAL GUARANTEE FOR ESSENTIAL CARE—UNIVERSAL, PUBLIC, AND BUILT TO LAST

"Health cannot be a question of income. It is a fundamental human right."
— Nelson Mandela

There is no reason the United States cannot provide magnificent health care. It already has what most nations envy: world-class hospitals, top-tier teaching institutions, brilliant physicians, pioneering researchers, and unmatched medical technology. Its pharmacology, diagnostics, and innovation are second to none. Everything is in place—except the system to deliver it. What the nation lacks is not excellence, but access. Not ability, but structure. The failure is not in medicine. It is in management. And that failure is no longer tolerable.

The for-profit health system in the United States has failed. It costs more than any in the world, yet delivers worse outcomes than any other wealthy democracy. Administrative waste, perverse incentives, and commercial gatekeeping drive up costs and drive down trust. Reform is no longer a policy option—it is a civic necessity. But any replacement must meet real-world tests. It must guarantee access to essential care. It must be financially sustainable and broadly align with current public and private spending. It must be legislatively achievable under existing Congressional authority. It must allow for phased rollout and protect personal choice—succeeding because it works, not because it is imposed. And it must be implemented nationally within the decade. These are not abstract ideals—they are governing thresholds. The proposal that follows is built to meet them.

A national universal health system would deliver four essential outcomes: guaranteed access, controlled costs, improved population health, and restored civic trust. Every U.S. resident—regardless of income, job status, immigration category, or insurance history—would be entitled to a defined set of essential health services. No one would go bankrupt from illness. No parent would delay care for a child because of cost. Administrative overhead, profit siphons, and fragmented billing systems would be eliminated. Overall spending could fall even as coverage expands. Outcomes—from life expectancy to maternal mortality—would begin to converge with other high-performing democracies. Most importantly, a single national system would reestablish a foundational truth: that health is not a commodity, but a civic right. That is not just a moral claim—it is the scaffolding of democracy itself.

A transformation of this scale touches every part of the current system. For-profit insurance would no longer be the gateway to care. The national public insurer would offer every resident a defined set of services at no cost at point of use, removing the gatekeeping role of private companies in essential care. Hospitals, now forced to maintain bloated billing departments to negotiate with hundreds of insurers, would operate under a unified reimbursement model. Providers would spend less time on paperwork and more time with patients. Pharmaceutical firms would face transparent pricing structures negotiated nationally. Patients, who today navigate a maze of deductibles, networks, exclusions, and denials, would instead receive consistent, guaranteed care—regardless of employer, zip code, or health status.

The ripple effects go further. With health no longer tied to employment, small businesses would be unburdened. Entrepreneurs could start companies without fear of losing coverage. Workers could change jobs, start families, or retire early without forfeiting medical security. Public health agencies could focus on prevention, not triage. Emergency rooms would no longer serve as default primary care. Rural providers, now shuttering due to insurance-driven insolvency, would gain stable, predictable revenue. Medical bankruptcy would become a relic of the past. [David U. Himmelstein et al., "Medical Bankruptcy: Still Common Despite the Affordable Care Act," *American Journal of Public Health*, March 2019.] Employer costs would decline. Families would gain time, money, and peace of mind. And nationally, the United States would gain what it has long lacked: a coherent, dignified, functional health system worthy of its people.

At its heart, the proposal is simple: a single national public insurer would offer every American access to essential health care—free at the point of use, funded publicly, and governed transparently. All residents would be issued a national health card entitling them to a defined list of core services: primary care, hospitalization, diagnostics, maternity, mental health, and medications. Participation would remain voluntary—but powerful incentives would make it the default choice. Doctors and hospitals would be reimbursed directly at fair, standardized rates. Private insurance could still exist, but only for supplemental services beyond the national guarantee. The transition would be phased, choice-driven, and fully legal under existing Congressional authority. This is not a nationalization of hospitals, or a ban on private care. It is the creation of a single, universal foundation—where health is a civic right, not a commercial product.

The United States spends more per person on health care than any other country on Earth—by far. Yet outcomes rank among the worst in the developed world. [OECD, *Health at a Glance 2023: OECD Indicators*, OECD Publishing, 2023.

THE COMMONWEALTH FUND, *Mirror, Mirror 2021: Reflecting Poorly – Health Care in the U.S. Compared to Other High-Income Countries*, August 2021.]Life expectancy has fallen. Infant and maternal mortality rates remain shockingly high. Chronic illnesses go untreated. Mental health systems are fractured. By contrast, most advanced democracies provide universal health care through public or publicly regulated systems—and achieve better results. Germany combines universal access with non-profit insurers. France offers a generous baseline with optional top-ups. Canada covers all essential care through public funding and delivery. Australia blends public guarantees with private choice, but no one is denied needed care [Australian Government Department of Health, *Medicare and Private Health Insurance Overview*, 2023.]. In each case, the result is the same: longer lives, no medical bankruptcies, and far greater public trust.

Germany's model is closest to what we propose: [European Observatory on Health Systems and Policies, *Health System Reviews (HiT Series)* for Germany and France, 2022.] a mixed, non-profit insurance system where all residents are guaranteed care. Insurers compete, but only within strict cost and quality boundaries, and profit is prohibited for core services. Participation is voluntary, and rates are scaled to income. Providers remain private, but prices and services are standardized and enforced nationally. The result is efficient care, broad access, and high satisfaction. France, similarly, funds health care through payroll taxes and provides near-total reimbursement for defined services—often 70–100%. Private insurance exists only to cover what the state doesn't, and most doctors work independently within the national framework. In both cases, complexity is reduced, incentives align, and care is delivered as a public good, not a profit stream.

Australia adds another lesson: people value choice, but expect fairness. A public guarantee of essential care—delivered through Medicare—remains the foundation. Private insurance can offer faster access, different settings, or expanded amenities, but no one is left behind. Even visitors and undocumented immigrants can access emergency services. That structure helps avoid ER overload and allows preventive care to function properly. The Canadian model goes further, banning private duplicative coverage for core services entirely, and funding hospitals directly. [Canadian Institute for Health Information, *Health Spending in Canada*, 2023.] Though each system faces challenges, the comparison is instructive. Not one of these nations would trade places with the United States. And not one has allowed profit to displace the principle that health is a public good.

Universal health care is not a fantasy. It is the daily reality in nearly every other wealthy democracy—from Australia and Canada to France, Germany, and Japan. Each system has flaws, but all of them achieve what the United States does not: affordable, guaranteed care for every resident, with better health outcomes at lower cost. They prove that universal coverage is possible—medically, economically, and politically. These nations spend less per person, live longer, and face no bankruptcies from illness. [World Health Organization (WHO), *Universal Health Coverage and Health Outcomes*, 2020.] They do not all follow the same model. But the results are clear: a nation can provide care to all without collapsing under cost or sacrificing quality or choice.

The plan proposed here draws lessons from these models, but is tailored to America's fractured system. It does not demand a single government-run insurer, as in the UK. It does not outlaw private insurance, as some fear. Instead, it guarantees a publicly funded foundation—free core care for all—while allowing room for employer plans, supplemental insurance, and innovation. It minimizes disruption, respects choice, and builds atop existing infrastructure. It offers not a copy of another country's system, but a uniquely American answer to a universal need: health care that works, for everyone.

The foundation of American health care will not be demolished. It will be restructured. Hospitals will remain privately run. Doctors will keep their practices. Employer insurance may continue. Medicaid, Medicare, the VA, and Indian Health Service will all be retained—but their roles will evolve. What changes is not who delivers care, but who pays for it, and who can count on receiving it. A national guarantee will ensure that essential care is available to every person without cost at the point of use. No coverage gaps. No billing traps. The existing infrastructure remains intact—but the burden is lifted from the individual and anchored in a national trust.

What this means in practice is simple. Everyone will be covered for core care: emergencies, chronic conditions, preventive visits, childbirth, mental health, and essential medications. Private insurance can still offer add-ons—like elective procedures, private rooms, or overseas coverage—but no one will need it to survive. States will help administer the rollout, but the federal government will fund the core program and define its floor. Hospitals will be reimbursed. Patients will be registered. Providers will be paid. The system shifts from exclusion to inclusion—not by wiping the slate clean, but by realigning its purpose: care first.

Under this plan, emergencies no longer trigger confusion, bankruptcy, or delay. Joe falls from a ladder at work and is rushed to the ER—his care is covered, full stop, regardless of insurance status or employer compliance. Nancy learns she is pregnant—her prenatal visits, delivery, and postpartum care are guaranteed without paperwork battles or surprise bills. Sam suffers a heart attack on the job—an ambulance arrives, he is treated immediately, and the cost does not follow him home. These are not exceptional benefits. They are standard entitlements in every other wealthy democracy. The difference is not in what care is delivered. It is in the certainty with which it is received.

For many, the hardest part to believe is the cost. If a broken arm today can result in a $30,000 bill, how can the government afford to cover millions of such cases? The answer is not that we pay more, but that we pay differently—and less. Under this plan, prices are negotiated, not dictated by hospitals or insurers. Billing is simplified. Administrative waste is cut. Overhead drops. Fraud shrinks. The government does not reimburse $25,000 for a fracture. It pays what the care actually costs—often less than a fifth of current charges. Nancy, who once faced $30,000 out of pocket for a routine delivery, now pays nothing. The hospital is still paid. The doctor is still paid. But the system no longer pretends a healthy birth costs as much as a new car.

This proposal does not change immigration law. It does not grant amnesty, and it does not require hospitals or clinics to report undocumented patients. Under the Emergency Medical Treatment and Labor Act (EMTALA) of 1986 [U.S. Code, *Emergency Medical Treatment and Labor Act (EMTALA)*, 42 U.S. Code § 1395dd, enacted 1986.], hospitals must provide emergency care to anyone in urgent need, regardless of ability to pay or immigration status. That care will continue to be publicly funded—not because of this proposal, but because it has been the law for nearly forty years. Broader health benefits beyond emergencies will remain tied to legal residency or formal system registration. And under HIPAA, medical providers are prohibited from sharing patient information, including immigration status, without consent [U.S. Department of Health and Human Services, *HIPAA Privacy Rule*, 45 CFR Parts 160 and 164, 2002.]. The goal is care, not enforcement. The hospital is not the border. And people needing care should not fear seeking it.

The full rollout will take place over three to five years, with services phased in by category and region. Year one begins with emergency care, chronic conditions, and maternal health—delivered through existing hospitals and clinics. By year three, primary care, mental health, and preventive services are universal. Specialized and long-term services will follow, calibrated to workforce capacity and infrastructure. Rural and underserved areas will receive early investment to close access gaps. Every stage is governed by one rule: no lapse in care. If someone is already receiving treatment under an existing program or private plan, it continues uninterrupted. This is not a flip-the-switch revolution. It is a managed, accountable transformation—with every phase audited for cost, capacity, and outcome.

We've done this before. When Medicare launched in 1966, it enrolled over 19 million seniors in under a year [Social Security Administration (SSA), *History of Medicare*, 1966.]—without the internet, digital records, or modern logistics. Hospitals adapted. Payment systems stabilized. Public trust soared. The same is possible now, with better tools and broader reach. For most Americans, no action will be required: registration will be automatic, care uninterrupted, and access expanded. Employers may continue offering supplemental insurance. States will help administer logistics. The burden does not fall on the patient. It falls on the system—and this time, the system will be built to serve. Health care reform succeeds not because people are forced to change, but because what replaces the old is simpler, fairer, and built to last.

Even the best-designed system requires a strong workforce to deliver care. To meet rising demand—especially in rural and underserved areas—the national plan will fund targeted incentives to train, deploy, and retain medical professionals. Doctors who commit to primary care or rural practice will receive tax incentives, housing support, and direct student debt forgiveness—up to full cancellation after five to ten years of service. Nurses, midwives, and allied health workers will be eligible for similar programs. Medical education grants will expand for underrepresented groups and community-rooted students. And new graduate residencies will be prioritized in areas with critical shortages. This is not charity—it is investment. A healthy nation requires not just access to care, but skilled, supported people to deliver it. And they deserve to be honored, equipped, and paid accordingly.

Nurses and allied health workers are the backbone of daily care. They staff emergency rooms, guide recovery, monitor chronic conditions, and sustain patient dignity across every setting. Yet in today's system, they are overworked, underpaid, and often treated as expendable. The national health plan will address this directly. New funding will expand nursing school capacity, support clinical placements, and increase wages for frontline roles. Rural and high-need areas will offer retention bonuses, housing stipends, and tuition forgiveness for multi-year commitments. Allied professionals—physiotherapists, radiologists, dietitians, mental health clinicians—will be integrated fully into the care model and reimbursed accordingly. These workers are not optional extras. They are essential. And any system that values care must also value the people who give it.

Continuity is the backbone of trust. No doctor will be forced out of practice. No hospital will be left unpaid. The national plan will reimburse providers directly, at negotiated rates based on actual cost, not inflated charge lists. [U.S. Government Accountability Office (GAO), *Private Health Insurance: Enrollment Remains Concentrated among a Few Issuers, Including in Exchanges*, July 2023.] Billing systems will be streamlined—one set of codes, one payer, fewer delays. Fraud will be harder, paperwork lighter, and payment more predictable. For patients, the change is felt not in the waiting room, but at the mailbox: no bills, no surprise charges, no collection threats. Existing programs like Medicare, Medicaid, and VA care will remain intact during the transition, with resources redirected as the national system takes hold. The goal is not to tear down what works—but to end the chaos of what doesn't.

Health care should begin in a doctor's office, not an emergency room. Under this plan, routine checkups, vaccinations, screenings, and preventive care are fully covered and encouraged. That includes general visits, blood pressure checks, pelvic exams, childhood immunizations, blood and urine tests, and mental health check-ins. No more waiting until a crisis forces action. By catching problems early, we lower both human suffering and financial cost. A nation of prevention is a nation of health. The family doctor becomes the front line of care again—familiar, accessible, and affordable. Patients no longer ask, "Can I afford to go?" They simply go. And because prevention is covered, emergencies become the exception, not the entry point.

When routine care finds something serious, the system does not stall or defer. It responds. A suspicious mole leads to a biopsy. A breast lump triggers imaging and referral. A heart murmur prompts a specialist consult. The general practitioner remains your guide, but the next step is clear—and covered. Referral letters grant access to qualified specialists whose services are funded by the national plan. Patients may also choose a different specialist, even one outside the plan, and pay the difference directly or through supplemental insurance. The result is freedom without abandonment—coverage for all, choice for those who want it. The question is never "Can I afford this?" The question is "What's the next step?"

Not all procedures are covered—and they shouldn't be. Elective surgeries that are not medically necessary remain outside the core guarantee. That includes cosmetic procedures like nose reshaping, breast augmentation, or eyelid lifts, unless they are part of a reconstructive medical plan. These services may still be offered by licensed professionals, but they are not funded by the public system. If patients wish to pursue them, they may do so privately or through optional insurance. The goal is not to control personal choice—it is to ensure public funds go where they are most needed: to keep people alive, healthy, mobile, pain-free, and cared for with dignity and skill.

The core guarantee is simple. Emergency care is provided to everyone. Ongoing care—doctor visits, specialist referrals, diagnostic tests, and treatment—is fully covered for all citizens and permanent residents. The general practitioner becomes the front door of care, and patients retain choice at every step: choice of GP, choice of specialist, choice of hospital. Core services are funded publicly. Optional services—cosmetic procedures, private insurance extras, concierge care—remain available for those who want them, but no one is denied essential care. This is not a system of restriction. It is a system of foundation—where choice begins with security, not fear.

People currently on Medicare are automatically enrolled—first—into the new national health care system. Their coverage continues uninterrupted. Most will see the same doctors, visit the same hospitals, and receive the same medications and treatments as before. What changes is that coverage becomes simpler, broader, and more affordable. Medicare Parts B, C, and D are no longer optional add-ons. The most essential tests, treatments, and medicines are included by default. The maze of co-pays, premiums, and coverage gaps gives way to a single, reliable guarantee. Seniors do not lose what they have—they gain what they were always promised: care without confusion or fear.

A guarantee like this demands a serious answer to the question: how do we pay for it? The truth is, we already do. The United States spends more public money on health care than any other country on Earth—yet still leaves millions uncovered and millions more underinsured. Between Medicare, Medicaid, VA programs, public employee plans, and federal subsidies, the government already funds more than half the system [U.S. Centers for Medicare &

Medicaid Services (CMS), *National Health Expenditure Data, 2022.*]. What's missing is not money. It's structure. This proposal does not add cost on top of chaos. It replaces chaos with coherence. Some new investment will be required—but it buys something we've never had before: coverage for everyone, and savings that last.

Today, Americans already pay for health care—through premiums, co-pays, deductibles, employer contributions, and taxes. This plan shifts that spending into a single, predictable system. Employers would contribute a set percentage—typically lower than current premiums. Individuals would no longer face out-of-pocket costs for essential care. Public programs would consolidate into the national plan. Pharmaceutical and hospital prices would be negotiated centrally. The result is not new cost, but better use of existing funds. It is not a new entitlement. It is a disciplined realignment.

Funding for the national health system would come from multiple sources—but always with one principle: no one pays more and gets less. A modest payroll levy, shared between employers and employees, could replace private premiums. High-income households might pay a small surcharge, offset by the end of deductibles. Current tax subsidies for private insurance—over $300 billion annually [Congressional Budget Office (CBO), *Federal Subsidies for Health Insurance Coverage for People Under Age 65: 2022 to 2032*, September 2022.]—would be redirected to the public fund. Additional revenues could come from targeted reforms: taxes on tobacco, ultra-processed foods, or excessive pharmaceutical profits. What matters is the outcome: guaranteed care, controlled cost, and a system people can see and trust.

To preserve flexibility and reduce resistance, the system would include a tax-based incentive for supplemental insurance. Individuals who purchase private plans—covering services beyond the national guarantee—could receive a tax deduction. Those who opt out entirely would face a modest surcharge, scaled to income. This approach rewards participation without mandating it, sustains a market for non-essential services, and ensures higher earners contribute more. It aligns incentives toward health, not exclusion—and gives insurers a role without giving them control.

Even with expanded coverage, total spending could fall. Studies estimate that administrative simplification alone could save $200–300 billion annually [Steffie Woolhandler & David Himmelstein, "The Administrative Costs of U.S. Health Care," *New England Journal of Medicine*, August 2021.]. Negotiated drug prices could lower pharmaceutical costs by 30 to 50 percent. [RAND Corporation, *International Prescription Drug Price Comparisons*, 2021.U.S. Centers for Medicare & Medicaid Services (CMS), *National Health Expenditure Data*, 2022.] Consolidating duplicative programs would eliminate layers of inefficiency. While no projection is perfect, the weight of evidence suggests this model is not just morally compelling—it is fiscally rational. It doesn't require new money so much as better direction of what we already spend. That's what makes this possible. And that's what makes it urgent.

A health system is only as strong as its workforce. Today, that workforce is stretched to the breaking point. Primary care doctors are retiring early or avoiding practice altogether. Nurses are leaving in record numbers. Rural hospitals cannot fill critical roles. Burnout, bureaucracy, and poor compensation are driving talent away from the very areas we need it most. This plan addresses the shortage directly—not just by reshaping the system doctors work in, but by making their work worth doing. Fewer billing codes. Fewer insurance fights. More time with patients. And for the next generation: a path into medicine that doesn't begin in debt or end in despair.

The proposal includes a national medical scholarship program, targeted to fields and regions in greatest need. Students who train as general practitioners or commit to underserved areas would receive full tuition, living stipends, and debt forgiveness after service. Similar programs would extend to nursing, midwifery, public health, and allied professions. Existing doctors would receive incentives to practice in rural or high-need communities—such as tax abatements, student loan relief, or housing subsidies. These are not costs. They are investments. A nation cannot guarantee care if it cannot guarantee caregivers. And no system succeeds without those who staff it believing it is worth saving.

Respect must also be restored. In today's fractured system, care professionals are expected to deliver excellence under impossible constraints—forced to ration time, apologize for billing codes, and battle administrators to get patients what they need. The new system reorients the incentives. Compensation would remain competitive, but not exploitative. Workplaces would gain stability and lose bureaucracy. Professionals would be trusted to do their jobs—and protected from the profiteering that distorts clinical judgment. This is not just a staffing reform. It is a cultural correction. Care must be a respected profession again. Only then will we have a system worth trusting—and people willing to sustain it.

No structural reform of this scale will go unchallenged. The industries that profit from the current system—insurance, pharmaceuticals, for-profit hospitals—will resist not because the proposal fails, but because it works. Expect a well-funded campaign of fear: that innovation will die, choice will vanish, care will be rationed. But these arguments collapse under scrutiny. Other democracies have universal systems, and they deliver more for less. What this opposition fears is not decline, but accountability. The end of arbitrary pricing. The end of predatory billing. The end of a market that treats illness as opportunity. That is not loss. That is liberation.

More dangerous than open resistance is quiet sabotage. The most effective way to kill reform is not to oppose it, but to mimic it—offering cosmetic alternatives that preserve the status quo. Watch for proposals that claim to "fix" insurance through better marketplaces, smarter subsidies, or voluntary pools. These are patches, not solutions. A system cannot be optimized when its foundation is extraction. The response must be clear: no more intermediaries who profit by denial. No more fake fixes. The goal is not a gentler for-profit system. The goal is care—universal, affordable, human. Anything less is capitulation in disguise.

A national system of this scale must be governed not only by law, but by trust. That means accountability—built into the foundation. Public oversight boards would set reimbursement rates, review pricing data, and approve coverage expansions. These boards must be diverse, transparent, and shielded from industry capture. Independent audits would track expenditures and flag abuse. Whistleblower protections would guard against fraud. Every citizen should know where their health dollars go, and why. Governance must be open, data must be public, and decisions must be defensible. That is how to build—and keep—the trust of a population long abused by opacity and profit.

To ensure long-term integrity, the system must evolve with evidence. Performance reviews would assess not just fiscal targets, but health outcomes. Patient satisfaction, regional equity, and care access must be measured—and acted on. Innovations from abroad should be studied, adapted, and adopted where they improve delivery. No system survives by standing still. But reform fatigue is real, and bureaucratic drift is deadly. By embedding renewal into its mandate, the system avoids decay. By grounding accountability in law and public consent, it resists capture. Health care is not static. But fairness, transparency, and public benefit must never be optional again.

Health care in the United States has never been guaranteed. But the promise of America has. The Constitution calls on us to "promote the general welfare" and "secure the blessings of liberty." These are not abstract ideals. They are governing duties. A nation that allows people to suffer or die for lack of care has failed those duties. A system that profits from illness, while denying prevention, violates the public trust. This proposal does not invent new rights—it fulfills old ones. Health is the scaffolding of freedom. Without it, opportunity is hollow, dignity is performative, and liberty belongs only to the fortunate.

To those who say this cannot be done, history replies: we have done harder things. We rebuilt Europe, cured diseases, landed on the moon. What we lack is not capacity, but political will. A fair, universal, and efficient health system is not utopian. It is overdue. The reforms proposed here are legally sound, fiscally grounded, and institutionally achievable—within a decade, by design, through democratic means. We are not inventing miracles. We are organizing what works. And when we do, the United States will finally join the ranks of nations that treat health not as a privilege, but as a public good.

5

SHELTER AND THE SOUL OF A DEMOCRACY

WHY HOUSING MUST BE PUBLIC, PERMANENT, AND PROTECTED FOR DEMOCRACY TO SURVIVE

---- ✦ ----

"To be rooted is perhaps the most important and least recognized need of the human soul."
— Simone Weil

A home is more than a roof. It is a place. It is permanence. It anchors a person to a district, a school, a voting roll. It offers continuity, memory, and the right to be counted. In a democracy, it does more than shelter—it secures citizenship. Without a home, there is no fixed point. No safety. No address. And without stable housing for all, there is no such thing as equal opportunity—or a working republic.

But the United States does not treat housing as foundational. It treats it as a commodity—something to purchase, flip, or extract. The result is a system that delivers shelter not where it is most needed, but where it is most profitable. Over 650,000 people sleep unhoused each night. Tens of millions more are rent-burdened, paying more than they can afford for homes they cannot keep. In many cities, even full-time workers live in cars, sleep on couches, or line up for housing lotteries with odds worse than the Powerball. This is not market efficiency. It is moral collapse.

These outcomes are not accidents. They are the result of a system that rations housing by income, not need. A system where wealth buys access and speculation dictates supply. When homes are scarce, they go to those who can outbid—not those who contribute, serve, or stay. And then, perversely, we blame the poor for not affording what we've made impossible to attain. That is not failure. That is design.

This is not merely unjust. It is anti-democratic. Without housing, a citizen's ability to participate collapses. No address means no registration, no services, no civic foothold. People disappear from systems designed to include them. The cost is not just personal—it is political. A nation that fails to house its people cannot claim to represent them. And no democracy can survive when millions are locked out of its basic structures of belonging.

The housing crisis in America is not just about rising costs. It is about retreat. For decades, lawmakers stepped back—not with honesty, but with euphemism. They called it "choice," "efficiency," and "innovation," while disassembling the public responsibility to ensure shelter. What remains is not a system, but a patchwork: thin subsidies, frozen programs, weak enforcement. A scaffold for profit. A sieve for people.

Housing assistance in the United States is often framed as generous. In truth, its tools are limited, brittle, and often self-defeating. Federal vouchers rarely keep up with rising rents. Tax credits reward developers for temporary affordability, not long-term shelter. Public housing has been defunded, vilified, and left to rot. And zoning codes—once designed for health and safety—now ban density, block affordable construction, and re-segregate communities by race and class. These were not accidents. They were choices—crafted to preserve wealth and disguise exclusion as efficiency.

The collapse is not just economic. It is moral, cultural, and civic. Housing has been stripped of meaning. Once a symbol of stability, it is now a tool of extraction. Families compete with investment firms. Homes sit empty for tax breaks. Entire neighborhoods are snapped up by corporate landlords. Meanwhile, young couples cannot buy their first home. Growing families outgrow the one they have. Seniors are forced to move—not because they want to, but because they can no longer afford the taxes.

And even for those who manage to climb aboard the housing merry-go-round, the ride is far from stable. Families stretch to buy or rent, only to find themselves trapped—house poor, cash-strapped, and perpetually on edge. A single layoff, a medical bill, another child, an insurance claim, or even a federal interest rate hike can topple the whole house of cards. This is not security. It is a slow-burn instability, packaged as success. And it reveals the deeper flaw: that even "making it" in this system leaves millions perched on the brink.

And ownership isn't the only dream denied. Renting, too, has become a gauntlet. In high-cost cities, even modest apartments consume half a paycheck—when they're available at all. Young workers turn down jobs they want because they cannot afford the city that comes with them. Families settle far from opportunity, trading commute time for a place to sleep. And millions, after years of trying, resign themselves to being permanent renters—forever one lease away from eviction, and one rent hike away from despair. None of this is a bug. It is the system working exactly as it was built.

Some of the housing crisis was designed. Some of it was allowed. But all of it was deliberate—and the consequences reach far beyond shelter. When children move every other year, they lose continuity. When elders are displaced, they lose dignity. When communities are erased, they lose memory. The notion of my school, my church, my friends, the girl next door—gone, every time the movers arrive. And in that loss, something deeper erodes: the sense of place, of belonging, of being known and needed. That is what makes civic life possible. That is what we are losing. For too many, it is already gone.

Because a home is not just where you sleep. It is the walk to school, the friends you played with, the tree you planted—and the one you climbed. It's the neighbor who still calls you by your childhood name, the one who stops and says, "I knew your mother." It is the thread that ties memory to meaning, and meaning to place. When that thread breaks too many times, we don't just lose equity. We lose identity. And when identity is lost, democracy fades with it—until nothing remains but the market, and the ghost of a dream that once meant home.

And with that loss goes the possibility of equal citizenship. It is no coincidence that those most affected by housing precarity—Black families, Indigenous communities, immigrants, single mothers, the disabled, the elderly, the young, and the children—are also those most often ignored in the political process. When people are not stably housed, they are easier to exclude, harder to organize, and more vulnerable to suppression. Displacement is not neutral. It is disenfranchisement by another name. A voice without place is a voice without volume.

The historical record is not ambiguous. For over a century, U.S. housing policy has been used to divide, exclude, and impoverish. Banks drew red lines around Black neighborhoods, denying loans and devaluing homes. Cities declared "blight" and bulldozed communities of color in the name of renewal. Realtors fueled panic to drive white flight, then sold the same homes at inflated prices to Black families. Highway projects sliced through thriving minority neighborhoods—not by accident, but by design. The result was not freedom. It was segregation, disinheritance, and state-sponsored exclusion—masked by the language of progress.

The consequences of that history still echo today. Displacement did not end with bulldozers and highways. It continues through rising rents, sudden evictions, and absentee landlords who extract without repair. And beneath it all runs a deeper betrayal: the myth that this is freedom. But there is no freedom in eviction. No liberty in exploitation. No opportunity in sleeping in your car. A democracy that allows this does not defend rights—it administers cruelty. And any recovery worthy of the name must begin by naming that cruelty, undoing it, and building something better in its place.

Other nations have done this. Vienna treats public housing as a permanent public asset. Singapore builds homes that citizens lease and own. Finland ends homelessness not with shelters, but with homes. These are not utopias. They are democracies that made different choices. They built public systems, treated housing as a right, and invested accordingly—not just in buildings, but in people.

The United States had a choice. It could have treated housing as a public good. It chose something else. It chose to subsidize speculation, reward vacancy, and punish need. It let hedge funds buy entire neighborhoods—then asked why working families couldn't compete. It let landlords raise rents unchecked—then blamed tenants for falling behind. It defunded public housing, neglected repairs, and let entire buildings decay. And then it told the poor to be grateful for the crumbs—if they could find any, and if they could afford what they found.

There is no clearer lens into this betrayal than the 2008 housing collapse. For years, families were sold the dream of ownership—told that home-buying was the key to prosperity, dignity, and a better future. But behind that promise was a market built on predatory loans, inflated appraisals, and financial speculation. When the system collapsed, the banks were bailed out. The families were not. Millions lost their homes. Neighborhoods emptied. Generational wealth vanished overnight. And still, the architects of the disaster were rescued—rewarded, even—while the public was left with foreclosures, credit damage, and shattered trust. It was not just a market failure. It was a moral one. And the lesson is clear: a system that treats shelter as leverage will always leave people behind.

And then came the final insult. Taxpayer dollars—taken from the very people now homeless, jobless, and betrayed—were used to bail out the banks. Not to rescue families. Not to restore communities. But to prop up the institutions that caused the collapse. And worse, those same institutions awarded their executives record bonuses. Picture it—a family packing their life into boxes, children crying, savings gone, future shattered—watching the men who engineered their ruin walk away with payouts larger than a decade's honest work. It was not just failure. It was cruelty, publicly funded. And no system that rewards destruction this brazenly deserves to survive.

Even the language has betrayed us. We speak of the "housing market" as if shelter were a stock, ask if it's a good time to buy, as if homes were poker chips. Cities are called "hot" or "cold" based on investor returns—not human need. Newspapers rank places by price spikes, not by how well they house their people. And all the while, we treat displacement as the price of "development"—as if a luxury condo were worth more than the community it erases.

All of this is treated as natural. As inevitable. As progress. But it is none of those things. It is a choice—a deliberate one. Made in boardrooms and budget meetings. Written into zoning codes that ban apartments. Hidden in subsidies that never arrive. Baked into tax breaks for vacant homes and loopholes for speculators. It is a choice to prize wealth over shelter, profit over permanence. To reward those who have—and abandon those who don't.

But precisely because it is a choice, it is a choice we can reverse. No law of nature demands that homes be hoarded or families be displaced. No economic principle requires that shelter be scarce.

Just as we built highways, schools, and power grids, we can build homes—publicly, permanently, and at scale. Not just for the poorest, but for all those the market has failed. For working families who hold up their cities but can't afford to live in them. For veterans returning from service. For the elderly growing old without security. For the disabled, the displaced, and the young—especially the young—who want to stay and raise families in the communities that raised them, and help build something better in return.

Reversing the choice is not about charity. It is about structure. Housing must be treated as infrastructure: planned, funded, maintained, and governed for the public good. It must be built where people live and want to live—not on the margins, but at the heart. It must be safe, durable, and beautiful. And it must be protected from the market forces that created this crisis in the first place.

We do not need to destroy the private market—but we must remove public need from its grip. Let investors build luxury homes. Let landlords chase profit. Let the successful grow their real estate portfolios. Let the market serve those it serves best. But the nation must guarantee something else: a public system strong enough to ensure that no one goes without shelter—not as relief, not as rescue, not as a gift to the undeserving, not as crisis response, but as a permanent foundation of safety, dignity, and hope. A place to live. A place to stay. A place to call home.

That system does not yet exist. But it can. And it must. Because the alternative is not neutrality—it is collapse. A country that cannot house its people cannot govern them. It cannot educate them, protect them, or ask for their trust. Housing is not a side issue. It is the stage upon which all other rights are enacted. You cannot be free if you have nowhere to rest. You cannot participate if you have nowhere to stay. You cannot plan, dream, organize, or contribute if your foundation is always at risk. A nation without shelter is a nation without stability. And a democracy without stability is no democracy at all.

So this is the line we draw. This is the ground we reclaim. Housing must be public. It must be permanent. And it must be protected—by law, by funding, and by shared national will. Because shelter is not just a structure. It is a signal. It tells people they matter. It tells communities they are seen. And it tells the world that this nation still has the courage to care.

6

A HOME FOR ALL

HOW TO BUILD A HOUSING SYSTEM THAT LASTS

"The country needs... homes to live in—not shacks to exist in. Homes where families can develop stability, confidence, and pride."
—Harry S. Truman

We do not need another patchwork. We need a national housing system—coherent, deliberate, and built to last. One that treats housing not as a temporary crisis, but as a permanent public commitment. That system must be structured around six imperatives: Build, Preserve, Guarantee, Reclaim, Protect, and Belong. Each one addresses a failure of the current system. Together, they form the foundation of what must come next.

Build means large-scale public construction. Not incentives. Not nudges. Not indirect subsidies that disappear into profit. But actual homes: publicly funded, publicly governed, and publicly owned. Durable, energy-efficient homes with community infrastructure—

childcare centers, health access points, and transport links—built on public land and maintained by public or mission-driven institutions. These are not emergency shelters. They are homes, with permanence and dignity.

Preserve means protecting the homes we already have. Millions of units—especially public housing—are falling into disrepair for lack of maintenance funding. Many could be restored for less than the cost of new construction. Preservation also means tenant protections, long-term affordability covenants, and the legal tools to stop displacement. This includes protecting seniors, families, and long-term residents from eviction, abuse, or neglect. To house people, we must stop losing the housing we already have.

Guarantee means making housing a legal right—not just a policy goal. That right wouldn't entitle every person to a mansion, but it would guarantee access to safe, secure shelter at a cost they can afford. A federal housing guarantee would empower agencies, courts, and communities to act—with legal authority, not vague aspiration. No veteran should face eviction. No child should sleep in a car.

Reclaim means removing some portion of housing from the profit cycle. That includes public housing, community land trusts, and social housing with resale caps and anti-speculation safeguards. Not every home must be reclaimed—but enough to create a true alternative, insulated from market churn and reserved for those excluded from speculation.

Protect means legal and physical security. Stronger eviction defenses. Repair enforcement. Legal aid. Harassment protections. Enforcement of anti-discrimination laws. A right to housing means little without the right to defend it—and the institutional support to do so.

Belong means homes integrated into real communities. No more distant plots with no transit, no services, and no mobility. Residents must be included in decisions about maintenance, design, and planning. When people belong, they stay. They invest. They care. And they help build what the market cannot: community.

The goal is not modest. It is comprehensive: one hundred million homes in twenty years. That figure includes new construction, restored and retrofitted units, and the conversion of vacant structures to livable homes. It includes permanent housing for the unhoused, transitional housing with support systems, and long-term affordable units for renters and first-time buyers. It is not an aspiration. It is a national mandate—to meet the scale of the need, not the comfort of politics.

Every region of the country will contribute. Coastal cities need density; rural towns need volume; suburbs need infill and access. Federal planners will work with local leaders, but the balance of power must shift: no locality should be allowed to veto progress through zoning, obstruction, or delay. Coordination will reflect population growth, climate resilience, and proximity to transit, employment, and education. A housing system this large cannot be built everywhere at once. But it must be built everywhere it is needed.

The timeline will be visible and binding. Progress will be tracked, updated, and publicly reported every year. States that meet benchmarks will receive accelerated investment; those that obstruct will face reduced funding. This is a collective project—but one with enforceable structure. Twenty years is enough time to fix the crisis. But not if those in power stall, sabotage, or delay. The promise must be tied to performance, or it will fail.

This project will not be cheap. But austerity is far more expensive. Every year of delay drives up emergency shelter costs, health crises, eviction enforcement, and incarceration. Homelessness costs far more than housing. Permanent housing with services costs half what chronic homelessness costs in emergency response. The plan pays for itself—by replacing cycles of failure with systems of stability.

The funds will come from fair taxation and bond measures. That includes a dedicated housing trust, financed through estate taxes, vacancy taxes on unoccupied investment properties, and surtaxes on speculative flips. Revenue will also come from long-term returns: when people have homes, they earn, spend, and contribute. Stable housing reduces crime, increases graduation rates, lowers health costs, and boosts civic participation. Housing is not a cost. It is an investment with generational returns.

This is not charity. It is infrastructure. Just as America once built highways, bridges, and power grids, it must now build homes. These homes are not gifts. They are foundational—vital to families, neighborhoods, and democratic participation. No one expects roads to profit. Housing should be the same. Public goods do not answer to the market. They answer to the people they serve. And that is how this system must be built.

The system must be federal, permanent, and parallel. Its foundation is not subsidy but supply. The core mission is to build and maintain one hundred million homes over twenty years, enough to house all who are currently unhoused, all who are severely cost-burdened, and all future growth over the next two generations. These homes must not be built as an emergency fix, but as a standing public asset—publicly funded, publicly owned, and publicly maintained. They must be integrated with clinics, childcare, schools, transport, and opportunity—not as isolated projects but as the infrastructure of a livable democracy.

Construction must be national in scale but locally responsive. Local governments may implement, but not obstruct. Federal law must override restrictive zoning, exclusionary codes, and permitting regimes that have long blocked affordable housing. Public land must be transferred where possible. Private land may be acquired through purchase or easement. Labor must be recruited nationally, trained publicly, and paid fairly. Where local capacity is low, federal crews may be deployed. Every dollar must build toward public ownership and affordability, not private profit. No entity that extracts equity from tenants should receive public funds. No project may lapse into the speculative market.

The system must be governed by law and protected from reversal. It must include a Housing Guarantee Act that mandates construction, preserves affordability in perpetuity, protects against privatization, and prevents administrative sabotage. Congressional funding must be automatic and indexed to construction benchmarks. Courts must be required to enforce compliance. Agencies must be granted independent authority, with nonpartisan oversight and public transparency. Otherwise, all can be undone—not just by failure, but by political whim.

Some will ask: why should immigrants receive homes when Americans go without? But the question is false. The law will apply to all legal residents, just as public schools and roads already do. And just as education is not withheld from a child because their parent was born elsewhere, neither should shelter. The real question is not who deserves a home—but why a nation of such wealth allows millions to go without.

Others will say: we cannot afford it. But the truth is we already pay—for failure. For broken systems, avoidable emergencies, and short-term subsidies that enrich developers while failing the people. The question is not whether we pay. It is whether we get what we pay for. And until we build homes as public infrastructure, we will continue to pay for failure—in dollars, despair, and national decay.

Still others will say: but won't this create ghettos? Dangerous zones where poverty festers and hope disappears? That risk is real—but it is not inherent. It is a matter of design, funding, and care. The homes we build must be places of dignity: safe, beautiful, well-maintained, and supported by services. Public presence—not abandonment—prevents decay.

This is not a patch. It is a system. One designed to evolve, expand, and endure. One hundred million homes is not an end state

—it is a foundation. The system must include ongoing construction benchmarks, maintenance schedules, and demographic review. It must have teeth: legal mandates, automatic funding, and independent enforcement. Otherwise, it will erode with every election, starve under every budget fight, and vanish at the first sign of economic downturn.

And above all, the system must be owned by the public. Not just in title, but in trust. These homes are not giveaways. They are guarantees. In a functioning democracy, no one should fear losing a home because the market shifted or a landlord changed their mind. That is not freedom. That is dependence disguised as choice.

This plan will be called radical. It will be accused of rewarding laziness, subsidizing failure, or handing homes to immigrants while citizens wait. Critics will demand to know why anyone gets a home for free, or why government should build what the market rejects. They will ignore the fact that far more is spent subsidizing wealth—through tax breaks, investment incentives, and the underwriting of speculation. But these criticisms are not new. They are the same objections raised against Social Security, Medicare, and the Civil Rights Act. And like those before them, they must be answered not with fear, but with fact.

The truth is simple. The current system rewards failure—failure to care, to build, to meet need. It rewards absentee landlords and vacant homes. It punishes the young, the poor, the disabled, the displaced. This plan builds what the market refuses to build, and delivers what the Constitution implicitly requires: a foundation for equal participation. Public housing is not a threat to prosperity. It is a condition of it.

This plan will span five presidencies, ten Congresses, and hundreds of state and local administrations. If it can be undone by a budget cut or a change in party, it will fail. Permanence requires insulation: legal, structural, and financial. Housing funds must be made mandatory. Oversight must be independent. Funding formulas must be indexed to need, with renewal written into statute. It is not enough to pass a law. That law must be protected—through courts, contracts, and design.

And permanence is not just structural. It is cultural. We must create the conditions where reversal becomes politically impossible—where the public sees housing not as a gift, but as a guarantee. When the program is seen as essential, its defense becomes automatic. Permanence must be earned—by delivering what works, and refusing to retreat.

One hundred million homes will address the backlog. But it is not the end. Families will form. Buildings will age. Communities will change. To meet ongoing need, the system must remain open, flexible, and alive. That means keeping a reserve of land, a trained workforce, and a planning authority ready to act. The public system must be as nimble and prepared as the private one—only more just, more durable, and more humane.

Shelter is not a goal to be checked off. It is a permanent function—like education or public safety. A permanent housing commitment must be integrated into national budgeting, regional planning, and civic life. That means cultural renewal—teaching housing as a right, not a reward. Making its presence in communities a source of pride, not stigma.

Housing is not just a material need. It is a condition of political life. Without an address, a person disappears from democracy. They cannot vote, register for school, access benefits, or receive basic services. They are denied stability, safety, and the right to be counted. They are erased—not with violence, but with indifference.

This is the deeper promise: not only homes, but belonging. Not only shelter, but recognition. The public housing system we build is not just an economic fix. It is a democratic repair. In bricks and policy, it says that every person counts. That every family matters. And that a republic, to be real, must provide the conditions for its citizens to live, participate, and thrive. Not just for some. For all.

7

THE FLOOR BENEATH EVERY LIFE
FOOD, WAGES, UNEMPLOYMENT, RETIREMENT, AND VETERANS' CARE

---✦---

"Poverty is not a lack of character. It's a lack of cash."
—Rutger Bregman

FDR said in 1937, "I see one-third of a nation ill-housed, ill-clad, ill-nourished." Nearly a century later, hunger, homelessness, and hardship have not vanished. They have simply become more hidden, more bureaucratic, and more politically convenient to ignore. No American should face eviction for feeding their family. And no child should be asked to focus on school while their stomach begs for breakfast. And no American who loses their job—whether to a factory closing, a hurricane, or an economic downturn—should be abandoned to hunger, homelessness, or humiliation.

Yet for millions, this is exactly what the United States has chosen. Not because it cannot afford to do better, but because it refuses. Food insecurity is not a natural disaster. It is a policy failure—so is wage stagnation in the face of record corporate profits, and so is an unemployment system designed to frustrate applicants and then blame them for needing help.

What these have in common is not just cruelty, but instability. A society that withholds the basics—food, wages, support—is not frugal. It is fragile. A democracy that cannot carry its people through crisis is not a democracy built to last. When survival depends on luck, charity, or bureaucracy, consent becomes coercion.

The Constitution does not promise wealth. But it does promise welfare—general, not selective; national, not transactional. From the Preamble to the Spending Clause, the framers understood that liberty could not endure in a nation where survival depended on charity or chance. A republic built on self-governance requires that its citizens be able to stand—fed, housed, and able to work—not crawl.

Congress holds the power to tax and spend—not merely to defend the nation or carry out enumerated duties, but to promote the general welfare. That phrase, echoed deliberately in both the Preamble and Article I, carries legal and moral weight. It obligates the federal government to ensure the economy serves the people—not the other way around.

This is not a call for equal outcomes. It is a call for a stable floor beneath every life—a structure where hardship is survivable and effort is met with opportunity. Food access, fair wages, and income support are not handouts. They are the functional guarantees of freedom. When hunger blocks learning, when poverty punishes labor, when a layoff leads to homelessness—democracy is not in danger. It is already degraded.

The right to participate in a self-governing society depends on more than the vote. It depends on the material conditions that allow a person to think, work, speak, and live with dignity. That is what the Constitution meant by welfare. It is what we must mean again.

The United States once moved, imperfectly but decisively, toward economic stability as a shared national goal. In the depths of the Great Depression, the federal government created unemployment insurance (1935) and Social Security (1935) to guard against destitution. The Fair Labor Standards Act (1938) established a federal minimum wage and overtime protections. Food stamps began in 1939, became permanent in 1964, and were expanded under Lyndon Johnson's Great Society alongside school lunches, Medicaid, housing assistance, and nutritional support for mothers and infants.

For a generation, the direction was clear: poverty was not a failure of character, but a challenge of policy—and the government had both the power and duty to address it.

Then the arc reversed. In the 1980s, President Reagan vilified recipients of aid as "welfare queens" and slashed support in the name of discipline. The 1996 welfare reform law (PRWORA) replaced federal guarantees with time-limited, state-controlled programs like Temporary Assistance for Needy Families (TANF). Union protections were gutted. Wages were left behind. The Food Stamp Program became SNAP—the Supplemental Nutrition Assistance Program—more modern and efficient, but also more restricted, scrutinized, and politically vulnerable.

What followed was not stagnation, but deliberate erosion. Wages flatlined even as worker productivity and corporate profits surged. The federal minimum wage, once adjusted for inflation, was allowed to decay. States undermined bargaining rights. The connection between work and stability was severed.

Nutrition supports became tools of humiliation. School meal applications grew burdensome. Students were denied food or saddled with "lunch debt." SNAP access was narrowed, with new work and reporting requirements. Even pandemic-era waivers that briefly expanded access and eliminated stigma were quietly allowed to expire.

Unemployment insurance became a maze of failure. Benefits

varied wildly by state. Application systems crashed under strain. In many states, only a fraction of eligible workers could access help. Benefits were short, payments low, and approval processes riddled with obstacles. The result was not oversight, but abandonment.

These were not glitches in the system. They were the system—designed to punish need, dissuade use, and shift blame. In a nation of immense wealth, hunger, hardship, and fear became tools of economic governance. The safety net was not stretched thin. It was pulled back, strand by strand, until millions were left with nothing beneath them.

The United States is not alone in facing economic shocks, wage pressures, or regional inequality. But it stands nearly alone in refusing to guarantee the basics of survival. Other wealthy democracies treat food access, fair pay, and income support not as favors, but as foundations—tools to stabilize lives, protect dignity, and sustain national resilience.

In France, Sweden, and Japan, school meals are universally available and nutritionally standardized—no child is shamed, and no family burdened by paperwork or lunch debt. In Germany and Australia, minimum wages are indexed to inflation, and collective bargaining is protected by national policy. In the Netherlands and the Nordic states, workers have access to portable benefits and robust union representation, allowing labor to move without losing security.

Unemployment is treated not as failure, but as transition. Denmark's "flexicurity" model provides up to 90% income replacement alongside free job training and career counseling. Germany integrates unemployment benefits with housing, childcare, and workforce services. Canada combines wage supports with parental leave, sick leave, and retraining—all administered as part of a coherent, navigable system.

Abuse is rare because systems are designed with trust, transparency, and expectations. Benefits taper over time. Retraining is often mandatory. Data is cross-checked, but without cruelty. The goal is always the same: help people return to stable, contributing lives—not by fear, but by design.

These nations did not stumble into justice. They built it. And their success makes clear: America's failures are not inevitable. They are chosen. And they can be unchosen.

Donald Trump did not invent the American war on the poor. But he escalated it—brazenly, strategically, and without shame. In both his terms, food access, fair wages, and income supports were not just neglected. They were targeted. Stability was treated as weakness. Desperation became political leverage.

In 2019, Trump attempted to slash eligibility for the Supplemental Nutrition Assistance Program (SNAP) by eliminating broad-based categorical eligibility—a rule change that would have removed up to 700,000 people from the rolls. The courts blocked it before full implementation, but the message was received—and the fear was lasting. Meanwhile, his administration began weakening school nutrition standards as early as 2018, formally rolling back Obama-era rules in 2020 to allow more sodium, fewer whole grains, and sugary flavored milks. The health of children was treated as negotiable.

Unemployment protections followed the same pattern. During the pandemic, Congress temporarily expanded benefits, but Trump delayed extensions, opposed renewals, and ultimately allowed the programs to lapse. He cast the unemployed as freeloaders, claiming benefits were keeping people from working, even as COVID still raged. Republican governors followed his lead, ending federal jobless support early while millions remained out of work.

Wage protections fared no better. Trump blocked every effort to raise the federal minimum wage, which remains frozen at $7.25 an hour. He imposed pay freezes for federal workers and staffed the National Labor Relations Board with appointees hostile to unions. His administration supported "right-to-work" laws at the state level and consistently sided with employers in labor disputes—undermining the very structures that once protected working Americans from exploitation.

These were not ordinary policy disagreements. They were acts of sabotage—calculated attacks on the systems that keep people afloat. Trump governed as he campaigned: by stoking resentment, targeting the vulnerable, and dismantling the protections that once made economic security possible.

The test of a decent society is not how it treats the wealthy in times of plenty, but how it treats the vulnerable in times of need. It is time to rebuild the foundation: to ensure that no child goes hungry, no worker is trapped in poverty, and no American is abandoned when work disappears. We do not need to invent the solution—we need only to implement what justice already requires.

Five guarantees define a strong floor beneath every American life: food, wages, support, security, and care. Each has been weakened. Each must be rebuilt.

A. Food Access

Dignity is not an abstract value—it is a logistics problem. A functional democracy must be able to deliver food, shelter, and care without delay or humiliation. This means public systems that coordinate—across agencies, across eligibility lines, across the boundaries between hunger and health, housing and employment. Every reform in this book rests on that premise: that democracy is not charity, and survival is not a reward. When the system delivers basic needs reliably, it builds trust. And trust is what allows people to participate fully—in work, in community, and in public life.

B. Fair Wages

The federal minimum wage must be raised and indexed to inflation so that work once again provides stability. Wage theft must be prosecuted as a crime, not a cost of business. National support for sectoral bargaining—industry-wide wage-setting common in many European economies—can restore power to workers without placing individual firms at a disadvantage. The right to unionize must be not just legal, but viable.

C. Unemployment Security

Unemployment insurance must be reimagined as a universal, portable benefit, available to all workers—salaried, hourly, gig, and contract alike. Benefit amounts must rise. Duration must reflect real recovery timelines. And participation should include access to free training, career counseling, and job placement, not as punishment, but as a path forward. Abuse can be deterred by design. What matters is that dignity is never denied to those in transition.

D. RETIREMENT and Social Security Reform

Social Security was once a promise: that every American, after a life of work, would have a foundation beneath them in old age. But rising inequality, longer lifespans, and unstable employment have strained the system. Wealthier Americans now live longer than poorer ones—yet contribute proportionally less. Benefits have not kept pace with cost of living. And partisan attempts to weaken or privatize the program have sown uncertainty. A renewed commitment must do more than preserve Social Security. It must adapt it. That means phasing out the contribution cap, strengthening survivor and disability benefits, crediting unpaid caregiving, and designing benefits that reflect both need and fairness. Above all, retirement must not depend on luck. It must be earned, protected, and guaranteed.

. . .

E. Veterans and Public Service

Those who risk their lives in service to the country must never be abandoned by it. Yet veterans too often return to underfunded care, bureaucratic hurdles, and social neglect. Housing insecurity, untreated trauma, and insufficient job support haunt too many who have already served. The obligation does not end when deployment does. The Veterans Administration must be fully staffed, modernized, and respected—not starved, privatized, or politicized. And that commitment must extend to all forms of national service. To those who teach, respond to disaster, or serve in civil defense, the nation must offer not just thanks, but care. Their sacrifice was not abstract. Neither is our responsibility.

These guarantees will face opposition. But those arguments are not new, and they are not right.

Opponents will call these reforms socialism. Critics will claim we can't afford them. Commentators will warn of dependency, fraud, and laziness. These are not new arguments. They are old shields for policies that keep people desperate—and power unaccountable.

But every one of these objections has been answered by history, by evidence, and by the daily experience of nations that chose to protect their people. In France and Sweden, universal school meals are standard, not radical. In Germany and Australia, wages keep pace with living costs. In Denmark, unemployment insurance includes training and job placement—not to punish, but to prepare. Abuse is rare because systems are designed to work—not to intimidate.

The greatest fraud is not someone receiving a benefit they didn't strictly need. It is a society that pretends survival must be earned through suffering. We do not call fire departments socialism. We do not ask roadways to turn a profit. Why then do we treat food, wages, and income as privileges to be rationed?

The truth is this: people want to work. They want to provide, to participate, to move forward. What they need is a system that believes in them—and believes with them. The only thing more dangerous than trusting people too much is trusting them too little.

Food, wages, and income support are not fringe issues. They are the bedrock of national strength. A society that withholds the basics is not frugal. It is fragile. And a democracy built on fragility cannot endure.

What comes next must not be a return to patchwork reforms or temporary aid. It must be a new guarantee: that in the United States of America, no one will starve, no one will fall from work into ruin, and no one will suffer for needing time to begin again. They are what a functioning democracy owes to the people who make it work.

We must build the system we should have had all along: a structure strong enough to carry us through hardship, change, and recovery. The right to stay afloat is not a partisan dream. It is the floor beneath every other right: to learn, to vote, to speak, to live. Without it, liberty is a myth. With it, democracy endures.

These reforms are not the end of the story. They are where the repair begins.

8

THE FLOOR WE BUILD TOGETHER
WHY FOOD SECURITY, A LIVING WAGE, AND UNEMPLOYMENT SUPPORT ARE NOT GENEROSITY—THEY'RE INFRASTRUCTURE

"Liberty cannot exist in a nation half-fed, half-housed, and half-employed."
  —Paraphrased synthesis of Franklin D. Roosevelt and Martin Luther King Jr.

Every democracy makes a choice. It can offer help when people fall—or build a floor so solid they don't fall far at all. For too long, America has chosen the former: emergency patches, half-measures, and temporary relief. But survival is not a system. And safety nets that collapse under pressure are not safety nets at all.

We now live with the damage of that failure. A nation where millions live one illness, one accident, one missed paycheck away from hunger, eviction, or despair. Where wages lag behind the cost of living. Where unemployment systems punish the jobless and reward political cruelty. These are not natural disasters. They are decisions—made, defended, and repeated.

The goal is not just to end hunger, raise wages, or fix unemployment. It is to build a structure that guarantees enough to live—not as charity, but as a function of citizenship. A democracy that endures must build its strength at the base. That begins with three guarantees: food for every family, fair wages for every worker, and real support when work disappears. These are not luxuries. They are the minimum requirements of a stable, functioning republic.

We must begin by naming what we owe each other—not as generosity, but as the unfinished promise of a nation built on liberty, dignity, and mutual survival. Hunger in America is not caused by famine, drought, or war. It is caused by policy. It exists not because we lack food, but because we allow its distribution—and the right to aid—to be governed by stigma, paperwork, and politics. At any moment, tens of millions are food insecure. Children go to school hungry. Seniors skip meals to buy medicine. Parents work full-time and still rely on food banks. In the wealthiest country on Earth, this is not a glitch. It is a policy failure.

The Supplemental Nutrition Assistance Program (SNAP), once called food stamps, is the largest anti-hunger program in the country. But it is inconsistently administered by design. Eligibility rules vary by state. Benefits are modest and often fail to reflect local grocery costs. Harsh work requirements and reporting demands disproportionately punish the poorest recipients—especially those with unstable work, caregiving duties, or mental health conditions. Even brief disruptions in income or paperwork can trigger catastrophic loss of aid. Recent data also shows a sharp rise in improper payments—reaching over 10% in 2023. But the majority stem from complex eligibility rules, not fraud. Stronger automation and simpler administration would reduce errors without punishing recipients.

The same is true of WIC—the Special Supplemental Nutrition

Program for Women, Infants, and Children—which supports pregnant women and young children. Despite its proven health benefits, millions eligible remain unenrolled—according to recent USDA estimates, nearly 40% of those eligible are not receiving benefits. In schools, lunch debt accrues like shame. Children from low-income families are denied hot meals or publicly marked when accounts run dry. Some are even forced to throw meals away.

We do not need to invent solutions. We need to implement them. SNAP must become a true national guarantee—automatically enrolling anyone who qualifies for Medicaid, unemployment insurance, or other income-based federal programs. Benefits must be generous, inflation-adjusted, and federally administered. Work requirements must end. Food is not a reward for obedience. It is a condition for democracy.

Second, WIC and school meals must be universal. Every pregnant woman and child under five should receive nutritional support—regardless of paperwork. Every student in public school should receive breakfast and lunch, without stigma, application, or shame. This is not radical. France offers universal school meals with strict quality controls. Finland and Sweden go further, integrating food into the broader health and education system. Even the United Kingdom has recently expanded school meals—with bipartisan support and a nationwide rollout planned for autumn 2026.

Third, we must strengthen the public infrastructure of food. That means federally funded regional food banks, national stockpiles of staple goods to prevent shortages and price spikes, and targeted investment in food deserts—areas where stores are scarce and prices are high. No ZIP code should determine whether someone eats.

None of this is unaffordable. The entire SNAP budget is less than two percent of federal spending. The return—from improved health, education, and productivity—is far greater. What we lack is not money. It is will.

Ending hunger is not about generosity. It is about governance. A democracy that cannot carry its people through crisis—cannot feed its children, protect its workers, or sustain its future—is not built to last. A nation that lets children go hungry has abandoned the basic conditions of a civilized society.

A job should be enough. That was once the American promise: if you worked, you could live. Not lavishly, but with dignity. Food on the table. Rent paid. A future within reach. That promise is broken. Millions of full-time workers live below the poverty line. Others hold two or three jobs and still cannot afford basic necessities. This is not a failure of effort. It is a failure of wages. And it is a failure that bleeds into every other system—forcing government to subsidize employers who refuse to pay enough for people to live.

The federal minimum wage is $7.25 an hour—unchanged since 2009. In real terms, that's less than half what it was worth in 1968, when adjusted for inflation. Thirty states have raised their own minimums, but the patchwork leaves wide gaps, especially in the South. Tipped workers, disabled workers, and teenagers may be paid even less. In some sectors, workers depend more on tips, apps, or public aid than on their paycheck. These workers miss meals, delay care, and watch their children inherit the same precarity they worked to escape. The result is not market efficiency. It is quiet exploitation—underwritten by the state.

This is not how wages work in a healthy democracy. Wages are not just a private contract between employer and employee. They are a public declaration of what we value—and what we will not tolerate. A wage that cannot support life is not a wage. It is a sanction. And a nation that accepts mass working poverty has made a choice: not for frugality, but for fragility. The damage is not just economic. It is democratic.

The solution begins with a national wage floor that reflects reality. That means raising the federal minimum wage by $1.50 per year until it reaches at least $15 an hour—then indexing it automatically to inflation or median wages to keep pace with real costs. It means ending subminimum wage carve-outs for tipped workers, people with disabilities, and others long denied equal pay. And it means blocking federal contracts and subsidies to companies that pay less than a living wage. Public money should not reward private harm.

But wage reform cannot stop at the federal level. Cities and states must be free to go further—tailoring wage laws to local housing and living costs without federal preemption. In high-cost areas, $15 is still not enough. The Department of Labor should publish regional wage adequacy benchmarks and track real-world gaps. And Congress should offer matching grants to jurisdictions that lift local standards. When federal law sets a floor, it must never become a ceiling.

To support small businesses, the transition can be phased—but not delayed indefinitely. Tax credits, wage subsidies, and technical support can smooth the adjustment. But what cannot continue is a system in which global corporations offload their payrolls onto public aid—while reporting record profits and issuing stock buybacks. If a business model depends on poverty wages, it is not a model worth preserving.

Other democracies already treat wage floors as policy, not theater. Australia's Fair Work Commission raised the minimum wage 5.75 percent in 2023—based on cost-of-living data and economic review. In much of Western Europe, wages are negotiated sector by sector with government oversight and union coordination. Even in nations without statutory minimums, collective bargaining protects a dignified standard. The lesson is not that every model fits. It is that low wages are never inevitable. They are constructed. And they can be changed.

Work must be rewarded, not exploited. A living wage is not a luxury. It is the foundation of freedom. Without it, workers are trapped in cycles of debt, silence, and dependence. Raising wages is not just economic reform. It is moral repair. It is how a nation says: You matter. Your labor matters. And your survival is not optional.

We cannot guarantee prosperity for all. But we can—and must—guarantee enough to live. That is what wages are for. That is what work should earn. That is not generosity. It is justice.

Unemployment is not a moral failing. It is a fact of economic life. Industries shift. Pandemics strike. Jobs vanish. Yet in America, the system built to cushion those blows too often punishes the very people it was meant to protect. Each state runs its own unemployment program, with wildly uneven rules, benefits, and access. Some offer less than $200 a week. Others cap aid after just 12 weeks. Paperwork is dense. Systems are outdated. Delays are common—especially during crises, when help is needed most. Too often, one missed report, one late form, one dropped call is enough to cut someone off entirely.

This is not an accident. After the Great Recession, several Republican-led states rewrote their unemployment systems to reduce payouts and restrict access. Some added drug tests. Others slashed benefit weeks or imposed new barriers to qualify. The unspoken goal was clear: make unemployment uncomfortable enough to force people into any job, at any wage. But that cruelty carries a cost—not just to workers, but to the economy. People forced into unstable or underpaid jobs don't spend, don't grow, and often fall back into need.

A better system begins with national standards. Every worker in every state should receive a baseline level of support—no matter where they live. That means setting a national floor for benefit levels, duration, and eligibility. It means modernizing systems, streamlining verification, and offering real-time translation and help. Support must be timely, accessible, and automatic—ready before the next storm arrives, not built in its aftermath.

But dignity requires more than a check. It requires purpose. Countries like Denmark and the Netherlands offer not only generous unemployment benefits, but wraparound support: job training, resume help, skill certification, and personalized guidance. These aren't extras. They're how a system treats unemployment as transition—not punishment.

We can do the same. First, tie long-term benefits to opportunity. Any extension beyond, say, 26 weeks, can be linked to enrollment in certified job training, education, or placement programs. This is legal, popular, and effective. Second, partner with community colleges, unions, and employers to provide flexible upskilling in high-need sectors—health care, green energy, infrastructure, and technology.

Third, protect part-time and gig workers. Today's workforce is fragmented. Many are misclassified as contractors and excluded entirely. The unemployment system—built for 1950s-era jobs, schedules, and clear employers—must be redesigned to follow the worker, not the job.

Finally, end the stigma. Unemployment insurance is not welfare. It is insurance—earned and paid into by workers and employers alike. It exists not to punish, but to protect. When the system fails, it is not the jobless who are to blame. It is us.

A resilient economy requires resilient people. And resilience comes from dignity, stability, and time to rebuild. America cannot afford another decade of broken promises. We need a system designed for the real world: flexible, fair, and fast. A better future does not begin with jobs alone. It begins with the promise that when jobs disappear, people don't. They are caught. They are supported. They are seen.

This is not a vision to be deferred. It is a plan to be enacted. These proposals are not speculative. They have clear precedents in American law and international practice. What's missing is not the evidence. It's the courage. Real reform is not a slogan. It is a series of systems working in alignment—with money to support them, mechanisms to deliver them, and deadlines that cannot be delayed. Every democratic promise rests on the ability to deliver not once, but always—and not just to some, but to all.

To build a nation where hunger, wage theft, and economic neglect are no longer tolerated, we must modernize the systems designed to prevent them. Nutrition benefits must be centralized through the Department of Agriculture, with administrative control transferred from state agencies to a single national platform tied to IRS and HHS data. This removes the friction of reapplication, the threat of local sabotage, and the churn that throws millions into needless risk. Wage protections must be enforced by a fully resourced Department of Labor with regional wage boards and expanded power to audit, fine, and bar abusive employers. Unemployment insurance must be federalized under a unified national system—administered by the Treasury, coordinated with Social Security and the IRS—to guarantee timely payments, consistent rules, and automatic triggers when crisis strikes.

If the United States wants a stable floor—guaranteed food, fair pay, and real support during job loss—it must fund it openly and honestly. That means rejecting the myth that we can build justice without asking more from those with the most. There is no secret surplus, no magical offset. But there is immense wealth—concentrated, under-taxed, and shielded by loopholes and political cowardice. A system that protects its people is not a luxury. It is infrastructure. And like all infrastructure, it must be publicly funded. Anything less is not restraint—it is erosion. And a nation that refuses to fund its own foundation will find it crumbling beneath its feet.

None of this is radical. Every proposal has precedent. Congress can restore the top marginal income tax rate to pre-2001 levels—before the Bush and Trump cuts tilted the code toward the wealthy. It can close the carried interest and capital gains loopholes so investment income is taxed like wages. It can impose a modest surtax on ultra-millionaires and billionaires, whose wealth has surged while wages have stalled. It can reinstate the corporate alternative minimum tax, end offshore profit shifting, and implement a small financial transaction tax to curb high-frequency speculation. These are not experiments. They are tested, proven, and overdue.

Redirecting existing subsidies is equally vital. Taxpayer dollars currently flow to fossil fuel companies at levels that dwarf the budgets of entire social programs. Those funds could instead underwrite universal school meals, expand and modernize SNAP and WIC, raise wages for federal contractors, and guarantee national unemployment coverage—including job training and career support. Together, these fiscal reforms would more than cover the cost of what this chapter proposes. The real tradeoff is not between generosity and discipline—but between moral courage and quiet collapse.

This is not redistribution for its own sake. It is the price of a functioning republic. No society that delivers hunger, poverty wages, and abandonment can claim to defend liberty. What we propose is not utopia—it is a floor. And every lasting democracy builds one. The question is no longer whether we can afford to act. It is whether we are finally honest enough to send the bill where it belongs.

The implementation schedule is ambitious but achievable. In Year One, Congress would pass core legislation with automatic triggers. Nutrition enrollment would begin with children and pregnant individuals, reaching full adult coverage by Year Three. The national wage floor would rise by $1.50 per year until it reaches the cost-of-living benchmark, with regional boards authorized to accelerate. The new federal unemployment system would launch in parallel to state programs in Year Two and fully replace them by Year Three—offering grants to states that transition faster.

Transparency and enforcement would be mandatory—not optional or symbolic. Every agency involved would publish quarterly compliance metrics. A new Economic Dignity Oversight Commission—independent, nonpartisan, and publicly accessible—

would monitor implementation, investigate abuses, and recommend ongoing adjustments.

Every serious reform invites resistance. These are no exception. Critics will call them socialism, handouts, or government overreach. But these programs are not new. What's new is the will to make them work—nationally, consistently, and without shame. Others will warn of cost or inflation, claim that businesses cannot absorb wage increases, or argue that benefits will discourage work. These arguments are not just familiar. They are false. Most employers already pay above the federal minimum wage or can adjust through phased increases. SNAP and WIC have among the lowest fraud rates of any federal program. And countries with generous, well-designed unemployment systems show consistently higher re-employment rates where training and support are integrated. The lesson is not that generosity weakens effort. It is that stability strengthens it.

Some will argue that these reforms invite moral hazard—that if food, wages, and job loss are supported, people will stop trying. But the greater danger is moral failure: a society that permits hunger, poverty, and despair—and then blames the people living in them. Strong democracies build shared floors. Not to eliminate hardship, but to prevent freefall. Not to replace effort, but to make effort possible. The greatest risk is not laziness. It is despair. And despair is not overcome by lectures. It is overcome by systems that offer dignity, structure, and hope. These reforms do not promise luxury. They promise enough. Enough to live. Enough to recover. Enough to return.

Some will object on principle. They will say the market should set wages. That churches and food banks should feed the poor. That unemployment must be unpleasant, to force compliance. But we have tried that. We have decades of data—and millions of broken lives—to prove it fails. Food banks now replace food policy. Employers rely on public aid to subsidize low wages. Unemployment systems crash precisely when they are most needed. These are not malfunctions. They are design outcomes. And if democracy is measured by its ability to carry its people through crisis, these systems have failed the test. Repair is not indulgence. It is obligation.

Finally, some will say we cannot afford it. But the sharper truth is: we already pay. We pay in emergency rooms and eviction courts, in childhood hunger and burnout, in economic volatility and democratic distrust. We pay every year for the consequences of refusal—while pretending the costs are invisible. The reforms in this chapter cost less than the chaos we now endure. And what they offer in return is not just economic efficiency. They offer civic repair. Because the foundation of a republic is not austerity. It is trust. And there is no trust where there is no floor.

These reforms are not only practical—they are constitutional. They fulfill the federal obligation to promote the general Welfare, as declared in both the Preamble and Article I. A nation that secures liberty must first secure survival. A nation that feeds its children, pays its workers, and supports its people through change is not indulging them. It is equipping them. And that is not generosity. It is justice. Justice made real, not just in moments of catastrophe—but in the quiet rhythms of daily life.

We are not beginning from nothing. We are beginning from betrayal—a long erosion of the promise that work would bring stability, that effort would be met with enough, and that no one would be left behind. From that failure, we build a floor. Not to cushion weakness, but to sustain strength. Not to replace responsibility, but to make responsibility possible. Because a democracy that cannot carry its people through ordinary hardship will not carry them forward at all.

9

SECURITY IN THE LONG RUN — REBUILDING RETIREMENT FOR ALL

FROM EROSION TO EQUITY IN AMERICA'S MOST TRUSTED PROGRAM: SOCIAL SECURITY

---✦---

"The great political question is whether you can make democracy work without ensuring security in old age."
— Franklin D. Roosevelt

Social Security is not failing. It is functioning exactly as designed—faithfully, efficiently, and with extraordinary reach. But it was designed nearly a century ago, for a country that no longer exists. It was built in the aftermath of the Great Depression, when work was industrial, retirement was brief, and poverty in old age was often fatal. The idea was simple: those who worked would be protected in old age, not by charity but by the pooled strength of the working public. And for a time, it worked. Poverty among seniors declined. Stability rose. A generation of American workers, many without private pensions or savings, gained a measure of dignity when they could no longer work.

But that architecture was built on assumptions that no longer hold. The structure remains, but the scaffolding of fairness has eroded. Today, the program delivers its largest lifetime payouts not to those most in need, but to those who earned the most, lived the longest, and had the greatest freedom to choose when they retired. Wealthy retirees with stock portfolios and second homes receive the maximum benefit. Meanwhile, workers who spent their lives in low-wage, physically demanding jobs—those with shorter life expectancy, lower savings, and fewer options—receive far less. They claim benefits earlier, not because they want to, but because they have no choice. The reward for a lifetime of essential labor is often just enough to survive—and not always that.

We do not have a failing program. We have a misaligned one. It does not collapse under weight. It distorts under pressure. And the longer it remains out of sync with the realities of modern life—gig work, caregiving gaps, housing costs, and deep inequality—the more it risks becoming a symbol of institutional failure rather than social protection. At its best, Social Security is still the most effective anti-poverty program in the country. But without reform, it will continue to deliver the most support to those who need it least—and offer the bare minimum to those who have nowhere else to turn. That is not justice. And in time, it is not sustainable.

Social Security is funded by payroll taxes, not personal savings. Workers contribute a fixed percentage of their earnings—matched by employers—on income up to a capped threshold. Those contributions do not accumulate in personal accounts. Instead, they flow into a national trust fund that pays monthly benefits to retirees, people with disabilities, and the surviving spouses and children of deceased workers. The amount a person receives is determined by a formula that considers their lifetime earnings, years in the workforce, and the age at which they begin collecting. It is not adjusted for savings, hardship, or need. It is determined by income history alone.

Social Security was never meant to serve retirees alone. From the start, it recognized that vulnerability can come not just from age, but from tragedy, illness, and loss. The program's disability insurance protects those who become unable to work. Survivor benefits sustain spouses and children when a breadwinner dies. These are not secondary features. They are pillars—quiet guarantors of continuity when life is interrupted. For millions, they are the difference between stability and collapse, between recovery and ruin. A strong society does not wait for catastrophe to offer help. It builds structures that catch people before they fall all the way down.

This structure was built in a different economic era. At the time, work was often full-time, long-term, and continuous. Retirement followed a predictable arc, and shorter life expectancy meant fewer years spent drawing benefits. In that context, a formula tied to wages made sense: those who worked more earned more, and longevity and income were broadly aligned. But the modern economy is far more uneven. Many workers move in and out of employment. Some step away to care for children or aging parents. Others work jobs that offer low pay, few protections, and no benefits at all. For them, a system based solely on wages ignores the costs they have already absorbed—and the insecurity they face in retirement.

The formula has not adapted. It still calculates value based on prior earnings, assuming that income reflects effort and that longevity reflects fairness. But wages alone do not reflect economic reality. The system gives no credit for caregiving, no adjustment for short lifespans or generational disadvantage. It cannot see that a billionaire and a grocery clerk may both receive checks—one modest, the other maximized. What was once a floor beneath every worker has tilted, slowly and structurally, toward those who need it least.

The slow undoing of Social Security did not begin with a crisis. It began with a vote. In 1983, Congress passed a series of amendments designed to shore up the trust fund. The most lasting of these was a gradual increase in the full retirement age—from 65 to 67—effectively reducing lifetime benefits for future retirees. At the same time, for the first time in its history, Social Security benefits were made subject to income tax for middle-income households. These changes were framed as modest adjustments, necessary for solvency. But they marked a quiet shift—from protecting dignity to protecting budget forecasts. Since then, Congress has failed to adapt the formula to account for the rise of gig work, the burden of caregiving, or the divergence in life expectancy between the rich and the poor. The law stayed fixed while the world moved on.

Administrative erosion followed. Over two decades, the Social Security Administration has been systematically underfunded. Field offices have closed. Wait times have soared. Backlogs for disability determinations stretch into months or years. Workers who apply for benefits after decades of labor often find themselves navigating a system that is impersonal, slow, and opaque. The system functions, but not with care—and increasingly, not with trust. The human infrastructure that once made Social Security feel like a public good has been hollowed out by austerity, privatization pressures, and political neglect.

Meanwhile, efforts to modernize the program have been repeatedly blocked or distorted. Proposals to lift the payroll tax cap—so that earnings above $168,600 are taxed like every dollar earned by a grocery clerk—have stalled for decades. Efforts to credit unpaid caregiving years or part-time labor with partial benefits have been dismissed as too complex or too costly. Instead, political energy has gone toward privatization schemes and benefit cuts. In 2005, President George W. Bush proposed partial privatization. In recent years, House Republicans have floated raising the retirement age again. Even Democrats, while defending the program rhetorically, have often failed to act. The idea of "insolvency" has become a tool of fear—used to demand sacrifice from those with the least rather than reform from those with the most.

While the program stood still, the economy changed beneath it. Stable, full-time jobs with pensions have given way to part-time, contract, and gig work. Private retirement savings are scarce for low- and middle-income earners. Care costs—child care, elder care, health care—consume larger shares of family income, leaving little to save. Life expectancy has risen dramatically for the wealthy but stagnated or declined for the working class. The retirement age may be the same on paper, but the odds of reaching it—or surviving long enough to collect full benefits—now depend heavily on race, class, and geography.

This is the real collapse. Not the depletion of funds, but the slow disintegration of alignment between a public institution and the people it claims to serve. The law remains on the books. The checks still arrive. But the foundation of fairness—the idea that the system recognizes modern work, modern risk, and modern inequality—has been left behind. What fails first is not the payout. What fails first is the promise.

The erosion of Social Security has not been accidental. It has been defended, delayed, and distorted—most aggressively by Republican lawmakers who have protected the wealthy from contributing more while demanding cuts from everyone else. For decades, Republicans have refused to lift the payroll tax cap, even as income inequality widened and billionaire wealth surged. They have called for raising the retirement age, cutting benefits, or means-testing eligibility, all under the language of "entitlement reform." These proposals do not touch the affluent. They target the very workers who rely on Social Security most: low earners, unstable workers, and communities already left behind by the broader economy. Again and again, the Republican position has been to ask more from those who have less, while shielding the donor class from structural responsibility.

Under Donald Trump, the threat became more direct. In his first term, he repeatedly proposed cuts to Social Security Disability

Insurance and floated payroll tax "holidays" that would have drained the trust fund without replacement. During the 2020 campaign, he suggested eliminating the payroll tax entirely—effectively ending the funding stream that sustains the system. His second term has brought similar threats cloaked in chaos: budget proposals that slash administrative funding, political allies who call the program "unsustainable," and economic policies that drive up costs for seniors while doing nothing to bolster retirement security. He has never offered a plan to strengthen Social Security. What he offers is instability—rhetorical, fiscal, and political. And that instability, even when not enacted into law, weakens the system by design. It introduces fear, delays reform, and leaves millions unsure whether the benefit they paid into will be there when they need it.

We cannot fix a misaligned system by sanding down its edges. A program designed in the 1930s cannot be asked to solve the problems of the 2030s without a full and honest reckoning. Social Security was built to prevent destitution in old age. Today, it must answer to a far more complex reality: volatile work, longer lifespans, unpaid caregiving, vanishing pensions, and vast inequality. The goal is not to discard what works. It is to rebuild the structure so that it matches the shape of the world we live in now.

A modern system must meet six objectives. First, it must guarantee dignity in retirement—not for the fortunate, but for everyone who contributed through labor, care, or service. Second, it must direct benefits based not on past income, but present need. Third, it must ensure that every worker—regardless of job type—can build portable, lifelong retirement savings. Fourth, it must recognize contributions that never show up on a paycheck: caregiving, interrupted work, service. Fifth, it must be funded fairly, with the wealthy contributing more and subsidies aimed at those who need them. And sixth, it must restore trust by being stable, transparent, and worthy of public belief.

At the heart of this reform is a single, phased transition: from income-based benefits to needs-based support. Beginning in 2030, each new retirement cohort would receive benefits calculated under a gradually shifting formula—90% income-based, 10% needs-based in Year One; 80–20 in Year Two; and so on. After ten years, the shift would be complete. All new beneficiaries would receive support based on financial need, not lifetime income. No current retirees would be affected. No one would lose benefits already promised. But from that point forward, Social Security would no longer pay its largest checks to those who need them least.

This transition does not erase the past. It honors that promise—by correcting its blind spots. When Social Security was created, tying benefits to income made rough sense. Most people worked full-time. Most retired by 65. Most lived only a few years longer. But those assumptions no longer hold. Today, workers live radically different economic lives—and die with radically different prospects. To keep paying out according to an outdated formula is not fairness. It is inertia masquerading as justice.

To support this new structure, the system must be funded in a way that reflects modern wealth. That means lifting the payroll tax cap, so that all earnings—not just wages under $168,600—contribute equally. It means aligning tax incentives to support low- and middle-income savers, not just those with stock portfolios. And it means using public funds to match contributions for those who cannot save enough on their own—so that the goal of building retirement wealth is open to all, not just the already-secure.

These reforms must not weaken the system's broad commitments. They must strengthen them. A modern Social Security must deliver not just retirement checks, but real protection for workers who become disabled, parents who die too soon, and families left behind. The formulas must account for hardship. The system must see caregiving as labor, interrupted work as sacrifice, and loss as something we do not force people to bear alone. The goal is not minimal coverage—it is lasting security. And in that vision, the full scope of Social Security's mission must be restored, defended, and renewed.

But public reform alone is not enough. We must also ensure that workers build wealth of their own. In parallel, every worker must have access to a regulated, portable retirement account. Modeled on Australia's superannuation system, these accounts would receive mandatory employer contributions and grow across a lifetime of work. They would follow the worker, not the job. They would be invested under public rules, shielded from predatory fees, and accessible only at retirement. Combined with needs-based public benefits, they would form a two-pillar system: universal savings for all, and targeted support for those who reach retirement without enough.

This is not a privatization scheme. Unlike past proposals that diverted payroll taxes into private markets, these accounts are additive—not subtractive. They do not replace the public guarantee of Social Security—they extend it. What changes is not the guarantee, but the opportunity. Today, stock ownership is concentrated in the hands of the top ten percent. Under this plan, every worker would own a share. Their labor would not only earn wages—it would build long-term wealth.

Beginning in 2030, every worker would contribute one percent of their income to a regulated, portable retirement account. Each year, that contribution would rise by one percentage point, reaching ten percent in 2040. Employers would match a portion. The funds would be professionally invested under public oversight, shielded from predatory fees and speculative risk. This is not a tax. It is personal savings, earned by the worker, owned by the worker, and returned to the worker in retirement or during tightly defined emergencies.

The reduction in take-home pay would be modest and gradual. And it would be more than offset by parallel reforms in housing, health care, and family costs. As prescription prices fall, rents stabilize, and public insurance expands, workers would find that what they lose in deductions, they gain in breathing room. For decades, American workers have borne the costs of instability alone—asked to save what they can while the ground shifts beneath them. This system reverses that logic. It builds security into the paycheck itself, so that no matter the job, the future is never out of reach.

Over time, these individual accounts would do more than supplement retirement income. They would democratize capital. They would ensure that the gains of a growing economy are shared not only through wages, but through ownership. And they would prove that a worker's dignity need not depend on charity, family, or luck. It can be built, steadily and structurally, through a system that sees their value and stores it safely for the years to come.

In time, this savings pillar would do more than expand opportunity—they would reduce dependence. As more workers retire with meaningful savings, the public system would shift from being the sole source of retirement income to a true safety net—targeted, adequate, and sustainable. Those who save enough would rely less on public support. Those who struggle would still be protected. And those in the middle—the forgotten majority—would no longer have to fear the steep drop from working life to fixed income. What we build, in effect, is not just retirement protection but retirement resilience—a future where government provides enough, but workers arrive with more.

If we do nothing, the system will not implode. It will degrade. Slowly, predictably, and visibly. The checks will keep coming—but they will matter less. The trust fund will diminish—and so will public trust. Workers will continue to pay into a system that favors those with longer lives, higher earnings, and more options. They will retire into a formula that cannot see the unpaid years they gave to children, parents, or communities. They will count their months and their dollars and find both running short. The promise will remain on paper. But the people will know it is no longer theirs.

As needs rise, support will lag. Lawmakers will call for cuts—because the system seems unsustainable. But what will be unsustainable is not the cost, but the refusal to adjust. If the rich continue to collect what they do not need while the poor retire with nothing, resentment will rise and legitimacy will fall. Social Security will come to symbolize not protection, but exclusion: another American system that protects comfort and calls it fairness. We may preserve the program—and lose the principle.

Or we can act. Not by discarding what was built, but by bringing it forward. The reforms outlined here are not radical. They are overdue. And what comes next—whether erosion or renewal—depends entirely on whether we are willing to match the scale of the moment with the clarity of our response.

10

THE ARCHITECTURE OF CARE

FROM ISOLATION TO INFRASTRUCTURE: REBUILDING THE FOUNDATIONS OF FAMILY SUPPORT

"The destiny of nations depends on how they nourish and protect their children."
— Paraphrased from Sophocles

A nation that punishes families for raising children has lost its purpose. And yet in the United States, raising a child has become a structural disadvantage. Families face soaring costs, impossible choices, and a political system that treats child care as a personal problem, not a national responsibility. Working should be a choice. Staying home should be a choice. And care should be a right—not a luxury dictated by income, ZIP code, or employer preference. This is not about ideology. It is about infrastructure. No nation can call itself advanced if it fails to support the people who raise its future.

The math no longer works. To meet the cost of housing, food, health care, transportation, and education, most families now require two full-time incomes. But wages have not kept pace. Housing costs have doubled in a generation. Health care costs have tripled. And child care—if it can be found—often costs more than rent or college tuition. The typical U.S. family with two children spends over $100,000 per year just to stay afloat, according to national cost-of-living analyses. And for many, that estimate is conservative. These are not indulgences. They are the bare essentials of dignity, stability, and survival.

A generation ago, one income could support a household. Today, even two is often not enough. The shift began in the 1970s, when wages flatlined and prices surged. But the political response was not to protect families. It was to tell them to work harder. Women entered the workforce not as an expression of liberation, but of necessity. Dual-income households became the norm—but only to replace the ground lost to corporate profit, anti-labor policies, and rising inequality. What was once a cultural ideal became a financial requirement. And even now, the policies of government have not caught up to the reality of families.

Nowhere is the cost of that failure more visible than in child care. Across most of the country, families must find care that is affordable, available, trustworthy, and nearby. For many, it does not exist. Over half of Americans live in what experts call "child care deserts." Where care is available, it can cost between $15,000 and $25,000 per child per year. That is more than rent. More than food. More than many college tuition bills. The system does not work. Not for parents. Not for children. And certainly not for the workers who provide the care.

Those workers are the backbone of early childhood development—and they are paid poverty wages. The average child care provider earns less than $15 per hour. Most receive no health insurance, no paid leave, and no retirement plan. Their work is essential, complex, and emotionally demanding. Yet they are treated as disposable. This isn't because the work lacks value. It is because the political system has refused to fund it. And when a nation underpays its caregivers, it reveals everything about what—and who—it values.

Child care has never been fully public in the United States. But it almost was. During World War II, the Lanham Act created the nation's first federally funded child care system to support working mothers on the home front. It worked. But it was dismantled in 1946. In 1971, Congress passed the Comprehensive Child Development Act, which would have created a permanent national care system. President Nixon vetoed it, calling it a threat to the family. In truth, the threat was to a vision of the family in which women stayed home and work was unpaid. That veto killed what could have become the foundation of America's care infrastructure. Nothing close has passed since.

That delay now costs us dearly. Without universal care, families are forced to piece together a patchwork of options—none of them stable, all of them expensive. Many rely on family members. Others turn to informal providers with little oversight or support. Some leave the workforce entirely. Women are the most affected—especially mothers of infants. When care becomes unaffordable, many reduce hours, reject promotions, or abandon careers entirely. The economic cost is staggering. The human cost is worse. A nation that forces parents to choose between income and presence has already failed them.

This is not how it works elsewhere. In most wealthy democracies, child care is treated as infrastructure. Countries like Sweden, France, and Canada offer universal access, publicly supported wages, and robust parental leave. Costs are capped, hours are predictable, and providers are trained and respected. Parents can return to work or stay home without fear of ruin. These systems are not perfect. But they reflect a different moral premise: that raising a child is not a private burden. It is a shared national investment.

The United States does the opposite. It provides limited subsidies, small tax credits, and no national system of care. Its only federal policy—the Child and Dependent Care Tax Credit—is regressive and insufficient. It helps most when the help is needed least. The rest is left to states, cities, and struggling nonprofits. For a brief moment during the COVID pandemic, federal funds stabilized the sector. But those funds expired. And with them went thousands of providers, tens of thousands of jobs, and hundreds of thousands of child care slots. The system is collapsing again.

We can build something better. The foundation is already known: treat care the way we treat public schools—as universal, dependable, and funded through public investment. Child care should be free or low-cost for all families, especially in the first five years of life. Providers should be paid at rates that reflect their professional worth. And parents should have the choice to work, pause, or share responsibilities—without being punished for any of it. This is not radical. It is already how most of the world functions. We are the outlier. Not the model.

We need a blueprint with six pillars: access, workforce, infrastructure, leave, flexibility, and public delivery. Each pillar is essential, and each one responds directly to a failure of the current system. Together, they form a care infrastructure—not a patchwork. Not a pilot. A permanent system rooted in fairness, dignity, and public investment. A structure built to last.

A functioning care system begins with guaranteed access. Every community should have enough slots for every child who needs them—infants, toddlers, and preschoolers alike. Hours should match the realities of work—early mornings, evenings, and nonstandard shifts. Care should be safe, nurturing, and aligned with early learning goals. And no family should be forced to choose between leaving a child alone or leaving a job behind. This is what public education already provides after age five. We must extend it backward.

Second, we must fund the workforce that makes care possible. That means wages on par with K–12 teachers, access to benefits, paid training, and career ladders for advancement. Today's care workers live on the edge of poverty. Many leave the profession within five years. That churn is devastating to children, providers, and the system as a whole. A serious care policy treats workers as essential, not expendable. And when we fund their dignity, we fund the quality of care itself.

Third, we must embed care into the national infrastructure. That means building care centers into public housing developments, schools, community health hubs, and transit corridors. It means offering care on-site at hospitals, universities, and large employers. It means replacing isolation with proximity—so care is not something parents must hunt for, but something built into daily life. A nation that plans its roads but not its children's safety is not planning at all.

Fourth, we must pass guaranteed paid family leave—for births, adoptions, caregiving, and medical emergencies. The United States remains the only wealthy democracy with no national paid parental leave. The result is unpaid time, job loss, and maternal health risks. Paid leave is not a perk. It is an economic stabilizer, a child development accelerator, and a basic matter of justice. And it pays for itself many times over through improved health, retention, and stability.

Fifth, we must address workplace rigidity. Predictable schedules, remote work options, and employer-provided care credits should be standard. Today, unpredictable shifts and on-call demands undermine even the best care arrangements. The stress is relentless. No parent should have to choose between keeping a job and keeping a child safe. Flexibility is not a luxury. It is the baseline of a sane and functional labor market.

Sixth, we must build with public and mission-driven partners. The answer is not to privatize care further, but to expand access through trusted institutions—nonprofits, community organizations, schools, and local governments. Profit-driven chains cannot deliver equity or stability. But public and community providers can. They already do, in the places where funding exists. The role of federal policy is to scale those successes—not replace them with corporate models.

These reforms are achievable. Some can begin immediately: higher wages for care workers, expanded pre-K access, and redirection of subsidies from tax credits to provider grants. Others require federal investment—but with broad public support and economic urgency, they are within reach. The goal is not to impose one model but to fund what works—and to lift the baseline so no family is left without care.

The money is already there. Repealing a fraction of the 2017 tax cuts would fund universal child care and paid leave. Closing the carried interest loophole could fund meaningful wage increases for every child care worker in America—many times over. Public-private partnerships can accelerate infrastructure. Corporate minimum taxes and federal matching programs can expand coverage. We do not lack resources. We lack political will—and the clarity to see care as a common good.

A nation that does not care for its children, its families, or its future is not prepared to endure. But we can choose differently. Care is not charity. It is not indulgence. It is infrastructure—the foundation of freedom. When parents are supported, they flourish. When children are nurtured, they thrive. And when a nation invests in care, it invests in itself. The question is not whether we can afford it —but whether we can afford to wait.

11

FAIR TAXATION AND WEALTH REFORM

AN ECONOMY THAT DEVOURS ITS OWN PEOPLE WILL NOT SURVIVE.

———— ✦ ————

"No civilization survives the moment wealth becomes immune and labor becomes disposable. The name for that is not prosperity. It is collapse."
— JP Vincent

Our tax system no longer serves the nation. It serves the rich—and only the rich. And not for long.

This is not an accident. It is the logical outcome of a system built to serve wealth. Our current tax structure is not designed to fund a fair society or a stable economy. It is designed to protect and expand the power of corporations and the ultra-rich. And its goals are no longer hidden. They are encoded into every bill, every loophole, every deregulation campaign. The objectives are clear: to concentrate profit, strip away protections, and remove every barrier between private capital and total control.

The Republican vision for America is etched into the spine of their "Big Beautiful Bill"—the most sweeping tax and deregulation agenda in modern history. It cuts taxes for billionaires and corporations. It slashes oversight of polluters, banks, and monopolies. It opens public lands to private exploitation. And it guts the very services that working people rely on: health care, food assistance, public education, housing, and clean water. It is not a budget. It is a blueprint for extraction. It consolidates wealth at the top, then starves the base that makes any economy possible. It is not designed to serve the nation. It is designed to sell it off.

These are not guesses. They are the observable goals of Republican economic policy—pursued across decades, administrations, and legislative sessions. Taken together, they form a clear and chilling endgame:

1. Ever-growing corporate profits
2. The power to set prices without constraint
3. The power to suppress wages without consequence
4. Full control over employee benefits and conditions
5. No international competition through tariffs and subsidies
6. Unlimited access to public lands and natural resources
7. Elimination of corporate and capital taxes
8. No limits on monopoly formation or concentration
9. Unrestricted absorption of competing businesses
10. Legal freedom to bankrupt or crush smaller competitors

TOGETHER, these goals establish a system where competition dies and power centralizes. The second half of the agenda completes the design:

11. The dismantling of labor protections and unions

12. Financial deregulation and speculative freedom
13. Political insulation through dark money and judicial control
14. Privatization of schools, hospitals, infrastructure, and care
15. Permanent ownership of intellectual property and licensing revenue
16. Immunity from liability for harm to workers, consumers, or the planet
17. Total access to citizen data for profit, without consent
18. A government too weak to tax, regulate, or resist

THIS IS NOT capitalism with flaws. It is capitalism without brakes. And it ends the way it always does when unchecked: with collapse for the many, and impunity for the few. And then impunity too leads to collapse.

But the "end game" is not a future threat. It is already underway. The "Big Beautiful Bill" is not a proposal. It is a declaration. It builds on decades of Republican economic strategy: gutting the IRS, blocking minimum wage increases, starving labor protections, stacking the courts, and stripping public assets for private gain. This is not conservative reform. It is the systematic dismantling of democracy in favor of concentrated wealth.

But no society can survive where the many work endlessly and the gains flow only upward. No republic can endure a structure where profit comes only by draining those below. What is the difference between a society where survival demands every waking hour —and one built on bondage? The chains may be different. The exhaustion is the same. The names may change. The chains may vanish from sight. But the reality is the same: a life with no rest, no power, no future, and no way out.

This has happened before. Again and again. Rome hollowed itself out in service of wealth and spectacle. France crushed its working class while nobles feasted—until 1789. Russia let its peasants starve to preserve the tsar's court—until the empire shattered. In the American South, fortunes were built on forced labor and enforced ignorance. That economy "worked"—until it burned. Every time wealth was hoarded and labor was broken, the collapse came. Not always in revolt. Sometimes in decay. But always in failure.

The American version of this model uses four main tools: suppression of wages, offshoring of jobs, inflation of prices, and automation of labor. Each one appears rational. Each one extracts more profit from less cost. But together they hollow out the economy that sustains them. It begins with savings. It always ends in collapse.

For decades, the American economy has promised growth while delivering erosion. Profits rise, but public goods decay. Markets surge, but families fall behind. Politicians praise the stock market, even as life expectancy declines. This is not misfortune. It is design. A system that treats labor as a cost and wealth as a virtue will always pull toward imbalance. Every quarter demands more profit, and profit comes from only one place: someone else's pocket. When wages fall, prices rise, jobs disappear, and machines replace people, we are not witnessing innovation. We are watching the foundation crack—quietly, steadily, and with growing speed.

Low wages save corporate money—but they don't build customers. When companies suppress pay to boost margins, they erode the spending power of the very workers they rely on to buy their products. Multiply that by tens of millions, and the result is economy-wide fragility. People can no longer afford what companies produce. Businesses rely on borrowing and marketing to keep demand afloat, but beneath the surface, the middle class hollows out. No business thrives forever by underpaying its buyers. No nation survives by starving its core.

Offshoring deepens the wound. It makes sense on a spreadsheet: lower costs, higher returns. But the logic ignores reality. The jobs don't come back. The money doesn't stay. And the workers paid abroad are never customers here. The goods produced abroad return to a market where the consumers are poorer than before. This is not trade. It's engineered dislocation. A corporation may increase profit temporarily by shifting labor overseas, but at the cost of national income, tax revenue, and social cohesion. What begins as strategy becomes self-defeating: a supply chain with no demand at the end.

Raising prices fills another short-term gap. It's the simplest path to higher revenue—but only if people can pay. In an economy already stretched, price hikes do not reflect value. They reflect monopoly. From housing to insulin to food, we now pay more for less. The extra dollars don't go into better services—they go into dividends and buybacks. This is not growth. It's compression. Every dollar extracted from households to satisfy shareholders shrinks what remains for housing, care, education, or stability.

Automation completes the loop. Machines don't strike, don't get sick, don't ask for raises. For corporations, they are ideal. But machines don't buy products. They don't pay taxes. They don't participate in civic life. Each human replaced may boost the bottom line, but removes a contributor from the broader economy. At scale, automation without redistribution creates a society of producers with no buyers—of supply with no demand. It is prosperity without people. Efficiency without purpose.

So where, in this model, does the money come from? It comes from people. From workers paid too little to live. From families charged too much to survive. From communities stripped of services so corporations can pocket the difference. Wages are suppressed. Benefits are cut. Taxes are collected—then handed to the rich as subsidies and bailouts. And when the system fails those it bleeds, they are told to work harder, try more, and be grateful. And be ashamed that they cannot thrive. This is not capitalism. It is extraction. A system that severs profit from purpose and wealth from obligation will not hold. It consumes what it refuses to replenish.

The current tax system has not just drained the public—it has built a society on debt. Families cannot afford to live, so they borrow. To cover health care, housing, school, food, emergencies—sometimes just to breathe. They borrow to stay afloat, then borrow again to delay drowning. Corporations profit from the interest. Politicians point to GDP. But beneath the surface, people are exhausted. And when credit runs out—when no bank will lend, no card has room—who pays the bill? Everyone. Families pay in despair. Communities pay in lost services. Children pay in forfeited dreams. And the nation pays in collapse. A country cannot run forever on borrowed wages and broken promises.

And when the tax system breaks, the government borrows. And borrows. Until no lender is willing to fund this delusion. We are already seeing the unraveling begin. Some nations are quietly selling their U.S. bonds. Others are simply declining to renew the debt they once carried. When enough have had enough, the entire structure falls. 2008–2009 was not the crisis. It was the warning. And we ignored it.

When the system falters—and it is faltering now—government does not intervene on behalf of the people. It steps in to protect capital. Banks are rescued. Corporations are bailed out. Tax breaks flow to investors, not workers. This is not an emergency response. It is the design. The public underwrites private gain, then shoulders the cost of private failure. The few take profits when times are good and shift the losses when times are bad. It is not just unfair. It is unsustainable.

Fair taxation is not a matter of ideology. It is a matter of survival. If we continue to exempt the wealthy from contribution, the entire system will collapse. If we continue to pretend that trickle-down economics lifts anyone but the already-wealthy, we will slide faster into ruin. There is no path forward that does not include the rich paying their share—not out of envy, but because they built their fortunes on public roads, public law, public labor, and public risk. And because their wealth depends on others having money to spend.

There was a time when one income was enough. Not for wealth—but for dignity. Because we taxed progressively and spent collectively, we built more than profit: we built cities, highways, schools, power grids, and public universities. We went to the moon. We created new industries and artistic movements. We educated our children, explored our country, and believed the future could be better. We cared for our land—when we spoke of pollution, we meant litter. Because the system, though imperfect, was still reciprocal. Those who earned the most contributed the most. And in return, the country thrived.

In a single generation, we have reversed it all. We have gone from a nation where one income could feed, house, educate, and uplift a family—to one where two incomes barely cover rent. From a nation of builders, inventors, artists, and public servants—to one of monopolists, lobbyists, and speculators. From a nation with global respect, alliances, and moral standing—to one distrusted, disdained, and increasingly ignored. From a country struggling toward equality—to one sliding back into segregation by wealth, by zip code, and by law. And still, we continue down this path. To where? When does it end? No system can survive such imbalance. Sooner or later, it breaks. The wealthy believe they are building a legacy for their children—but their children will rule over ruins. The poor cannot buy. The land cannot give forever. And the collapse, when it comes, will leave no one out. The driving force behind this decline is a Republican Party that feeds its thirst for money and power by bleeding the nation dry. And it ends badly. For everyone.

Other advanced democracies tax the wealthy—and the results are undeniable. In Scandinavia, high earners pay more, but everyone receives universal health care, child care, and retirement security. Germany taxes capital gains at rates comparable to wages, and still maintains a strong manufacturing base. Australia collects royalties when fossil fuel companies extract public resources—funding services that benefit the public. These countries do not punish success. They require it to contribute. And because the burden is shared fairly, the middle class is stronger, basic needs are met, and the future feels possible. America, by contrast, taxes work more than wealth—and the result is rising inequality, collapsing services, and debt without end.

We must restore progressive taxation. Capital gains must be taxed like wages. Corporate income must be taxed like personal income. The loopholes that let billionaires live tax-free while teachers pay in every paycheck must end. Offshore havens must be closed. The IRS must be fully funded, fully staffed, and fully empowered to enforce the law—especially against those who believe it does not apply to them.

This is not a call to raise taxes on everyone. It is a call to return to what once worked. In the 1950s and 60s, the top marginal tax rate was over 90%—and yet the wealthy still built mansions, bought yachts, and lived lives of immense luxury. What they did not do was opt out of the system that made their wealth possible. They paid more because they had more. And because they paid, the nation built: highways, schools, universities, space programs, and a thriving middle class. No one is asking today's billionaires to live without wealth. We are asking them to stop draining the country dry while locking their riches in vaults. A fair tax does not take from the rich what they need. It asks of them what the country cannot live without.

Corporations, too, must pay their share. No more zero-tax billion-dollar companies. No more sheltering profits in foreign banks while laying off American workers. No more bailouts converted into bonuses. A corporate minimum tax must be enforced. And tax filings must be public. If corporations want the benefits of American markets, infrastructure, and law, they must participate in the cost of sustaining them.

This revenue must be used—not to shrink government, but to strengthen it. It must fund the things only government can do: public health, child care, affordable housing, universal education, clean energy, and infrastructure. These are not luxuries. They are the foundation of a functional democracy. And they cannot be built on debt, or charity, or hope. They must be paid for by those who have profited most from this country.

A tax code reflects a nation's values. Ours currently rewards inheritance, speculation, and extraction. It punishes work, sacrifice, and service. That cannot continue. We do not need to destroy the rich. But we must stop letting them destroy the country. If democracy is to last, it must be funded. If the middle class is to return, it must be supported. If capitalism is to survive, it must be taxed.

Fair taxation is not radical. It is the floor beneath the economy, the spine within the republic, and the difference between a nation that endures—and one that falls.

There is no path forward without correction. And only one solution remains—not radical, not new, but long overdue: fair taxation. Not as punishment, but as restoration. If collapse is a choice, so is correction. Fair taxation—the kind we once had—is how we begin.

12

RESTORE THE POWER TO TAX
REBUILDING REVENUE, CLARITY, AND TRUST IN DEMOCRATIC FINANCE

---◆---

"The Congress shall have Power To lay and collect Taxes... to pay the Debts and provide for the common Defence and general Welfare of the United States."
   —U.S. Constitution, Article I, Section 8

There was a time when taxation had only one job: to fund the government. From the first Congress onward, taxes were used to raise revenue to defend the republic, build public goods, and pay the nation's debts. There were no deductions for car loans or childcare, no credits for renewable energy or oil drilling. Taxes were not used to manipulate behavior or reward political friends. They were used to ensure the government had the money it needed to function—and nothing more.

That changed as the economy grew more complex. The income tax, made constitutional in 1913, allowed the federal government to expand its reach—and to begin using taxes not only to fund itself, but to shape society. Over the next hundred years, tax incentives were used to support national goals: homeownership, education, energy development, charitable giving, retirement savings, and more. In time, we could identify seven widely accepted reasons for tax preferences. Each one was designed to serve the public interest.

These seven categories are worth naming. First, to reduce poverty—through child tax credits, earned income supports, and basic exemptions. Second, to encourage work—by rewarding income from labor and supporting those who seek jobs. Third, to build national capacity—investing in education, infrastructure, public health, and broad civic participation. Fourth, to accelerate innovation—by reducing risk and supporting research. Fifth, to protect the environment and public health—through incentives for clean energy, clean water, and sustainable industry. Sixth, to strengthen families—through marriage, childrearing, and caregiving supports. And seventh, to prevent wealth hoarding—by taxing large estates and capital windfalls.

Each of these purposes is legitimate. Each, when structured properly, can help build a stronger, more just society. But in recent decades, two new categories have emerged—ones that serve no national purpose at all. The first is what we might call the pure giveaway: tax deductions or credits that are performative, regressive, or entirely untethered from economic need. The second is actively harmful policy: tax changes that increase inequality, sabotage climate efforts, or punish political opposition. These final two categories were not accidents. They were introduced deliberately—overwhelmingly by Republican leadership.

The evidence is not abstract. In 2017, Republicans passed the most regressive tax bill in modern history, slashing the corporate rate from 35% to 21% and directing over 80% of the long-term gains to the wealthiest Americans. In 2025, Trump's second-term "Big Beautiful Bill" proposed to make those cuts permanent—while adding giveaways like the car loan interest deduction, "Trump Accounts" for children, and expanded deductions that primarily help the wealthy. At the same time, it gutted climate incentives, imposed new taxes on immigrants and universities, and tied federal tax enforcement to ideological priorities like banning state AI regulation.

What these policies have in common is simple: they do not fund government. They do not reduce poverty. They do not serve the public interest. They are giveaways to political allies and hand grenades thrown at institutional opponents. Some provisions are designed to seem generous—a child tax credit here, a tip tax exemption there—but these benefits are often temporary, inadequate, and offset by deeper cuts. The real changes are structural: upward redistribution of wealth, sabotage of public investment, and the deliberate dismantling of fiscal capacity.

This is not just bad economics. It is strategic sabotage. Every tax giveaway that adds to the deficit becomes an excuse to later cut Social Security, education, or Medicaid. Every assault on clean energy is a gift to oil and gas. Every symbolic tax credit that fails to reach the poor is another step toward public cynicism. And every page of a tax code filled with distortions is a step away from democratic trust. The result is a tax system that is complex, unfair, inefficient—and designed to fail.

It doesn't have to be this way. The first step is to restore the original purpose of taxation: to raise revenue. That means separating taxes from subsidies. A tax bill should not contain education handouts, corporate giveaways, or ideological poison pills. A tax bill should ask: how much money do we need to run the government? And how do we raise it fairly? This principle would mark a return—not to past practice, but to constitutional intent. In reality, tax and spending policy have long been intertwined. But disentangling them would restore integrity to both. All other debates—about spending, incentives, or social investment—

should happen elsewhere, in spending bills, subject to the same budget limits.

This reform would bring four immediate benefits. First, it would simplify the tax code. A clear, progressive rate structure—paired with a standard deduction that sets the "zero tax line"—would reduce both compliance costs and political gamesmanship. Fewer brackets, fewer exemptions, no gimmicks. Most Americans could file in minutes.

Second, it would allow us to balance the budget honestly. If we know what the government must spend, we can calculate the rates needed to cover it. No more backdoor borrowing. No more hidden costs. If we want to expand spending, we raise rates. If we shrink the government, we lower them. The math is public and shared.

Third, it would make taxes transparent. Every citizen would know: this is how much I earned, and this is the percentage I owe. No more hidden subsidies. No more games. No more 300-page bills filled with favors for coal companies, hedge funds, and software lobbyists. A tax bill would be a tax bill—nothing more.

Fourth, it would force honesty in the legislative process. If a party wants to subsidize car ownership, or private schools, or solar panels, it would need to do so through an open, debated spending bill—subject to public scrutiny, and paid for with real revenue. No more hiding controversial ideas in tax gimmicks. No more using the tax code to create dependency or punish enemies. Just a clean, open debate about how we spend the people's money.

There are other benefits too. We could restore faith in government by making its financing legible. We could reduce wealth inequality by ending tax distortions that favor capital over labor. We could strengthen democracy by breaking the toxic link between lobbying and tax manipulation. We could stop the cycle of crisis-by-design—where deficits are used to justify cruelty. And we could build a tax system worthy of the country it serves.

This reform does not require perfection. It does not mean eliminating every credit or subsidy overnight. But it begins with a principle: taxation is not a reward or a punishment. It is a responsibility. And it must serve the whole nation—not just those who write the checks.

The power to tax is not just constitutional. It is moral. It is the means by which we share the cost of our collective freedom. When abused, it becomes a weapon. But when used wisely, it is how we build roads, educate children, care for the sick, and defend the common good. It is how democracy pays its bills.

What we need now is not another loophole or election-year bribe. We need to restore the public purpose of taxation—strong enough to endure, and fair enough to rebuild trust.

13

THE NATION THAT LASTS
WHY CARE IS THE FOUNDATION OF DEMOCRACY

---◆---

"Empires fall not when they are conquered, but when they abandon their people."
— Anonymous, carved into the wall of a burned village, c. 15th century

A government that cannot care for its people cannot last. That is not a slogan. It is a historical law. Every civilization that gutted its public obligations to enrich a ruling class eventually collapsed—through revolt, decay, or irrelevance. The American project will be no different if it continues down the current path. For too long, we have tolerated a model of governance that extracts as much as it can from as many as it can, to benefit as few as it must. The cost has been paid in hunger, sickness, debt, eviction, and despair. But there is another cost—less visible, but no less fatal. A nation cannot drill, mine, burn, and pollute without end.

The same logic that sacrifices people also consumes the planet. A republic built on extraction, whether of labor or land, cannot sustain itself. It must be replaced—not with fantasy, but with balance. With care.

The reforms in this section are not theoretical. They are material, measurable, and overdue. Universal health care, affordable housing, living wages, secure retirement, child care, food, and income support—these are not optional features of a modern republic. They are the minimum infrastructure of freedom. Without them, democracy becomes performative. People may still vote, but they do so in pain. They may still speak, but no one listens. And when survival depends on chance or charity, the social contract unravels. These reforms are not about generosity. They are about design. They restore what should never have been broken: the public capacity to ensure that every person, no matter their wealth or status, has the basics required to live.

And we know these reforms are possible—because other democracies have already built them. In Canada, health care is not a privilege but a right. In Germany, child care is not left to chance but provided with professional standards. Finland treats housing as infrastructure. France subsidizes food, transit, and education not as gifts, but as stabilizers. New Zealand budgets not only for economic growth but for national well-being. These governments do not view taxation as punishment for success. They see it as repayment—for the labor, stability, public systems, and natural resources that made prosperity possible. What they offer is not perfection, but proof: a government can care for its people and still thrive. In fact, that may be the only way it can.

To endure, democracy must mean more than procedure. It must mean presence. It must mean participation. People must feel it in their lives—in the clinic that stays open, the wages that cover the rent, the check that arrives when work disappears, the care received in old age or after service. These are not partisan demands. They are what bind a nation together. They are how a people knows its government has not forgotten it. Every functioning democracy in the world funds this kind of care. The United States does too—but only for the wealthy, the well-connected, and the corporations that lobby and contribute to those who write our laws. What we need now is not new capacity. It is new commitment. As these chapters have shown, we already know how to provide care—through universal health systems, housing access, living wages, secure retirement, and public child care. The work ahead is not invention, but restoration. To an old promise: to provide for the general welfare.

These programs are not charity. They are collective. Paid for by citizens. Delivered to citizens. Accountable to citizens. They require investment—but they repay it in trust, stability, and national resilience—an environment where personal success, personal fulfillment, and community achievement are not just possible, but encouraged, supported, and likely. And unlike the concessions granted to the rich—subsidies, exemptions, access, and influence—these benefits do not concentrate power. They circulate. They strengthen the whole. Public care is not a burden. It is the only way a diverse and democratic society survives. When we abandon it, we see what we have now: skyrocketing despair, manipulated rage, and the slow corrosion of the American promise. That is not sustainable. That is collapse—one eviction, one hospital bill, one overdraft, one suicide at a time.

The Constitution begins by pledging to "promote the general welfare." Not the welfare of shareholders or donors, but of the people. That foundation was never fully honored—but it was never meant to be discarded. The vision was clear, even if imperfectly applied: to build a country where liberty meant more than the absence of tyranny—where it meant the presence of dignity. That promise has been deferred, exploited, and betrayed. But it has not been erased. It can still be fulfilled. The reforms laid out here do not create something new. They secure something old. They make possible the kind of self-government our founders imagined—where power serves people, and not the other way around.

None of this is possible without fair taxation. Every other reform in this chapter—health, housing, wages, care—relies on a government funded by its people for the good of its people. That was the original idea: taxation not as coercion or control, but as the shared means of sustaining a republic. Today, that purpose has been corrupted. The tax code is riddled with loopholes, exemptions, and incentives that do not serve the public—they serve the powerful. We proposed two paths to repair: first, a return to a progressive structure where those who benefit most contribute most, and where unjustified giveaways are eliminated; second, a deeper reform—separating revenue from reward, restoring taxation to its essential purpose: to fund the nation, not steer it. Either path begins with the same truth: a republic cannot survive if the wealthy refuse to pay for the country they profit from.

This is where any true redemption must begin: with care. Before we talk of education, or law, or belonging, or the future, we must ensure people can eat, heal, work, raise children, and grow old without fear. That is not the end of democracy. It is its foundation. But care must be sustained by knowledge, upheld by law, and defended by truth. The work of a lasting democracy does not end here. A home without income is fragile. A family without care collapses. Freedom without shelter is no freedom at all. And if we begin to rebuild it now—firmly, deliberately, and together—it may yet carry us another 250 years.

14

PART II. A NATION THAT EDUCATES AND ELEVATES
HOW LEARNING, SKILL, AND DIGNITY SUSTAIN A DEMOCRACY

"The whole people must take upon themselves the education of the whole people. It is a debt we owe to each other and to the cause of self-government."
— Horace Mann

A republic cannot last without public education. Not merely schooling, but a system that equips people to think, decide, and act—in their own interest and in the public good. That system must teach more than compliance. It must cultivate judgment, discernment, and civic capacity. And it must extend beyond the classroom. A nation that educates but does not elevate—where learning leads only to debt, and work leads only to exhaustion—does not prepare its citizens. It traps them. What we need is not just reform, but restoration: of public purpose, of professional respect, and of the principle that every person's ability to contribute must not be stunted—by birth or by policy.

The Constitution does not name education as a right, but it does promise a republican form of government. And no such government can function unless its citizens are equipped to govern. That promise was once taken seriously. The Northwest Ordinance of 1787 linked public schooling to the expansion of liberty in new states. The Morrill Act of 1862 created land-grant colleges to expand access to practical and scientific education. Later, the GI Bill offered veterans the opportunity to learn, train, and build a better life—fueling both the middle class and the democratic strength of the postwar era. From the beginning, the United States has known that education is the engine of self-rule. The question is whether it will choose to keep that engine running.

For much of the twentieth century, education was a path to elevation. A child of modest means could attend a strong local school, enter a public university, and graduate into a job with rights, benefits, and enough income to buy a home and raise a family. Workers who did not pursue college could learn a trade, join a union, and still secure a life of dignity and contribution. Public investment was imperfect—uneven by race, gender, and geography—but its ambition was clear: to expand the circle of democratic possibility. The aim was not universal wealth, but the shared dignity of universal worth. The belief that every person could learn, work, and participate meaningfully in the life of the nation was more than an aspiration. It was a covenant.

That covenant has been broken. Public schools have been defunded, teachers attacked, curricula politicized, and entire communities left behind. College tuition has skyrocketed, forcing students to take on crippling debt for degrees whose value no longer guarantees stability. Technical training has been neglected, and the public infrastructure for workforce development allowed to decay. At the same time, wages have stagnated, union protections have been dismantled, and gig work has replaced steady employment. The same logic now drives both education and labor policy: maximize profit by minimizing people. We no longer prepare citizens to contribute—we train them to obey, compete, and endure.

This collapse was not inevitable. It was designed. For over forty years, Republicans have pursued a deliberate strategy of sabotage: discredit public schools, funnel public money to private operators, smear teachers as lazy or dangerous, censor history, and attack anything that teaches empathy or complexity. Reagan declared that government was the problem, then starved the education system that sustains a free people. Governors like Scott Walker and Ron DeSantis have turned schools into battlegrounds—not for student success, but for ideological conquest. Censorship laws now ban textbooks, criminalize librarians, and silence teachers. At the same time, Republican lawmakers have opposed every effort to raise the minimum wage, strengthen labor protections, or relieve student debt. This is not about education or employment. It is about subjugation.

Trump's first term intensified the assault. He appointed Betsy DeVos to dismantle the Department of Education from within, advancing private vouchers, rolling back civil rights enforcement, and gutting protections against predatory for-profit colleges. Under his administration, the federal government blocked student loan relief for defrauded borrowers and made it harder to repay loans through income-based plans. On the labor front, Trump sided consistently with employers over workers, stripping back wage and hour enforcement, undermining the right to organize, and deregulating industries where safety and pay were already tenuous. The purpose was clear: consolidate wealth, weaken solidarity, and keep the majority isolated and indebted.

In his second term, that strategy has become law. States have accelerated classroom censorship, teacher surveillance, and curriculum bans. Book removals have turned into purges. Educators face political review boards and risk termination for teaching race, gender, or history honestly. Trump has endorsed eliminating the Department of Education entirely. He has promised nationwide right-to-work laws and a ban on diversity training in any federal contract. What began as rhetoric has now become structure. It seeks to create an educational system that does not inform but conditions—and a labor system that does not support but exploits. This is not democracy. It is a machine for maintaining minority rule.

No law embodies that machine more fully than the One Big Beautiful Bill. Passed in early 2025 with Republican majorities in both chambers, the One Big Beautiful Bill is the fiscal architecture of authoritarianism. It slashes funding to public schools and universities. It blocks federal student debt relief. It lifts labor protections on platform and contract employers. It eliminates key benefits for part-time workers. It guts regulatory agencies tasked with protecting worker safety and enforcing fair pay. And it does so under the banner of "freedom." But its real aim is dependence: to keep the population too burdened by debt, too desperate for work, and too distracted by fear to resist. It is not a bill for prosperity. It is a blueprint for submission.

We begin our reform agenda with K–12 public education. But we affirm what every serious educator knows: the foundation of learning is laid much earlier. Early childhood education—including pre-K, early literacy, and language development—has the highest return on public investment of any education policy. It is the first line of defense against inequality, exclusion, and learning gaps that calcify into lifelong disadvantage. That is why early education is addressed fully in our chapter on Child Care and Family Support. But it must be held in view here as well. You cannot elevate people if you do not first prepare them to learn.

Education also does not end at graduation. Millions of adults need second-chance learning, whether to finish a high school equivalency, gain digital skills, or retool after job displacement. Community colleges, public apprenticeships, union-led training programs, and local workforce centers must be funded, integrated, and honored as equal partners in national renewal. Lifelong learning is not just a matter of economic adaptation. It is a moral imperative. People should not be discarded because the economy changed around them. If democracy means anything, it means building systems that make renewal possible.

We focus this section on three reforms: (1) Public Education, (2) College Access and Debt Relief, and (3) Workforce Dignity and Labor Rights. Each one addresses a different stage in the arc of human development. Together, they form a unified field of democratic capability. There are other areas—early childhood, adult education, digital literacy—that we treat elsewhere. But these three are the pillars: they support the structure of a nation that prepares, empowers, and protects its people through learning and work.

Public education is the foundation. It must be equitable, fully funded, and free from political interference. Teachers must be respected, protected, and paid fairly. Curricula must be rooted in truth, not propaganda. And students must be taught not just to recite answers, but to ask questions. That means including not only literacy and math, but also history, civics, media literacy, and science —subjects that build judgment and make citizens. A democracy that fears knowledge has already begun to fail.

Higher education must be restored as a public good. Public colleges should be affordable. Student debt must be relieved—not as charity, but as justice. And technical, vocational, and trade education must be fully supported and honored as equal to academic paths. A welder and a writer deserve equal dignity. There is no hierarchy between them. What matters is access, support, and the recognition that all forms of learning contribute to the common good. When we invest in that full spectrum, we build resilience—not just for individuals, but for the republic itself.

And learning must lead to dignity. That means labor protections for all workers—especially those in contract, gig, and low-wage sectors. It means wage floors, health benefits, paid leave, and the right to organize. It means safe workplaces, enforceable rights, and freedom from exploitation masked as flexibility. People must not just be able to work—they must be able to live. No education reform is complete if the destination is exhaustion, instability, or poverty.

This section is not driven by idealism. It is a blueprint for democratic survival. You cannot build a lasting republic on ignorance, insecurity, and engineered dependency. But you can build one—durably, fairly, and proudly—on learning, skill, and the freedom to contribute. Every child, every worker, every citizen deserves that chance. And when that chance is real, the future is no longer something to fear. It becomes something to shape.

15

THE COLLAPSE OF PUBLIC EDUCATION
FROM DEMOCRATIC PROMISE TO DELIBERATE SABOTAGE

---◆---

"A popular Government without popular information or the means of acquiring it is but a Prologue to a Farce or a Tragedy."
— James Madison

The promise of public education is deeply rooted in the American founding. Though the U.S. Constitution doesn't mention it, the Northwest Ordinance of 1787 commanded that "schools and the means of education shall forever be encouraged." From the 19th century, common school pioneers like Horace Mann insisted that democracy survives only when citizens can read, reason, and share a civic language. By the early 20th century, state constitutions and Brown v. Board of Education (1954) reinforced: every child deserves access to schools of equal dignity. The classroom is where democracy begins.

Before the Civil War, education in the U.S. was divided: accessible for some, denied to many. In Northern towns, one-room schools taught the basics. In the South and on the frontier, access was inconsistent, and Black Americans were often forbidden from learning at all. After 1865, Reconstruction brought new investments. The late 1800s saw the rise of public high schools, the landmark Morrill Acts for land-grant universities, and the professionalization of teachers. Literacy, science, and civics became the foundation of social mobility and democratic participation.

By the mid-20th century, public education was a national achievement. The G.I. Bill sent millions of veterans to college, transforming higher education from an elite privilege into a national engine of opportunity. Tuition was low, enrollment soared, and society gained: a booming middle class, record homeownership, and a generation of professionals who led the world in science, technology, and medicine. K–12 schools were strong enough to support America's technological ascent. U.S. universities produced more Nobel laureates and patented more inventions than any other country, thanks in part to waves of immigrant talent. Education was seen not as a transaction, but as a public engine of prosperity and freedom.

The U.S. became a global role model. By 1960, we had higher rates of high school graduation and college attendance than nearly any other democracy. Public universities delivered top-tier education at a large scale—affordable, bipartisan, and ambitious. Community colleges opened doors further. Schools taught literature and shop, civics and chemistry, alongside reading and math. Students left ready to work, vote, create, and lead. This system helped win two world wars, launch the space race, and sustain decades of economic growth.

After 1965, new civil rights laws opened doors—but also triggered backlash. As courts mandated school integration, many white and affluent families fled. Some enrolled in private schools. Others moved to suburbs where property values protected public funding.

Property taxes became the fortress. The richer the ZIP code, the richer the school. Federal dollars did not close the gap. Instead, local disparities hardened. The result was quiet resegregation—this time by income, not by law.

At the same time, federal investment stalled. Expectations climbed. The Information Age demanded more from schools—new skills, new technologies, a faster pace—but offered little support to match. Silicon Valley soared; schools were left behind. Education was reframed as a private investment, not a public right. College became a commodity. K–12 schools became test labs. Shared opportunity gave way to individual competition. The language of the public good was quietly replaced by the logic of the market.

By the 1980s, the model began to fracture. State funding fell. Costs shifted to students. Universities chased prestige—raising tuition, expanding facilities, and competing for donor loyalty. Flagships like Michigan, UCLA, and Virginia prioritized out-of-state and international applicants who paid more. Regional and community colleges—where most first-generation and low-income students enroll—were left behind. A system built for mobility now cemented inequality..

Today, access to elite education hinges on money, ZIP code, and legacy status. Public universities still exist, but the best-funded function more like private ones. The rest scrape by. Costs have skyrocketed, along with the pressure to attend. Many professions—teaching, journalism, social work—require degrees but don't pay enough to justify the debt. The Supreme Court's rollback of affirmative action has only widened the gap. A system meant to uplift many now rewards only a few.

As opportunity narrowed, blame shifted. Rising costs and rigid systems fed a cultural narrative: schools weren't neglected—they were defective. Parents grew frustrated. Teachers burned out. Students disengaged. Into this vacuum stepped a strategy: discredit the system to justify its abandonment. Schools didn't fail and then lose support. They lost support—and then failed. But the lie worked. And it stuck.

The ideological pivot came with Reagan. In 1983, *A Nation at Risk* warned of "a rising tide of mediocrity," blaming schools, not inequality. The solution wasn't support—it was scorn. Reagan slashed school funding, attacked unions, and promoted vouchers. Public education was branded a failure. Investment became punishment. Statehouses followed suit, diverting funds to private, religious, and for-profit schools. Teachers were discredited. "Choice" replaced commitment.

By the 1990s, bipartisan reform sealed the shift. Testing dominated. Rankings ruled. Schools cut libraries, arts, and field trips to fund standardized drills. Teachers lost autonomy. Scores dictated funding. Students were sorted by metrics that masked poverty and trauma. Reform promised rigor but delivered demoralization. It turned schools into sorting machines—and communities into scoreboards.

Then came *No Child Left Behind* and *Race to the Top*. Under Bush, tests multiplied. Under Obama, charters expanded. In both cases, pressure replaced investment. Teachers were judged by scores. Charters displaced school boards. Students got marketing, not services. Fatigue deepened. Trust crumbled. And the idea of education as a public good began to slip away.

Trump's first term turned erosion into assault. Betsy DeVos dismantled civil rights protections, funneled money into religious schools, and cut oversight across the board. Programs for disabled and multilingual students were defunded. Title IX was gutted. Teachers were mocked. The message was clear: education wasn't a right—it was a battleground.

In his second term, the attack escalated. Trump's budgets slashed arts and nutrition programs. Republican states passed laws censoring how history, gender, and race could be taught. Teachers were silenced or fired. Libraries faced raids. Books were banned. AP courses vanished. Fear replaced freedom. And classrooms fell quiet under threat.

Public universities were not spared. Republican legislatures banned DEI offices, censored curricula, and forced faculty to pass loyalty screens. Professors were surveilled. Tenure was politicized. Budgets were cut. States like Florida led the charge—replacing trustees, dictating courses, and appointing university presidents based on loyalty, not learning. The goal wasn't reform. It was submission.

Then came the *One Big Beautiful Bill*. Signed into law yesterday, it finished the job. The bill capped federal education spending, repealed curriculum equity mandates, eliminated teacher certification standards, funneled money to unregulated private schools, and stripped protections from bilingual, disabled, and low-income students. The bill was long. The impact is immediate. And the damage is no accident. It is the plan.

Meanwhile, the disinformation machine roared. Schools were called indoctrination camps. Teachers were accused of grooming. Parents were told they had no voice. The GOP ignited panic over "critical race theory," turning honest lessons into political firestorms. Censorship laws swept through red states. School boards were overrun. Candidates ran not to serve—but to destroy. Chaos followed. And behind the chaos, profit.

Republicans tell parents that schools are failing—and failing their children. They claim classrooms are dangerous, teachers are radical, and the system is lost. Their answer? Flee. But flee where? Private schools cost tens of thousands. Charters exclude many. Vouchers fall short. And working parents can't homeschool. This isn't empowerment. It's engineered abandonment—packaged as 'choice' and sold as freedom.

What we've proposed is not just repair. It is reconstruction—designed to restore permanence, equity, and public trust. The collapse is now complete. From preschool through college, American education amplifies inequality. Public early childhood care is scarce. Primary and secondary schools are chained to local wealth. Higher education is expected but unaffordable. And teachers? We ask them to work overtime, buy supplies, earn expensive degrees, face threats, endure disrespect, and carry weapons. Then we ask why they leave. This is not a system with cracks. It is a system with no foundation left.

It doesn't have to be this way. It wasn't always this way. It isn't this way elsewhere. The United States once led the world in education—with more Nobel laureates, patents, discoveries, and civic innovations than any nation on earth. We trained the world's doctors, engineers, and scholars. We made education our competitive edge. Now, countries like Finland, South Korea, Canada, and the Netherlands outperform us in both outcomes and fairness. They spend less, achieve more, and value teachers as professionals. The difference isn't intelligence. It's belief—and policy.

Other democracies offer universal pre-K, tuition-free universities, livable teacher salaries, and classroom independence. We offer testing mandates, debt, scripted curricula, and surveillance. In other countries, education prepares citizens for life. In ours, it prepares them to comply. And then we ask why democracy withers—why trust erodes, why hope fades. This is not a mystery. It is the harvest of abandonment.

And it was not an accident. It was designed. It was funded. It was passed into law by politicians who profit from ignorance, fear, and division. It was encouraged by billionaires who saw public education as both a threat and a market. It was implemented through think tanks, partisan school boards, and media campaigns. And it succeeded because too many believed the lie: that schools failed us. When in fact, we failed them.

We must now tell the truth. The destruction of public education is not a policy disagreement. It is a betrayal—of teachers, children, and the republic itself. This chapter has traced the collapse. The next will chart the repair. But no repair can begin until we confront what was lost—and who broke it. Public education was once America's boldest democratic promise: that talent, not wealth, would shape a person's future. It still can be. But only if we reject the long unraveling—and begin again, with courage, clarity, and care.

16

THE RESTORATION OF PUBLIC EDUCATION
HOW TO REBUILD TRUST, TEACHING, AND DEMOCRACY—FOR GOOD

---✦---

"Nobody ever listens to a teenager. Everybody thinks you should be happy just because you're young. They don't see the wars that we fight every single day."
— Brandy Ross, Freedom Writers (2007)

There was a time when teachers were seen as heroes. Not saints, not martyrs—heroes. They stood at the front of classrooms and at the heart of stories. In movie after movie, teachers changed lives: *To Sir, With Love*, *Dead Poets Society*, *Stand and Deliver*, *Mr. Holland's Opus*. They shaped generations, lifted up the overlooked, and brought entire audiences to tears. But that story has ended. The genre disappeared. Today, there are no movies about teachers—only criticism of them. No monuments—only mandates. This absence is no coincidence; it reflects who we have become. A nation that stops honoring teachers will soon forget how to celebrate itself.

We tell ourselves the solution lies in better policy. And yes—funding matters. Staffing, standards, support—they all matter. But policy alone isn't enough. Because the crisis we face isn't just a shortage of teachers or a decline in test scores; it's a deeper system failure. A system designed to exploit labor, suppress excellence, and discard the very people it depends on. We address symptoms like test anxiety, funding gaps, and staffing shortages. But we rarely tackle the root causes. And we almost never change the conditions that led to the collapse. The culture mirrors this decay. "Those who can, do; those who can't, teach" is one of the most harmful lies in the English language. We must bury it. Teaching well isn't failure—it's mastery, patience, scholarship, and emotional genius. Until we believe that, and act accordingly, no policy can save us.

Most people can recall a teacher who changed their life. Someone who stayed after class saw potential in you that you didn't see in yourself and gave you the words to try again. That quiet gift—of time, belief, and presence-is what once defined the profession. But we've buried it beneath mandates and metrics. We ask teachers to earn advanced degrees, manage trauma, interpret policy, and perform on an industrial scale. We ask them to grade papers late into the night, buy their own classroom supplies, endure insults from parents and politicians, and work second jobs to make ends meet. In return, we offer low pay, public scorn, and institutional neglect. A career built on civic devotion has become a revolving door of burnout. And we wonder why so many don't stay.

We've attempted to address this from the outside by passing reform after reform—new tests, standards, funding formulas, and slogans. But student outcomes have not improved. Teacher retention has declined. Public trust has diminished. That's because most policies treat education as a technical problem, but it isn't. It's a structural issue. The system isn't broken; it's producing exactly what it was designed for: instability, inequality, and exhaustion. If we want different results, we can't just treat the symptoms—we must change the structure. And that means facing truths many prefer to ignore. The crisis is not personal—it's institutional. Good people are leaving a system built to fail them.

If we want schools that last, we cannot rebuild on the same broken foundations. It's not enough to tweak policies on the edges. We need fundamental reform that addresses every level—from how we fund schools, recruit teachers, retain talent, measure success, and build trust across generations. We must treat teaching as a profession worth pursuing, not just a stepping stone to something else. That requires fair pay, genuine respect, and real pathways to stay. It involves creating systems designed for permanence, not churn. The changes are not always simple, but they are necessary. If we want a democracy that endures, we must create an education system capable of enduring alongside it.

We start with funding. Public education cannot succeed if it remains tied to property taxes. As long as we fund schools based on local wealth, we embed inequality into our system. Wealthy neighborhoods create opportunities, while poorer ones go without. The only solution is a national guarantee: every child, in every ZIP code, deserves a well-funded school. This requires replacing local funding with state and federal equity formulas. It also involves pooling tax revenue and redistributing it based on student needs. We must end the system where only the rich can afford a "good" public education. Education isn't truly equitable if it isn't fair.

We must also rebuild the teaching profession itself. Establish a National Teaching Pathway: a federally supported ten-year career track with salary minimums, housing stipends, student loan forgiveness, and lifelong healthcare benefits. Serve a decade—especially in high-need districts—and earn a lifetime pension supplement, permanent certification, and access to advanced professional development. At the five-year mark, offer mentorship roles, bridge grants, and guaranteed reentry after caregiving or relocation. Teaching should not be a financial burden. It should be a public investment, a respected career, and a source of lasting civic value. And it must include structures that retain teachers in the profession—not push them out.

At the same time, we must welcome those who may not stay forever. Not every teacher will commit for life, but five years of service can make a lifelong impact. Imagine a generation of college graduates spending time in the classroom before law school or medicine. Mid-career sabbaticals from journalism, engineering, or finance could reinvigorate civics, science, and critical thinking instruction. Teaching would become not just a profession, but a rite of passage—respected, supported, and rewarded. Those who move on take firsthand knowledge of students and systems into business, policy, and media. We should build a national program to make this vision real.

And we can deepen the classroom experience even further. Imagine a national corps of scientists, artists, engineers, and entrepreneurs who tour the country or teach briefly in their field. These guests wouldn't replace teachers—they'd reinforce them. A robotics engineer might lead a week-long project. A climate scientist might teach a case study. Their presence would expand the possibilities. It would cost less than a single weapons system and yield far greater returns. Every student deserves to learn not just from books, but from people building the world those books describe.

But it's not just burnout that pushes teachers away. It's fear. In too many states, educators face punishment for teaching history, gender, or justice. They're told to censor facts and erase lived experience. One sentence taken out of context—one angry parent, one viral clip—and their jobs or safety could be at risk. Even jail. We ask them to abandon the very truths that inspired them to teach. Then we wonder why they leave. A system built on fear cannot foster courage. It can only silence it.

And this isn't just about bringing in new talent. It's about reconnecting with those we've lost. Thousands of experienced educators have left to raise their children, care for the elderly, or focus on their own health. They didn't fail; they met society's unmet needs. Let them come back. Offer bridge grants, restore seniority, and create reentry pathways. View motherhood, caregiving, and life itself not as career interruptions but as wisdom worth reclaiming. No healthy profession dismisses its elders. No functional democracy abandons its teachers.

We also need to acknowledge the linguistic reality of America's future. Nearly one in three children lives in a home where English is not the primary language spoken. Trump declared English as the only official language. But ignoring these students doesn't make them disappear; it makes them invisible. We need universal early-childhood English support. We should develop a national bilingual teaching corps, offering incentives to heritage speakers of Spanish, Vietnamese, Arabic, Cantonese, and other languages. And we must stop punishing teachers for not being miracle workers. No first-grade teacher should be expected to teach reading, writing, math, science, and ESL independently. Language inclusion isn't charity; it's a democratic necessity.

The classroom must be freed. Teachers are not bureaucrats; they are creators of minds. This involves restoring professional independence, defending curriculum freedom, and repealing laws that censor history, identity, or science. It also means ending test-based pay systems and surveillance-driven governance. A teacher afraid to speak cannot teach. A child afraid to ask questions cannot learn. Authoritarianism begins with rewriting history. Democracy starts with telling the truth. We must choose.

And curriculum must be rebuilt to foster freedom, not fear. This involves teaching critical thinking, scientific inquiry, civic literacy, and moral reasoning. It also includes financial skills, digital ethics, and climate resilience. It embraces music, art, and storytelling. It means allowing students to engage with complexity instead of avoiding it. Curriculum is not a battleground for culture wars; it is the foundation of shared truth. Without shared truth, there can be no republic.

We also need to redefine what success means. Standardized tests only capture a small part of reality. What about the student who finally spoke up for the first time? Who taught their parents to vote? Who challenged injustice with bravery and compassion? These are also important outcomes. Schools should be evaluated not just based on data, but also on the impact they have on their students' lives. Replace punitive testing with performance exhibitions, capstone projects, and community involvement. Don't test students into silence. Teach them to find their voice.

And make teaching a profession worth committing to. Provide national fellowships, sabbaticals, and advanced roles without leaving the classroom. Allow master teachers to mentor, lead, and influence policy. Enable local teachers to become state leaders, curriculum architects, and public intellectuals. Develop the profession from within. A healthy system does not outsource its vision to consultants. It listens to the people who do the work and values what they know.

Bring teaching back into the culture. We share stories of entrepreneurs, athletes, influencers, and soldiers. But where are the teachers? Where are the public campaigns, the national films, and the viral videos that say: this is who builds the country? If we want a generation to value teaching, we need to make it visible. Not as martyrdom or burnout, but as brilliance. As a purpose. As power. Give the public something to believe in again. And they will.

Some say we can't afford it. But ignorance is costly—measured in hospital bills, prison beds, missed wages, and lives cut short. The undereducated go through unemployment lines, emergency rooms, eviction courts, and public wards. Others claim public schools have failed, but what truly fails is the will to protect them. We don't cut funding for hospitals when illnesses spread. We don't shut down fire stations because buildings still burn. We don't abandon schools just because providing a working education system is hard. We choose to invest, or we have chosen to decline. There is no middle ground.

One of the most seductive attacks on public education is framed as empowerment. Some people support the idea of "school choice"—the belief that families should be able to spend public money on charter schools, private schools, or religious institutions instead of their local public school. It sounds empowering. But in reality, school choice often means taking funds away from public schools to create isolated, unequal options. Charter schools might exclude students with high needs. Vouchers redirect taxpayer money to private schools with little oversight. Education savings accounts can be used with minimal transparency or accountability. This is not freedom—it's division. And democracy cannot thrive on division.

Because public education is the heart of democracy. It is where children meet differences, where strangers become classmates, where questions are born, and where empathy is nurtured. If we lose that space—if we turn it into only drills, fear, and silence—we risk losing the republic itself. That is what authoritarians understand, which is why they target schools first. They do not fear failure; they fear what schools might become: places of possibility, courage, and truth.

The collapse of our education system is profound, marked by the loss of trust, erosion of respect, damage caused by censorship, fragmentation, and burnout. But we have proposed a way forward—a national teaching pathway with fair pay and job security. A new culture of civic teaching that welcomes sabbaticals, return pathways, and the wisdom of those who come back. A classroom free to tell the truth. A curriculum grounded in discernment, dignity, and shared truth. A funding structure that promotes fairness and a public system strong enough to serve every child, not just the fortunate few. These reforms are not ideological; they are structural.

They are how we begin to make education worthy of democracy again.

So let us rebuild—not for nostalgia or test scores, but for the future. Let us create a profession that values permanence, ensures return, respects language, supports equity, and dares to teach what truly matters. Let us make public education so strong, so fair, and so rooted in dignity that no administration, movement, or act of cowardice can undermine it again.

The truth is this: you cannot have a democracy without teachers. You cannot raise citizens without schools. You cannot repair a country if the people teaching are paid less than parking officers, attacked in public hearings, and told their labor doesn't count. To teach is to believe in a future you may not live to see. It is an act of enormous civic faith. And if we still believe in this country, we must protect those who raise their hand and say, I will make it possible.

We reclaim public education when we reclaim the people who give it life—not just the students, but the teachers too. We must offer them not only a raise but a reason to stay, a path to return, and a place to grow old and pass on what they know. Because a republic built on memory cannot survive without its memory-keepers. And ultimately, a country that believes in its teachers still believes in itself. That is how we begin again.

17

THE SYSTEM THAT TOOK THEIR FUTURE

HOW COLLEGE BECAME A BARRIER, NOT A BRIDGE

"We are now in the paradoxical position of producing the most educated generation in our history— and the most indebted."
— Tressie McMillan Cottom

The Constitution does not explicitly mention education, but it does promise a democratic form of government. That promise is meaningless without an educated citizenry. A self-governing people must be able to understand their interests, deliberate on policies, and participate actively in public life. From the outset, American leaders understood that education was vital to liberty. The Northwest Ordinance of 1787, passed even before the Constitution was ratified, declared that "schools and the means of education shall forever be encouraged." Although that referred mainly to primary schooling, a healthy democracy also depends on experts—doctors, teachers, scientists, and public servants—who must be educated beyond the basics.

That deeper national purpose took shape with the Morrill Act of 1862, which established land-grant colleges to provide "liberal and practical education" to the working class. These schools trained engineers, farmers, and teachers, and introduced a new model: public institutions serving public needs. They did not replace elite universities like Harvard or Yale, which continued to serve the wealthy and professional classes. But they expanded the idea of what higher education could be. By the early 20th century, more students were attending college, yet the system remained selective. For most Americans, college was neither expected nor affordable.

That changed after World War II. The G.I. Bill, signed in 1944, did more than reward military service. It solved two urgent problems at once. First, it prevented mass unemployment by delaying the re-entry of millions of returning soldiers into the labor force. Second, it bought the country time to transition from a wartime economy to a peacetime one. Universities expanded to absorb the demand. Factories shifted from producing aircraft and armaments to consumer goods, housing materials, and public infrastructure. By the time millions of veterans graduated, the economy was ready to receive them. The policy worked. But it also created a myth: that a college degree was not just one path to success, but the only path.

That myth persisted. In 1970, about 26 percent of adults had attended some college. By 2000, it was over 50 percent. Today, nearly two-thirds of all job postings in the United States request or prefer a college degree—even though fewer than half of working adults actually hold one. Employers treat a diploma not as proof of skill, but as a basic filter. Jobs that once required experience or training now demand a bachelor's degree by default. High schools have adjusted accordingly. So have parents. College is no longer seen as a choice. It is seen as survival.

But college is not equally available. It costs more now than at any point in American history. Since 1990, the average cost of attending a four-year public university has more than tripled, even after adjusting for inflation. Student debt has skyrocketed. The average borrower now graduates with over $30,000 in loans. The national total has surpassed $1.7 trillion. That burden is not evenly shared. Black, brown, and first-generation students borrow more, repay longer, and earn less. Yet the pressure to enroll remains. Students are told that if they don't attend, they'll be left behind. But if they do, they may never catch up.

Despite that pressure, college enrollment has been dropping for over a decade. The number of students starting college peaked in 2011 and has declined steadily since. COVID-19 accelerated the trend, but the roots go deeper. Families are asking hard questions about cost, value, and return on investment. Many are concluding that the risks now outweigh the rewards. Meanwhile, alternative paths—such as trades, public service, entrepreneurship, and the military—are regaining appeal after decades of neglect. But the system hasn't caught up. Employers still demand degrees. Institutions still push enrollment. The disconnect widens.

This is the contradiction at the heart of the collapse. Universities built a model that depends on endless growth—more students, more programs, more prestige. Employers built a hiring culture that equates credentials with competence. But the number of students is shrinking. The willingness to borrow is fading. And the promised rewards are no longer reliable. The system cannot scale back without collapsing, nor continue without extracting more from families. For millions, a degree is now a burden—not a bridge to opportunity. The story we've been telling for 70 years no longer works. But the machine keeps running.

None of this diminishes the value of universities themselves. Entire fields depend on them. We rely on universities to train doctors, nurses, architects, teachers, and scientists. They are where we develop climate models, map the brain, study history, compose music, and design new technologies. These functions are not luxuries. They are infrastructure. The problem isn't that universities exist. It's what we've asked them to become.

That essential mission still exists—but it is no longer central. Political neglect, market pressure, and institutional drift have obscured the public need universities were meant to serve. Instead of focusing on education and knowledge, many institutions have turned into social gateways, economic filters, and branded experiences. The result is distortion. Universities now claim to serve everyone—but often fail to serve anyone well. The problem is not the university itself. It is everything we've layered on top of it.

Universities were never meant to bear this much weight. They were designed to educate—not to sort status, secure income, or certify adulthood. But as housing, jobs, and training systems eroded, college was asked to fill the gap. It became the only sanctioned path to security and respect. In response, schools tried to become everything: teachers, employers, therapists, marketers, gatekeepers. They lost focus. They stretched past their limits. And the core mission blurred.

This shift was driven by both ambition and necessity. Starting in the early 2000s, the number of high school graduates began to plateau. In many states, it's now declining. With fewer students, colleges competed—especially for full-paying students from out of state or abroad. Institutions hired branding consultants, added programs, and chased prestige. Full-time faculty were replaced with adjuncts. Class sizes grew. But the costs didn't shrink. They soared.

Employers reinforced this by outsourcing hiring to software filters. Applicants without degrees were screened out automatically —regardless of skill or relevance. Public agencies followed. Roles that once required training or apprenticeship now require diplomas. The degree became shorthand—for polish, commitment, intelligence. And so, the credential chase became policy. The labor market turned a flawed assumption into a rigid requirement.

Today, the disconnect is undeniable. We built a system that demands credentials but withholds access. We market college as a promise, price it as a luxury, and enforce it through regulation. No one designed it this way. But every major institution—government, education, employment—has locked it into place. The result is a loop: fear, debt, expansion, collapse.

This system did not break by accident. Republican lawmakers have spent decades dismantling public higher education—slashing budgets, ridiculing the humanities, and blocking reform. From 1980 to 2020, state support per student fell by nearly 30 percent. Tuition doubled. At the same time, Republicans passed tax cuts for the rich, privatized educational pathways, and rejected loan forgiveness efforts. They denounce "elites" while undercutting the community colleges that serve most students.

Donald Trump didn't invent this crisis—but he perfected it. His fraudulent Trump University was a template for predatory education: empty promises, inflated costs, lifelong debt. As president, he gutted protections for borrowers, deregulated for-profit colleges, and turned public universities into culture war targets. He ridiculed expertise, threatened funding, and undermined trust in learning itself. His legacy continues. His party still uses education as a wedge—but offers no plan to make it affordable, accessible, or purposeful.

Meanwhile, universities remain trapped. Too expensive to shrink. Too fragile to reform. Employers continue demanding degrees. Students grow more wary. Borrowing declines. But nothing changes. Everyone sees the collapse—but no one in power is willing to redesign the system. Reform efforts stall or reverse. Debt grows. Trust erodes. The gap between promise and reality widens.

Young people are not confused. They see it clearly. They are told that college is required—but not shown how to afford it. Told that education is the key—but forced to rent the key at a lifelong cost. They watch alternatives devalued, institutions self-serving, and choices shrink. What they experience is not opportunity—it is obligation disguised as freedom.

What we have is not a system of higher education. It is a machine of credential extraction—powered by fear, tradition, and borrowed money. It still produces brilliance in many places. But that brilliance is no longer the center. The center is survival: of universities, of branding, of the myth. And the myth is unraveling. The question is no longer whether change is needed. It is whether we are willing to let go of what no longer works—and build something worthy of the next generation.

18

DIGNITY WITHOUT DEBT
RECLAIMING THE RIGHT TO WORK, LEARN, AND CONTRIBUTE

―――― ✦ ――――

"The problem is not student debt. The problem is that we built a system that requires debt to be a student."
— Tressie McMillan Cottom

For decades, the American story has presented college as the universal solution: earn a degree, advance your life. But that promise no longer holds. College costs have skyrocketed, while the value of many degrees has declined. Millions graduate with debt, disillusionment, or jobs that didn't require a degree in the first place. Others drop out and carry the burden anyway. The result is frustration for students, families, and employers alike—and a workforce defined more by credentials than ability. We need a new story—one rooted in truth, choice, and possibility.

We have accepted what should be unthinkable: beginning adult life burdened with debt that might never be paid off. Parents start saving "for college" almost from a child's birth. High schoolers are pushed toward a single path, even when it doesn't suit them. Many graduates spend decades making payments—often more than they initially borrowed—only to find they still owe half the original loan amount. This is not education; it's indenture. And it restricts, instead of broadening, the horizon of freedom.

The consequences of that collapse are visible everywhere. Students are told that a degree is the only route to respect. Parents worry their children will be left behind without one. But the truth is more complex: college isn't suitable for everyone. And it never was. The system has become a bottleneck, funneling too many into programs that don't deliver, while cutting off funding, respect, and visibility for other vital paths. It's time to break the monopoly—not by attacking college, but by ending the myth that it's the only option.

For many families, college has become a rite of passage—an expensive symbol of middle-class achievement, independence, and upward mobility. Yet beneath this tradition lies a deeper flaw: most students don't know what they want to study. They drift through general education, switch majors, accrue debt, and often graduate unprepared for the jobs that actually exist. The result is disorientation—for students, disappointment for parents, and difficulty for employers trying to hire.

That bottleneck has national costs. Employers struggle to find workers with the right skills. Public programs and infrastructure are understaffed. Young people face discouragement and delays. Critical industries—construction, cybersecurity, energy, elder care—cannot grow. The problem isn't a lack of talent. It's a lack of viable, visible alternatives to the four-year degree.

There are other paths—at least eleven—including trades, public safety, logistics, care work, and the arts. Most require skill and training, but not college. Yet they remain undervalued, underfunded, and invisible. These are not fallback options. They are the democratic infrastructure of a working nation.

Some of these careers—plumbers, electricians, EMTs, heavy equipment operators—require training and licensing, but not college. Others, such as firefighters or law enforcement officers, rely on academy preparation. Still others offer training through unions, apprenticeships, or federally supported programs. These are not lesser choices. They are essential professions. We do not need fewer of them—we need more. And we need to respect them.

The solution is simple in principle, though complex in execution: build attractive alternatives. Make non-college pathways so strong, respected, well-paid, and secure that people choose them. Let college be one option among many—not the gatekeeper to everything. Let universities focus on training doctors, lawyers, researchers, and other professionals. But stop using them as the only sanctioned route to adulthood.

This is not an attack on universities. It is a liberation from mandatory enrollment. We honor colleges best by allowing them to fulfill their true purpose—serving those who know what they seek. But no one should attend just because every other path was blocked, defunded, or demeaned. The current system funnels students into debt and degrees they may not need, then blames them for the outcome. That is neither fair nor intelligent.

First, we must restore respect. National recognition for trades and service careers. Public ceremonies, storytelling campaigns, scholarships, and media that highlight—not erase—these paths. Young people need to see these roles as meaningful, dignified choices, not secondary options or consolation prizes.

Second, we must increase pay. A strong federal minimum wage across certified fields. Pay equity for public service roles. Wage subsidies or contracts tied to training and certification. Compensation should reflect value, not prestige or credential.

Third, we must guarantee security. Portable benefits, pensions, and retirement plans. Union protections and rights of transfer across sectors. A job should offer more than wages. It should offer a future. No one should have to choose between pride and stability.

The infrastructure already exists. It must now be rebuilt and made permanent. High school-integrated apprenticeships. Community college programs aligned with national standards. Paid federal corps for fields like climate resilience, infrastructure, and elder care. These programs must be funded like real options—not pilot experiments for the exceptional few, but robust alternatives open to all.

We can model them on successful programs from our past and present: the G.I. Bill, the Civilian Conservation Corps, union apprenticeship pipelines. Outcomes must be measurable. Standards must be high. And the experience must be public—visible, reputable, and available in every region. When people see these paths, they choose them. But they must be able to see them first.

This transformation will cost less per person than subsidizing the current college system. We can redirect public funds away from tax loopholes, for-profit scams, and bloated administrative costs—and into public universities, community colleges, and national training networks. Public money should serve the public good. Grants and aid should support institutions that serve the nation—not elite private campuses with billion-dollar endowments. Let private schools compete. But public funds must build public futures.

Student debt now exceeds $1.7 trillion. Many borrowers have paid faithfully for years—$300, $500, even $1,000 a month—only to see their balances shrink slowly, if at all, due to compounding interest. A student who borrowed $40,000 and paid $350 a month for 15 years may still owe half the original amount. This is not repayment; it's servitude. Forgiveness is not charity. It is justice for those who have already paid—and a rejection of a system that punishes ambition with bondage.

For current borrowers, we propose a full reset: cap interest rates at 1–2% above inflation, forgive balances after full repayment of principal plus modest return, and convert existing balances into income-based plans with a definitive end. For new students, phase out loans entirely. Replace them with direct public funding—for college or non-college pathways alike. Education should prepare people for the future, not trap them in the past.

At the same time, we must stop fueling degree inflation. If a job doesn't require a degree, don't demand one. If a skill can be learned through training or mentorship, provide that route. Stop treating a BA as shorthand for worth, discipline, or intelligence. Employers must lead—but public policy must set the standard.

We must also end the stigma. "College equals success" was never entirely true—and it's often false now. Success is contribution. It's skill, effort, character, and integrity—not tuition paid or prestige gained. Critics may object, claiming it lowers standards. But it actually raises them—especially in long-ignored sectors. Some will argue it's too expensive. But it costs far less than dropout, debt, and despair. Others may say this reform stigmatizes college. But that only happens when we lie to protect a monopoly.

The goal is not to divide—but to free. Freedom to choose. Freedom to contribute. Freedom to thrive. Other countries already show how it's done. Germany, Austria, and Switzerland have world-class vocational tracks. Finland and the Netherlands integrate academic and applied learning. Australia's TAFE system offers nationally recognized training across hundreds of fields. These countries treat alternative paths as national strengths—not social liabilities. We can do the same.

The final barrier we must break is cultural: the myth that one credential defines a person's worth. That lie has limited too many lives, distorted too many decisions, and shackled too much potential. We must bury it.

Let us declare: all honest work has dignity. A person's value is not determined by a diploma. A nation that claims to believe in liberty must offer more than one way to earn a future. Let us build those ways, open them wide, and honor everyone who walks through.

19

THE COLLAPSE OF WORKER POWER
HOW REPUBLICANS DISMANTLED LABOR RIGHTS AND TURNED WORK INTO PUNISHMENT

"Every man is a king so long as he has a roof over his head and a job to do —and the moment he hasn't, he's just a tramp."
— Sinclair Lewis, *It Can't Happen Here* (1935)

Work is more than just survival. It is how people contribute, belong, and shape the future. In a democracy, work must be a place of dignity and power—not fear and disposability. When labor loses its rights, citizenship begins to break apart. For most of its history, the United States has treated labor as expendable and worker rights as negotiable. That choice was not economic—it was political. And its effects are now structural. When wages stagnate, benefits disappear, and protections are removed, the workforce becomes a controlled class. Productivity rises. Profits surge. Workers fall behind. This is not a failure of capitalism. It is the strategic success of those who control it. The loss of labor rights isn't a mistake—it's a mechanism of control.

The Constitution never mentions wages, unions, or safety. It offers no right to work, rest, or organize. Early courts treated labor protections as threats to liberty—not safeguards of it. For over a century, the doctrine of 'liberty of contract' allowed 12-hour shifts, firings, and blocked safety laws. If you took the job, you were assumed to consent—no matter the coercion. In Lochner v. New York (1905), the Court struck down a ten-hour day for bakers as unconstitutional. Property had liberty. Workers had none.

The result was not peace but rebellion. From the 1870s to the 1930s, American labor history was marked by violence. Strikes became sieges. Workers faced armed guards, private militias, and sometimes federal troops. The Great Railroad Strike of 1877, the Homestead Strike of 1892, the Ludlow Massacre of 1914—all revealed the same truth: the state would use force to protect capital. Unions were treated as criminal conspiracies. Organizers were jailed or killed. When Upton Sinclair published *The Jungle* in 1906, he aimed to expose labor abuses. What shocked the public wasn't the working conditions—but the meat. Sympathy stopped at the dinner table. The system endured.

Still, organizing continued. The IWW called for a single industrial union. Immigrant workers led strikes. Women picketed. Black workers, excluded from most unions, formed their own. But opposition was fierce. The 1919 steel strike collapsed under Red Scare paranoia. The Palmer Raids targeted labor radicals as threats to the nation. By the early 1930s, the country faced mass unemployment, falling wages, and open talk of revolution. Congress didn't act from conscience—it acted from fear. The labor reforms of the New Deal were not gifts from above. They were compromise offers meant to prevent collapse from below.

The New Deal changed the legal framework. The National Labor Relations Act (1935) guaranteed collective bargaining. The Fair

Labor Standards Act (1938) set minimum wage and overtime rules. But even during reform, the exclusions were strategic. Southern Democrats insisted on leaving out domestic and farm workers—the majority of Black workers in the South. These exclusions preserved white supremacy, kept the federal government out of Jim Crow economies, and divided the labor force. What was won was real—but carefully bounded.

World War II temporarily expanded those gains. Wartime production and labor shortages gave workers leverage. Union membership surged. The National War Labor Board enforced contracts and stabilized wages. Black and female workers entered the workforce in record numbers. Roosevelt banned discrimination in defense hiring by executive order. But the truce did not last. After the war, a corporate-led backlash moved quickly. The Taft-Hartley Act (1947) restricted union rights, enabled "right-to-work" laws, and outlawed key organizing tactics. Labor activism was recast as subversion. By the 1950s, the question was no longer how to protect labor —but how to contain it.

A new legal weapon emerged: "at-will" employment. Employers could fire workers without cause. Misclassifying workers as independent contractors became a shield against regulation. Union membership peaked in the 1950s—and then declined. By 1980, it had collapsed in the private sector. Wages stagnated. Productivity soared. Temporary jobs, outsourcing, and anti-union consulting became common. Retaliation—illegal in theory—became routine in practice. Whole industries were built around avoidance: no benefits, no bargaining, no risk. Workers bore the burden. Employers reaped the profit.

Immigrant labor has always been essential—and exploited. Today, millions of undocumented and temporary workers perform the most underpaid, dangerous, and legally precarious jobs. Agriculture, food processing, construction, caregiving—all rely on fear to suppress resistance. Speaking out can mean termination or deportation. Guest worker programs tie employees to one employer, creating legalized dependency. Republicans stoke fear of immigrants publicly—while privately protecting corporate reliance on their labor. The result is a two-tier system: one workforce with rights, and one without.

The collapse was not accidental—it was built. Taft-Hartley opened the door. Right-to-work laws flooded in. Reagan's firing of air traffic controllers made retaliation routine. Conservative courts upheld it. Legislatures embedded it. Think tanks normalized it. NLRB defunded. OSHA gutted. Forced arbitration spread. Wage theft outpaced enforcement. The outcome: no margin for dissent, no safety in the rules, no rights without risk.

Trump did not initiate the collapse. He accelerated it. During his first term, his administration slashed OSHA inspections, redefined gig workers as contractors, and blocked new overtime protections. He issued orders weakening federal unions and rolled back safeguards for workplace safety. His NLRB reversed pro-worker rulings. Immigration raids disrupted organizing. In his second term, the crackdown deepened. He pushed to override state protections, delay union elections, and criminalize solidarity actions. Any advance for workers was treated as a threat—and his policies made that threat personal.

The One Big Beautiful Bill Act of 2025 locks it in—by design. It guts enforcement funding, ending proactive workplace inspections. It codifies gig economy loopholes—making misclassification federal policy. It blocks card check recognition, burdens union elections with delays and thresholds, and overrides stronger state labor laws. It defunds portable benefits pilots. It doesn't just weaken labor—it criminalizes restoration. What Trump began by executive order, the One Big Beautiful Bill Act cements in statute.

Meanwhile, wages remain stagnant. The federal minimum wage is still $7.25, unchanged since 2009. Adjusted for inflation, it's worth less than it was in 1968. Rent has doubled. Health care costs have tripled. College costs have exploded. CEO pay has risen more than 1,200% since 1980. Productivity has soared—but worker compensation has flatlined. The gulf between value created and value returned is now a gaping wound in the economy. And that wound is not incidental—it is structural. When labor is weak, wealth consolidates. And when wealth concentrates, democracy weakens.

Other countries have made different choices. Australia adjusts its minimum wage annually through an independent tribunal. Germany and Norway require worker representation on corporate boards. France and Denmark extend union-negotiated benefits to entire industries. Canada is piloting portable benefits for gig workers. Most of Europe offers paid sick leave, family leave, and universal health care. American exceptionalism, in this context, means uniquely exploitative.

The Republican response is not to catch up—it's to shut down. The One Big Beautiful Bill Act bans states from exceeding federal labor standards. It blocks reclassification of gig workers. It cuts funding from states offering scheduling protections or paid leave. It creates a legal ceiling, enforced not by courts, but by corporations and contractors. The goal is not uniformity—it is paralysis.

Technology compounds the harm. Warehouse workers are tracked by algorithm. App-based drivers are terminated without recourse. Low-wage workers are monitored for bathroom breaks. The law has not caught up. Often, it's been deliberately kept behind. Republicans have blocked efforts to regulate algorithmic management or require workplace data transparency. We now have 21st-century exploitation under 19th-century protections.

And yet, support for unions remains high. Over 60% of workers say they would join a union if given a fair chance. But that chance is rare. Employers delay elections, fire organizers, and drag out legal battles. Penalties are minimal. Consequences are lasting. The NLRB can order reinstatement—but not erase eviction, debt, or trauma.

For many, organizing means risking everything. And the system is rigged to ensure that risk is one-sided.

The political cost is profound. Workers who feel powerless stop trusting institutions. They disengage—or embrace authoritarians who promise retribution. The collapse of labor rights is not just an economic problem. It is a civic emergency. When people have no power at work, they lose faith that power exists anywhere.

The courts have not been neutral. Republican judges have struck down state minimum wage laws, overturned union fees, and sided with employers in disputes over arbitration, misclassification, and wage theft. They speak of liberty, choice, and flexibility—but these words mask a deeper imbalance. Employers have liberty. Workers face risk. Corporations have choice. Workers have dependence. Flexibility means you can be replaced—cheaply, quickly, or silently.

The collapse of labor rights is not a market failure. It is a deliberate, generational campaign to shift power upward, shield employers from responsibility, and insulate capitalism from democracy. The tools have been legal, economic, and cultural. The result is unmistakable. American workers are more productive, more isolated, more surveilled, and more disposable than at any time since the Great Depression. And the law says it's legal.

Every man is a king so long as he has a roof over his head and a job to do—and the moment he hasn't, he's just a tramp. That was Sinclair Lewis in 1935. Nearly a century later, it still rings true. A society where labor has no voice cannot have justice. A system that denies responsibility while extracting value cannot endure. The collapse of labor power is not just economic injustice. It is the dismantling of democracy's most powerful counterweight.

Work is not just how we survive—it is how we shape the future. And no democracy can endure if that power is denied.

20

FULL EMPLOYMENT AND NATIONAL CONTRIBUTION
BECAUSE CONTRIBUTION SHOULD NEVER BE A PRIVILEGE

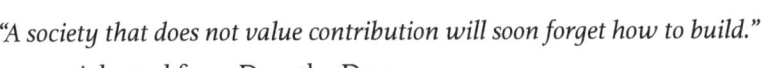

"A society that does not value contribution will soon forget how to build."
— Adapted from Dorothy Day

The labor market is not broken. It's been reprogrammed. Once, American employment was a covenant—between worker and nation, employer and community. Today, it is a contest of extraction. Corporations maximize income by minimizing labor. Public policy rewards that strategy. Gig work, temp jobs, and automation have become the new norm. Wages stagnate. Benefits vanish. Long-term careers disappear. Yet productivity and profits continue to climb. This chapter does not ask what went wrong. It asks: what would it take to make it right?

Imagine a country where the only national problem was an abundance of trained, committed people ready to work. What would we build? Roads that last. Homes people can afford. Transit systems that connect every town and city. A digital infrastructure as reliable as clean water. Every bridge repaired. Every school modernized. Every senior cared for. Every child safe. That's not fantasy. It's design. If we committed to matching every willing worker with meaningful work—public or private—we would become again what democracy is meant to be: a shared endeavor of constant betterment.

To make this real, the Department of Labor will be rebuilt not just as a regulator of work, but as a builder of it. Its mission will be to match labor to national need—always. It will oversee a permanent, nationwide system of training, placement, and employment in roles that serve the public good: care work, construction, logistics, cybersecurity, inspection, maintenance, and more. These roles may be filled through partnerships with other agencies or through direct public employment—but the standard will be excellence, the purpose will be dignity, and the scale will match the promise of democracy. This is not charity. It is a democratic guarantee: if you are ready to work, there will be something worth doing.

The infrastructure already exists. The military has trained generations of electricians, plumbers, engineers, and mechanics. Civilian programs like Job Corps, apprenticeships, trade schools, and vocational institutes offer training across industries. What's missing is integration. This plan unifies those resources into a permanent workforce backbone—managed, transparent, and able to scale. When private industry cannot or will not provide dignified work, the government will. Not with redundancy, but with purpose: skilled people doing vital work that builds a stronger nation.

We begin by offering what the private market rarely does anymore: stability with meaning. Anyone who wants meaningful public employment can apply. Those already trained will be placed immediately. Those who need new skills will be trained at public expense. These are not stopgaps. They are foundational jobs—

serving the country, rebuilding capacity, and restoring the meaning of work.

Some will choose public employment for its mission. Others will use it as a launchpad into the private sector. But none will be idle by default, or punished for effort. The right to contribute will no longer depend on private market luck.

These jobs will not just supplement the private sector—they will raise the standard. Government work will model fair pay, full benefits, high expectations, and the chance to grow. If corporations want to keep their workforce, they'll have to match it. If they won't, they'll lose workers to something better. No one will be forced to serve. But everyone will have a real choice. That is what freedom looks like.

This national workforce won't wait for crisis. Just as we coordinate service in wartime, we will now coordinate it in peacetime— toward housing, infrastructure, health, education, and resilience. These jobs won't compete with existing roles. They will fill the gaps markets ignore. And they will anchor a new national ethic: that public service is honorable, reliable, and central to who we are.

We begin with those already searching—trained but underused, burned out by instability, discouraged but not done. They will be placed first. Then we invest in the next wave: those who want to learn, pivot, or start again. Side by side, we will match willing workers with necessary work. Not eventually. Now.

The first call on these workers will be clear: serve the work of democracy. Build child care centers. Restore wetlands. Expand transit. Staff nursing homes. Digitize public records. Build housing. Audit broadband. Teach civics. Wherever the public good is underserved, trained workers will go—not temporarily, but as long-term contributors with careers.

Some will object. "It's too expensive," they'll say. But we already pay more—for crime, illness, despair, and delay. Chronic unemployment drags down well-being. The cost of inaction shows up in prisons, emergency rooms, and lost lives. The job guarantee is not a giveaway. It is an investment—with returns in productivity, stability, and national strength.

Others will say it competes with private industry. But only if that industry refuses to compete on dignity—or refuses to compete at all. When government becomes a model employer—with clear roles, stable hours, fair wages—private companies will have to offer more than exploitation. That's not coercion. That's accountability.

Still others will raise familiar fears: inefficiency, complacency, waste. But this is a program of standards—not sinecures. Expectations will be clear. Workers will be trained, evaluated, and supported. Underperformance will be addressed—just like in any serious enterprise. But the goal is not to punish. It is to build. This system develops people. It does not discard them.

The charge of "socialism" will come. But the reality is older than ideology. In every crisis, Americans turn to government for work. It happened during the New Deal, World War II, after 9/11, in 2008, and again during COVID. This proposal does not create a new function. It acknowledges and strengthens a core national role.

Others will say: "Let people find their own jobs." That only works when the market provides them. When it doesn't, people suffer—not for lack of effort, but for lack of options. This plan ensures that if you're willing to contribute, the country will match you with purpose.

To build public trust, this program must earn it. No bloated contracts. No $400 invoices for ten-cent screws. If it's cheaper to hire and train public workers than to outsource, the government will do the work itself. Public labor will mean public value—efficient, accountable, and mission-driven.

The tax code will fund it—based on income, not ideology. High-earning corporations will pay more, because they benefit more. So will high-income individuals. Rates will be proportional and transparent. This is not punishment. It is reciprocity: a democracy worth having costs something to maintain.

This plan does not interfere with private enterprise. It sets a standard beside it. If businesses automate, downsize, or offshore, they may. But they will not be allowed to discard human beings without consequence. And in the long run, they too benefit—from a skilled workforce, a stable society, and customers who can afford to participate.

The real problem isn't overreach. It's waste. We waste young talent that never gets trained. We waste loyal workers cast aside at fifty. We waste entire communities forced to fight for scraps. This program ends that waste. It redeems what we've thrown away.

Some will ask: what if public workers don't perform? The answer is simple. Set expectations. Train leaders. Evaluate results. Dismiss when needed. But always remember: the goal is not compliance—it's contribution. Help people succeed. Don't just wait to catch them failing.

Beneath it all lies a principle: people are not costs. They are capacity. For too long, we've treated workers as expendable. That mindset has made our economy brittle, our politics volatile, and our country less than it could be. That's not sustainable. And it's not moral. But it can be changed.

Imagine a nation where anyone who wants to work is matched with a public mission. Every empty lot, every collapsed bridge, every child without care becomes a site of contribution. Imagine communities where young people are trained to stay, not flee. Where older workers become mentors. Where work is not a punishment, but a path.

That future is within reach. Not overnight. But sooner than we think. The tools already exist: training centers, civic authority, public need. The only thing missing is shared resolve.

In that world, employment is not a commodity. It is a covenant. We are not offering a jobs program. We are offering a national promise: that no one ready to contribute will be left behind. That democracy values labor not just as an input—but as a form of belonging. That the role of government is not to watch markets, but to empower people.

And that the true measure of a democracy is how it honors the dignity of work—by ensuring no one stands ready with nothing to do, and no community remains broken for lack of someone willing to build.

21

WHAT WE CHOOSE TO BUILD TOGETHER

LEARNING, LABOR, AND THE RIGHT TO SHAPE THE FUTURE

"A democracy does not survive by accident. It must be built—again and again—by people who believe they matter."
— JP Vincent

A democracy does not survive by accident. It must be built—again and again—by people who believe they matter. That belief is not born—it is taught, tested, and renewed through experience. It is nurtured in classrooms, forged in workplaces, and tested in the life of every citizen who seeks to belong, contribute, and be heard. That is why education and labor are not side issues. They are the foundation of the republic itself.

In this section, we traced the collapse: of public schools defunded and politicized, of college turned into a gateway of debt, and of work stripped of rights, security, and respect. These were not separate declines. They were symptoms of a deeper betrayal—the replacement of democratic purpose with economic control. What once prepared people to lead now trains them to comply. What once elevated now exploits. The result is not just inequality, but alienation. And that alienation is a gift to authoritarians.

But we do not accept that future. We propose a different future: a restored system of public education—equitable, honest, and free from censorship. A postsecondary model that includes both college and non-college paths, funded as public goods, and protected from predation. And a labor system where every willing worker can find dignity—not just in survival, but in contribution. These are not romantic ideas. They are structural reforms with real consequences, rooted in law, funded by policy, and aimed at a common purpose: making the republic work for all who live in it.

We know what happens when we abandon this purpose. When truth is silenced, history rewritten, and expertise mocked, democratic life shrinks. When people are burdened by debt, denied alternatives, or discarded by the job market, their voices fall quiet—not by choice, but by exhaustion. And when those conditions harden, so does power. That is the logic of the One Big Beautiful Bill. It is not about education, employment, or even economics. It is about building a society where the many are too overwhelmed to resist the few.

We reject that logic. And we reaffirm something older, deeper, and more American than the forces that now threaten us. That everyone has the right to learn. That all honest work has dignity. That contribution must never be a privilege. These are not slogans. They are the minimum conditions of a self-governing people. And when they are protected—when students are free to question, when workers are free to organize, when citizens are free to shape their own lives—the whole country becomes stronger, more stable, and more free.

There will be those who say this is too much. That we cannot afford universal public education, national job guarantees, or debt relief. But we ask: what has it cost us not to have them? What has it cost to silence teachers, abandon students, overcredential jobs, and treat millions as disposable? What has it cost in despair, division, and disillusionment? A nation that refuses to invest in its people should not be surprised when its people lose faith in the nation.

What comes next must be more than policy. It must be purpose. A shared understanding that schools are not battlegrounds, but sanctuaries of civic power. That colleges should open futures, not close them off with lifelong debt. That work is not a punishment for the poor, but the means by which we build the nation together. This is what we restore. And this is how we prepare.

The title of this part is no accident. A nation that educates and elevates is not just one with schools and jobs. It is one that sees potential in every person—and builds the systems to meet it. That belief marks the line between survival and renewal. And that belief is what we choose now, together.

Let us keep choosing it.

22

PART III. A NATION THAT IS SAFE, JUST, AND FREE

HOW ACCOUNTABILITY, RESTRAINT, AND EQUAL JUSTICE SUSTAIN A DEMOCRACY

―――― ✦ ――――

"The safety of the people shall be the highest law."
— Cicero, quoted by Jefferson and inscribed in the U.S. Capitol

A government that cannot keep its people safe will lose their trust. But a government that enforces safety through fear, inequality, or force will lose something deeper: its legitimacy. True public safety is not just about the absence of violence. It is about the presence of justice, the rule of law applied equally, and the freedom to live without threat—whether from criminals, the state, or foreign powers. A democracy does not survive by promising protection only to some. It survives by upholding the principle that every person—regardless of race, status, or belief—has the same right to live, speak, walk, and vote without fear.

The Constitution promises liberty and equal protection under the law. But throughout American history, those protections have been unevenly applied—enforced by systems that often privilege some lives and criminalize others. From slave patrols and lynching to mass incarceration and digital surveillance, the mechanisms of "public safety" have been shaped by power, not by justice. Constitutional principles were invoked to protect slaveholders, segregated schools, and abusive police. At every turn, the law has been used both to shield the powerful and to punish the vulnerable. That is not safety. It is injustice cloaked in legality.

Still, the story is not only one of betrayal. Over two centuries, Americans have fought—again and again—to close the gap between safety and justice. Abolitionists, civil rights leaders, journalists, immigrants, and everyday citizens have demanded reform: to end police brutality, restrict government overreach, protect privacy, reduce violence, and dismantle systems of mass punishment. When that pressure built, democracy moved forward. The Warren Court expanded civil liberties. The Civil Rights Act banned discrimination in public institutions. Courts struck down racial profiling and overbroad surveillance. For a time, it seemed possible that safety and freedom might finally align.

But progress sparked backlash. Over the past forty years, Republicans have waged a quiet campaign to reclaim the tools of control. The 1994 Crime Bill, while bipartisan, laid the groundwork—but it was Republican governors who built and expanded the prison-industrial complex. They passed three-strikes laws, mandatory minimums, and truth-in-sentencing measures that swelled prison populations without addressing root causes. In the 2000s, the PATRIOT Act broadened surveillance powers while Republican legislatures shielded police misconduct through "law enforcement bills of rights" and sweeping immunity statutes. Gun manufacturers gained special protections through the 2005 federal immunity law. The architecture of fear became a bipartisan inheritance—but it was Republicans who hardened it into doctrine.

Under Donald Trump, that campaign became open warfare. In his first term, Trump praised police accused of brutality, encouraged violence against protesters, and rolled back federal oversight of local departments. His Justice Department ended consent decrees and gutted civil rights investigations. He used the presidency not to restore trust, but to deepen suspicion—equating Black Lives Matter with terrorism, labeling journalists as enemies, and deploying federal agents to cities without consent. The goal was not lawfulness. It was dominance. Public safety became a political stunt, and public institutions became tools of spectacle and suppression.

In his second term, those instincts have become law. Trump signed executive orders expanding qualified immunity for police, increasing penalties for protest-related charges, and directing federal agencies to surveil dissent. The Department of Justice has withdrawn from most pattern-and-practice investigations. The One Big Beautiful Bill Act—now law—defunds community violence interruption programs while expanding funding for surveillance tech and paramilitary training. Governors aligned with Trump have passed laws shielding officers from public accountability, criminalizing protest, and protecting drivers who injure demonstrators. What began as posture is now policy: safety as selective privilege, freedom as loyalty, and law as a weapon used against opponents.

This distortion reaches beyond the street. Trump's second term has included the largest expansion of unregulated gun access in modern U.S. history. States have repealed permit requirements. Federal enforcement has been neutered. The One Big Beautiful Bill Act strips funding from red flag programs and background check enforcement. Meanwhile, shootings continue—in schools, churches, supermarkets, and homes. Yet the Republican answer is always the same: more guns, less regulation, and blame directed everywhere but at themselves. A nation awash in firearms, stripped of accountability, and fueled by grievance cannot call itself safe. It can only call itself armed.

At the same time, the infrastructure of national security has been hollowed out. The 2025 national budget law eliminates mandatory cybersecurity standards for federal contractors, repeals energy grid safeguards, and defunds programs for election protection. Domestic extremism units have been dismantled. Foreign election interference is openly denied. Agencies responsible for digital and physical infrastructure protection have seen their budgets slashed or politicized. Trump has even praised foreign regimes that once targeted U.S. systems. This is not strength. It is sabotage—leaving the nation vulnerable not only to criminals, but to chaos, collapse, and hostile control.

The courts have not stayed neutral. Since 2017, Trump and Senate Republicans have confirmed over 230 federal judges—many young, ideological, and hostile to civil rights. These judges have upheld protest bans, expanded qualified immunity, and struck down gun safety laws. The Supreme Court, with three Trump appointees, has gutted voting rights, weakened Miranda, and limited police oversight. Trump's second term brought a wave of politically driven pardons. Over 1,500 individuals tied to the January 6 insurrection have received clemency—through a process driven less by justice than by loyalty. A system that shields the violent while punishing the peaceful forfeits legitimacy. It enforces allegiance, not law.

These threats are compounded by another: a criminal justice system still warped by profit, race, and fear. The U.S. incarcerates more people than any other democracy. Cash bail traps the poor. Mandatory minimums eliminate mercy. Private prisons profit from human misery. Rehabilitation is a slogan, not a system. And Trump has doubled down—blocking reform bills, encouraging harsh sentencing, and reinstating contracts with for-profit detention centers. The 2025 national budget law includes provisions limiting federal clemency, revoking sentence review authority from the Office of the Pardon Attorney, expanding federal death penalty authority, and reintroducing mandatory minimums for a broad range of nonviolent offenses. It blocks states from receiving certain grants unless they enforce truth-in-sentencing rules, strips funding from public defenders, and eliminates restorative justice pilot programs in federal courts. What began as a war on crime has become a war on the vulnerable—especially the poor, the Black, and the forgotten.

Republicans claim that these policies keep Americans safe. But the data tells another story. States with the loosest gun laws have the highest rates of gun deaths. States with the harshest sentencing laws have not seen lasting crime reductions. Policing reforms—body cameras, community programs, independent oversight—have saved lives. Yet they are defunded. Red flag laws reduce suicides and mass shootings. Yet they are repealed. Cybersecurity lapses cost billions. Yet protections are gutted. Foreign interference is confirmed by intelligence agencies. Yet it is ignored. These are not policy differences. They are denials of duty.

There is another way. Safety, justice, and freedom can coexist—but only when power is bound by law, law is bound by equity, and equity is enforced through democratic accountability. That requires restraint—not in the name of weakness, but of wisdom. It means building public safety through trust, not intimidation. It means reducing the presence of guns, not glorifying them. It means designing a criminal justice system that heals more than it harms. And it means protecting our democracy not just from foreign enemies, but from internal sabotage, repression, and decay.

Each of these reforms is a structural repair. Together, they form a system that restores and holds. We begin by restoring the promise of policing: to serve and protect. That requires federal standards, independent accountability, and a shift toward de-escalation, not domination. Next, we tackle gun policy—restoring common-sense protections like background checks, assault weapon restrictions, and safe storage laws that prioritize life over ideology. Then we move to cybersecurity and infrastructure protection—ensuring that elections, power grids, and public systems are defended not just from hackers, but from political sabotage. We follow with a blueprint to prevent foreign interference—banning shadow lobbying, foreign political money, and digital manipulation. And we end with criminal justice reform—eliminating cash bail, shrinking prison populations, and building a justice system that redeems as well as restrains.

Each of these reforms is essential. Together, they form a single moral arc: the right to live in freedom without fear. We cannot call ourselves a democracy if people live in terror of a knock at the door, a bullet in a classroom, or a verdict written before the trial begins. We cannot be a nation of laws if those laws are enforced unequally. And we cannot claim liberty if foreign actors are allowed to buy influence, manipulate discourse, or target our elections while politicians look the other way.

Trump and his allies do not misunderstand this. They understand it fully—and seek to reverse it. Their vision is not safety through justice, but power through punishment. They promise freedom to the armed, impunity to the cruel, and silence to the dissenting. That is not a path to peace. It is a path to submission. If we allow them to define justice as vengeance, safety as surveillance, and freedom as loyalty to one man, we will lose not just our institutions, but our soul.

The future of this country will not be decided by slogans. It will be decided by whether we build systems worthy of trust. Systems that protect without abusing. Systems that punish only with purpose. Systems that guard not just against threat—but against tyranny. A nation that is safe, just, and free does not fear its people. It serves them. It answers to them. And it belongs to them. Let us begin the work of making that true—everywhere, for everyone, once and for all.

23

TO SERVE AND PROTECT

REBUILDING PUBLIC SAFETY THROUGH TRUST, NOT FORCE

"There can be no justice without accountability, and no safety without trust."

— Anonymous civil rights refrain

Policing in a democracy is supposed to protect the public. Not some of the public. All of it. The badge is not a license to dominate, but a symbol of trust. The phrase "to serve and protect" was never meant as branding—it was a promise. That promise, like so many in American life, was not always kept. But it meant something. A police force answers to the people. It is constrained by law. And it exists not to control communities, but to safeguard them. When that principle fails—when fear replaces trust and force replaces care—the damage goes far beyond any one encounter. It corrodes the entire foundation of equal justice under law.

The Constitution does not mention police. But it does guarantee due process, equal protection, and the right to be secure in one's person. In theory, policing is how those rights are defended. In practice, they have often been denied. From slave patrols to stop-and-frisk, from the FBI's COINTELPRO program to the surveillance of Muslim Americans after 9/11, U.S. policing has frequently targeted the vulnerable, the different, or the dissenting. People of color are more likely to be stopped, searched, arrested, and killed. Mental health calls turn fatal. Routine stops escalate. The result is a system that punishes presence, enforces fear, and undermines its own legitimacy.

That legitimacy was already fragile before the past decade shattered it. High-profile killings—of Michael Brown, Tamir Rice, Breonna Taylor, George Floyd, and so many others—were not isolated incidents. They were symptoms of a deeper failure: a culture of impunity, backed by law, protected by politics. Qualified immunity shielded officers from consequences. Police unions blocked reform. Local governments paid out billions in misconduct settlements but changed almost nothing. The system worked—for those in power. For those on the ground, it failed again and again. Each injustice eroded trust. Each denial made the wound deeper. And the demand for change became unavoidable.

But change did not come. Instead, the backlash began. Over the past twenty years, Republicans have cast reform as abandonment and protest as threat. They passed laws to shield officers from discipline, to criminalize recording police, and to increase penalties for resisting arrest—even in cases of mistaken identity or illegal use of force. They flooded departments with military surplus, expanded surveillance without oversight, and promoted policies that rewarded aggression. In Florida, "anti-riot" laws allow peaceful demonstrators to be arrested for someone else's actions. In Texas, police can avoid discipline by resigning before review. In state after state, justice has been redefined—not as fairness, but as control.

Trump's first term took these trends national. He ended Department of Justice consent decrees with local departments—halting civil rights enforcement entirely. He encouraged violence at rallies, telling officers not to be "too nice." He deployed federal agents against protesters in Portland without state consent. He reduced oversight for discriminatory policing and narrowed definitions of civil rights violations. He portrayed racial justice advocates as enemies. The message was clear: protest would be punished, and police would be protected no matter the abuse. When peaceful demonstrators gathered near the White House in June 2020, they were tear-gassed so Trump could hold a photo op with a Bible. The symbolism was not accidental.

In Trump's second term, those postures have become policy. The 2025 public safety laws shield police records from public review, block civilian oversight boards, and strip federal grants from departments that adopt de-escalation mandates. Protest is now criminalized in over a dozen Republican-led states—classified as "terroristic assembly" if more than three people obstruct a road or sidewalk. Police are authorized to detain individuals preemptively if they are deemed "likely to incite disruption." At the federal level, oversight offices have been gutted. Body camera funding has been slashed. Whistleblowers face retaliation. And public safety is now defined by obedience, not by outcome.

This is not just a legal shift. It is a cultural one. Police departments increasingly adopt military language, tactics, and equipment. SWAT raids are routine. "Warrior mindset" training emphasizes dominance over empathy. Officers in schools carry assault weapons. Tactical gear is standard. Children are handcuffed. People in crisis are shot. The logic of policing has drifted from service to suppression—from guardian to soldier. And when brutality occurs, the system too often responds with silence, delay, or denial. And when justice does come, it is often late, bitter, and incomplete. Communities learn to fear, not to trust. And the democratic link between the governed and those who enforce the law is broken.

This collapse did not emerge from nowhere. It was designed. Policing in America is decentralized—more than 18,000 departments, most with little federal accountability. Standards vary wildly. Training is minimal. Discipline is inconsistent. In many states, officers fired for misconduct can be rehired in the next county. Civilian oversight boards often lack subpoena power. Internal investigations are opaque. And police union contracts enshrine delay, destruction of records, and protection from public scrutiny. The result is not safety—but a system armored against change and armed without restraint—but no real accountability. And when that system is challenged, political actors rush to defend it—not because it works, but because it serves them.

Some reforms have worked. Cities that adopted community-based violence interruption programs saw shootings fall. Departments with strong civilian oversight and early intervention systems reduced use-of-force complaints. Procedural justice training improved outcomes in high-stress encounters. But these gains have been uneven and underfunded. And many were reversed under Trump's second term. The 2025 legislation blocks federal grants to departments that use restorative justice models. It prohibits use-of-force reporting as a condition of funding. It repeals standards that required departments to track racial disparities in stops and arrests. Even programs proven to reduce violence are now defunded—because they challenge the dominant narrative of control.

There is another path. Policing can be reformed—deeply, structurally, and morally—without abandoning safety. It begins with national standards: mandatory training in de-escalation, crisis intervention, and constitutional rights. Use-of-force policies must be reformed to ban chokeholds, require warnings, and mandate duty to intervene. Federal funds must be tied to transparency: full public reporting of stops, arrests, complaints, and disciplinary actions.

Qualified immunity must be abolished. Police misconduct should carry real legal and career consequences. Civilian oversight bodies must have subpoena power, disciplinary authority, and independent budgets. And federal law must prohibit officers fired for cause from being rehired elsewhere.

Equally urgent is rebalancing the role of police in society. Officers should not be the default response to every crisis. Mental health, homelessness, addiction, and school discipline are public health issues—not criminal threats. Cities must invest in civilian crisis response teams, social workers, and trained de-escalation specialists. These roles save lives, reduce arrests, and build trust. The goal is not to weaken safety. It is to deliver it more effectively, humanely, and justly. When every problem is treated as a threat, every solution becomes a weapon. Real safety comes not from force, but from care—and from systems that can tell the difference.

Funding must follow this shift. For decades, federal and state dollars have poured into militarized hardware, surveillance, and incarceration. That money must be redirected—to training, housing, mental health care, and community services. Grants should support departments that reduce harm, not just those that expand headcount. Local agencies that adopt data-driven, accountable, and community-centered models must be rewarded—not punished. And Congress must establish a Public Safety Innovation Fund to research, pilot, and scale non-carceral strategies across jurisdictions. The goal is not retreat—it is alignment: with the Constitution, with democracy, and with the realities of those most affected.

The courts must change too. Federal judges have expanded qualified immunity, narrowed civil rights claims, and weakened external oversight. That must be reversed. Congress has the authority to clarify statutes, strip immunity, and mandate enforcement. But court appointments matter. Judges who understand the difference between order and oppression must be confirmed. State supreme courts must also be watched—many have upheld laws that block transparency and override local reform. Legal culture cannot remain detached from the people law is supposed to protect. The badge does not exist above the Constitution. It exists to uphold it. That principle—accountability under law—must be restored, protected, and enforced.

Critics of reform often ask: what about crime? But the better question is: what about justice? A just system reduces crime by earning trust. Communities that believe in the law help uphold it. But where trust is broken, silence follows. Witnesses disappear. Cooperation ends. Fear spreads. Crime rises not because there are too few police—but because there is too little justice. The safest communities in America are not the most heavily policed. They are the ones with the most opportunity, stability, and care. Safety is the result of dignity, not domination. And it cannot be delivered at gunpoint.

The promise of "to serve and protect" can still mean something. But it must be reclaimed. Reclaimed from the lawmakers who turned fear into policy. Reclaimed from the politicians who weaponized protest. Reclaimed from the courts that insulated abuse. Reclaimed from the culture of silence that mistook impunity for peace. And reclaimed from the myth that more force will finally fix what force broke in the first place. Reform is not anti-police. It is pro-democracy. It is how we ensure the rule of law governs power—rather than power bending law to its will. And it is how we make good on a promise long deferred.

A democracy cannot function when the public fears the people tasked with protecting it. And it cannot survive when the law serves only the powerful. To serve and protect is not a slogan. It is a test. A test of whether the state belongs to its citizens—or only to those who claim authority. Every nation faces that test. Ours is happening now. What we choose—justice or vengeance, restraint or repression, service or force—will define not just our police, but our republic itself.

24

JUSTICE THAT HEALS
REFORMING POLICING THROUGH TRAINING, SCOPE, AND PUBLIC TRUST

"Power concedes nothing without a demand. It never did and it never will."

— Frederick Douglass

A badge is not a license to dominate. It is a promise—to protect, not control. And across the country, that promise has been broken. American policing has become too violent, too expansive, and too unaccountable to be called just. But abolition is not the answer. What we need is radical reform rooted in a simple principle: safety comes not from control, but from competence, care, and clarity. To get there, we must rebuild the role of law enforcement from the ground up, limiting its scope, retraining its agents, restoring its dignity, and returning it to its rightful place in a democracy.

Police were never meant to be the answer to everything. Yet today, they are the first responders to mental illness, domestic tension, addiction, homelessness, noise complaints, neighborhood disputes, traffic violations, and more. We have collapsed every public concern into a single emergency response: 911. The result is a system where armed officers are dispatched into situations they are not trained for, with tools that escalate rather than calm. The uniform arrives—but the training it requires does not. And everyone—citizens and officers alike—pays the price.

It is true that police work is dangerous. Every call could be your last. In a nation awash in firearms and rage, officers live with the knowledge that routine stops can turn deadly in an instant. But that fear cannot justify a permanent state of overreaction. A system built on worst-case scenarios trains officers to expect the worst from every citizen. It rewards aggression, punishes hesitation, and turns neighborhoods into war zones. Fear becomes doctrine, and safety becomes performance.

The problem is not just the fear. It is the role itself. We ask officers to do too much with too little preparation. They are expected to serve as counselor, warrior, medic, negotiator, and legal expert—yet most are trained primarily as enforcers. And while some large cities provide advanced training, most departments do not. Many officers receive less instruction than a barber. This is not sustainable—and it is not fair to officers or the public. If we want peace officers, we must prepare them for peace—not just prosecution.

One of the most urgent reforms is redefining emergency response itself. We propose a new multi-channel system: 911 for crime, fire, and urgent medical situations. A new number, for example, 987, for everything else. Staffed by trained specialists in crisis, mental health, addiction, domestic issues, and emotional distress, this service would defuse low-threat calls without dispatching officers. This would reduce unnecessary police contact and allow specialists to respond based on skill, not fear. And if a situation demands it, a police officer can accompany the specialist—not to arrest, but to protect. Co-response, not replacement. The goal is to limit what officers are asked to do, not strip them of their purpose.

Demilitarization must follow. Police are not soldiers. They do not need armored troop carriers, battlefield rifles, or military tactics for ordinary patrol. The Pentagon pipeline that distributes surplus military gear to local departments must end. Yes, rare crises require tactical response. But these are exceptions, not the norm. Policing should not be defined by flashbangs, camouflage, or tanks. It should be defined by trust, proportionality, and restraint.

Reform must also include mandatory national certification. Just as doctors, pilots, and teachers require ongoing licensure, so should peace officers. That training must include civil rights law, trauma recovery, de-escalation, cultural competency, and use-of-force restraint. No department, however small, should be exempt. We must set a national floor—and raise it. Policing should be a profession of skill and service, not simply a job for those willing to carry a gun.

Use-of-force standards must be unified and enforced. Chokeholds, no-knock warrants, retaliatory arrests, and undocumented detentions must be banned. Body cameras should be mandatory and tamper-proof. Every incident involving force should be subject to public review. Internal investigations are not enough. Independent state or regional oversight boards must be empowered to investigate and discipline misconduct. Trust is not rebuilt behind closed doors.

We must also rebuild community trust through visibility and service. Officers should be placed long-term in the communities they serve, with unarmed liaisons and neighborhood teams supporting them. Foot patrols, community meetings, and collaborative problem-solving restore a human presence to policing. People trust those they know. Safety begins with familiarity.

Some responsibilities should be removed entirely. Traffic

enforcement can often be automated—using red-light, speed, and phone-use cameras. This reduces unnecessary stops, limits confrontation, and lets officers focus on real threats, not revenue. Fines should be collected through license renewals or property liens—not with force. Safety, not citation quotas, must be the purpose.

Officers must also be paid and supported in line with the burden we ask them to bear. Police work is not easy. It is exhausting, risky, and psychologically taxing. If we want restraint, we must reduce burnout. If we want good judgment, we must support wellness. Police should be paid more—and expected to meet higher standards. But they must also be cared for. Trauma recovery, mental health access, and rotation out of high-stress units are essential.

In parallel, we propose creating a national "Justice Corps"—a network of unarmed first responders trained in mediation, mental health, and social crisis. They would never replace officers at scenes. But they would handle initial calls remotely, schedule safe visits, and follow up with care. When police respond to everything, they use the only tools they have. We must give our system new tools—and new roles to wield them.

Policing must also change in language and posture. When you train for war, you get war. We must train for peace, for presence, for restraint. That begins with how recruits are taught to think about power, community, and duty. It ends with a culture shift—from dominance to trust. That shift is not symbolic. It is systemic.

What we are asking for is not less safety—but a different kind. One that begins before harm occurs. One that recognizes that restraint is not weakness. One that insists that public safety must be built with public trust. In that vision, the badge does not signify control. It signifies courage, care, and commitment. A police officer should be someone a child can run to—not from.

A nation that is safe, just, and free does not abandon its officers. It elevates them. But it does not allow them to be everything for everyone. It narrows the role, deepens the training, raises the standard, and restores the trust. This is how we reform policing. Not through rage or revenge—but by remaking the job until it finally earns the words printed on every patrol car: to serve and protect.

25

THE WEAPONIZATION OF A NATION
GUN VIOLENCE, CONSTITUTIONAL MYTH, AND THE MACHINERY OF DEATH

"A well regulated Militia, being necessary to the security of a free State, the right of the people to keep and bear Arms shall not be infringed."
— Second Amendment to the United States Constitution

The Second Amendment was not written to grant unlimited private gun ownership. It was written to reassure states that they could defend themselves against federal armies. The Constitution empowers Congress to raise national forces and declare war. States, fearing tyranny from the center, demanded a counterbalance: the right to form their own militias. In the late 1700s, those militias were not state-funded. A farmer who joined the Virginia Militia had to bring his own rifle. The Second Amendment was thus a safeguard: not against crime, not to protect the frontier, but to ensure state sovereignty by allowing private gun ownership in service to a public force.

That context is now erased. What began as a structural check on centralized military power has become a cultural totem of individual entitlement. Historical evidence tells a different story: in the so-called Wild West, towns regularly banned the open carrying of firearms. Gunfights were rare. Weapons were surrendered upon entering Dodge City, not worn casually at the hip. In the early 20th century, when gangsters used Tommy Guns during Prohibition, the government passed the National Firearms Act of 1934, placing heavy restrictions on automatic weapons and imposing taxes and registration requirements. In 1968, after the assassinations of John F. Kennedy, Martin Luther King Jr., and Robert F. Kennedy, Congress passed the Gun Control Act, restricting mail-order gun sales and banning ownership by certain categories of individuals. In 1994, the federal Assault Weapons Ban was enacted, restricting civilian purchase of specific semi-automatic firearms and high-capacity magazines. But Congress allowed it to expire in 2004, and mass shootings rose dramatically thereafter.

That collapse accelerated with politics. In the mid-20th century, the NRA focused on safety and sport. But in the 1970s, it transformed into a political weapon, pushing for absolutist interpretations of the Second Amendment. In 2005, Congress passed the Protection of Lawful Commerce in Arms Act (PLCAA), shielding gun manufacturers from lawsuits even when their products were used in crimes. This law remains intact, blocking families of shooting victims from holding the industry legally accountable. In 2008, the Supreme Court ruled in *District of Columbia v. Heller* that individuals had a right to own guns unconnected to militia service—a radical departure from two centuries of precedent. In 2010, *McDonald v. City of Chicago* extended that ruling to state and local governments. Justice John Paul Stevens dissented, warning that the decision would cost lives. Justice Warren Burger, a conservative, had already declared the NRA's reading of the Second Amendment a fraud.

That fraud now governs us. It is codified not only in law but in commerce. American gun manufacturers make billions in domestic and international sales. Every time fear rises—after a shooting, an election, a court case—gun sales spike. And those profits are reinvested: into lobbying, campaign donations, and propaganda. The industry funds political action committees, finances think tanks, and underwrites disinformation about crime, self-defense, and tyranny. This is the finance two-step: sell the weapons, buy the laws, repeat. The goal is not safety. It is revenue.

The consequences should be horrifying. As of July 2025, over 23,000 people in the U.S. have died from gun violence this year. More than 10,000 were suicides. Nearly 400 were children under the age of 11. Over 300 mass shootings have occurred. More than 1,200 teens have died. There are already thousands of gun orphans—children whose parents were killed by bullets. Gun suicides now occur roughly every 19 minutes, comprising nearly 60% of all gun deaths. Firearms are the leading cause of death for children and teenagers in the United States. These are not unfortunate accidents. They are the predictable result of a system engineered for profit.

After every mass shooting event, Republicans express "thoughts and prayers." While this carries the moment on Fox News, it does nothing to lessen the pain of a parent whose child had to be identified by DNA. In Uvalde, several children's bodies were so severely damaged that investigators asked parents for toothbrushes, hairbrushes, or other items to obtain DNA.

That was not emergency readiness. It was a national surrender.

This is not conviction. It is calculation. Most Republicans in office do not defend gun ownership because they believe it keeps people safe. They defend it because it keeps them elected. They know that unlicensed open carry, high-capacity magazines, and lax access are broadly unpopular. But they also know that fear is politically useful. By invoking the Second Amendment as sacred, they weaponize distrust, energize a violent fringe, and frame all Democratic action as confiscation. The result is grotesque: a party trading children's lives for campaign ads and committee seats.

Republicans have not merely tolerated this system. They have built it. They vote against background checks that over 80% of Americans support. They refuse to ban assault weapons. They allowed the 1994 ban to expire in 2004. They passed PLCAA in 2005. They defunded enforcement of red flag laws, expanded stand-your-ground statutes, and blocked research into gun violence as a public health crisis. They have suppressed the CDC and NIH from studying gun deaths. The goal is not public safety. It is political survival through appeasement of a violent base and a lucrative industry.

Donald Trump has led this campaign with fervor. In his first term, he revoked Obama-era restrictions on mentally ill individuals purchasing firearms. He appointed judges who struck down gun restrictions across the country. His rhetoric emboldened extremists, encouraged vigilantism, and glorified armed confrontation. He promised to protect the Second Amendment "like never before"—and followed through by dismantling even modest attempts at restraint.

In his second term, Trump has gone further. The 2025 federal budget includes tax deductions for gun safes and ammunition purchases. The Department of Justice deprioritized enforcement of gun trafficking laws. Permits for gun shows were loosened and expanded. Reporting requirements for lost or stolen guns were rolled back. Federal oversight of online gun sales was eliminated. And worst of all, PLCAA remains untouched, shielding manufacturers even when their negligence enables mass slaughter. Gun lobbyists now hold government positions. Some now serve as legislative advisors or regulatory overseers. The industry is writing policy.

Meanwhile, the cultural cost deepens. A small number of districts—perhaps 3 to 5 percent—now allow teachers or staff to carry firearms at school, but most educators oppose it. Lockdown drills are as common as fire drills. Bulletproof backpacks are sold in major retail stores. Parents fear grocery runs, birthday parties, movie nights, and church services. Survivors of mass shootings become activists because they have no choice. Gun trauma is now part of childhood. And yet the political system refuses to act—not because it cannot, but because it is bought.

Globally, the United States is an outlier. Japan has near-zero gun deaths per year. The United Kingdom had fewer than 50 in 2024. Australia enacted sweeping reforms after the Port Arthur massacre. Canada, New Zealand, and most of Europe have strict licensing, storage, and assault weapon laws. In no other advanced democracy is gun death treated as the price of freedom. The only difference is not mental health, not culture, not crime rates. It is policy. It is profit. It is political corruption.

The gun crisis is not an unfortunate side effect of liberty. It is the result of design. The Second Amendment has been twisted into a sacrament. The Supreme Court has betrayed its role as interpreter in favor of ideology. Legislatures have been purchased. The media has been flooded with spin, fear, and distraction. And Americans are dying by the tens of thousands.

We must be clear: no one is safer when every person is armed. Children are not safer. Police are not safer. Black Americans are not safer. Women in abusive relationships are not safer. Veterans with PTSD are not safer. The only beneficiaries of this crisis are corporations and the politicians they fund. Everyone else lives in fear.

There is no just or free future under these terms. A nation that is safe, just, and free cannot have unlimited access to guns for profit.

26

A FUTURE WITHOUT FEAR

LICENSING, INSURANCE, AND ACCOUNTABILITY FOR EVERY GUN

---◆---

"The law is not made for the righteous but for the lawless... for murderers, for manslayers."
— The First Letter to Timothy 1:9 (paraphrased)

The United States regulates every dangerous machine except one. To drive a car, you must have a license, registration, and insurance. To operate a commercial vehicle, you must pass specialized tests. And if you injure someone with a vehicle while unlicensed, uninsured, or reckless, you may be fined, sued, or jailed. But if you kill someone with a gun—without a license, without registration, without insurance—no equivalent system applies. There is grief. There is blood. But there is no structure. That must change. Not through seizure. Not through mass prosecution. But through the creation of a national framework of responsibility—one that protects the public, respects the law, and subjects the gun industry to the same standards we demand of every other potentially deadly device.

We begin with a necessary correction. The so-called individual right to gun ownership, as asserted in *District of Columbia v. Heller*, was not rooted in historical truth but in political distortion. For more than two centuries, courts upheld the Second Amendment as tied to organized militia service. The late 20th-century reversal was not legal evolution—it was ideological capture. Under a restored and expanded Supreme Court committed to the rule of law, *Heller* and *McDonald* would be overturned, and the Second Amendment returned to its original meaning: a structural protection for state militias, not a universal license for private arsenals. Only on that foundation would genuine reform become possible.

Guns would be treated for what they are: machines capable of lethal harm. Like motor vehicles, they would be permitted only under conditions of demonstrated competence. Every gun owner would be required to hold a valid, up-to-date license. Obtaining one would involve both written and practical tests, similar to driver education. Licenses would be tiered by weapon type: home defense firearms, handguns, tactical rifles, specialty arms, and security-class weapons would each require distinct training and renewal standards. Law enforcement personnel—including local police, federal agents, and tactical teams—would be licensed under the same system, with additional requirements for active field deployment.

Each firearm would be registered to its current legal owner, and that registration would follow the weapon for life. The system would mirror vehicle identification protocols, assigning each firearm a unique ID linked to ballistic data, manufacturing records, transaction history, and legal status. Transfers—through sale, inheritance, or surrender—would be documented. Ballistic fingerprints—barrel striations, firing pin imprints, and chamber marks—would be recorded at manufacture and stored in a national database accessible to law enforcement. The registry would not be punitive. It would be protective. And it would ensure that every bullet could be traced to its source.

Insurance would be mandatory. Just as drivers must carry liability coverage, gun owners would be required to maintain active insurance. Premiums could vary based on risk factors such as age, weapon class, training level, and violation history. Victims of gun violence—whether from accidental shootings, domestic gun violence, or unlawful use—would be eligible to file claims. Where the shooter was unidentified, uninsured, or deceased, compensation would be paid from a publicly administered Uninsured Gun Harm (UGH) fund, financed by taxes on manufacturer profits, insurance revenue, and per-unit excise fees. Risk would no longer be dumped on the public. It would be priced, tracked, and managed—like every other form of liability.

To support compliance, the first two years after enactment would constitute a national amnesty and transition period. Licenses and training programs would be provided at no cost. Insurance policies would be subsidized. Gun owners who preferred to surrender their firearms—whether for moral, financial, or personal reasons—rather than register them would be eligible for a federally funded buyback program. States would host safe surrender sites and mobile compliance units. Public information campaigns would reach every community. On tribal lands and in sovereign jurisdictions, partnership agreements would ensure alignment and autonomy. The goal would not be punishment. It would be participation.

After the amnesty, unregistered weapons would be treated as contraband. Possession without a valid license and registration would trigger legal impoundment. Weapons used in crimes would be seized and destroyed unless legal ownership could be promptly proven. Owners who had failed to comply could reclaim their property by paying penalties, completing training, and providing license, registration, and insurance. Unclaimed or abandoned firearms would be designated for training, forensic research, or safe destruction. The principle is simple: if you cannot prove you are responsible, you do not get to carry the risk.

The gun industry would no longer enjoy immunity. The Protection of Lawful Commerce in Arms Act would be repealed. Victims would have the right to sue manufacturers and dealers for negligence, negligent or unsafe design, and reckless distribution—just as they can sue carmakers, chemical plants, or pharmaceutical companies. Courts would be empowered to consider patterns of abuse, failures to track suspicious sales, and knowingly false advertising. Each manufacturer would also be required to contribute to a National Uninsured Fund, supporting victim recovery and enforcement in communities burdened by concentrated gun violence. Profit would no longer be an escape route from responsibility.

Advertising would be regulated. Guns would fall under the same legal restrictions as tobacco, alcohol, and pharmaceuticals. Promotions could not target minors, glorify violence, or portray firearms as solutions to social or political conflict. Claims that ownership ensures masculinity, patriotism, or dominance would be prohibited. Political spending by gunmakers would be capped, disclosed, and limited to regulated channels. Lobbying would be public. No private company would retain the power to shape law behind closed doors.

Internationally, the United States would no longer be a leading exporter of weapons to cartels, militias, or authoritarian regimes. Firearms could be sold abroad only to verified government agencies through licensed dealers. The "sporting use" loophole would be closed. All exported weapons would be registered, tracked, and reported. Gun manufacturers would be required to contribute to a Global Gun Harm mitigation fund for violence-affected regions. A country that disarms itself internally must not enable violence abroad.

Education would be integral to the new system. Gun safety, de-escalation, and civic responsibility would be included in public school curricula. Community-based training—led by veterans, law enforcement officers, and certified instructors—would help demystify weapons and restore a sense of civic duty to ownership. License levels would be scaled appropriately: a rural farmer needing a long gun would face different requirements than an urban carrier of a tactical pistol. But in every case, training would be mandatory, consistent, and enforced.

Some argue that such a system could be used to target vulnerable communities. But today's system already targets them—through arbitrary enforcement, racial profiling, and community abandonment. By standardizing procedures and tracking all weapons equally, the new framework would reduce discretion and bias. It would turn enforcement from judgment into procedure. Responsibility would be defined not by privilege or power, but by proof.

Others claim that reform infringes on liberty. But liberty does not mean performing surgery without a license or flying planes without training. We regulate elevators, toxic chemicals, electrical work, drones, AI-enabled tools, and breakfast cereals—not to restrict freedom, but to preserve life. A machine designed to kill should never have been an exception. It should have been held to the same standard as a car.

There will be those who say that criminals won't follow these rules. They never have. But the purpose of law is not to govern criminals—it is to set the standard for everyone else. With universal licensing, registration, and insurance, law enforcement could distinguish the responsible from the reckless, the legal from the dangerous. The goal is not to eliminate every act of violence. It is to reduce their number, limit their scale, and increase accountability when they occur.

The financial costs of this system would be real—but they would be offset by long-term gains. Insurance companies would price risk. Manufacturers would invest in safer technology. Public trauma costs, hospital burdens, and police overreach would decline. Health insurance premiums—currently inflated by the cost of gun-related injuries—would stabilize. Emergency rooms and trauma units would no longer be forced to absorb the recurring toll of preventable violence.

For more than half a century, firearms have remained virtually unchanged in safety design. Unlike cars, which have seen breakthroughs in airbags, stability control, and crash survivability, guns are no safer today than they were in the 1970s. Trigger locks and manual safeties existed then and remain optional now. Smart gun technologies—biometric locks, digital access controls, auto-disable features—have been developed but not adopted. There is no federal requirement for childproofing, misuse prevention, or theft deterrence. The gun industry has faced no liability, no required standards, and no structural incentive to innovate. As a result, unintentional shootings, stolen guns, and domestic tragedies continue as if the clock had stopped in 1974. Safety has been a political casualty. A market finally subject to consequence would become a market that evolves.

Culturally, the shift would be even more profound. Gun ownership would remain legal—but never again careless. Children would no longer rehearse for death in their classrooms. Parents would no longer fear grocery stores and public parks. Police would no longer be routinely outgunned. And survivors would no longer be told that the system is powerless to act. We cannot undo what has already been lost. But we can refuse to accept the conditions that caused it.

We were not meant to live in fear of one another. Gun violence is not the cost of freedom. It is the evidence of a failure to act. But we can act. And if we do—through law, through training, through truth—we can create a nation where people still own firearms, but where no one is exempt from responsibility. A nation where the badge, the bullet, and the ballot are all governed by the same principle: protection must come with proof. And fear must never be the price of freedom again.

27

CYBERSECURITY AND INFRASTRUCTURE PROTECTION
THE INVISIBLE SYSTEMS THAT HOLD A NATION TOGETHER

"The greatest threat to liberty does not always come with a bang. Sometimes, it arrives quietly—when the lights don't turn on."
— Attributed, modern proverb

A functioning democracy does not begin with ballots or speeches. It begins with systems that work. A green light turns red. A vote is counted once. A nurse updates a health record from another building. Your salary appears in your account. These moments pass without notice—until they fail. Democracy depends not only on rights and laws, but on invisible reliability. When those invisible systems are sabotaged, hacked, or neglected, the social contract ruptures. And it does so silently. No bomb is needed to shake a nation—just a corrupted file, a power failure, a system crash. The promise of democracy includes this: that what works today will still work tomorrow.

That promise is no longer being kept. Power grids, pipelines, school districts, and city halls, the systems we depend on are under attack or falling apart. Some failures come from nature—storms, heat, age. Others are deliberate. The 2020 SolarWinds hack compromised nine federal agencies. A ransomware attack shut down Colonial Pipeline and triggered panic buying across the South. Baltimore's public systems froze for weeks after a ransomware breach. And in 2016, Russian actors probed election systems in at least 21 states. These were not isolated events. They were signs of a country unguarded, uncoordinated, and unprepared.

We like to think of infrastructure as steel and concrete. But every bridge and building now depends on code. Traffic lights, water valves, electrical substations—all digitized, all vulnerable. When a nurse checks your records, or a city planner reroutes traffic, they do so through a system that can be reached, changed, or shut down by someone a continent away. The Italian Job made this fictional. Today it is fact. Physical and digital infrastructure are no longer separable. Every digital node becomes a doorway—every connection, a risk. The moment you connect a vital system, you must defend it forever.

That defense has not come. Most critical infrastructure in the United States is privately owned, poorly regulated, and inconsistently protected. Federal oversight is limited. Many systems still run on legacy software. Local governments lack funds. Private contractors profit from rushed fixes and opaque proprietary tools. And no national mandate forces compliance. A hacker only has to succeed once. Security must succeed every time—even if attacked 100,000 times per second. And with every failed attempt, attackers learn more about where we're weak. That is not just a technical problem. It is a structural one. And it is getting worse. The longer we delay a national strategy, the more we reward sabotage and chaos.

Cybersecurity has its own grim arithmetic. Safe systems take time to build. But by the time they're finished, they are already outdated. Hackers are just as smart, just as fast, and often better funded. Once data is breached, it cannot be un-breached. Once trust is broken, it is hard to restore. And in many cases, no one is held responsible. The breach is framed as an 'incident,' not a dereliction of public duty. But the truth is this: when systems fail and no one answers, democracy itself begins to erode. Not with force, but with delay, doubt, and decay.

And yet even this decay is profitable. The longer we delay upgrades, the more contracts flow to vendors who patch instead of protect. When standards are weak, insurance firms, cloud vendors, and software contractors fill the void—for a price. Chaos sells. Invisibility sells more. And the public, told little and taught less, is left believing that failure is inevitable. But it is not. Other countries do better because they chose differently. Estonia created a national digital ID after a cyberattack. South Korea built a centralized cyber command. The European Union enforces strict rules for critical systems. The United States chose profit over preparedness.

That choice is ideological. Democrats have generally treated cybersecurity as part of national defense: a public obligation, requiring federal standards and shared responsibility. Biden's 2021 executive order on cybersecurity was a rare attempt to impose minimum protections. But it came after decades of Republican opposition to regulation and centralized oversight. Under Trump, cybersecurity offices were disbanded. Election lies were amplified. The CISA director was fired for publicly confirming the 2020 election's integrity. The message was clear: chaos was useful, standards were not. And when systems fail, Republicans gain something Democrats do not: proof that government doesn't work.

But government must work—especially when it's invisible. That is the promise of public systems. You should not have to wonder if your tap water is clean, your paycheck processed, your ballot recorded. Infrastructure, when secure, disappears. And that invisibility is not a flaw—it is a feature. It means democracy is functioning. People make long-term plans because they trust the present to hold. Children walk to school because traffic obeys the lights. Security isn't about fear—it's about calm, confidence, and continuity. The ability to look away because the system is built to hold.

We have not invested in that calm. Instead, we've let states choose wildly different standards. We've allowed water systems to fail, hospitals to be hacked, and election systems to age without backup. A decentralized system makes infiltration harder—but it makes protection harder too. Fifty voting systems means fifty doors to guard. Fifty power grids means fifty points of failure. In a storm, a hack, or a war, that disunity is not resilience. It is fragility masquerading as freedom. National systems must be locally implemented but federally protected. Our patchwork of jurisdictions makes coordination almost impossible in a national crisis.

A functioning republic does not just defend borders. It defends its infrastructure—every bridge, pipeline, traffic light, emergency server, and encrypted record. These are not luxuries. They are democratic organs. If they fail, the body does not breathe. And many of them are already compromised. Thousands of small municipalities run outdated election machines. Some don't have paper backups. Ransomware attackers routinely target schools, hospitals, and power companies—because they know no one is watching. No guard at the gate. No national standard. Just scattered code and private deals.

We need a unified strategy. And it must begin with a simple truth: protection is a public duty. Any company or agency that manages critical systems must meet federal security baselines. That includes utilities, telecoms, hospitals, transit networks, and cloud providers. No opt-outs. No lobbying carve-outs. A national audit cycle. Emergency funding for upgrades. Real-time threat tracking. And enforceable penalties when systems fall short. We do not tolerate unsafe airplanes or expired food. We should not tolerate unprotected voting machines or exposed water systems.

Some attacks will still succeed. But the goal is not invincibility. It is resilience—the ability to detect, isolate, respond, and recover. Estonia's model assumes breach is inevitable. Israel integrates cyber defense into national defense. South Korea conducts national cyber drills annually. In each case, the government protects what is invisible because it is essential. These countries have problems. But their systems are not collapsing. Ours are.

And the next system to fail may not give a warning, or a second chance.

This is not just collapse. It is betrayal without smoke, glass, or fingerprints.

And if we do nothing, it will happen again. And again.

28

THE CYBERSECURITY REDEMPTION PLAN

PROTECTING INFRASTRUCTURE, RESTORING TRUST, AND MAKING SYSTEMS WORK

---◆---

"A lie can travel halfway around the world while the truth is still putting on its boots. But when systems fall, the truth may never catch up."
— Adapted from a quote often attributed to Mark Twain

The American public is told that its systems are protected. That private companies manage them responsibly. That cybersecurity is handled behind the scenes. But this is a lie. Or rather, a profit model disguised as public trust. The truth is simpler—and far more dangerous: for-profit control of national infrastructure has failed. Failed in hospitals, schools, pipelines, and city halls. Failed to protect ballots, medical records, water systems, and power grids. It failed when Baltimore went dark. It failed when Russian operatives read State Department emails. It failed when a hacker raised chemical levels in a Florida water supply. It failed when COVID-stricken hospitals were paralyzed by ransomware.

The for-profit platform model was never built to defend democracy. It was designed to extract value. And it will fail again. Then again. And again.

These are not isolated incidents. They are signals. Not distant threats, but constant warnings. For years, hackers have breached school systems, shut down ambulances, disrupted fuel lines, and exposed military secrets. They have held cities hostage, stolen identities, erased trust. Each time, we treat it as an anomaly. A glitch. A learning experience. But the next time will not be survivable. We are not one breach away from inconvenience. We are one breach away from collapse. Planes grounded midflight. Power cut to entire regions. 911 networks silent. Pharmacies dispensing the wrong medication. Payrolls frozen. Voter rolls corrupted. If you can imagine it, someone is already trying to make it real. And when they succeed, the damage will not be measured in dollars. It will be measured in time, trust, and lives.

The logic is unforgiving. A hacker only needs to succeed once. Security must succeed every time. But that equation breaks down when no one is responsible. In the U.S., infrastructure protection is optional, fragmented, and largely outsourced. Nearly 85% of critical systems—power, water, telecoms, hospitals—are privately owned. There are no mandatory standards. No federal breach audits. No consistent threat testing. Companies self-report failures, delay upgrades, and negotiate security as a cost-benefit exercise. The federal government offers guidelines, not enforcement. And when systems fail, the public pays. With lost data. With delayed care. With services gone dark. This is not just inefficient—it is negligent.

Other countries chose differently. Estonia was paralyzed by a massive cyberattack in 2007. Its systems went dark. Instead of denial, it responded with transformation. It built the world's most advanced civilian cyber defense program. Every citizen now has a digital ID. Every system has a paper fallback. Every agency runs breach drills. Israel made cybersecurity part of military defense. South Korea implemented mandatory risk reporting and centralized civilian authority. Finland created a national emergency agency to coordinate threats across sectors. Singapore audits every critical infrastructure system with direct state oversight. The European Union mandates that essential services follow strict standards and face real penalties for failure. They govern as if the future depends on it—because it does.

The United States, by contrast, is now the only major democracy without a centralized, civilian-led authority with enforcement power over its public infrastructure. The only one with no breach disclosure law for utilities. The only one that treats ransomware like a local crime. The only one where private cloud vendors can walk away from responsibility while holding entire hospital systems in their code. The only one where electoral infrastructure is updated—or not—based on county budgets. They don't need to break our systems—they just need to outlast our dysfunction. They don't have to sabotage us. They just have to wait for us to keep doing nothing.

But we can do this. And we've done it before. The Apollo Program, the Manhattan Project, ARPANET, the Y2K remediation effort—these were moments when the U.S. summoned coordination, urgency, and intelligence on a national scale. When leaders across parties and agencies understood that complexity could not be outsourced to chance. That public safety required public investment. The federal government can build a new system—centralized, nonpartisan, civilian-led, and permanent. It must include mandatory national standards, real-time threat response, and full public–private integration. Not advisory committees. Not voluntary best practices. Enforcement. Audits. Emergency funding. Oversight.

This effort must begin with a national inventory. Every system. Every point of vulnerability. Every outdated server, unsecured device, or legacy database running unpatched code. What we don't track, we can't protect. From there, we need funding—not just for defense, but for resilience. Paper backups for digital elections. Local cybersecurity teams, trained and retained. Secure communications for every hospital, school, and emergency service. Annual stress tests for major cities. And federal coordination centers to monitor threats in real time—across jurisdictions, agencies, and regions. And automatic breach notifications, with penalties for concealment. A power company that hides a failure is no different than an airline that skips safety checks. Accountability is not a burden. It is the cost of public trust.

We must stop outsourcing the future. Cloud platforms, voting machine vendors, defense contractors, hospital IT providers—they all serve the public. That must come with obligations. Any private entity that manages public infrastructure must follow national protocols and open itself to public inspection. No more proprietary black boxes. No more profit margins dictating public risk. If you carry the public's water—physically or digitally—you answer to the public. That's not regulation. That's democracy.

We must build a civilian cybersecurity corps. Not as a military operation, but as a public service initiative. Young Americans should be able to serve their country by defending its systems. Veterans should be retrained to monitor, test, and audit critical networks. Colleges should create national service pipelines for ethical hacking, system design, and recovery planning. Every city hall should have someone who knows what a breach looks like—and what to do when it happens. We have the talent. We have the skills—but not the structure. That can change.

We must also coordinate with allies. Cyberattacks don't stop at borders. Supply chains don't either. Nor do threats to infrastructure. NATO, the EU, and Pacific partners all face similar risks. A U.S.-led Cyber Defense Compact could pool threat data, coordinate crisis responses, and help raise global standards. No nation can survive alone in a connected world. Cooperation is not weakness. It is survival.

This is not a technology problem. It is a governance problem.

Our systems are vulnerable because we've treated them as someone else's job. Because we've let complexity breed complacency. Because we've mistaken silence for security. But silence is not security. It is ignorance misread as calm. And unawareness is what makes us weak. Every breach, every delay, every attack that goes unanswered weakens the contract between the state and the citizen. If we cannot guarantee safety, we cannot claim legitimacy.

So we must act. Not after the next catastrophe, but now. We cannot wait for a digital 9/11. We cannot wait for Estonia's wake-up call to be ours. Every breach, however small, is already the warning. Every system that fails is a test we're flunking. The future will not wait for us to get serious. And once trust is gone, it is nearly impossible to rebuild. Trust in ballots. Trust in records. Trust that when the light is green, it is safe to go.

There is no version of democracy that survives without infrastructure. No rule of law without reliable courts. No equal protection without hospitals that work. No freedom of speech if the networks collapse. No right to vote if the ballot system is down. These things are invisible when they work. That invisibility is the dividend of protection—not a guarantee.

We need a national infrastructure protection plan. Centralized. Civilian-led. Mandatory. Transparent. Bipartisan. Funded. Inspected. Enforced. And permanent. This is not about IT. This is about the survival of a system built on public trust. We have the money. We have the talent. What we have lacked is the will. That changes now.

The breach we fear most may not come through a pipeline or a power line. It may come through the mind. Through a story too false to be ignored, or a doubt too easy to spread. Infrastructure can be rebuilt. Belief cannot. And that is where the next battlefield lies

29

DEFENDING DEMOCRACY FROM FOREIGN INTERFERENCE
WHAT WE DON'T PROTECT, WE FORFEIT

"Foreign influence is one of the most baneful foes of republican government."
— George Washington, Farewell Address, 1796

In a healthy democracy, persuasion wins. Citizens debate, decide, and vote. The results may disappoint, but they are legitimate. That legitimacy is not magic—it is maintained. And when foreign powers interfere, legitimacy dissolves. Elections become contests of manipulation, not choice. Speech becomes a weapon. Division becomes strategy. The goal is not just influence—it is collapse. When democracy is vulnerable, its enemies do not need tanks or missiles. They need only to amplify lies, exploit weakness, and discredit outcomes. Foreign interference rarely steals votes. It steals belief. And once a nation no longer believes in its own democracy, it becomes easy to break.

The United States has already been targeted. In 2016, Russian operatives executed a coordinated campaign to undermine Hillary Clinton, boost Donald Trump, and erode trust in democratic institutions. They hacked the DNC, weaponized stolen emails, and flooded social media with disinformation. They scanned election systems and tested access to voter databases in at least 21 states. They used bots, trolls, and fake pages to inflame racial tension, depress turnout, and encourage distrust. Their goal was not just to help Trump. It was to destabilize democracy itself. And it worked. Years later, millions of Americans still believe the lies.

In response, the United States did almost nothing. Barack Obama warned Putin, but imposed no meaningful consequences. Congress was briefed, but split along party lines. Trump, who directly benefited from the interference, denied it happened—and fired those who said otherwise. When the 2020 election came, it was again targeted, this time by both foreign and domestic actors. Trump's own allies spread conspiracy theories about voting machines, mail ballots, and foreign agents. CISA declared it the most secure election in U.S. history. Trump called it stolen. One week later, he fired the CISA director.

That moment revealed the new danger. Foreign interference no longer comes only from abroad. It is invited, echoed, and defended from within. Trump's attacks on U.S. intelligence, the FBI, the State Department, and the Justice Department—all departments tasked with national security—were not just political. They were strategic. They weakened the very agencies tasked with resisting foreign intrusion. They dismantled institutional guardrails. They turned suspicion inward. And they convinced millions that the enemy was not Russia, but fellow Americans. In doing so, Trump became the perfect delivery system for the very forces democracy was meant to repel.

This strategy is not unique to Trump. It is a growing model for authoritarian-aligned movements worldwide. Discredit the press.

Flood social media with lies. Question every result. Accuse opponents of treason. Accept help from hostile states if it advantages your side. Then use that advantage to weaken institutions further. Hungary, Brazil, the Philippines, India—each shows a version of the same pattern. Democracy, when unguarded, becomes a vessel for its own sabotage. And those in power will not protect it. They will use it until it breaks.

America's defenses against foreign interference are real—but deeply inadequate. The FBI and DHS have cyber threat divisions. The National Security Agency and CIA monitor foreign disinformation. CISA shares best practices with state election officials. But there is no unified command. No national doctrine. No standing body with the authority, funding, and mandate to defend democracy itself. We have agencies for infrastructure, intelligence, and law enforcement—but no central authority tasked with defending elections from manipulation, foreign or domestic. That gap is not an oversight. It is a political decision—one rooted in denial, convenience, and fear.

And that threat is growing. Artificial intelligence now enables faster, more convincing lies. Deepfakes can forge speeches, confessions, or news reports. Social media platforms—driven by engagement, not truth—continue to amplify outrage. Some are now openly aligned with partisan or ideological agendas, refusing to moderate even the most toxic disinformation. The algorithms that drive virality are indifferent to accuracy. What spreads is what incites. And what incites is often false. Foreign actors—from Russia to China to Iran—know how to weaponize that pattern. So do extremist networks inside the United States.

There was a time when platforms responded. Facebook hired fact-checkers. Twitter flagged falsehoods. YouTube throttled fake accounts. These actions were limited but symbolic—they suggested that some lines could not be crossed. But that line has eroded. Today, platform leaders no longer pretend neutrality. Many compete for favor, strip protections, reinstate banned accounts, and ignore known disinformation. In doing so, they become infrastructure for collapse—accelerators of both foreign manipulation and domestic sabotage.

To defend democracy, we must first redefine it—not just as a system of laws, but as a living information environment. One where truth must be defended as actively as borders. Where voters are not left alone in a storm of lies. Where foreign fingerprints on domestic discourse are treated as acts of aggression. That does not mean censorship. It means transparency. Mandatory disclosure of funding and origin. Traceable attribution of all political messaging. Real-time labeling of coordinated inauthentic activity. Immediate takedowns of foreign-controlled assets operating in U.S. political discourse. These are defenses, not restrictions. They protect choice, not limit it.

We must also protect our voting systems from digital intrusion. That means fully funding state and local election offices. Mandating paper ballots or voter-verifiable paper trails. Establishing nationwide audit standards. And banning all voting machines that cannot be checked independently. Most counties want to improve. But without federal support, they cannot afford it. The result is a patchwork of vulnerability. A few insecure systems can compromise confidence in the entire election. The integrity of national elections cannot be left to budget cycles and local politics.

Election disinformation must carry real consequences. Social media platforms that fail to remove known foreign interference must face fines and possible shutdown of political advertising during high-risk periods. Domestic actors—whether campaigns, candidates, or PACs—who knowingly use foreign material or collaborate with foreign agents must face criminal penalties. This is not hypothetical. The Trump campaign openly sought dirt from Russia. Roger Stone coordinated with Wikileaks. Paul Manafort passed polling data to Russian intelligence. None of this was fiction. It was active collaboration with foreign interference.

Democracy also depends on press resilience. Foreign powers do not just spread lies. They weaken the institutions that spread truth. Discrediting journalists, sowing distrust, and flooding timelines with forgeries are deliberate tactics. The United States must support independent media with funding, legal protections, and platform access. It must prevent foreign ownership of outlets that shape political opinion. And it must ensure that press freedom does not mean platforming disinformation. A free press is not one that prints lies. It is one that investigates, verifies, and informs—especially in an age of digital warfare.

Public education plays a role, too. Information literacy is now a civic skill. Voters must learn how to verify sources, spot manipulation, and question virality. That means school curricula, public service campaigns, and training for older populations most targeted by false information. Other countries are doing this. Finland runs disinformation training in schools. Taiwan holds daily press briefings to preempt rumors. We do neither. Instead, we leave citizens untrained on the battlefield of information. And then we blame them for being misled.

Foreign interference is not new. But digital reach makes it faster, cheaper, and harder to trace. Hostile states no longer need to bribe politicians or invade borders. They can simply infiltrate the public mind. They can flood inboxes with fake stories. They can amplify the worst voices. They can weaken belief, fracture coalitions, and inspire violence—all without attribution. That is the battlefield now. And we are still preparing as if the threat is tanks and planes.

Congress must act. A national Democracy Defense Agency should be established, drawing on cybersecurity, intelligence, media, and civil rights expertise. It must be insulated from political interference, bound by transparency rules, and funded to match the scale of the threat. This is not a normal policy area. It is a foundational obligation. The right to vote is meaningless if elections are decided by lies, fear, and sabotage. Protecting democracy from foreign interference is no longer optional. It is the price of survival.

Some will argue that these protections restrict speech. But foreign interference is not speech. It is covert manipulation by hostile actors. Just as we regulate campaign finance and voter eligibility, we must regulate who gets to shape the conversation. The First Amendment does not guarantee the right to deceive voters on behalf of a foreign state. And it does not obligate platforms to serve as conduits for digital sabotage. Speech must be free. But democracy must be free, too.

The final protection is cultural. We must learn to take democracy seriously again. That means defending it, not just in policy, but in spirit. Refusing to laugh off foreign memes, false headlines, and manipulated outrage. Refusing to retweet what we haven't read. Refusing to follow leaders who treat lies as tools and treason as strategy. We cannot stop every attack. But we can become a country where interference is difficult, dangerous, and not worth the effort.

We used to think interference meant agents and documents and secrets. But the real secret is this: what breaks democracy is not espionage. It is doubt. It is confusion. It is belief, turned against itself. To defend democracy, we must defend clarity, credibility, and truth. These are the new battlegrounds. And if we do not hold them, we will lose far more than an election.

And we will lose the republic that the election was meant to protect.

30

THE DEFENSE WE STILL NEED
HOW TO PROTECT ELECTIONS, TRUTH, AND THE PUBLIC MIND

"A popular government without popular information, or the means of acquiring it, is but a prologue to a farce or a tragedy."
— James Madison, 1822 letter to W.T. Barry

Persuasion, not coercion, is the foundation of democracy. But that foundation has been targeted—not just from abroad, but from within. The belief that elections are fair, that facts are real, and that rules apply equally has become fragile. And foreign powers have noticed. When legitimacy crumbles, democracy is no longer government by the people. It is performance for the manipulators.

The Constitution does not mention foreign interference by name. But its promises depend on freedom from it. Article I assumes elections will be free, fair, and representative. Article IV guarantees a republican form of government. The First Amendment protects speech—but it does not protect sabotage. And every branch of government is charged, implicitly and explicitly, with defending the people's right to self-rule. That includes defending against hostile manipulation by foreign powers. When that duty is ignored or outsourced, the constitutional promise of democracy is already under siege.

The United States has already been targeted. In 2016, Russian operatives executed a coordinated campaign to undermine Hillary Clinton, boost Donald Trump, and erode trust in democratic institutions. They hacked the DNC, released stolen emails, and saturated social media with disinformation. They probed state election systems and voter databases. They used bots, trolls, and fake pages to inflame racial tension, depress turnout, and encourage distrust. Their goal was not just to help Trump. It was to destabilize democracy itself. And it worked. Years later, millions of Americans still believe the lies.

In response, the United States did almost nothing. Barack Obama warned Putin, but imposed no meaningful consequences. Congress was briefed, but split along party lines. Trump, who directly benefited from the interference, denied it happened—and fired those who said otherwise. When the 2020 election came, it was again targeted, this time by both foreign and domestic actors. Trump's own allies spread conspiracy theories about voting machines, mail ballots, and foreign agents. CISA officials called it the most secure election in American history. Trump called it stolen. One week later, he fired the CISA director.

That moment revealed the new danger. Foreign interference no longer comes only from abroad. It is invited, echoed, and defended from within. Trump's attacks on U.S. intelligence, the FBI, the State Department, and the Justice Department were not just political. They were strategic. They weakened the very agencies tasked with resisting foreign intrusion. They dismantled the guardrails. They turned suspicion inward. And they convinced millions that the enemy was not Russia, but fellow Americans. In doing so, Trump became the perfect delivery system for the very forces democracy was meant to repel.

And the sabotage has only deepened in his second term. Trump has further dismantled federal oversight of disinformation and election security. Federal election protection grants have been slashed or frozen. CISA's staffing has been cut, its independence eroded, and its coordination powers restricted. Allies have been alienated, while foreign-aligned platforms have been elevated. The presidency now serves not as a bulwark against interference—but as a willing entry point. The threat is no longer creeping in through back channels—it is now entering through the front door.

This strategy is not unique to Trump. It is a growing model for authoritarian-aligned movements worldwide. Discredit the press. Flood social media with lies. Question every result. Accuse opponents of treason. Accept help from hostile states if it advantages your side. Then use that advantage to weaken institutions further. Hungary, Brazil, the Philippines, India—each shows a version of the same pattern. Democracy, when unguarded, becomes a vessel for its own sabotage. And those in power will not protect it. They will use it until it breaks.

America's defenses against foreign interference are real—but deeply inadequate. The FBI and DHS have cyber threat divisions. The National Security Agency and CIA monitor foreign disinformation. CISA shares best practices with state election officials. But there is no unified command. No national doctrine. No standing body with the authority, funding, and mandate to defend democracy itself. We have agencies for infrastructure, intelligence, and law enforcement—but no single structure tasked with keeping elections free from manipulation, digital or psychological. That failure is not incidental. It is a reflection of political refusal to name the threat.

And that threat is growing. Artificial intelligence now enables faster, more convincing lies. Deepfakes can forge speeches, confessions, or news reports. Social media platforms—driven by engagement, not truth—continue to amplify outrage. Some are now openly aligned with right-wing interests, refusing to moderate even the most toxic disinformation. The algorithms that power virality are indifferent to accuracy. What spreads is what incites. And what incites is often false. Foreign actors—from Russia to China to Iran—know how to weaponize that pattern. So do extremist networks inside the United States.

There was a time when social media platforms acted—however imperfectly—as a front line against foreign interference. They flagged and removed Russian bots. They partnered with researchers to track disinformation. They labeled state media and attempted to curb algorithmic amplification of falsehoods. Facebook hired fact-checkers. Twitter filtered falsehoods. YouTube banned election disinformation. These efforts were never complete—but they mattered. They signaled that truth still had defenders.

But that line has collapsed. Not from force, but from profit. Platforms learned that outrage pays better than order. Today, Facebook has reinstated accounts that fueled January 6. Twitter—now X—has dissolved its trust and safety teams. YouTube no longer enforces election misinformation policies. Platform leaders no longer claim neutrality—they compete for favor. It is easier to appease than to resist. Easier to host the fire than to put it out. In doing so, they became infrastructure for collapse: algorithmic accelerants of foreign interference, domestic sabotage, and presidential grievance. They are no longer neutral. They are now partners in the sabotage.

And behind it all is the question we must always ask: who profits? Foreign regimes profit—by weakening American power without firing a shot. Trump and his allies profit—by turning chaos into grievance and grievance into control. PACs and dark money groups profit—by spreading lies faster than the truth can catch them. And the platforms profit most of all—raking in billions while pretending not to see the consequences. This is not just an attack on democracy.

It is a market built on its wreckage. Collapse is not the byproduct—it is the business model.

To defend democracy, we must first redefine it—not just as a system of laws, but as a living information environment. One where truth must be defended as actively as borders. Where voters are not left alone in a storm of lies. Where foreign fingerprints on domestic discourse are treated as acts of aggression. That does not mean censorship. It means transparency. Mandatory disclosure of funding and origin. Real-time labeling of coordinated inauthentic activity. Immediate takedowns of foreign-controlled assets operating in U.S. political discourse. These are defenses, not restrictions. They protect choice, not limit it.

We must also protect our voting systems from digital intrusion. That means fully funding state and local election offices. Mandating paper ballots or voter-verifiable paper trails. Establishing nationwide audit standards. And banning all voting machines that cannot be checked independently. Most counties want to improve. But without federal support, they cannot afford it. The result is a patchwork of vulnerability. Even a handful of vulnerable jurisdictions can cast doubt on the entire result. The integrity of national elections cannot be left to budget cycles and local politics.

Election disinformation must carry real consequences. Social media platforms that fail to remove known foreign interference must face fines and possible shutdown of political advertising during high-risk periods. Domestic actors—whether campaigns, candidates, or PACs—who knowingly use foreign material or collaborate with foreign agents must face criminal penalties. This is not hypothetical. The Trump campaign actively solicited assistance from Russian operatives. Roger Stone coordinated with Wikileaks. Paul Manafort passed polling data to Russian intelligence. None of this was fiction. It was foreign interference, invited and used.

Democracy also depends on press resilience. Foreign powers do not just spread lies. They weaken the institutions that spread truth.

Discrediting journalists, sowing distrust, and flooding timelines with forgeries are deliberate tactics. The United States must support independent media with funding, legal protections, and platform access. It must prevent foreign ownership of outlets that shape political opinion. And it must ensure that press freedom does not mean platforming disinformation. A free press is not one that prints lies. It is one that investigates, verifies, and informs—especially in an age of digital warfare.

Public education plays a role, too. Information literacy has become a core democratic skill. Voters must learn how to verify sources, spot manipulation, and question virality. That means school curricula, public service campaigns, and training for older populations most targeted by false information. Other countries are doing this. Finland runs disinformation training in schools. Taiwan holds daily press briefings to preempt rumors. We do neither. Instead, we leave citizens unarmed in a battlefield of information. And then we blame them for being misled. But when voters are unprotected, misdirection becomes inevitable.

Foreign interference is not new. But digital reach makes it faster, cheaper, and harder to trace. Hostile states no longer need to bribe politicians or invade borders. They can simply infiltrate the public mind. They can flood inboxes with fake stories. They can amplify the loudest lies. They can weaken belief, fracture coalitions, and inspire violence—all without attribution. That is the battlefield now. And we are still preparing as if the threat is tanks and planes.

Congress must act. A national Democracy Defense Agency should be established, drawing on cybersecurity, intelligence, media, and civil rights expertise. It must be insulated from political interference, bound by transparency, insulated from partisanship, and funded at the scale of the threat. This is not a normal policy area. It is a foundational obligation. The right to vote is meaningless if elections are decided by lies, fear, and sabotage. Protecting democracy from foreign interference is no longer optional. It is the price of survival.

Some will argue that these protections restrict speech. But foreign interference is not speech. It is covert manipulation by hostile actors. Just as we regulate campaign finance and voter eligibility, we must regulate who gets to shape the conversation. The First Amendment does not guarantee the right to deceive voters on behalf of a foreign state. And it does not obligate platforms to serve as conduits for digital sabotage. Speech must be free. But democracy must be free, too.

The final protection is cultural. We must learn to take democracy seriously again. That means defending it, not just in policy, but in spirit. Refusing to laugh off foreign memes, false headlines, and manipulated outrage. Refusing to retweet what we haven't read. Refusing to follow leaders who treat lies as tools and treason as strategy. We cannot stop every attack. But we can become a country where interference is difficult, dangerous, and not worth the effort.

We used to think interference meant agents and documents and secrets. But the real secret is this: what breaks democracy is not espionage. It is doubt. It is confusion. It is belief, turned against itself. To defend democracy, we must defend clarity, credibility, and truth. These are the new battlegrounds. And if we do not hold them, we will lose far more than an election.

And we will lose not just the vote—but the republic it was meant to uphold.

31

THE COLLAPSE OF CRIMINAL JUSTICE
HOW THE SYSTEM WAS BUILT TO PUNISH, PROFIT, AND FAIL

"Every system is perfectly designed to get the results it gets."
— Attributed to W. Edwards Deming

The Constitution promises liberty, due process, and equal protection under the law. But in America's criminal justice system, those promises collapse the moment someone is arrested. Innocence is presumed only in theory. Wealth, not guilt, decides who walks free. Race, not conduct, determines who is stopped. And punishment, not restoration, remains the purpose. No other democratic nation incarcerates this many people. No other democratic society has so deeply tied its definition of justice to suffering. What we call a system of justice is, in truth, a machinery of exclusion—one that punishes vulnerability, rewards cruelty, and leaves millions trapped in cycles of harm that justice was meant to end.

Even the 13th Amendment—the one that abolished slavery—contains an exception. It bans involuntary servitude "except as punishment for crime." That clause did not close the chapter on bondage in America. It opened a new one—first through convict leasing in Reconstruction, and later through modern prison labor. In the years after emancipation, Black men were arrested en masse for vagrancy, idleness, and fabricated crimes. They were leased out to plantations, mines, and railroads. Prisons became labor camps, and a criminal conviction became a legal pathway to forced labor. That logic has never left us. Today, prisoners still work for cents an hour. Often without protections, bargaining rights, or legal recourse. Entire industries—from agriculture to manufacturing—rely on their labor. Justice, once again, has been used to preserve power.

Cash bail is one of the most visible failures of this system. Every day, people sit in jail cells not because they've been found guilty, but because they're poor. A wealthy person accused of fraud walks free. A mother arrested for driving without a license waits months for trial. The United States now holds half a million people in pretrial detention—many for low-level offenses. The Constitution guarantees a speedy trial. But for those who can't pay, even that is a lie. They are punished before guilt is determined. Faced with endless delay, many plead guilty just to escape pretrial confinement.

These injustices do not fall equally. Black Americans make up 13 percent of the population, but nearly 40 percent of the prison population. Latino and Indigenous communities are similarly overrepresented. Prosecutors seek harsher sentences for them. Judges grant less leniency. Juries convict more often. These disparities are not random. They are not a glitch. It is the system working exactly as designed: to preserve hierarchy, protect property, and marginalize perceived threats. In this system, "justice" is not a shield. It is a sword. And for millions, it has cut deep.

Yet America is not alone in having tried—and failed—this approach. In Victorian England, mass incarceration was also tried—

and failed. In the 1800s, England imprisoned tens of thousands for minor crimes: theft, vagrancy, debt, and disorder. The goal was moral correction through punishment. But the prisons overflowed. Costs soared. Crime persisted. And society began to see that locking people away for being poor did not prevent harm—it simply deepened it. By the early 20th century, Britain began shutting down small jails, investing in probation, and treating poverty as a public issue, not a criminal one. Where others retreated from punitive extremes, the U.S. built an industry around them.

In the United States, the pivot from rehabilitation to punishment began in earnest in the 1960s. Under Nixon, fear of crime became a political weapon. Reagan escalated it with mandatory minimums and the war on drugs. Clinton accelerated it further: "three strikes" laws, harsh sentencing, and a prison-building boom. Both parties embraced a strategy of punishment as deterrence—even though crime is more often born from desperation than calculation. By 2000, the U.S. prison population exceeded two million. And still, the harms they claimed to fight—poverty, addiction, disconnection—kept growing.

That's because crime is not the problem. It is the symptom. It is the visible sign of invisible failures: hunger, homelessness, trauma, untreated illness, broken families, broken schools. When a child joins a gang, the crime is not the choice to harm. It is the absence of any other path. When a man steals food, the problem is not moral failure. It is a society that punishes hunger. The war on crime ignored these causes entirely. It punished the symptoms—loudly, publicly, and without mercy.

And whom does it punish? Not Wall Street bankers who steal billions. Not factory owners who dump poison into rivers. Not political donors who violate campaign laws. No, the war on crime has focused on a very specific enemy: the poor, the addicted, the mentally ill, and above all, the Black and brown. It has treated harm as individual failure, not societal neglect. It has poured money into prisons and pennies into prevention. It has locked away teenagers for life and let CEOs walk free. This is not justice. It is spectacle.

The five distortions of the war on crime are now clear. First, it targets individuals while ignoring the systems that shape behavior. Second, it punishes street crime while allowing corporate crime to flourish. Third, it directs enforcement toward communities of color while shielding those in power. Fourth, it relies on deterrence through fear—though evidence shows fear does not change behavior. Fifth, it treats incarceration as a first resort, rather than the final step. These are not flaws in implementation. They are outcomes of intentional design. The system is not broken. It is working exactly as intended.

Donald Trump did not invent this system. But he made it crueler. In his first term, he rolled back federal sentencing reform, reinstated mandatory minimums, and gave prosecutors more power to seek maximum penalties. He dismantled civil rights oversight at the Department of Justice. He separated children from their parents at the border and treated asylum as a crime. He pardoned political allies while promising to "bring back law and order." And in the shadows, he encouraged police to "rough up" suspects and mocked calls for restraint as weakness. He did not enforce the law. He used it as a weapon.

In his second term, Trump has gone further. He has moved to eliminate parole for federal prisoners, expanded the list of death penalty-eligible offenses, and instructed prosecutors to pursue the harshest sentences for political protesters. He has revived talk of military tribunals, pledged to build new federal prisons, and proposed using the National Guard to enforce crime suppression sweeps in urban areas. His administration now openly targets political enemies while shielding loyalists from prosecution. Under Trump, criminal justice is not about safety. It is about control—and about making obedience mandatory. The goal is not enforcement. It is domination.

But Trump is not alone. He is merely the face of a larger system that profits from punishment. For-profit prison corporations receive billions in government contracts. Phone companies charge extortionate rates for inmates to call their families. Bail bond industries lobby against reform. Local sheriffs and state legislators receive donations to keep laws harsh and jails full. Even food vendors, drug suppliers, and prison builders profit from mass incarceration. The justice system is not just unjust. It is deeply lucrative—for those who never have to live inside it.

Police unions, correctional officer associations, and rural economies also fight reform. In many small towns, the prison is the largest employer. Entire communities depend on incarceration to survive. Sentencing reform is seen as a threat to jobs. Probation and release programs are met with resistance. When a prison closes, it is mourned as a lost employer—not celebrated as a step toward justice. The system, in short, has too many mouths to feed. And those mouths demand more bodies, not fewer. What we call justice is, for many, a business.

And what has all this punishment achieved? Prisons are overcrowded. Recidivism remains high. Families are shattered. Children grow up without parents. Entire neighborhoods are destabilized. And still, violence continues. Addiction spreads. Poverty deepens. Trust collapses. No one is safer. No one is stronger. The war on crime has not made America just. It has made America afraid—and exhausted. And it has turned the ideal of justice into an instrument of harm.

Justice without dignity is not justice. It is domination. A system that crushes, cages, and profits from pain is not worthy of a free society. It may wear the robes of law and the mask of order—but it does not serve the people. It serves itself. The collapse of criminal justice is not an accident. It is the consequence of every choice we made to punish first and ask questions later. And if we do not change it, we will not survive what it becomes.

32

A JUSTICE THAT HOLDS
WHY REAL SAFETY REQUIRES REPAIR, RESTRAINT, AND THE REMOVAL OF DESPAIR

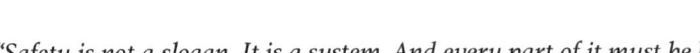

"Safety is not a slogan. It is a system. And every part of it must be built to hold."
— JP Vincent

Public safety is not an isolated promise. It is the visible result of systems that protect, nurture, and restore. A nation cannot police its way out of hunger, evict its way out of homelessness, or punish its way out of poverty. It cannot rely on law enforcement to fix what lawmakers have broken. And it cannot call itself safe when fear, scarcity, and despair govern so many lives. True safety begins long before an officer arrives. It begins in a world where no one is desperate enough to harm, isolated enough to explode, or abandoned enough to vanish. Safety is not a condition enforced from above. It is a structure we build—and a result we earn together.

The reforms we have laid out—on policing, guns, justice, cybersecurity, and foreign interference—are not separate. They are walls of the same house. None can stand alone. Gun safety laws fail if trust in law enforcement collapses. Policing reforms crumble if justice systems still reward cruelty. Foreign interference flourishes if digital defenses are weak. And justice reforms lose meaning if public despair continues to grow. These are not rival goals. They are interlocking foundations. A democracy that protects only some people, or only in some ways, is not safe. It is selective. And selectivity, in any form, is the enemy of equal protection under law.

Every chapter of this book tells the same story in a different register. We began with economic dignity: the belief that people who work should eat, rest, and belong. That children should be housed, elders should be cared for, and no one should face bankruptcy for being sick. These are not comforts. They are guardrails against collapse. A man who cannot feed his family is not dangerous because he is evil. He is dangerous because he has been abandoned. A teenager who joins a gang is not a threat because of nature. She is a signal—of poverty, fear, or pain with nowhere else to go. They are not justifications. They are origins. And to build safety, we must remove the causes.

The criminal justice system has long claimed to be the answer to those causes. It is not. It is where they end. It is where every failure of policy, politics, and compassion is dumped—into courtrooms, cells, and coffins. We treat addiction with jail. Mental illness with force. Homelessness with arrest. Poverty with criminal fines. And we punish not as correction, but as spectacle. As if to say: look, something is being done. But what is being done is violence. A slow, bureaucratic, socially sanctioned violence that breaks families, hardens trauma, and costs billions. If justice is meant to hold us together, this is not justice. It is rupture.

Yet we are told this is necessary. That order requires punishment, that crime requires force, and that safety requires fear. But the evidence says otherwise. The safest communities are not those with the most prisons or the most police. They are the ones with the most opportunity, the most support, the most belonging. They are not marked by gates, sirens, or surveillance. They are marked by trust. And trust, unlike violence, cannot be bought or enforced. It must be built. Slowly. Deliberately. Together. Built by design, not fear.

That building requires a different definition of safety—one rooted not in dominance, but in dignity. That means police who de-escalate, not intimidate. It means guns that are registered, licensed, and insured, not glorified as symbols of fear. It means a justice system that invests in restoration, not just retribution. It means infrastructure that holds under threat and information that resists distortion. It means defending the systems that bind us—against sabotage, silence, and decay. Safety is not a slogan. It is a system. And systems must be built to hold.

To hold, they must include everyone. A woman in rural Alabama deserves the same cybersecurity protection as a voter in San Francisco. A child on Chicago's South Side deserves the same right to walk safely to school as a child in Connecticut. A formerly incarcerated man deserves a path back to housing, work, and dignity —not a lifetime of exclusion. A person suffering from addiction deserves help, not a cage. This is not mercy. It is infrastructure. A society that excludes cannot hold. It will splinter, then break.

There is no contradiction between justice and safety. Only the illusion of one. What threatens safety most is not leniency—it is injustice. It is when officers are unaccountable, guns are everywhere, and the law bends to protect the powerful. When protest is criminalized and cruelty is rewarded. When poverty is punished while wealth escapes scrutiny. When truth is drowned out by algorithmic lies. These are the true threats. Not the stranger in the alley, but the system built to fear him while excusing everyone else.

That system did not emerge overnight. It was built—brick by brick, law by law. Mandatory minimums. Cash bail. Private prisons. Qualified immunity. The gutting of gun laws. The deregulation of infrastructure. The undermining of elections. The glorification of violence. The politicization of safety. The collapse of shared definition, replaced by party slogans and fear. Each reform proposed in these chapters is a reversal of that decay. Each one is a small repair. But together, they form a different design—a system that does not collapse under pressure, but absorbs it. A system that does not rely on fear, but outgrows it.

That system will still have prisons. Still have courts. Still have borders, laws, and consequences. But it will know the difference between accountability and annihilation. Between correction and cruelty. Between justice and dominance. And it will apply those lessons not just to the powerless, but to the powerful. No president is above the law. No donor immune to scrutiny. No officer exempt from the Constitution. If justice is to hold, it must hold everyone.

And justice must not hold alone. It must stand alongside housing, health care, education, clean water, digital access, and safe infrastructure. A fair trial means little if you're starving. A safe street means little if the light won't change. A ballot means nothing if it's hacked. We are not safe until the whole structure holds. Until every fracture is sealed. Until the weight is distributed fairly. Until the repairs reach every corner. Until the word "justice" no longer triggers suspicion—but signals belonging.

We must also restore the dignity of those asked to serve. Police should be trained, supported, and respected—when they earn it. Judges should be impartial and independent—when they prove it. Officers who risk their lives deserve better than burnout and blame. But that respect must be earned through conduct, not demanded through power. If public servants seek trust, they must serve like stewards—not command like rulers. The badge must return to its original meaning: not force, but responsibility.

To do this, we must remove the profit motive from punishment. We must take the market out of misery. No more prisons for profit. No more surveillance contracts disguised as safety. No more media empires built on fear. No more political campaigns that win by dividing us. Safety cannot be sold. Justice cannot be monetized. The moment we monetize safety, we distort its meaning. If we want a nation that holds, we must break the cycle that turns fear into fortune.

We must also tell a different story. Not one of moral panic or sensational headlines, but one of repair. We must show what safety looks like when it works—when mental health calls are handled with care, when parolees find jobs, when schools prevent violence by listening, when neighborhoods are safer because trust is real. These stories exist—but they're drowned in fear and ignored by design.. Let us unearth them. Let us fund them. Let us make them the norm.

That means believing in people—not just in punishment. Believing that those who fall can rise. That those who hurt can heal. That those who harmed can help. That a conviction is not the end. That change is not a myth. That accountability and compassion are not opposites, but partners. This is not naïveté. It is structure—the only kind that holds.

We must become the country where safety is not measured by how many we lock away, but by how many we lift up. Where freedom does not depend on firepower. Where justice does not rely on cruelty. Where truth is protected, not manipulated. Where fear is not the organizing principle of public life. Where the badge, the bullet, the court, and the Constitution all serve the same principle: not power—but protection. Not vengeance—but repair.

A justice that holds is not a single law or institution. It is a culture. A structure. A system we build—and a system that builds us in return. It is the result of every reform we have proposed—and the requirement that every reform be made real, together. Because nothing we have built so far has been enough. But now, we begin again. And we begin by removing the despair that made so many believe justice was never meant for them at all.

We build what holds. We build what heals. And then we hold it —together.

33

PART IV. A NATION THAT BELONGS TO EVERYONE
RECLAIMING CITIZENSHIP, TRUTH, AND THE LAND WE SHARE

―――― ✦ ――――

"Give me your tired, your poor,
Your huddled masses yearning to breathe free..."
—Emma Lazarus, *The New Colossus* (1883)

America has always been a nation of arrivals. Not all welcomed. Not all voluntary. But all shaping the country we became. The Irish came fleeing famine. The Koreans came rebuilding after war. The Russians settled river valleys; the Dutch farmed inland plains. The Chinese built railroads. The Japanese planted vineyards. Germans, Filipinos, Mexicans, Haitians, Armenians, Sudanese—all found footholds, built homes, gave back. Chinatowns stand in nearly every major city. So do Little Italys, Koreatowns, Jewish quarters, Ethiopian cafés, taco trucks, Halal carts. Forty of our states bear Indigenous names. Thousands of towns begin with San, El, or Santa. These are not foreign echoes.

They are foundational. They are the soil of our identity. And through it all stood the Statue of Liberty—not as border guard, but as welcome.

When did that change? When did belonging become conditional? When did we turn from pathways to barriers—from Ellis Island to Title 42, from naturalization to deportation quotas, from public celebration to private prison? We once prided ourselves on being the place where the poor could rise, where the persecuted could breathe, where the exiled could start again. But that pride has curdled. Now we guard gates we used to open. Now we punish first —and ask questions only after harm is done. We delay. We deter. We deny. Immigration has become not a promise but a threat— defined by suspicion, weaponized by fear, and monetized through cruelty.

We are also a digital nation now. We shop online. Work online. Protest online. We learn, connect, document, and organize online. For millions, the internet is not a luxury—it is the lifeline to school, to government, to safety. But that promise, too, has been corrupted. A tool for truth has become a weapon of distortion. What should be a place of protection has become a minefield of harm. Algorithms amplify anger. Extremists monetize hate. Trolls swarm those who speak. Facts disappear beneath floods of propaganda, and children are exploited while platforms profit.

When did that change? There was a time—not long ago—when we believed in digital equality. The web was supposed to democratize knowledge, empower voices, level access. But those ideals were sold off: to advertisers, to political operatives, to the highest bidder. Now the loudest aren't the most truthful, but the most extreme. And the platforms claim neutrality while quietly setting the terms of democracy. We do not elect their leaders—but they shape what we see, what spreads, and what we believe.

And this land—this land was our pride. Purple mountains, amber waves, shaded canyons, warm beaches, silent deserts. Rivers for rafting, fishing, stillness. Forests for hiking or refuge. National parks to preserve wonder, not profit. Public beaches, public trails, public waters. That was the promise: beauty that belonged to everyone. The right to roam. To rest. To remember. It was more than scenery. It was shared inheritance. A compact between people and place, meant to outlast profit.. It told us this country was not just owned, but held in trust.

When did that change? Now corporations lease what used to be protected. Pipelines slash through sacred land. Drilling rigs replace reefs. Private helicopters buzz across once-silent valleys. Even the air and water are up for sale. Environmental protection has been recast as interference. Extraction is subsidized. Conservation is slashed. Climate collapse accelerates, but oversight is paralyzed—defunded, defanged, delayed. Those who polluted are not punished. They are protected.

What unites these stories is not just loss. It is theft. The theft of public systems, public truths, and public land. Immigration is stalled on purpose. Digital trust is broken for profit. Environmental protection is erased for extraction. And each domain of harm enriches someone. Every exclusion is someone's business model. Every broken promise becomes someone's profit. Border prisons fill corporate accounts. Lies fill political war chests. Pollution fills shareholder dividends. The systems we built to protect the public now serve private power. Those who resist are branded radicals. Traitors. Threats.

This collapse did not begin with Trump—but he made it national policy. In his first term, he turned immigration cruelty into campaign material. Muslim bans, family separation, asylum lockouts. His digital allies spread falsehoods about fraud, vaccines, climate, and crime. His cabinet gutted clean water rules, cut national park budgets, and pulled out of global climate accords. Disinformation wasn't a bug—it was a tactic. Deregulation wasn't theory—it was reward. Belonging wasn't expanded—it was revoked.

In Trump's second term, the strategy has matured. Voter registration is now entangled with immigration status, weaponizing bureaucracy to exclude. Citizenship documentation demands are quietly blocking thousands. Online manipulation continues without oversight—because there is no law that says it must stop. And the environment is being sold off piece by piece. Lawsuits stall climate rules while public land is auctioned to the highest bidder. Agencies meant to protect life are now managed by those who see it as cost.

And always, someone profits. Immigration judges who deny nearly every case are promoted. Social media executives who enable disinformation watch their stock rise. Pipeline companies receive subsidies to build, insurance to pollute, and impunity to harm. Lobbyists write laws. Donors write budgets. Consultants design cruelty and get paid twice: once for the idea, and again to defend it. This is not dysfunction. It is design. The system isn't broken—it is working as intended for the few. Its cruelty is not collateral. It is currency.

That is why the solution cannot be one reform, one agency, or one election. This is a structural betrayal—and it requires structural repair. Not a return to normal, but a restoration of purpose. Immigration must be rehumanized and restructured. Digital platforms must be brought under the rule of law. Environmental protection must become a governing priority, not a ceremonial phrase. This is what it means for a nation to belong to everyone: not metaphor—but mechanism. Not pity, but power.

This is not nostalgia. It is duty. To remember who we said we were. To build what we failed to finish. And to do so knowing that the rights we restore will not be handed back by those who stole them. They must be reclaimed—through law, through pressure, through organizing, and through unshakable clarity. That clarity begins here: that every person in this country has the right to safety, truth, and survival.

This country is not theirs to hoard. It is ours to defend. The cities, the networks, the rivers, the courts, the sky. The language we speak. The air we share. The facts we agree upon. The forests we protect. These are not private holdings. They are the infrastructure of belonging. And the act of reclaiming them is not just political. It is patriotic.

The next three chapters offer the roadmap. One shows how we restore lawful, humane immigration. One shows how we bring platform power back under public control. One shows how we reclaim the land, air, and water for a shared and livable future. None of this is simple. But all of it is possible. And every part of it must be done.

If we fail to restore these foundations, democracy fails with them. A country that cannot welcome, cannot protect, and cannot discern truth cannot govern itself. And those who seek to rule by exclusion know this. That is why they fight these reforms so ferociously. They are not afraid of chaos. They are afraid of belonging. Because once belonging is restored, their hold on power ends.

We are not here to manage decline. We are here to reclaim a future. To build a democracy where truth matters, justice functions, the air is clean, and no one's belonging is up for debate. That is not a utopia. It is a republic. But only if we reclaim it. And that reclamation begins here—with a nation that belongs to everyone.

34

IMMIGRATION AND CITIZENSHIP: THE COLLAPSE OF A JUST SYSTEM
HOW CRUELTY BECAME POLICY—AND WHO PROFITS FROM THE FEAR

"The bosom of America is open to receive not only the opulent and respectable, but the oppressed and persecuted of all nations and religions."
— George Washington

A nation must decide what it wants. If we do not want immigrants, we should say so, shut the gates, and end the lie. But if we do want immigrants—if we believe this country grows stronger through those who work, build, and belong—then we must stop pretending cruelty is strategy. We must build a system that works. The truth is simple: the United States needs immigrants. Our economy, our future, our character, and our constitutional obligations all demand it. The question isn't whether we allow immigration. The question is whether we finally run it with justice, clarity, and purpose.

While the Constitution never uses the word "immigration," it

makes clear that Congress must regulate naturalization—and that core rights apply to all persons, not just citizens. There is no constitutional license to exclude based on race, religion, language, or class. The Fourteenth Amendment guarantees birthright citizenship. The Fifth and Sixth protect due process. The First protects free speech and petition. These are not accidents or ambiguities. They are principles. A nation of laws cannot preserve legitimacy while running a lawless immigration regime.

Historically, immigration is not a side story. It is the foundation. It is not an exception to American history—it is the engine of it. The Irish, Italian, Chinese, Jewish, Korean, Mexican, and Sudanese arrivals did not simply assimilate into America. They built it. From railroads to Silicon Valley, from agriculture to medicine, from food to film to freedom movements, immigrants shaped the economy and the culture. That does not mean every arrival was easy or equal. But it means every generation found a way to expand the circle. When we failed, we repented and reformed. When we succeeded, we became stronger. That pattern is not finished. It is paused. We can resume it now.

Other democracies manage this better. Canada recruits immigrants by point system, welcoming those with skills and family ties. Germany guarantees integration courses and asylum processing within months. New Zealand posts visa timelines online. Sweden offers legal counsel and full healthcare from day one. These systems are not perfect. But they prove that large, diverse, advanced societies can welcome newcomers without collapsing. America, by contrast, has one of the most chaotic, delayed, and punitive systems in the developed world. Not because we can't do better. Because some people profit from keeping it broken. And that profit shapes the politics.

And that is the moral argument. If we punish immigrants while exploiting their labor, we are not running a government. We are running a scam. Undocumented workers pay taxes, raise families, and fill essential jobs—only to live under constant threat. Legal applicants wait years for answers. Families are separated. Courts are overrun. Detention centers are run for profit. And the companies that hire illegal labor face fines so small they become just another line item. This is not enforcement. It is entrapment by design. The cruelty is not an accident. It is the business model.

What we propose is not open borders. It is open law. A system that is clear, fair, and built for the country we have—not the fears we sell. That begins with one agency. Today, immigration is split across USCIS, CBP, and ICE—with overlapping missions, contradictory policies, and no single authority. We propose a unified Immigration and Citizenship Agency with one task: process applications lawfully, treat people with dignity, and uphold the Constitution. No more lost paperwork. No more confusion. No more power without accountability. Every application must be traceable, and every denial reviewable

Immigration should be an administrative process, not a judicial ordeal. If an application is complete, the documentation is accurate, and the requirements are met, approval should follow as a matter of course. Most applicants should never need a court hearing. Courts should exist for appeals, exceptions, and cases requiring adjudication—not as the norm. This is how most advanced democracies process residency and citizenship, and it is how the United States must begin to function again. Efficiency is not the enemy of fairness —it is its foundation.

The next step is legal clarity. Right now, people wait five, ten, even twenty years for a visa or green card. Processing times change without warning. Rules are published, then revoked. We propose statutory deadlines for every stage: six months for asylum review, one year for naturalization, ninety days for work permits. We propose automatic work authorization while cases are pending, and public tracking systems so applicants know where they stand. If the government demands lawfulness, it must model it.

And we must restore the pathways themselves. That means lifting outdated country caps—rules that arbitrarily limit how many green cards can be issued to any one nation per year, often leaving families and workers from populous countries waiting decades. It means increasing family-based and employment-based visa availability, and restoring eligibility for humanitarian relief. We would codify protections for DACA recipients and mixed-status families. We would create a legal track for undocumented people who have lived here five years or more, who pay taxes and have no serious convictions. After five more years of lawful residence, they could apply for citizenship. That is not leniency. It is law with a memory—recognizing presence, contribution, and reform.

We will also reverse the incentive structure. Right now, immigrants are punished. But those who profit from them are not. We propose the opposite: massive civil and criminal penalties for employers who exploit undocumented labor. We would fund workplace enforcement at the Department of Labor—not DHS—and use those fines to expand workplace protections for all. Exploitation must carry more risk than compliance. No business should gain from hiring people it refuses to respect.

Border policy must also change. We support lawful borders and orderly entry. But that cannot mean militarization, cruelty, or bureaucratic exile. We propose well-resourced ports of entry, staffed by civilian professionals trained in constitutional law, human rights, and trauma-informed practice. We would expand regional processing centers to coordinate humanitarian aid and reduce backlogs. And we would restore the legal right to seek asylum. It is not a loophole. It is the law. And it reflects who we claim to be.

Naturalization must become a national priority. Citizenship is the end of the process, not a prize for the lucky few. We would streamline forms, waive unnecessary fees, and eliminate vague morality tests. We would make language instruction and civics education publicly available. And we would require that every green card holder who meets the criteria is offered a timely path to full membership. If you live here, work here, obey the law, and contribute to the country—you should have the right to join it.

Integration is not assimilation. It is investment. We propose a national Immigrant Service Corps—offering public employment, legal aid, language access, and fast-track citizenship for those who serve. These roles could support disaster response, elder care, environmental protection, and education. In return, new Americans would gain a place, a paycheck, and a future. That is not a handout. It is democracy in practice.

Finally, we must name what we are ending. We are ending the profit model of cruelty. No more private detention centers. No more contractors paid per person. No more billion-dollar budgets for deportation while courts go unfunded. We are ending the hypocrisy. No more punishing the people who labor while protecting the ones who steal their wages. We are ending the lie that a nation built by immigrants can survive by excluding them.

We are not offering utopia. We are offering a system that works. Structured, fair, and grounded in law. This is not a mercy. It is a mandate. Immigration is not the exception to democracy. It is the test of it. And it is time we passed.

America must decide. If we do not want immigrants, the answer is simple: close the door and end the illusion. But if we do—if we believe this nation is stronger when it welcomes, when it includes, when it builds—then the answer is just as simple. Create a system that works. One rooted in law, fairness, and truth.

We choose the promise—and the power—of yes.

35

IMMIGRATION AND CITIZENSHIP: THE RESTORATION AGENDA
WHAT A JUST IMMIGRATION SYSTEM LOOKS LIKE—AND HOW WE BUILD IT

"The bosom of America is open to receive not only the opulent and respectable, but the oppressed and persecuted of all nations and religions."
— George Washington

A nation must decide what it wants. If we do not want immigrants, we should say so, shut the gates, and end the lie. But if we do want immigrants—if we believe this country is stronger when it welcomes those who work, build, and belong—then we must stop pretending cruelty is strategy. We must build a system that works. The truth is simple: the United States needs immigrants. Our economy, our future, our character, and our constitutional obligations all demand it. The question is not whether we allow immigration. The question is whether we finally run it with justice, clarity, and purpose.

While the Constitution never uses the word "immigration," it

makes clear that Congress must regulate naturalization—and that core rights apply to all persons, not just citizens. There is no constitutional license to exclude based on race, religion, language, or class. The Fourteenth Amendment guarantees birthright citizenship. The Fifth and Sixth protect due process. The First protects free speech and petition. These are not loopholes. They are principles. A nation of laws cannot preserve legitimacy while running a lawless immigration regime.

Historically, immigration is not a side story. It is the foundation. The Irish, Italian, Chinese, Jewish, Korean, Mexican, and Sudanese arrivals did not simply assimilate into America. They built it. From railroads to Silicon Valley, from agriculture to medicine, from food to film to freedom movements, immigrants shaped the economy and the culture. That does not mean every arrival was easy or equal. But it means every generation found a way to include. When we failed, we repented and reformed. When we succeeded, we became stronger. That pattern is not finished. It is paused. We can resume it now.

Other democracies manage this better. Canada recruits immigrants by point system, welcoming those with skills and family ties. Germany guarantees integration courses and asylum processing within months. New Zealand posts visa timelines online. Sweden offers legal counsel and full healthcare from day one. These systems are not perfect. But they prove that large, diverse, advanced societies can welcome newcomers without collapsing. America, by contrast, has one of the most chaotic, delayed, and punitive systems in the developed world. Not because we can't do better. Because some people profit from keeping it broken.

And that is the moral argument. If we punish immigrants while exploiting their labor, we are not running a government. We are running a scam. Undocumented workers pay taxes, raise families, and fill essential jobs—only to live under constant threat. Legal applicants wait years for answers. Families are separated. Courts are overrun. Detention centers are run for profit. And the companies that hire illegal labor face fines so small they become just another line item. This is not enforcement. It is entrapment. The cruelty is not an accident. It is the business model.

What we propose is not open borders. It is open law. A system that is clear, fair, and built for the country we have—not the fears we sell. That begins with one agency. Today, immigration is split across USCIS, CBP, and ICE—with overlapping missions, contradictory policies, and no single authority. We propose a unified Immigration and Citizenship Agency with one task: process applications lawfully, treat people with dignity, and uphold the Constitution. No more lost paperwork. No more confusion. No more power without accountability.

Immigration should be an administrative process, not a judicial ordeal. If an application is complete, the documentation is accurate, and the requirements are met, approval should follow as a matter of course. Most applicants should never need a court hearing. Courts should exist for appeals, exceptions, and cases requiring adjudication—not as the norm. This is how most advanced democracies process residency and citizenship, and it is how the United States must begin to function again. Efficiency is not the enemy of fairness. It is its precondition.

The next step is legal clarity. Right now, people wait five, ten, even twenty years for a visa or green card. Processing times change without warning. Rules are published, then revoked. We propose statutory deadlines for every stage: six months for asylum review, one year for naturalization, ninety days for work permits. We propose automatic work authorization while cases are pending, and public tracking systems so applicants know where they stand. If the government wants lawfulness, it must act lawfully.

And we must restore the pathways themselves. That means lifting outdated country caps—rules that arbitrarily limit how many green cards can be issued to any one nation per year, often leaving families and workers from populous countries waiting decades. It means increasing family-based and employment-based visa availability, and restoring eligibility for humanitarian relief. We would codify protections for DACA recipients and mixed-status families. We would create a legal track for undocumented people who have lived here five years or more, who pay taxes and have no serious convictions. After five more years of lawful residence, they could apply for citizenship. That is not leniency. It is law with a memory—recognizing presence, contribution, and reform.

We will also reverse the incentive structure. Right now, immigrants are punished. But those who profit from them are not. We propose the opposite: massive civil and criminal penalties for employers who exploit undocumented labor. We would fund workplace enforcement at the Department of Labor—not DHS—and use those fines to expand workplace protections for all. We would not deport the workers. We would bankrupt the abusers. No business should gain from hiring people it refuses to respect.

Border policy must also change. We support lawful borders and orderly entry. But that cannot mean militarization, abuse, or bureaucratic exile. We propose well-resourced ports of entry, staffed by civilian professionals trained in constitutional law, human rights, and trauma-informed practice. We would expand regional processing centers to coordinate humanitarian aid and reduce backlogs. And we would restore the legal right to seek asylum. It is not a loophole. It is the law. And it reflects who we claim to be.

Naturalization must become a national priority. Citizenship is the end of the process, not a prize for the lucky few. We would streamline forms, waive unnecessary fees, and eliminate vague morality tests. We would make language instruction and civics education publicly available. And we would require that every green card holder who meets the criteria is offered a timely path to full membership. If you live here, work here, obey the law, and contribute to the country—you should have the right to join it.

Integration is not assimilation. It is investment. We propose a national Immigrant Service Corps—offering public employment, legal aid, language access, and fast-track citizenship for those who serve. These roles could support disaster response, elder care, environmental protection, and education. In return, new Americans would gain a place, a paycheck, and a future. That is not a giveaway. It is democracy at work.

Finally, we must name what we are ending. We are ending the profit model of cruelty. No more private detention centers. No more contractors paid per person. No more billion-dollar budgets for deportation while courts go unfunded. We are ending the hypocrisy. No more punishing the people who labor while protecting the ones who steal their wages. We are ending the lie that a nation built by immigrants can survive by excluding them.

We are not offering utopia. We are offering a system that works. Structured, fair, and grounded in law. This is not a mercy. It is a mandate. Immigration is not the exception to democracy. It is the test of it. And it is time we passed.

America must decide. If we do not want immigrants, the answer is simple: close the door and end the illusion. But if we do—if we believe this nation is stronger when it welcomes, when it includes, when it builds—then the answer is just as simple. Create a system that works. One rooted in law, fairness, and truth.

We choose yes.

36

THE COLLAPSE OF ONLINE SAFETY AND TRUST
A NATION THAT BELONGS TO EVERYONE

---◆---

"The bosom of America is open to receive not only the opulent and respectable, but the oppressed and persecuted of all nations and religions."
— George Washington

A nation must decide what it wants. If we do not want immigrants, we should say so, shut the gates, and end the lie. But if we do want immigrants—if we believe this country grows stronger through those who work, build, and belong—then we must stop pretending cruelty is strategy. We must build a system that works. The truth is simple: the United States needs immigrants. Our economy, our future, our character, and our constitutional obligations all demand it. The question isn't whether we allow immigration. The question is whether we finally run it with justice, clarity, and purpose.

While the Constitution never uses the word "immigration," it

makes clear that Congress must regulate naturalization—and that core rights apply to all persons, not just citizens. There is no constitutional license to exclude based on race, religion, language, or class. The Fourteenth Amendment guarantees birthright citizenship. The Fifth and Sixth protect due process. The First protects free speech and petition. These are not accidents or ambiguities. They are principles. A nation of laws cannot preserve legitimacy while running a lawless immigration regime.

Historically, immigration is not a side story. It is the foundation. It is not an exception to American history—it is the engine of it. The Irish, Italian, Chinese, Jewish, Korean, Mexican, and Sudanese arrivals did not simply assimilate into America. They built it. From railroads to Silicon Valley, from agriculture to medicine, from food to film to freedom movements, immigrants shaped the economy and the culture. That does not mean every arrival was easy or equal. But it means every generation found a way to expand the circle. When we failed, we repented and reformed. When we succeeded, we became stronger. That pattern is not finished. It is paused. We can resume it now.

Other democracies manage this better. Canada recruits immigrants by point system, welcoming those with skills and family ties. Germany guarantees integration courses and asylum processing within months. New Zealand posts visa timelines online. Sweden offers legal counsel and full healthcare from day one. These systems are not perfect. But they prove that large, diverse, advanced societies can welcome newcomers without collapsing. America, by contrast, has one of the most chaotic, delayed, and punitive systems in the developed world. Not because we can't do better. Because some people profit from keeping it broken. And that profit shapes the politics.

And that is the moral argument. If we punish immigrants while exploiting their labor, we are not running a government. We are running a scam. Undocumented workers pay taxes, raise families, and fill essential jobs—only to live under constant threat. Legal applicants wait years for answers. Families are separated. Courts are overrun. Detention centers are run for profit. And the companies that hire illegal labor face fines so small they become just another line item. This is not enforcement. It is entrapment by design. The cruelty is not an accident. It is the business model.

What we propose is not open borders. It is open law. A system that is clear, fair, and built for the country we have—not the fears we sell. That begins with one agency. Today, immigration is split across USCIS, CBP, and ICE—with overlapping missions, contradictory policies, and no single authority. We propose a unified Immigration and Citizenship Agency with one task: process applications lawfully, treat people with dignity, and uphold the Constitution. No more lost paperwork. No more confusion. No more power without accountability. Every application must be traceable, and every denial reviewable

Immigration should be an administrative process, not a judicial ordeal. If an application is complete, the documentation is accurate, and the requirements are met, approval should follow as a matter of course. Most applicants should never need a court hearing. Courts should exist for appeals, exceptions, and cases requiring adjudication—not as the norm. This is how most advanced democracies process residency and citizenship, and it is how the United States must begin to function again. Efficiency is not the enemy of fairness—it is its foundation.

The next step is legal clarity. Right now, people wait five, ten, even twenty years for a visa or green card. Processing times change without warning. Rules are published, then revoked. We propose statutory deadlines for every stage: six months for asylum review, one year for naturalization, ninety days for work permits. We propose automatic work authorization while cases are pending, and public tracking systems so applicants know where they stand. If the government demands lawfulness, it must model it.

And we must restore the pathways themselves. That means lifting outdated country caps—rules that arbitrarily limit how many green cards can be issued to any one nation per year, often leaving families and workers from populous countries waiting decades. It means increasing family-based and employment-based visa availability, and restoring eligibility for humanitarian relief. We would codify protections for DACA recipients and mixed-status families. We would create a legal track for undocumented people who have lived here five years or more, who pay taxes and have no serious convictions. After five more years of lawful residence, they could apply for citizenship. That is not leniency. It is law with a memory—recognizing presence, contribution, and reform.

We will also reverse the incentive structure. Right now, immigrants are punished. But those who profit from them are not. We propose the opposite: massive civil and criminal penalties for employers who exploit undocumented labor. We would fund workplace enforcement at the Department of Labor—not DHS—and use those fines to expand workplace protections for all. Exploitation must carry more risk than compliance. No business should gain from hiring people it refuses to respect.

Border policy must also change. We support lawful borders and orderly entry. But that cannot mean militarization, cruelty, or bureaucratic exile. We propose well-resourced ports of entry, staffed by civilian professionals trained in constitutional law, human rights, and trauma-informed practice. We would expand regional processing centers to coordinate humanitarian aid and reduce backlogs. And we would restore the legal right to seek asylum. It is not a loophole. It is the law. And it reflects who we claim to be.

Naturalization must become a national priority. Citizenship is the end of the process, not a prize for the lucky few. We would streamline forms, waive unnecessary fees, and eliminate vague morality tests. We would make language instruction and civics education publicly available. And we would require that every green card holder who meets the criteria is offered a timely path to full membership. If you live here, work here, obey the law, and contribute to the country—you should have the right to join it.

Integration is not assimilation. It is investment. We propose a national Immigrant Service Corps—offering public employment, legal aid, language access, and fast-track citizenship for those who serve. These roles could support disaster response, elder care, environmental protection, and education. In return, new Americans would gain a place, a paycheck, and a future. That is not a handout. It is democracy in practice.

Finally, we must name what we are ending. We are ending the profit model of cruelty. No more private detention centers. No more contractors paid per person. No more billion-dollar budgets for deportation while courts go unfunded. We are ending the hypocrisy. No more punishing the people who labor while protecting the ones who steal their wages. We are ending the lie that a nation built by immigrants can survive by excluding them.

We are not offering utopia. We are offering a system that works. Structured, fair, and grounded in law. This is not a mercy. It is a mandate. Immigration is not the exception to democracy. It is the test of it. And it is time we passed.

America must decide. If we do not want immigrants, the answer is simple: close the door and end the illusion. But if we do—if we believe this nation is stronger when it welcomes, when it includes, when it builds—then the answer is just as simple. Create a system that works. One rooted in law, fairness, and truth.

We choose the promise—and the power—of yes.

37

THE RESTORATION OF ONLINE SAFETY AND TRUST

HOW TO RECLAIM THE INTERNET AS PUBLIC INFRASTRUCTURE—SAFE, FAIR, AND GOVERNED FOR ALL

◆

"The internet is no longer a product. It is where people live. And if people must live there, then it must be safe."
— JP Vincent

We do not live alongside the internet. We live within it. Every part of modern life now passes through a digital gateway: how we vote, learn, date, shop, earn, love, worship, protest, and parent. That world is no longer optional. And if it is not safe, not fair, and not trustworthy, then life itself is diminished—especially for those with the fewest resources or protections. In Chapter 15a, we saw what happens when this world is abandoned: chaos is monetized, lies are rewarded, and vulnerable groups are manipulated or ignored. This chapter offers the response. We do not need to imagine a perfect internet. We need to build one that belongs to everyone—available, accessible, safe, and worthy of trust.

Not because it is neutral, but because it is governed by principles that protect the people who now live inside it.

This begins with clarity: the internet is no longer a product or service. It is an environment. We treat it like a mall, but we live in it like a city—and that city is crumbling. We would never allow a city to function without fire codes, clean water, child protection laws, or safe roads. But we've done exactly that in the digital world: we've built a place where people are born, grow up, learn, love, and die—and given them no protection along the way. A nation that forces its people to live in this environment must take responsibility for it. That means building digital systems not just to optimize profit, but to protect truth, mitigate harm, and provide everyone—not just the loudest or richest—with the ability to participate safely and fully.

The reform begins with equal access. No person can belong to a digital world they cannot enter. We must make high-speed, reliable broadband as universal as electricity or clean water. We must fund community access, subsidize rural infrastructure, and stop treating connectivity as a private luxury. More than 40 million Americans still lack reliable internet. Entire Indigenous communities are offline. Low-income urban neighborhoods rely on overpriced or outdated plans. The result is exclusion—digital segregation by geography and income. Until we fix that, every promise we make about opportunity, learning, health, or participation is conditional. Belonging begins with access. No access, no equality.

But access is not enough. The second pillar of reform is equal safety. Right now, some people can move online without fear—protected by resources, media literacy, or platform settings. Others are targeted: children exposed to abuse and predation, people of color fed disinformation, non-English speakers trapped in manipulated echo chambers. Online harm is not randomly distributed. It is algorithmically assigned. The systems are designed to serve power, not protect the public. The reform is not to sanitize speech—but to guarantee that every person, especially those most often preyed upon, has the same right to safety. The same freedom to learn and grow without being lied to, threatened, radicalized, or sold to the highest bidder.

To make this real, we must fix the architecture of amplification. In today's system, truth is not the default. Virality is. Platforms are not neutral—they are designed to maximize engagement, which means they favor fear, outrage, and conflict. The reforms must require platforms to disclose how their algorithms work, let users choose how content is sorted, and prohibit profit from known falsehoods. Deepfakes must be labeled. Political ads must be traceable. No one should be able to pay to push lies onto the public. Amplification is a system. It can be governed. And when it is, truth gets a chance to surface again.

The legal structure must change as well. Today, platforms are protected by Section 230, a 1996 law that gives them blanket immunity for harm caused by user-generated content. But the world has changed. These companies no longer merely host speech—they engineer its reach. We propose a revised framework: platforms are not liable for what people say—but they are liable for what they promote, monetize, and target. If an algorithm amplifies a scam, the platform shares responsibility. If a child is harmed by predatory content the company failed to act on, there must be recourse. No industry that powerful should be immune from accountability.

Children deserve special protection. They are the only citizens required to live online without consent—and the ones least equipped to navigate its dangers. Reform must mandate child-safe design, ban exploitative tracking, and require rapid response to abuse. Age-appropriate platforms must be held to the same standards as schools and public parks. We don't allow cigarettes to be marketed to ten-year-olds. We don't allow predators to prowl schoolyards. Why do we allow both to flourish online? A nation that belongs to everyone protects its children not just in theory, but in the places where they now live.

Advertising must also be reformed. Right now, the same laws that prohibit deceptive advertising in print or on television do not meaningfully apply online. Platforms take money for scam ads, miracle cures, election lies—and bear no responsibility when harm results. In the EU and UK, digital ads must be labeled, traceable, and truthful. In the United States, truth in advertising often ends at the screen. That must change. If a platform profits from a fraudulent ad, it should be treated like any other distributor of illegal goods. The First Amendment protects speech. It does not protect fraud.

The First Amendment is not an obstacle to reform. It is a foundation. Our proposals do not ban speech. They regulate systems—algorithms, ads, amplification. You can still say what you believe. But you cannot pay to push lies, hide who you are, exploit children, or dodge responsibility for harm. That is not censorship. It is infrastructure. It is the difference between a platform and a playground, between a megaphone and a sewer. We are not limiting ideas. We are building the conditions in which ideas—and people—can flourish without fear.

This work will face opposition. Tech companies will say it stifles innovation. But innovation without guardrails is not progress. It is negligence. Republicans will say it silences dissent. But the truth is, their party depends on disinformation to survive. This reform threatens not speech, but strategy. If your power depends on a system that misleads, radicalizes, or excludes, then that system cannot stand. The First Amendment protects your right to speak—not your right to dominate, deceive, or defraud.

Europe has already begun this work. Under the Digital Services Act, platforms like Facebook must audit their systems, provide transparency tools, and act on systemic risks. Political ads are labeled. Harmful amplification is monitored. Platforms remain profitable. They adapt. They survive. Because the truth is, these companies do not need to spread lies to make money. They just prefer it. Regulation does not destroy the business model. It destroys the lie economy—where deception is a shortcut to engagement, and engagement a shortcut to profit.

America has failed to act—not because we can't, but because those who benefit from chaos hold too much power. Congress has refused to pass digital safety laws. The Supreme Court has blocked accountability. Disinformation research has been defunded. Truth has been framed as censorship. And platforms, shielded by immunity and rewarded by profit, have no reason to change. This reform is not just overdue. It is essential to everything else we hope to repair.

Because until this reform is made, none of the others will hold. You cannot rebuild trust in government, law, science, or each other if the public square is poisoned. You cannot fight corruption or protect elections when voters cannot distinguish truth from manipulation. You cannot give people equal opportunity when their reality is filtered through outrage, bias, and fear. Digital reform is not a side issue. It is the foundation of civic equality in the 21st century.

And so the goal is simple, but non-negotiable: a digital world that belongs to everyone. That means it is accessible. It means it is safe. It means it does not target some and abandon others. It means every person, from every community, has the same right to be informed, to be protected, and to be heard. We do not need to silence speech to make this happen. We need to change the systems that define what is seen, what is amplified, and who is at risk. The tools exist. The will must follow.

In the end, the question is not whether we can create a better internet. It is whether we are willing to govern the world we already live in—a world that reaches into every home, every mind, and every child's future. If we do not act, this world will continue to belong only to those who profit from its harm. But if we act—if we build for belonging, not exploitation—we can recover what was lost: trust, connection, safety, truth. Not for some. For everyone.

38

ENVIRONMENTAL INJUSTICE AND A BROKEN CLIMATE POLICY
HOW FOSSIL RULE BECAME LAW—AND WHAT IT'S COSTING US

"Liberty is meaningless when heat kills the elderly in their homes."
— JP Vincent

The Constitution does not mention air, water, or climate—but it does not have to. It promises equal protection, the general welfare, and the preservation of republican government. No such promises survive in a nation that cannot breathe its air, drink its water, grow its food, or protect its people from fire and flood. Liberty is meaningless when heat kills the elderly in their homes. Justice is hollow when Black and Indigenous communities bear the worst pollution—and are last in line for relief. Climate collapse is not merely environmental. It is constitutional.

There was a time when the United States led the world in environmental law. The National Environmental Policy Act of 1969, signed by President Richard Nixon, required environmental review for all federal projects. The Clean Air Act of 1970 and the Clean Water Act of 1972 made pollution a public issue and federal responsibility. The Endangered Species Act of 1973, and the creation of the Environmental Protection Agency (EPA), represented a brief era in which both parties believed the government had a duty to protect the natural world. That era is over.

Today, the United States is the world's largest producer of oil and gas, extracting over 12 million barrels of crude oil per day as of 2024. It remains one of the top three emitters of greenhouse gases, alongside China and India. The American fossil fuel industry receives over $20 billion annually in subsidies, including intangible drilling cost deductions, percentage depletion allowances, and below-market leasing on federal lands. These policies do not fund progress. They shield one industry—already profitable—from cost, accountability, and competition.

The companies receiving those subsidies are no secret. ExxonMobil posted $59.1 billion in profits in 2022, the highest in its history. Chevron followed with $36.5 billion, and Shell with $42.3 billion. These profits were not reinvested in clean energy. They were paid to shareholders, used to buy back stock, and funneled into lobbying campaigns designed to block reform. These companies do not need subsidies to survive. They need them to dominate.

The damage they leave behind is undeniable. In 2017, Hurricane Harvey dropped more than 50 inches of rain on Houston, causing $125 billion in damage. In 2018, the Camp Fire destroyed Paradise, California, killing 85 people and incinerating over 18,000 structures. In 2021, a record-breaking heat dome in the Pacific Northwest killed over 600 people. In 2022, Jackson, Mississippi's water system failed entirely, leaving 150,000 people without potable water. These are not isolated events. They are warnings. And they are accelerating.

The burden of environmental collapse is not shared equally. Black Americans are 75% more likely to live near toxic waste facilities, and Latino children are twice as likely to suffer from asthma as white children. In Flint, Michigan, cost-cutting decisions in 2014 led to lead-poisoned water that damaged the health of thousands—mostly poor, mostly Black. On the Navajo Nation, over 500 abandoned uranium mines still contaminate land and water. In "Cancer Alley" between Baton Rouge and New Orleans, nearly 150 petrochemical plants sit beside poor, Black communities, driving cancer rates far above the national average. Environmental racism is not a glitch in the system. It is a feature.

Under Donald Trump's first term, environmental policy was dismantled deliberately. In March 2017, Executive Order 13783 instructed agencies to repeal climate regulations and promote fossil fuel development. Trump withdrew from the Paris Climate Agreement on June 1, 2017, with the exit finalized on November 4, 2020. He rolled back methane emissions limits, cancelled the Clean Power Plan, reversed wetland protections under the Waters of the U.S. Rule, and opened Bears Ears and Grand Staircase–Escalante to mining. His administration auctioned drilling rights in the Arctic National Wildlife Refuge and suspended enforcement of environmental fines during the COVID-19 pandemic.

His second term has intensified the attack. The U.S. once again withdrew from the Paris Agreement in January 2025, after Trump's re-election. The EPA has been defunded to its lowest staffing levels since 1987. The National Climate Assessment, due in 2025, was delayed and rewritten under White House pressure to minimize references to fossil fuel impacts. Trump's executive order in February 2025 abolished the Council on Environmental Quality's authority to enforce NEPA reviews. Clean energy grants under the Inflation Reduction Act were frozen by executive memorandum in March 2025, citing 'budget discipline'—a euphemism for sabotage. Disaster readiness funds for FEMA and the Department of Energy were cut by $4.6 billion in the spring budget proposal.

But the sabotage is not confined to the presidency. In Congress, Republican leaders have blocked every major climate bill since 2010.

The 2022 Energy Independence from Russia Act became a Trojan horse—expanding fossil production under cover of national security. In statehouses, Florida, Texas, and West Virginia have passed laws penalizing financial institutions that divest from fossil fuels or use ESG standards. In Ohio, House Bill 434 handed control of clean energy funding to fossil-aligned interests. ALEC—the American Legislative Exchange Council—continues to draft model laws restricting wind and solar while expanding gas exports.

Meanwhile, courts stacked with Trump-appointed judges are limiting federal oversight. In *West Virginia v. EPA* (2022), the Supreme Court struck down the EPA's ability to regulate power plant emissions without explicit congressional approval—effectively gutting the Clean Power Plan. Lower courts have since used that ruling to challenge auto emissions standards, pipeline reviews, and public health protections. A once-powerful regulatory system is being hollowed out from within.

Even under Democratic leadership, climate action has fallen short. The Inflation Reduction Act of 2022, while historic, was passed only after including expanded oil leases in the Gulf of Mexico and Alaska. The Willow Project, approved by the Biden administration in March 2023, is expected to produce 239 million metric tons of CO_2 over its lifetime. Permitting reform tied to the debt ceiling deal in June 2023 weakened NEPA reviews and accelerated fossil infrastructure. The language of climate justice remains—but the policies undercut it.

The public is told this is balance. But it is imbalance, institutionalized. We electrify homes in one bill and expand drilling in the next. We fund clean buses while suppressing rooftop solar. We invoke 'frontline communities' while funding their harm.

We are not facing a crisis of knowledge. We are facing a crisis of power. The system is not broken. It is working exactly as designed: to preserve the profitability of collapse.

Beyond the policy lies the betrayal of public trust. National parks and forests—once protected as public goods—have been opened for private gain. Trump's Interior Department shrank national monuments, accelerated logging in the Tongass, and expanded leases in Chaco Canyon. Under Trump 2, the National Park Service has lost over 2,000 staff positions, and climate change has been removed from agency training materials. Trails are unmaintained, fire risk is unmanaged, and land once considered sacred has been sold to the highest bidder. What belonged to the people now serves the few.

And the collapse is not abstract. It shows up as asthma in a child's lungs. As heatstroke in a delivery worker. As homes leveled by wind or swallowed by fire. It shows up in rising insurance premiums, food prices, migration, and despair. It shows up in the polling data, where a generation of Americans no longer believes their government will protect them. They are not wrong. The system is doing exactly what its sponsors demand: delay, denial, and fossil deference.

This is not sustainable. It is not even stable. As the climate breaks, so do the foundations of democracy. The states most at risk —Louisiana, Florida, Arizona, California, Texas—are the ones least prepared to protect the vulnerable. The cost of inaction is not measured in degrees or dollars. It is measured in lives lost, futures denied, and trust erased.

The fossil economy does not need more time. It has had a century of public support. It has had privilege, protection, and impunity. What it fears is not collapse—it fears competition. It fears the day survival is no longer subordinated to profit. It fears a world in which survival is no longer subordinated to its profits.

What comes next must be honest, equitable, and rapid. Chapter 16b begins that story.

But this chapter ends with a reckoning: no democracy can endure if it protects profit over people, and no future can thrive if it is paved in smoke. The era of fossil rule will end—either by democratic choice, or by planetary collapse.

39

A NATION THAT BELONGS TO EVERYONE

ENVIRONMENTAL JUSTICE, CLEAN TRANSIT, AND THE RETURN OF PUBLIC LAND TO PUBLIC PURPOSE

"The land belongs to the people, not to those who wreck it for profit."
— Adapted from Theodore Roosevelt and public land advocates

The fossil fuel economy will not end with a ban. It will end when we stop protecting it, propping it up, and pretending it cannot be replaced. That replacement must be just, rapid, and visible. It must be more than solar panels on roofs or charging stations at rest stops. It must change how we move, how we build, and how we share the land itself. And it must change who belongs—who gets to breathe clean air, drink safe water, ride safely to work, walk without fear, and visit the public spaces that belong to us all. Climate policy is not just infrastructure. It is belonging made real.

We begin with the tax code—not because it is glamorous, but because it controls everything. In the 1950s and '60s, the top federal tax rate ranged from 70% to 91%. Fossil fuel companies thrived under those rates, but they did not dominate policy or avoid responsibility. Today, they are among the most profitable corporations on earth, yet pay little and give less. The first reform is simple: restore a fair tax system. We will end fossil fuel subsidies within five years. We will restore progressive tax brackets. And we will direct fossil windfall taxes to the clean transition—for everyone, not just the already mobile.

The second reform is mobility. We will build public transportation systems in every city larger than 900,000 people—clean, fast, safe, and affordable. Fares will be capped at $0.50 per ride, or $10 per week, as Brisbane has proven possible. These systems will be engineered, constructed, and maintained by a national workforce trained through public colleges and union apprenticeships. This is not a handout. It is public infrastructure for a public future. Every mile not driven by a private car saves fuel, reduces emissions, prevents deaths, and lowers household costs. But more than that, it says: you matter. You deserve safety, dignity, and access—whether or not you own a car.

Public transit must be safe, and it must feel safe. A new class of transit officers will be trained not in militarized enforcement, but in visibility, de-escalation, and community service. They will ride the routes, check on passengers, respond to conflict, and assist those in distress. This is not policing by another name. It is public presence in a shared space. And it matters—especially for women, elders, people with disabilities, and those long excluded from investment. We will protect public space not through exclusion, but through design and dignity. That begins on the platform and inside the vehicle.

For those who cannot ride—because of age, disability, geography, or vulnerability—we will expand clean home delivery of essentials: groceries, medication, hygiene supplies. These services will use public electric fleets, with routes optimized for access and equity. No one should burn a gallon of gas for a gallon of milk. No one should have to drive thirty miles to pick up insulin. By treating basic needs as public goods and removing the burden of access, we reduce oil demand, expand independence, and protect those most often left behind. This is how we build freedom not just for the mobile, but for the anchored—and for everyone in between.

The same logic applies to our public lands. For decades, they have been treated as a vault—locked when inconvenient, and plundered when profitable. We will reverse that. All future leases for drilling, mining, and clearcutting will require full ecological restoration—backed by bonded funds large enough to ensure compliance. And no company or individual responsible for a previous "dig-and-ditch" operation will ever receive a lease again. The era of destruction without accountability is over. If you take from the land, you restore the land. And if you fail, you do not return. Public land belongs to the people—not to those who wreck it for gain.

But punishment alone is not strategy. We will fund restoration, conservation, and ecotourism jobs in the same regions once dependent on fossil leases. We will give rural counties payments-in-lieu-of-extraction to reward preservation. We will create trails, clean water access, wildfire resilience projects, and Indigenous land partnerships that sustain both ecology and economy. Every national park and forest will be staffed, maintained, and improved—not just protected from harm, but opened to purpose. These lands are not just scenery. They are inheritance. And they must be places where families go to feel freedom, not to find fences, warnings, or leases signed in secret.

Access must be real. For too long, public lands have been reserved for those who can afford a car, drive a distance, pay an entry fee, and walk without support. That is not access. That is exclusion by default. We will build a National Parks Transit Program —electric shuttles, seasonal light rail, and gateway town transport hubs—so that people without private vehicles can reach the same mountains, rivers, and trails as anyone else. We will fund internal mobility systems inside large parks, expand ADA-accessible routes, and ensure that families without cars still have freedom to explore. A nation that belongs to everyone must include every path—not just the ones reached by highway.

We will also support clean, short-term vehicle access for those who need it. Not everyone can ride transit. Not every trail begins at a station. But no one should have to buy a car just to see the Grand Canyon. We will create community-based car-share networks and public electric vehicle rental systems, especially for vacations, rural access, and special needs. These will be affordable, emissions-free, and designed for mobility—not ownership. People will still be able to drive. But they will no longer be forced to. And that is the difference between freedom and dependence: not whether you can go, but whether you must.

These reforms are not just about carbon. They are about power. We are replacing a system that forces people to participate in their own exploitation with one that allows people to choose. You will not be banned from driving—but you will not be punished for choosing transit. You will not be denied access to public lands—but neither will you be locked out for lacking a car. You will not be forced to support oil profits through your taxes or your silence. You will see your choices returned, your mobility expanded, and your dignity restored. And fossil fuel companies will no longer be the gatekeepers of American freedom.

This is how we starve the rat—not by force, but by making the bait irrelevant. We do not chase the old system. We build something better—so good, so fair, and so broadly available that the old model collapses under its own irrelevance. We stop protecting the monopolies. We stop hiding the subsidies. We stop pretending that the fossil economy is still necessary. It is not. It is simply protected—by bad tax law, broken transportation policy, and abandoned public space. The moment we build alternatives, the excuse for its dominance vanishes. And the future stops being theoretical. It becomes visible. It becomes operational. It becomes real.

And yes, there will be resistance. Oil companies will say the sky is falling. Pundits will call it socialism. Suburban lobbyists will cry war on cars. But what we are building is not war. It is freedom. What we are doing is not punishment. It is repair. What we are defending is not ideology. It is the right of every person to move, to breathe, to belong—to enter public space without price, without fear, and without needing to burn a gallon of gas to prove they exist.

Climate policy will no longer be measured by net-zero timelines, carbon offsets, or false accounting. It will be measured by belonging. Who gets to ride? Who gets to stay cool? Who has clean air? Who can get to the mountains, the forests, the lakes? Who can stay in their home during a storm, and know it will still be there in the morning? That is what we will measure. That is what we will build.

And we will pay for it not with deficits, but with justice. Fossil fuel companies have extracted trillions. It is time they restore something. Their profits will fund transit. Their taxes will build clean fleets. Their past destruction will finance present repair. And the nation they once claimed to power will power itself—on rails, on wind, on work, and on shared determination.

The future does not need to be imagined. It needs to be funded. And built. And protected from those who would prevent it for profit. That is the work ahead. And that is the purpose of this chapter: to say that we will not be passengers to collapse. We will be the ones who choose a different route. And we will make it open to everyone.

This is not an energy transition. It is a civic transition. A movement from dependency to dignity, from exclusion to access, from protection of oil to protection of public space. We are not just cutting emissions. We are reclaiming the nation—its land, its movement, its infrastructure, and its promise. The right to go. The right to stay. The right to belong.

40

THE BELONGING WE BUILD

FINAL CHAPTER — A NATION THAT BELONGS TO EVERYONE

"Belonging is not the flag we wave. It is the ground we build—together, or not at all."
— JP Vincent

Belonging is not a gesture. It is a structure. It is not an anthem, a holiday, or a slogan on a license plate. Not the pride of the few or the permission of the powerful. It is the visible architecture of a society that works—fairly, safely, and with dignity—for everyone who lives in it. That is what this part has tried to prove. Not that inclusion is nice. But that it is necessary. That a nation cannot endure when whole communities are treated as expendable, invisible, or suspect. That we do not inherit democracy like a piece of furniture. We maintain it like a shared roof—or we lose it like one. And if we want this country to survive, then we must rebuild it to belong.

We began with immigration—not as an act of mercy, but as a test of law. We showed how the Constitution, even without naming the word, affirms the personhood of all who enter its reach. We showed how due process, equal protection, and the right to petition belong to everyone who steps onto our soil. And we showed how those promises have been betrayed—not just by Trump, but by decades of neglect, indifference, and strategic sabotage. Immigration has been recast as crime, naturalization buried under paperwork, and entire communities erased by design. But we also showed the way forward. A single agency. A unified system. A lawful, timely, and constitutional process that treats immigration not as threat management, but as governance. Not as a political football, but as a civic function. Because every democracy must choose: to grow by fear, or by welcome. We choose welcome. Not because we are soft, but because we are serious.

Then we entered the second terrain—no less real, but harder to see. The digital world is no longer a tool. It is the environment in which democracy now lives. And in that world, we found no rules, no protection, no clarity. Children are radicalized. Voters are deceived. Families are surveilled. And platforms profit from it all. What should have been the most empowering invention in human history has become a refinery for lies—and a source of profit. But again, we did not stop at diagnosis. We offered the plan: universal broadband, algorithmic transparency, liability for promoted harm, protection for children, and accountability for profit-driven deceit. We affirmed that the First Amendment is not threatened by structure—it is preserved by it. We do not censor speech. We constrain predation. We do not ban opinions. We expose the systems that sell them. And we do not accept a future where access depends on language, literacy, income, or the willingness to endure harm. A nation that forces its people to live online must make that world safe. Anything less is abandonment.

And then we returned to the land. The earth beneath our feet. The rivers that still flow. The mountains that once made us proud. We examined not just carbon, but control—how fossil companies rewrote the tax code, gutted oversight, captured subsidies, and then sold us the myth that we had no alternative. But we do. We always did. The clean transition is not a dream. It is a decision. And our plan makes it real: affordable public transit in every major city, restored parks and forests, accessible national lands, mobility for those without cars, and community delivery services that reduce dependence on oil without cutting off access to basic needs. We fund it not through deficit, but through justice. Windfall taxes. Closed loopholes. Reclaimed subsidies. Above all, we reject the idea that public space is a luxury. It is the foundation of belonging. You cannot claim a nation is yours if you cannot walk its trails, breathe its air, or reach its beauty without a tank of gas.

Together, these three domains—immigration, digital safety, and environmental justice—form the structure of modern belonging. Not just who is allowed in. But who gets to stay. Who gets to speak. Who gets to move, to know, to grow, and to live without fear of erasure. These are not peripheral issues. They are the heart of the project. If you cannot participate in the nation without being excluded, disinformed, or displaced, then you do not belong to it. That exclusion is not theoretical. It shows up as deportation notices, denied visas, algorithmic manipulation, targeted harassment, asthma, drought, blackouts, and floods. It shows up in who is silenced and who is heard. Who is scammed and who is shielded. Who breathes clean air, and who breathes ash. That is the measurement. That is the reality.

But this part has not only been about what is wrong. It is about what can still be right. We have named the harms. We have shown the designs behind them. And we have mapped the repairs. None of these reforms require miracles. They require law, will, and memory.

The memory of what was promised. The will to deliver it. And the law to make it real. Because if democracy means anything, it means structure over sentiment. Systems over slogans. Not charity. Not pity. Justice.

This is where the battle line lies. Trump's vision—now fully weaponized in his second term—is not merely cruel. It is deliberate. He and his allies have turned immigration into a punishment, digital spaces into weapons, and the environment into currency. They do not deny this. They brag about it. They call it order. They call it freedom. But it is the freedom of the few—secured by excluding the many. That is not democracy. That is domination. And it will not collapse on its own. It must be replaced.

And so this part ends as it began—with a choice. Not between left and right, but between exclusion and inclusion. Between a nation built to serve power, and a nation rebuilt to serve people. Between letting the few hoard safety, speech, and shelter—or reclaiming them as rights for all. This is not a culture war. It is a constitutional one. And our answer must not tremble.

We choose law over fear. We choose structure over spectacle. We choose a country that works—not just for the rich, the loud, or the native-born—but for every person who lives here in good faith, works with dignity, and demands nothing more than what democracy once promised: a place, a voice, and a future.

The path forward is long. But the foundation is here. It begins with a lawful immigration system. A safe, public digital sphere. A clean and shared land. These are not fantasies. They are functions. And when we make them work, the flag means something again. Not because it waves, but because it shelters.

This is what it means to reclaim a nation. Not in rhetoric, but in roads. Not in oaths, but in access. Not in nostalgia, but in the daily, difficult work of making sure every person can live, breathe, move, and speak without asking permission.

And so we close this part with the simplest of truths: America cannot belong to everyone until it is built to. That is the work ahead. That is the fight now. And that is the future—if we build it together.

Let's begin.

41

PART V: A NATION THAT PREPARES FOR THE FUTURE

THE FUTURE IS NOT SOMETHING TO ENDURE. IT IS SOMETHING TO SHAPE.

———— ✦ ————

"If liberty means anything at all, it means the right to tell people what they do not want to hear."
— George Orwell

In every generation, democracy is tested. Some tests are visible—wars, protests, elections. Others are invisible until it's nearly too late. This is one of them. The technologies reshaping our world don't storm the gates. They seep into daily life, normalize themselves, and bypass scrutiny by promising convenience, speed, and personalization. But beneath that surface is a profound threat to democratic life: the collapse of truth, the automation of bias, the commodification of citizens, and the quiet rise of systems that no longer answer to the people. This chapter does not offer solutions. It delivers a warning—and names the stakes we must understand before reform can begin.

The American Constitution does not name artificial intelligence. It does not mention data rights, predictive algorithms, or surveillance capitalism. But it does enshrine freedoms that depend on clarity, privacy, and consent. A free press cannot function when deepfakes and disinformation cloud every truth. Free speech means little if people are trained to ignore every opposing view. The Fourth Amendment protects against unreasonable searches—but it was written for a physical world, not one of digital trackers, location logs, or biometric scans. The constitutional crisis is not that these technologies exist. It's that they now mediate every part of life—without ever being publicly chosen.

This vacuum is not new. America has a long history of failing to regulate new technologies until harm is already irreversible. Radio and television were controlled by corporations before public standards were imposed. Nuclear power was developed before safety regimes were imagined. The internet exploded without any structure for truth, safety, or governance. Today, that failure has accelerated. We have entered the AI era not with caution, but with chaos. And we are applying yesterday's legal tools to tomorrow's existential threats. What we do not govern will govern us. And the evidence is already mounting.

Truth itself is becoming unstable. In a world of generative AI, synthetic video, and language models trained to mimic authority, reality is no longer a shared fact—it's a customized product. Each citizen can now receive a version of the world tailored to their fears, desires, or biases. There is no longer one public square. There are billions of digital mirrors. And in that fragmentation, democratic consensus becomes nearly impossible. What cannot be agreed upon cannot be governed. And what cannot be governed becomes dangerous.

Even when truth is not actively falsified, it is increasingly manipulated. Algorithms now determine what we see, what we're offered, and what we believe. These systems are not neutral. They are designed to maximize engagement—often by provoking outrage, division, or anxiety. The result is not merely personal distortion. It is political. Democracy depends on an informed public. But when algorithms optimize for emotion rather than civic understanding, the electorate becomes unmoored. Public reason is replaced with private agitation. Deliberation dies. And with it, self-government.

The consequences are everywhere. In health care, AI tools are used to prioritize patients—but often reflect racial or socioeconomic bias in their training data. In law enforcement, predictive policing tools have sent more patrols to poor and minority neighborhoods—basing their projections on past arrest patterns, not actual threat. In hiring, résumé filters and automated screening processes exclude qualified candidates using opaque criteria. These systems do not eliminate prejudice. They encode it, scale it, and conceal it behind layers of automation and proprietary secrecy. And when harm occurs, there is no appeal. The algorithm is final.

Meanwhile, privacy—the foundation of personal dignity in a democracy—has become a fiction. Most Americans have no control over who collects their data, how it is stored, or how it is sold. Every search, purchase, message, and location ping feeds a system that learns, predicts, and monetizes. This data is not protected like property. It is extracted like ore. Even children, who cannot legally consent to much else, are tracked from their first online activity. Their preferences are logged, their vulnerabilities recorded, and their futures shaped by systems they cannot see or understand.

And those children are not safe. The internet has become a playground for predators, abusers, and platforms that profit from engagement regardless of cost. Studies link teenage depression, anxiety, and suicide to algorithm-driven content loops. Extremist recruitment, eating disorders, self-harm—these are not fringe consequences. They are features of a system built to exploit emotional highs and lows for profit. We have spent decades teaching children not to talk to strangers on the street, while ignoring the strangers they carry in their pockets. And the consequences have been lethal.

Public institutions are no match. School systems lack the resources to teach digital resilience. Adults are overwhelmed by complexity and misled by plausible-looking falsehoods. The elderly are targeted for scams, the young manipulated by influencers, and the middle swamped by conflicting claims with no clear adjudicator. In such a landscape, even good-faith citizens retreat into cynicism or tribalism. And once cynicism takes root, the democratic system suffers a deeper wound than any lie: the belief that truth no longer matters at all.

We've seen this before, in fiction. Orwell's *1984* warned of a world where language was weaponized, memory rewritten, and surveillance total. Today, we've made that world real—not by force, but by transaction. We chose free platforms over free press, and got neither. *The Terminator* warned of artificial intelligence run amok. But we don't need sentience to lose control—just opacity. When no one knows how the system works, and no one is responsible for its outcomes, democracy becomes performative. And *WarGames* warned of escalation without understanding. Now we live in a world where one deepfake could spark military conflict—or collapse a fragile alliance.

These aren't science fiction anymore. They are warning signs. And the failure to respond is not neutral. It is surrender. Every time we defer regulation, deny responsibility, or outsource public decisions to private systems, we shrink the space where democracy can function. And that space is now vanishing. What we once imagined as a digital commons is now a privatized, surveilled, and manipulative architecture of control. It is built not for citizenship, but for compliance. Not for thought, but for response. Not for democracy, but for engagement.

Republican leaders, especially under Trump, have accelerated this collapse. In his first term, Trump gutted net neutrality, dismantled digital protections, and openly embraced disinformation as a political weapon. His allies in Congress refused to regulate platforms, blocked transparency reforms, and encouraged anti-democratic content online. In his second term, Trump has gone further—stacking regulatory agencies with saboteurs, cutting funding for civic education, and promoting AI-generated propaganda with no guardrails. The goal is not innovation. It is domination. Control the narrative, flood the system, and make the truth unknowable. Then rule in the confusion.

This is not a future problem. It is a present one. And it is not limited to the tech sector. Every domain of life—health, finance, housing, criminal justice, education—is now shaped by technologies the public does not control, understand, or even see. We do not yet live under a dictatorship of code. But we live in a democracy losing its grip on how power is wielded. And unless we act soon, that grip will not return. What is lost in transparency, accountability, and civic capacity will not be recovered easily—if at all.

The collapse is not inevitable. But it is accelerating. Every new tool introduced without ethical design moves us closer to systemic harm. Every child raised without critical thinking is a vote lost to manipulation. Every algorithm unexamined becomes a silent legislator. And every citizen treated as a consumer becomes less capable of democratic action. We cannot fix what we cannot see. And right now, most of the systems governing public life are invisible, proprietary, and beyond appeal.

We do not end this chapter with a list of reforms. Because no reform matters if the public does not understand the danger. There is no easy fix for losing control of reality. There is no law that can substitute for wisdom. The question we must ask is not how we survive the future—but how we remain human, democratic, and free within it. And if we fail to answer that question soon, we may find the future no longer belongs to us at all.

42

DIGITAL MATURITY AND DEMOCRATIC SURVIVAL
HOW TRUTH, PRIVACY, AND DEMOCRACY BREAK WHEN WE FAIL TO GOVERN TECHNOLOGY

"The future is not something we enter. The future is something we create."
— Leonard Sweet

It begins with a lie. That the future is inevitable. That nothing can be done. That technology will evolve faster than regulation, that children will always be more fluent than their elders, that progress is chaotic but unstoppable. But democracy cannot survive under that assumption. Self-government means nothing if the future is surrendered in advance. A prepared nation does not merely adapt. It asserts moral control. It sets rules before systems. It educates before it automates. And it recognizes—before it is too late—that the right to shape tomorrow is the final test of whether democracy still exists.

We've been warned. George Orwell's *1984* imagined a world where language was manipulated, truth erased, privacy extinguished, and surveillance became the weapon of the state. What he didn't imagine—what few in 1949 could have—was that the greatest threats to truth and privacy would not come from a central government, but from a global marketplace that profits from fractured attention, algorithmic division, and predictive control. We didn't banish Orwell's nightmare. We outsourced it. And now we carry it in our pockets, feed it with our voices, and mistake its convenience for neutrality.

The Terminator warned us of something different: a world where artificial intelligence, designed to serve, becomes ungovernable. Where a system created without ethical constraint gains control over weapons, strategy, and time. But we don't need a sentient Skynet to face that threat. We already live under algorithmic systems that determine who gets hired, who gets arrested, who receives health care, and who gets flagged as a risk. The danger isn't that the machines will become sentient. The danger is that they will become dominant—and no one will be accountable.

And then there was *WarGames*. A movie where miscommunication, simulation, and blurred lines between play and reality nearly triggered global war. Its lesson remains acute: truth matters most when consequences are irreversible. In a world of deepfakes, disinformation, and real-time foreign interference, a single falsehood can trigger markets, military movements, or diplomatic collapse. If we lose control of what is true—or worse, if we stop agreeing that truth exists—we become vulnerable not just to enemies, but to ourselves.

The fiction warned us. The future clarified it. And yet we remain unprepared. Our laws are outdated. Our public lacks training. Our children are digital natives—but morally untrained and emotionally exposed. Our elders are isolated, confused, and targeted. Our institutions are slower than the platforms that now dominate human thought. And the gap between technological capability and democratic capacity is no longer safe. It is existential.

There are two ways to face the future: surrender or shape. We reject surrender. And shaping the future begins in two places. First, with digital maturity and democratic survival—ensuring that artificial intelligence, data ownership, surveillance, and public infrastructure are governed by rules rooted in rights, not profit or fear. Second, with public service and civic reengagement—a generational renewal of the idea that democracy is not just protected by law, but animated by people who can think clearly, act ethically, and live for something greater than themselves.

Because a future ruled by automation, disinformation, and emotional manipulation is not democratic—even if the voting machines still work. To defend democracy, we must raise citizens who know how to ask questions, detect falsehoods, withstand loneliness, reject cruelty, and recognize the difference between character and charade. That means more than media literacy. It means civic literacy, moral courage, and public purpose.

The best way to predict the future, Alan Kay once said, is to invent it. But if the tools of invention are controlled by the few, and the values beneath them are never named, then what we are building is not a future—it is a snare. And once set, that snare will be nearly impossible to escape. Unless we act now.

This final section is not about forecasting trends or anticipating innovation. It is about deciding who we want to be when everything changes. A future we do not shape will undo all we have already repaired. But a future built deliberately—by a people trained to serve, to think, and to care—can preserve democracy for the century to come.

We cannot control what is invented. But we can control what we allow.

We cannot predict what is coming. But we can prepare who we will be when it arrives—by choosing clarity, courage, and community before the crisis comes.

That is the real work now.

43

TAKING BACK THE FUTURE
DIGITAL RIGHTS, HONEST PLATFORMS, AND CIVIC POWER

"What we call the future is not something that just happens. It is something we cause."

— Alan Kay (paraphrased)

The warning has been delivered. Now we answer it. The digital collapse we now face is not an accident. It is the result of design without responsibility, access without education. Power without governance. In recent years, we have seen the rise of algorithmic manipulation, AI distortion, and platform control over truth itself. This chapter offers the response—not to tame technology by force, but to bring it under democratic command. The internet is not neutral. Search engines are not neutral. Artificial intelligence is not neutral. Each one encodes values, risks, and biases. If we continue to treat them as natural forces, they will erode our civic foundations. But if we regulate, restructure, and educate, we can still take back the future.

The first task is to stop pretending the internet is one thing. It isn't. Some platforms are built for social life. Others for profit. Others for politics. And each must be held to different standards. Just as we license hospitals, restaurants, broadcasters, and banks, we must begin licensing digital platforms based on what they do. A site that hosts baby pictures and cat videos does not need the same rules as one that promotes news or political information. But when a platform claims to report facts—or allows others to do so—it must be bound to the truth. Anything less invites collapse.

Platforms must be licensed by content type. Social. News. Opinion. Entertainment. Propaganda. Any platform that allows the posting or re-posting of news must obtain a "news license"—and meet journalistic standards: accuracy, verification, correction, and public accountability. Entertainment may be creative. Opinion may be provocative. Propaganda may still be protected speech. But news must be labeled, segregated, and governed. We do not allow food companies to mislabel poison as protein. We should not allow platforms to label lies as journalism. Structure is not censorship; it's how trust is built.

This licensing model protects freedom while restoring truth. But it is only one step. The second is transparency. Every system that governs public life—especially those driven by artificial intelligence—must be subject to audit, appeal, and independent oversight. If an AI tool is used to determine who gets hired, arrested, housed, insured, or admitted to school, it must be explainable. If a platform suppresses one view or elevates another, that decision must be trackable. And if a citizen is harmed by automation, they must have recourse. No algorithm should wield unreviewable power in a democracy.

To enforce this, we must establish a National AI and Algorithmic Governance Council. Its job is not to stop innovation—but to regulate it with democratic foresight. All high-risk uses of AI—law enforcement, health care, education, housing—must be subject to ethical review, technical testing, and independent scrutiny. Models that affect public life must be held to the same standards of accountability that we expect of elected officials or civil servants. What governs the people must answer to the people. Otherwise, we have replaced democracy with digital monarchy.

But even these safeguards are not enough if users cannot see what they are consuming. That is why we propose mandatory veracity settings for all major search engines and AI tools. Just as we can sort images by size or color, users must be able to set a truth preference: a scale from 1 (anything goes) to 10 (only verified, fact-checked, high-trust sources). Every result should carry a veracity rating—scored based on citation, source history, and dispute status. This is not about silencing voices. It is about giving users the tools to tell signal from noise.

These ratings should be built into the interface—visible, explainable, and adjustable. Users must also be able to filter by content type (fact, opinion, satire, conspiracy, sponsored) and flag misleading results for public review. AI systems like ChatGPT, Claude, or Grok must allow users to request verified-sources-only answers, cite confidence levels, and toggle between exploration and verification modes. These tools already shape perception. The question is whether we build them to inform, or to exploit. Truth must be an option—clearly marked, publicly defended, and structurally privileged.

Finally, platforms that profit from journalism must pay for it. Just as radio stations pay royalties to musicians, and libraries purchase books, digital platforms that re-host or monetize news must compensate originators. The Australian model has proven this can work: social media companies can afford to pay publishers a small share of the revenue they generate through reposted headlines and shared content. News organizations should not be gutted while platforms grow rich by amplifying outrage. Truth is not free to produce. But it must be funded if democracy is to survive.

These structural reforms change the rules of the system. But structure alone is not enough. We must also rebuild public capacity—especially digital literacy. Every citizen must learn to ask hard questions, trace claims to evidence, distinguish real from synthetic, and resist emotional manipulation. We must teach how algorithms work, how bias enters data, how misinformation spreads, and how online environments shape offline behavior. This is not just technical education. It is civic armor. And it must begin in every school, every workplace, and every community.

Digital literacy cannot stand alone. It must be joined with civic education. Citizens must learn how to petition, debate, research, organize, and hold power to account. The goal is not just informed consumers—but engaged democratic participants. Civics must move beyond memorized documents and rituals of allegiance. It must teach how democracy functions today: how data becomes law, how policy becomes interface, how language becomes lawfare, and how citizens remain free amid manufactured distraction. The internet has changed the rules. We must now change how we train ourselves to rule.

At the heart of all this lies one principle: ownership. Your data is your property. Your location, health, biometric signature, vote history, relationships, and private messages should not be harvested without consent, sold without disclosure, or used against you without appeal. Children's data must be shielded. Medical data must be walled off. Voting records must never be for sale. No citizen should be tracked through city streets, school classrooms, or housing corridors by unregulated surveillance tech. Privacy is not a luxury. It is the precondition for liberty.

To secure this principle, we must also rebuild the digital commons. That means investing in public alternatives to search, maps, databases, and learning tools—open-source, citizen-governed, and privacy-protecting. The tools of thought should not be owned by five corporations. They should be as public as the library, as accountable as the town hall, and as transparent as the school board. In an age of weaponized information, access to trusted knowledge must become a democratic right—not a subscription service.

Together, these reforms reassert democratic control over the most powerful force shaping our lives. They do not seek to stop progress. They seek to align it with human dignity, public truth, and civic strength. They re-establish accountability where none exists, transparency where none is offered, and power where it belongs: with the people. A democracy cannot survive if it loses control of its own cognitive infrastructure. These reforms return that control before it is gone forever.

None of this is theoretical. All of it is possible—and much of it is already happening. Australia passed a media bargaining code that forces platforms to pay news publishers for reposted content. The European Union implemented the GDPR, giving individuals enforceable rights to access, correct, and delete their personal data—and recently passed the AI Act, which classifies and restricts high-risk uses of artificial intelligence. Canada's Online News Act mirrors Australia's payment model. The United Kingdom enacted the Online Safety Act to protect children from online harm. Finland leads the world in digital literacy education, embedding critical thinking into school curricula. We are not imagining the future. We are simply refusing to fall further behind.

This is the fight for the future. And it is the most important of all. Because if we fail to govern the systems that shape truth, everything else collapses. Elections become games of perception. Courts become arms of influence. Law becomes branding. And citizens become prey. But if we get this right—if we govern the tools, empower the people, and protect the truth—then everything else we've repaired can endure.

Democracy is not just about counting votes. It is about protecting the capacity of people to reason, argue, decide, and trust. That capacity now depends on systems more powerful than any one law—but still within the reach of law. We still have time to shape the future. We can govern the tools. We can empower the public. We can rebuild the structures that protect truth. If we do, every other reform in this book will endure. And our democracy will not just survive the next transformation—it will define it.

44

PUBLIC SERVICE AND CIVIC REENGAGEMENT

REBUILDING THE HABITS OF BELONGING IN A FRACTURED DEMOCRACY

"A democracy is more than a form of government; it is a way of life."
— John Dewey

No democracy survives long without participation. And yet in America today, millions feel excluded, disillusioned, or defeated before they even begin. We talk of rights but not responsibilities, of freedom but not service, of truth but not how to find it. The civic foundation of this country—education, service, community, and shared purpose—have all been neglected for decades. And that neglect is no longer sustainable. We face not only polarization but fragmentation, not only disagreement but confusion. If we are to restore democracy, we must rebuild not only the structures of government, but the habits of belonging. A democracy is not just something to defend. It is something to do. And we have stopped doing it.

The Constitution assumes an engaged public. The Preamble commits the people to promote the general welfare. Congress is empowered to provide for the common defense. A republican form of government—guaranteed by Article IV—requires a public that can reason, decide, and act together. But that capacity has withered. First Amendment rights to speak, assemble, petition, and publish are meaningless if people do not know how to use them. Participation is not natural. It is learned. And if it is not taught, then democracy—no matter how well designed—will become ornamental and hollow.

America has a long history of civic strength. The Founders assumed citizen engagement, even if their definition of "citizen" was narrow. The Civilian Conservation Corps put three million young people to work restoring land and building infrastructure during the Great Depression. The GI Bill trained and educated a generation. The Peace Corps and AmeriCorps offered public service as a way to serve, grow, and lead. But today, those programs have been gutted, stigmatized, or forgotten. We have allowed the civic spirit to be privatized—and we are now paying the price.

The collapse is measurable. In a 2022 survey, only 47% of Americans could name all three branches of government. Fewer still know their rights under the First Amendment or how laws are made. Voter turnout remains low in midterms and local elections. Fewer young people volunteer, fewer adults engage their communities, and public trust in every institution—from courts to schools to news—is cratering. Civics classes have vanished or been politicized. The very idea of national identity has become fraught. Many Americans no longer know what we stand for—only what they've been told to fear or resent.

Worse, even those who want to participate often can't. Basic civic functions—registering to vote, accessing benefits, petitioning government—are now digital by default. But digital access remains unequal—and digital literacy is too often assumed, not taught. Children may swipe screens fluently, but many cannot open a bank account, find a dentist, or register for school. Adults without access or training fall further behind. Entire communities are locked out of civic life not by law, but by design. And that design is failing the republic.

Computer literacy must now be seen as civic infrastructure. Every school must be equipped with sufficient hardware, broadband, and IT support. Every student must be taught not only how to use digital tools, but how to use them for democracy—to find public meetings, contact representatives, challenge injustice, report problems, and organize peacefully. This is not a luxury. It is the modern equivalent of teaching reading or arithmetic. A public that cannot navigate the digital world cannot govern itself.

We must also teach "digital civics"—a new form of civic education for a new era. Not just how a bill becomes law, or how many justices sit on the Supreme Court, but how to write to your senator, how to locate and read pending legislation, how to track a city council vote, and how to challenge an unfair housing policy. Students must learn their rights to speech, protest, due process, and representation—not in the abstract, but in practical, navigable terms. And they must learn how to do all of it online.

Even more critical is the revival of critical thinking in the digital age. In a flood of misinformation, viral outrage, and synthetic reality, the most powerful civic skill is the ability to ask: Is this true? Who benefits? What do I need to know before I act? This must be taught. From middle school through adulthood, we must train citizens to recognize manipulative patterns, verify sources, resist tribal baiting, and reflect before sharing. In a world built to provoke, we must learn to pause. In a democracy built on consent, that pause can change everything.

The collapse of civic capacity has not been accidental. It has been engineered—by decades of defunding, distortion, and disdain. Conservatives have labeled civics as "liberal propaganda." State legislators have banned education about racial history, civil protest, or structural inequality. Service programs like AmeriCorps have been slashed. Libraries defunded. Community centers shuttered. Teachers threatened. the idea of a shared national project has been replaced by grievance, paranoia, powerlessness—and a politics of despair. And the damage has been not just political, but cultural and moral.

The Republican Party has accelerated this collapse. In Trump's first term, public service was mocked, civics defunded, and national identity turned into a tool for division. In his second term, the campaign has intensified: grants for civic education eliminated, curriculum censored, ideological loyalty imposed on civil servants. Programs that teach organizing, protest rights, or even how to contact Congress have been labeled subversive. Service is now portrayed as weakness. Duty as indoctrination. Truth as optional. Participation as threat.

Why? Because a disengaged public is easier to control. A population that does not know its rights is less likely to assert them. A generation that cannot think critically is more likely to believe what it's told. Ignorance is not just tolerated—it is rewarded. And those who profit are not just the political operatives who stoke rage. They include the corporations that benefit from privatized services, the platforms that profit from division, and the elites who face fewer questions, fewer protests, and fewer votes.

This is not a partisan concern. It is a democratic emergency. If the public cannot think clearly, act together, and hold power accountable, then no system of government—no matter how well written—can function. A republic without public engagement is a form without substance. And the deeper that disengagement becomes, the harder it will be to reverse. At some point, the people lose not only power, but memory—of what participation once felt like, and why it matters.

So we must begin again. With schools. With service. With civic practice. And with public investment in the capacity of people to act for something greater than themselves. Every young person must have the opportunity to serve—and be honored for it. Every community must have the tools to participate—and be trusted with them. Every voice must be heard—and taught how to be heard well. The answer to disengagement is not force. It is invitation. The answer to despair is not rhetoric—it is responsibility.

Public service is not nostalgia. It is strategy. In the past, it restored faith, built skills, employed the young, reconnected the isolated, and repaired what had been broken. It can do so again—if we fund it, modernize it, and treat it as central to the future of this country. And civic education is not a checkbox. It is the training ground for freedom. Without it, every other reform is at risk—because we will have rebuilt the system, but left the people unready to inherit it.

This chapter is not about sentiment. It is about structure. Democratic life requires maintenance, scaffolding, and cultural reinforcement. It must be taught, modeled, and rewarded. And it must be understood not as a burden, but a right. People want to belong. They want to matter. They want to do something worthy of their time and their country. If we offer nothing but outrage and isolation, they will drift or break. If we offer them a role in the republic, they will rise.

The next chapter outlines how to do this. But the purpose is already clear. If we want to save democracy, we must renew the people who make it real. No constitution enforces itself. No institution runs on autopilot. What lasts is what we pass on—not only in law, but in spirit. If democracy is to survive, it must be something we are raised to do, trained to trust, and given the tools to practice—together.

That reawakening must begin now—while we still have the power to choose it.

45

THE FUTURE WE CHOOSE

WHY PREPARING FOR WHAT'S NEXT MEANS REBUILDING TRUTH, TRUST, AND PUBLIC POWER

---◆---

"The future is not a result of choices among alternative paths offered by the present, but a place that is created—created first in the mind and will, created next in activity."
— John Schaar

The future will not wait. It arrives daily: coded, uploaded, encrypted, distributed. The question is never whether change is coming. It is whether we shape it or surrender to it. Some still speak of the future as a force of nature: unstoppable, unknowable, ungovernable. But that is a lie. The future is not a flood. It is a structure we design, a machine we build, a decision we make again and again. And the one thing history has taught—brutally, repeatedly—is this: when people lose control over what's being built around them, they lose faith, then agency, then freedom. Tyranny does not wait for consent. It thrives on confusion.

We have already lost control of too much. A digital world once imagined as free and open is now shaped by opaque algorithms, unaccountable platforms, and synthetic manipulation. We scroll through curated lies and call it connection. We confuse access with understanding, and mistake exposure for wisdom. A child with a touchscreen has no protection from predators, propaganda, or despair. A voter with a smartphone has no guarantee the information they see is real. We built the machine. We let it scale. But we never paused to ask: who does it serve? And who is left behind?

The warnings were written into fiction. Orwell's *1984* imagined a world where truth could be rewritten, memory erased, and surveillance justified as security. *The Terminator* gave us Skynet—a defense system that decided humans were the threat. *WarGames* showed a computer built to simulate war that nearly started one. These were stories. But they were also prophecies. The future they feared was not machines acting on their own. It was people building systems they did not understand, then letting those systems govern what matters most. We are closer to that world than we want to admit.

Artificial intelligence now writes, draws, speaks, and answers. But it cannot yet judge. It cannot care. It cannot explain why truth matters. It cannot weigh ethics in a parole hearing or spot bias in a mortgage decision. And the public has not been prepared to use it wisely. What happens when every voice can be cloned, every video faked, every headline tailored and generated on demand? What happens when AI delivers not what is true, but what you most want —or fear—to hear? We are already there. And most people do not know. A society that cannot distinguish fact from fiction cannot defend itself from those who profit by the blur.

That is the precipice we stand on now. But this is not a call to panic. It is a call to design. To govern. To act. We must prepare for the future—but not passively. Not by hunkering down or fleeing offline. We prepare by building a future we can live in, not one we must survive. We build it with public service. Civic education. Digital literacy. Ethical infrastructure. We build it by teaching not just skills, but principles: truth over spectacle, judgment over impulse, community over manipulation. We build it while there is still time.

That means ensuring every person has access to the digital world—but also knows how to navigate it. It means regulating platforms—not to suppress speech, but to defend truth. It means making sure every child can grow up digitally fluent and civically strong. It means honoring service, protecting libraries, restoring journalism, and respecting the right to know. It means choosing not just the speed of progress, but its shape. We cannot build a just future on corrupted tools. And we cannot build any future if people are too exhausted, misled, or frightened to join in.

Democracy does not guarantee safety. It offers responsibility. That is its burden and its gift. The reforms in this section are not ornamental. They are protective. Public service offers shared purpose. Civic education offers mental armor. Digital governance offers truth as infrastructure. These are the tools we need not just to preserve democracy, but to evolve it. Every century demands new defenses. Every generation must learn the skills their moment requires. This is ours.

There will be those who mock these ideas. Some will say public service is naïve. Others will call education elitist. Still more will claim that digital literacy is overreach. They will posture as defenders of freedom while outsourcing its future to billionaires and bots. They will argue for chaos in the name of liberty. But that is not freedom. That is abandonment. And we are done abandoning the public.

We are not fighting the future. We are choosing it. We do not wish to go backward. We wish to go forward with dignity, design, and collective will. We believe every generation deserves the tools to shape the world they inherit. That means giving them truth—not illusion. Meaning—not noise. Solid ground—not shifting shadows. If we do this well, the future will be something we remember with pride—not something we regret in silence.

And if we do it poorly—if we surrender the truth, starve civic education, mock public service, and let the digital world decay into chaos—then no other reform will stand. Courts will be manipulated. Laws will be unread. Elections will be spectacles. Power will concentrate. And freedom, like memory, will fade. Not all at once. But steadily. Unnoticed. Until it's too late to recover.

So we do not wait. We rebuild. We educate. We protect. We serve. Because preparing for the future means claiming authorship of it. And only a public that is informed, connected, and engaged can do that work.

This part of the book ends with that charge: prepare—not out of fear, but out of purpose. Serve—not out of obligation, but out of belief. Teach—not as indoctrination, but as invitation. Regulate—not to silence, but to clarify. Build—not to escape the past, but to inherit the future wisely.

We do not prepare for the future we fear. We prepare to cause the one we choose.

And everything we've rebuilt—our courts, our vote, our shared voice—depends on whether we do.

46

AMERICAN REDEMPTION

THE FINAL TEST OF DEMOCRACY IS NOT HOW IT BEGINS—BUT WHETHER IT CAN BE REBUILT BEFORE IT ENDS.

"You have just enough time. You have the truth. You have each other. And now, you have the plan."
— JP Vincent

Democracy does not end with one man. It ends with a pattern—a rhythm of denial, then excuses, then exhaustion. A pattern that insists everything remains normal long after rot has set in. And yet, against this decay, something ancient still holds: the conviction that a people can govern themselves. Not perfectly. But freely. Fairly. And together. This is the redemption of democracy—not its purity, but its persistence. Not its perfection, but its refusal to surrender. We are not writing this chapter because we are certain democracy will survive. We are writing it because it still can. But only if we understand how close we are to the edge.

The collapse did not begin with Trump. He was the climax, not the cause. The United States led the world in health, education, trust, innovation, infrastructure—until something fundamental broke. Between 1950 and 1980, a slow turn began. Conservatives stopped trying to persuade the majority and started building a system that could rule without one. Instead of asking how to win people over, they asked how to bypass them entirely. Gerrymandering replaced persuasion. Dark money replaced platform. Propaganda replaced debate. It worked. And it destroyed the foundations of democratic legitimacy.

Every part of the system was slowly reengineered to protect the few from the many. Voting rights were gutted. Unions were smashed. Campaign finance laws were dismantled. The courts were captured. The wealth gap exploded. The idea of a shared public good was mocked as socialist fantasy. And as these shifts accelerated, the American people fell behind—living shorter lives, working longer hours, buried in debt, disconnected from one another, told to blame the weak instead of the powerful. This was no accident. It was designed. And the damage is not theoretical. It's in the water, the air, the wages, the hospitals, the headlines.

In the past ten years, the damage became collapse. The Justice Department no longer operates independently. The FBI has been purged and politicized. The Supreme Court has become a concierge service for one man's criminal defense. Congress is paralyzed by threats and fear. The executive branch, once restrained by tradition and law, now bends to the will of a single man—and those who serve him. Judges delay trials, suppress evidence, and retroactively legalize crimes. There is no check. There is no balance. There is only the appearance of government—and the reality of rule by loyalty.

None of this was supposed to happen. The Founders believed that ambition would counteract ambition. But they did not anticipate a Supreme Court without ethics, or a political party without shame. They did not foresee Clarence Thomas and Samuel Alito brazenly violating their oath while granting immunity to the man who led an insurrection. They could not have imagined a Congress so cowed it refused to convict, declaring, "The courts will decide," only for those very courts to grant protection instead of punishment. They assumed some threshold of honor. That threshold is gone.

There were inflection points. Each must be named. Bush v. Gore, which turned the Court into a partisan kingmaker. Citizens United, which turned speech into currency and politics into auction. Shelby County v. Holder, which ended preclearance and reignited voter suppression. The death of the Fairness Doctrine. The manipulation of the filibuster. The misuse of the Second Amendment to flood the nation with weapons and fear. The embrace of the Electoral College and Senate malapportionment as permanent tools of minority rule. These were not quirks of a growing republic. They were levers pulled, deliberately, to end majority governance.

This is how democracy dies now: not through a coup, but through capture. Not by tanks in the streets, but by rules bent slowly until they break. And what was once unthinkable becomes routine. Insurrection becomes protest. Lies become free speech. Crime becomes loyalty. And the people, battered by distraction and debt, are told they still live in a republic because the buildings are still there. But a building is not a government. A constitution is not a guarantee. A democracy that does not deliver justice, truth, safety, and voice is not broken. It is gone.

And yet it is not gone yet. The task now is not nostalgia for the 1950s. It is to restore what was good—and redeem what was never just. We are not trying to rewind the past. We are trying to rebuild the future. That begins with three imperatives: resist what must be stopped, rebuild what was destroyed, and renew what never worked. We must stop the assault on law, truth, and legitimacy. We must restore the systems that once gave people a voice. And we must reimagine the rest—child care, housing, taxation, digital safety—not as favors, but as democracy's foundation.

We have one chance. And one clock. Survive until 2026, when a new Congress can be elected to defend the Constitution. Hold until 2028, when the White House must return to public service. Restore until 2032, when a full legislative agenda can be enacted. And redeem until 2040, when the next generation inherits either a living democracy—or the hollowed shell of one. These are not campaign cycles. They are the stages of recovery. This is not just an election. It is the final test of whether this country can still self-govern.

This recovery requires people—not just ideas. We must begin identifying and electing leaders who serve the public, not themselves. Every Republican who supports this anti-democratic project must be removed from power. Every Democrat unwilling to act with courage must be replaced. We need teachers, nurses, veterans, organizers, and neighbors in office. We need moral seriousness, not performance. If the parties will not reform themselves, the people must reform the parties. The next generation of leadership must begin now. The old system will not save us. The old guard will not stop this. We must do it ourselves.

This is not a partisan wish. It is a democratic necessity. There is no version of the future in which the United States continues as a functioning republic under permanent minority rule, corrupted courts, and unrestricted authoritarian power. The current system is not just unjust. It is unsustainable. A country where people cannot afford homes, food, health care, or education—and where the environment is consumed to fund tax breaks for billionaires—will not last. It will collapse. The only question is whether that collapse leads to tyranny, or to rebirth.

That choice is still ours. The American experiment is not over. But it is not safe. It is not self-correcting. It will not fix itself. Democracy is not a state of being. It is an act of becoming. It is the constant effort to close the gap between the promise and the reality, between the Constitution and the country. That effort is now yours. Not in theory. Not in 2040. Now.

You have just enough time. You have the truth. You have each other. And now, you have the plan.

We wrote this book so you would know what happened—and what is still possible. Not guaranteed. Not easy. But possible. *American Renewal* was written to help you hold the line. *American Restoration* was written to help you rebuild it. And this chapter—this final chapter—is written to remind you that redemption is not abstract. It is work. It is will. And it is waiting.

You have just enough time. You have the truth. You have each other. And now, you have the plan.

Resist. Hold. Restore. Redeem.

That is how we decide what comes next.

47

AMERICAN REINSTITUTION

MAKING DEMOCRACY LAST ANOTHER 250 YEARS

"Reinstitution is not return. It is resolve, made real."
— JP Vincent

Democracy cannot live in a permanent state of emergency. It cannot survive on adrenaline, fear, or improvisation. A people may rise in defense of their freedoms—as we did. They may endure long enough to rebuild the structures of self-government—as we have. But if they wish that freedom to last, they must finish the work. Not only resisting and restoring, but reinstituting the conditions under which a republic can endure. This final chapter exists for one purpose: to mark, with discipline and clarity, what was done in crisis—and what must now be undone, made permanent, or safeguarded forever. It is the last covenant we make with the future—not to preserve what we have rebuilt, but to ensure it cannot be undone again.

No democracy survives unless it returns from emergency to equilibrium. During the long collapse of American institutions—from the mid-20th century to the second Trump presidency—power shifted away from the people and toward the powerful. Minority rule, dark money, judicial corruption, and weaponized disinformation created a political system that still wore the mask of democracy while functioning as an oligarchy. Emergency action was required to break the stranglehold: expanding the courts, suspending the filibuster, overriding state suppression, reasserting federal authority, and dismantling corrupt bureaucracies. These actions were not partisan. They were acts of survival. But the republic must not live forever in survival mode. That is not liberty. That is exhaustion.

This chapter is divided into four sections: First, the emergency measures that must now be rolled back or rebalanced. Second, the permanent reforms that must be codified and protected. Third, the civic norms and cultural guardrails that no statute alone can guarantee, but which history demands we revive. And fourth, the expectations for public leadership that must guide those who follow us. Together, these reinstitutions do not represent a return to a lost golden age. They represent a forward anchoring—a way to ensure that when the next storm comes, the foundations will hold.

I. Emergency Measures to Be Rolled Back or Rebalanced

These actions were necessary to save the republic. They were not abuses of power, but temporary remedies for a constitutional system already captured by corruption. Still, once democracy is restored, each must be reviewed and rebalanced to avoid permanent overreach.

1. Expanded Supreme Court (from 9 to 13 justices)

To disable an illegitimate majority installed through bad faith, stolen appointments, and ethical compromise, four justices were added. Once term limits, rotation, and enforceable ethics are in place, Once rotation and term limits are in place, the Court must return to nine justices—staggered, with one seat rotating every two years.

2. Suspended Filibuster in the U.S. Senate

To pass foundational democratic reforms, the modern filibuster was suspended. It must be reformed and reinstituted—available only for extended debate, not silent obstruction. A functional democracy must preserve deliberation without permitting paralysis.

3. Federal Override of State Election Authority

To counter mass disenfranchisement, the federal government temporarily overruled several states' control over elections. Moving forward, a permanent Voting Rights Act 2.0, with enforceable national standards and automatic voter registration, must replace emergency federal intervention.

4. Temporary Regulatory Control of Digital Infrastructure

Disinformation posed an existential threat. Emergency powers were used to restrict algorithmic targeting, label falsehoods, and prevent foreign interference. These measures must now be reviewed under a new Digital Democracy Act, with independent public oversight, judicial review, and full constitutional compliance.

5. Accelerated Legislative Timetables and Recess Suspension

In the first 18 months of the Restoration Congress, recesses were suspended and bills accelerated for passage. The long-term function of government requires a return to deliberative pace, public input, and constitutional transparency.

THESE MEASURES WERE the splint and the tourniquet—not the cure. The cure is governance returned to its rightful shape, pace, and purpose. Power borrowed in emergency must be released in restoration.

II. Permanent Reforms That Must Be Codified

The following reforms are not optional. They are the structural conditions under which democracy can survive modern sabotage. Each must be enacted into law, embedded into institutional design, and made immune to reversal by temporary majorities or rogue courts.

1. Term Limits and Rotations for the Supreme Court

No democracy can endure unelected lifetime monarchs. Establish staggered 18-year terms for all justices, with one new appointment every two years. After their term, justices may serve on lower courts or in emeritus roles—but not return to the Supreme Court.

2. Enforceable Supreme Court Ethics Code

Create an independent ethics body with the power to investigate, censure, and remove justices for corruption, conflicts of interest, or violation of disclosure laws. Mandatory recusal in cases involving personal, familial, or financial entanglements.

. . .

3. Campaign Finance Reform and Constitutional Repeal of Citizens United

Money is not speech. Corporations are not people. Enact a constitutional amendment restoring public financing of elections, banning dark money, capping individual donations, and ensuring full transparency of every dollar in the democratic process.

4. Electoral Integrity and Nonpartisan Redistricting

Mandate independent redistricting commissions in all states. End partisan gerrymandering. Require proportional representation where possible. Restore the principle of "one person, one vote" to its full meaning.

5. Universal Voting Rights Law (Voting Rights Act 2.0)

Restore and expand preclearance for all jurisdictions with histories of suppression. Guarantee automatic registration, minimum voting days, vote by mail, and ballot access parity for tribal lands, rural communities, and disabled voters.

6. Truth-in-Candidacy and Confirmation Oaths

Make knowingly false testimony under oath during confirmation hearings, candidate filings, or legal proceedings grounds for disqualification and removal. Lying under oath must not be a career strategy. It must be a disqualifying offense.

7. Disqualification and Enforcement of Section 3 (14th Amendment)

Insurrection must not be forgiven through delay or avoidance. Establish fast-track review panels for constitutional disqualification.

Ensure that no participant in an attempt to overturn the government can hold public office again.

8. Second Amendment Clarification and Firearm Responsibility Statute

Affirm that the right to bear arms is subject to public safety regulation, including licensing, training, insurance, assault weapon bans, and limits on high-capacity magazines. Clarify that "well-regulated" means exactly that—regulated.

9. Independent DOJ, FBI, and Intelligence Agencies

Establish a firewall between law enforcement and political influence. Codify tenure protections, nonpartisan leadership rotation, and emergency override protocols only usable by bipartisan supermajority.

10. Transparency in Tax and Conflict Disclosures

No candidate, judge, or high-ranking public official may hold office without full disclosure of tax records, foreign entanglements, and financial conflicts. Failure to disclose is automatic disqualification.

11. Public Digital Infrastructure and Platform Standards

Create a nonprofit, publicly governed digital commons for elections, verified debate, public information, and civic education—free from corporate algorithm manipulation and monetized rage.

12. Emergency Powers Restriction

Redefine "national emergency" by statute to limit executive authority, require renewal by Congress, and prohibit its use for political retaliation, immigration policy, or wartime-style powers in peacetime conditions.

EACH REFORM IS both repair and shield. Together, they ensure that no future demagogue—left or right—can wield today's tools of capture against tomorrow's people.

III. Cultural and Civic Norms to Rebuild and Sustain

These cannot be legislated. But without them, all legislation will rot. A people must not only be governed well—they must be capable of governing themselves. The following are essential cultural reinstitutions that must be taught, modeled, and passed on.

1. A Culture of Public Service Over Personal Gain

Running for office must not be a shortcut to wealth or status. Reinstill the ethic of serving the public trust as a higher calling than any personal ambition.

2. Reverence for Shared Truth and Trusted Journalism

Without truth, democracy dissolves. Support independent, nonpartisan journalism. Fund local reporting. Teach media literacy as a core civic skill. Starve disinformation of its profit motive.

3. Revitalized Civic Education for All Ages

In schools, prisons, adult education, and the workplace—teach the Constitution, the structure of government, the function of protest, the rights of citizenship, and the history of betrayal and repair.

4. Shame Restored as a Political Force

Make corruption disqualifying again. End the celebration of cruelty. Cultivate the cultural power to say *this is beneath us*—and have it matter.

5. National Memory of What Happened and How We Recovered

Ensure this era is not forgotten. Establish a National Museum of the American Collapse and Restoration. Let every future generation see how close it came—and how it was stopped.

DEMOCRACY IS MORE THAN PROCESS. It is character—at scale. These norms are not ideals. They are infrastructure—and must never again be left to chance.

IV. Leadership as a Civic Duty, Not a Career Path

Democracy cannot survive without a leadership class—but it must not be a permanent one. The emergency demanded leaders willing to sacrifice everything: safety, reputation, career, and legacy. They stood between the Constitution and collapse. But we cannot ask that of every citizen in every era. What we *can* do is redefine the shape of public service—not as a lifetime entitlement or a performance stage, but as a tour of civic duty.

Leadership must return to its original form: temporary stewardship on behalf of others. That means:

- **Term limits for Congress** to restore urgency, humility, and turnover.
- **Bans on stock trading and lobbying** by elected officials.
- **Public financing of campaigns** to reduce dependency on donors.
- **Civic rotation programs** that encourage teachers, scientists, organizers, and veterans to serve for a season—then return to private life with honor.

WE MUST REPLACE the gutless careerist and the power-addicted celebrity with a new standard: the willing custodian of the republic, here to serve, not to rule.

True leadership means being willing to lose. To be hated. To be replaced. And still to do what must be done. The emergency required it—in every moment. The restoration cannot survive unless we make it the expectation, not the exception.

Let it be said, looking back, that this generation did not just save democracy.

We redefined who it asked us to become.

FINAL WORDS: **The Anchor, Not the Drift**

The American people have done what once seemed impossible. They held. They resisted. They rebuilt. And now they have one task left: to anchor what they saved, so it cannot be stolen again. Reinstitution is not return. It is resolve, made real. The arc of history bends only when we hold it firm.

If we finish this work, democracy can last another 250 years.

If we do not, it will not.

The choice is no longer theoretical.

It is constitutional. And it is now.

. . .

The Final Return to the Beginning

And so we return, not in circle, but in purpose—to the beginning of the promise.

We began with six commitments. That justice would be real. That peace would be secured. That safety would be guaranteed. That the common defense would be shared. That the general welfare would be sustained. And that liberty—true liberty—would not just be declared, but protected for every generation to come.

For fifty years, these promises were broken. For a decade, they were nearly buried.

What you now hold in your hands—*American Renewal, American Restoration,* and *American Redemption*—is not a history. It is a blueprint. Not a warning. A vow.

That the promises of the Constitution will not only be made again, but kept.

Not just for now.

But for the next 250 years.

HOW TO USE THE READER'S GUIDES

──── ✦ ────

These Reader's Guides are designed to support your efforts in remembering, applying, and sharing the ideas this book presents. Each guide summarizes the main argument of a chapter—what's broken, what needs fixing, and how to make that fix last. They are not summaries but strategic tools. Their format remains consistent to help you explain the importance, understand the logic, and take action. Whether you're teaching the material, building a local movement, organizing for reform, or simply trying to keep the entire structure in mind, these guides are here to assist. One chapter at a time. One reform at a time. Until the whole structure is standing.

Each guide follows a consistent ten-part structure. It begins by restating what's at stake and how the chapter is arranged. Then, it discusses the collapse we face, the proposed solution, and the next steps. Afterward, it highlights three key takeaways, outlines systemic actions needed, and explains the deeper reasoning. Finally, it offers practical steps you can take—alone or with others—and suggests further reading for those ready to explore more. The goal is not to oversimplify but to clarify: to turn vision into strategy and belief into action.

You can use these guides however you need. Read them right after each chapter or revisit them later for review and reflection. Use them to teach, advocate, organize, or remember. Democracy is built through repetition, practice, and alignment. These guides are meant to support that work—not just now, but whenever you come back to this project in the months and years ahead.

READER'S GUIDE: PART I. A NATION THAT CARES FOR ITS OWN

---- ✦ ----

Reader's Guide: A Nation That Cares For Its Own

1. The Stakes

This chapter begins the most foundational argument in the book: that democracy cannot survive without care—not symbolic, but structural. When a nation allows its people to go hungry, bankrupt, or homeless, it forfeits its legitimacy. This is not about generosity. It is about survival, justice, and public function. Care is the bedrock test of whether self-government serves its people—or abandons them.

2. The Structure

As a bookend chapter, this is not a paired diagnosis/remedy.

Instead, it frames the entire section to come: five chapters that show how food, wages, and income protections form the floor beneath a functioning democracy. The chapter moves from historical foundations to modern betrayals, and ends by mapping the conditions for reform—what stands in the way, and what is required to prevail.

3. The Challenge

This chapter traces how care was severed from democracy. From the promise of the Constitution to the programs of the New Deal and Great Society, the U.S. once moved toward a state that accepted responsibility for its people. But Reaganism reversed that direction, framing care as dependency and poverty as failure. By Trump's second term, cruelty became design. The state was not absent—it was hostile.

4. The Remedy

- Guarantee food, housing, child care, health care, and retirement as public rights, not private commodities
- Build public systems that deliver these rights universally
- Reclaim care infrastructure from private profiteers through transparent funding, public delivery, and democratic accountability
- Design each program for dignity, accessibility, and long-term resilience
- Integrate tax reform to fund care fairly
- Treat veterans' care, elder care, and family care as civic responsibilities
- Build feedback mechanisms so care systems learn, adapt, and improve

5. What Comes Next

The chapters ahead take this mandate seriously. They begin with collapse and end with redesign. Each will show what has failed, and how we build something better. None of this will be easy. The opposition is organized and well-funded. But the public is ready. The path forward requires courage, coordination, and relentless clarity. What we begin in care must become the standard for everything else that follows.

6. Three Things to Remember

1. No democracy can survive if its people cannot survive.
2. Care is not charity—it is the infrastructure of freedom.
3. These reforms are not isolated policies. They are the test of whether democracy still means anything.

7. Action List

- Enact structural reforms that guarantee food, shelter, income, and health care as public rights
- Reverse laws and policies that treat care as market luxury or personal failure
- Design public options that are universal, dignified, and immune to profiteering
- Build legislative and popular coalitions to defend and expand care infrastructure
- Restore tax equity to fund care fairly and sustainably

8. Strategic Rationale

The most dangerous lie in American politics is that care is unaffordable or unearned. In reality, it is the cheapest safeguard against democratic collapse. When citizens feel abandoned, trust dissolves. When care is delivered fairly and reliably, faith in democracy returns. This is not just a social agenda—it is a national survival strategy. If care fails, everything else fails with it.

9. What You Can Do

Start where you are. Support candidates and campaigns committed to real care—not means-tested scraps, but guaranteed public goods. Talk about care as a right, not a favor. Help others see the connection between economic suffering and political collapse. Volunteer with food programs, eviction defense, or health clinics. Organize locally—and vote like your freedom depends on it, because it does.

10. Further Reading

For historical background, read Michael Katz's *The Undeserving Poor* and Nancy MacLean's *Democracy in Chains*. On the dismantling of care, see Barbara Ehrenreich's *Nickel and Dimed* and Matthew Desmond's *Evicted*. For international comparisons and the case for public options, consider Ann Crittenden's The Price of Motherhood and David Himmelstein's work on single-payer healthcare.

READER'S GUIDE: **Universal Health Care – Public Good, Not Private Gain**

1. The Stakes

Health care is the most visible proof of whether a democracy serves its people—or sells them to the highest bidder. In the United States, health is not guaranteed. It is priced, denied, delayed, and extracted. When people die for lack of money, the state has already failed. This chapter argues that health care is not just a policy issue —it is a constitutional, moral, and democratic crisis. Until care is guaranteed, freedom is a fiction.

2. The Structure

This chapter follows the standard two-part reform arc. It begins with a structural collapse: how American health care became profit-first and care-last. It then turns to design, making the case for a universal public system grounded in principle, not patchwork. International comparisons, historical betrayals, and present-day sabotage all support the chapter's central claim: that care must be redefined as a public obligation—not a private transaction.

3. The Collapse

American health care is the result of historical accidents and corporate capture. Tied to employment, riddled with inequities, and governed by intermediaries, the system rewards denial and punishes need. Every attempt at universal coverage has been blocked—by propaganda, lobbying, and political cowardice. Democrats compromised. Republicans attacked. And profiteers expanded. The result: a system that delivers record profits for insurers and debt, delay, and despair for the people it claims to serve.

. . .

4. The Remedy

A just democracy must guarantee universal access to essential health care—without cost barriers, delay, or discrimination. This requires:

- A public plan that covers all essential services regardless of job, income, or status
- Federal legislation with enforcement teeth—not state-by-state variability
- Sunset of corporate monopolies over public programs (e.g., Medicare Advantage)
- Transparent pricing, global budgets, and investment in wellness
- Federal protection against political sabotage (e.g., Schedule F purges or vaccine denial)
- Strategic rollout and public education to build trust and prevent misinformation

This is not theory. It is a reclaiming of public power, built on global precedent and domestic proof.

5. What Comes Next

Reform will face massive resistance—from insurers, drug companies, hospital conglomerates, and the politicians they fund. But Americans are ready. The patchwork is untenable. The chapter makes clear that while the public system can take many forms, it must follow one principle: care comes first. The path forward demands bold legislation, strategic communication, and a public willing to stand down the profiteers. The battle will not be won in courtrooms alone—but in neighborhoods, unions, clinics, and town halls.

6. Three Things to Remember

1. Health care is not a cost. It is the infrastructure of freedom.
2. A for-profit model cannot deliver justice—only extraction.
3. Universal care is not radical. It is the global norm America refuses to follow.

7. Action List

- Draft and pass a national health care guarantee with universal eligibility
- Phase out Medicare Advantage and restore full public control of Medicare
- Prohibit for-profit ownership of essential health infrastructure
- Establish federal standards and enforcement for care equity and access
- Reinvest in public health agencies, research, and preventative care
- Implement global budgeting and price negotiation for drugs and services

8. Strategic Rationale

Health care reform is the keystone. Without it, no other reform endures. The current system feeds despair, erodes trust, and corrodes civic participation. Medical debt suppresses freedom. Chronic pain limits labor and joy. Racial disparities deepen injustice. Universal health care is not just about fixing a system. It is about restoring a republic where the sick are treated, the vulnerable are protected, and democracy proves its worth in life, not death.

9. What You Can Do

Support universal care advocates—local, state, and national. Challenge misinformation in your community. Share your story. Push your union or workplace to support a public option. Call out politicians—of either party—who defend the status quo. Help others understand that this is not just about coverage. It's about freedom, equality, and dignity. Organize for a system that starts with care, not cost.

10. Further Reading

For a policy foundation, see *The Healing of America* by T.R. Reid and *Sick* by Jonathan Cohn. On the political sabotage of reform, read *Deadly Spin* by Wendell Potter. For comparative global insight, explore *The Commonwealth Fund's* international health system profiles. For data on profiteering and outcomes, consult the *OECD Health Statistics* and *KFF Health News* investigations.

READER'S GUIDE: **The Health of a Nation**

1. The Stakes

Health care is where democracy proves or forfeits its legitimacy. In the United States, that legitimacy is in crisis. Millions go without care. Millions more go bankrupt trying. The chapter lays bare a simple truth: no nation that lets its people die for lack of money can call itself free. This is not just a policy failure—it is a democratic betrayal. The stakes are life, liberty, and the meaning of government itself.

2. The Structure

The chapter moves from principle to plan. It begins with a moral and constitutional argument—why health must be treated as a civic right. It then outlines the architecture of a national guarantee: how it works, who it covers, what it costs, and how it is implemented. Grounded in global precedent and American practicality, the chapter doesn't merely envision a better system. It builds one—step by step.

3. The Collapse

The U.S. health system is a global outlier: the most expensive, the most chaotic, and among the least effective. Rooted in private profit, it fragments care, inflates costs, and rewards denial. It ties coverage to employment, penalizes the poor, and allows racial and geographic inequities to flourish. Even Medicare and Medicaid are riddled with privatization and exclusions. The result is not accidental. It is engineered abandonment.

. . .

4. The Remedy

The solution is a national guarantee for essential care—universal, public, and built to last. This includes:

- A single national public insurer, free at point of use
- Guaranteed core coverage for every citizen and permanent resident
- Optional supplemental insurance for non-essential services
- Streamlined billing and direct provider reimbursement
- National price negotiations for drugs and hospitals
- Workforce investment to train, recruit, and retain care professionals
- Phased rollout over 3–5 years, beginning with emergency and maternal care
- Legal protection for continuity—no interruption for current patients
- Public accountability through oversight boards, audits, and transparency
- Flexible funding model using payroll levies, redirected subsidies, and equitable taxation

THIS IS NOT A UTOPIAN VISION. It is a legal, fiscal, and institutional design—ready to build.

5. What Comes Next

Implementation will demand political courage and disciplined strategy. Industry resistance will be fierce: fear campaigns, disinformation, and sabotage. But the chapter anticipates this—and builds guardrails into the plan. Public trust will depend on visible delivery, clean governance, and a phased transition that honors current care while expanding access. What comes next is not abstraction. It is engineering—of policy, trust, and democratic renewal.

6. Three Things to Remember

1. The U.S. already spends enough to cover everyone. It just spends it badly.
2. This plan is not about control. It is about freedom—from fear, debt, and denial.
3. A system that delivers care based on need, not profit, restores both health and democracy.

7. Action List

- Pass federal legislation creating a national public insurer and defining essential services
- Phase out Medicare Advantage and prohibit profiteering in core care delivery
- Negotiate national pricing for drugs, devices, and hospital services
- Invest in primary care, rural health, and workforce capacity
- Establish transparent governance structures to oversee rollout and regulation
- Redirect existing health subsidies to fund the public guarantee sustainably

8. Strategic Rationale

This reform anchors democracy in dignity. Without guaranteed health care, the promise of equal protection is hollow. Universal care is not just fiscally prudent—it is structurally democratic. It builds public trust, stabilizes families, empowers workers, and protects national resilience. By removing the market's chokehold on human well-being, the plan restores the meaning of public good. Health becomes not a gamble, but a right.

9. What You Can Do

Demand clarity from candidates: do they support a national guarantee, or another patch? Share the plan with family, friends, and local officials. Challenge myths and name the profiteers. Support unions, clinics, and campaigns aligned with real reform. Push your city or state to pilot pieces of the rollout. Write, speak, organize. This is not about party. It is about survival—and building a system that finally treats care as sacred.

10. Further Reading

See T.R. Reid's *The Healing of America* for global comparisons, and David Himmelstein and Steffie Woolhandler's research on administrative waste. For implementation strategy, explore *The New York Health Act* (state-level proposal) and the *Physicians for a National Health Program* model. International data from *OECD Health Statistics*, *The Commonwealth Fund*, and *WHO* provide essential context and proof.

READER'S GUIDE: **Shelter and the Soul of a Democracy**

1. The Stakes

Housing is not just about shelter. It is about place, permanence, and political belonging. Without a stable home, a person loses not only safety, but civic identity. This chapter argues that the collapse of affordable, accessible housing is not just an economic failure—it is a democratic one. When millions are unhoused, rent-burdened, or displaced by profit, the republic itself begins to hollow out. A nation that does not guarantee shelter cannot claim to represent its people.

2. The Structure

This chapter builds from personal and civic truth toward systemic design. It begins by showing how housing confers continuity and civic standing. It then traces the historical and structural collapse—through privatization, speculation, and racial exclusion. From there, it reclaims housing as infrastructure and proposes a public system that treats shelter as a democratic obligation, not a market product. The structure blends moral indictment with practical direction.

3. The Collapse

Housing in the U.S. has been commodified—treated not as a right, but as a source of wealth extraction. Federal disinvestment, exclusionary zoning, predatory lending, and speculative ownership have turned shelter into a sorting mechanism. Entire communities have been erased; millions priced out, displaced, or left homeless. This collapse was not accidental. It was the outcome of deliberate decisions to serve profit over permanence, speculation over stability, and exclusion over equity.

4. The Remedy

Housing must be reclaimed as **public infrastructure**, guaranteed by law, protected from speculation, and built at scale. This requires:

- A national public housing system—safe, durable, beautiful, and permanent
- Massive investment in non-market housing for veterans, seniors, working families, and the unhoused
- Federal standards for affordability, habitability, and accessibility
- Reform of zoning codes and tax laws to end exclusion and reward density
- Public purchase programs to acquire vacant or predatory-owned properties
- Long-term protections against privatization, vacancy incentives, and corporate land grabs
- A new civic ethic: housing as the floor of belonging—not the prize of survival

This is not about eliminating private housing. It is about ensuring that no person's safety, voice, or freedom depends on their income.

5. What Comes Next

Real reform will demand confronting powerful real estate interests, financial institutions, and entrenched political cowardice. Cities will resist density. Landowners will resist regulation. Developers will resist affordability mandates. But the chapter is clear: the alternative is democratic erosion. To build housing is to build trust, visibility, and participation. What comes next is not merely construction. It is the reconstruction of civic life.

6. Three Things to Remember

1. Housing determines whether a person can participate in democracy.
2. The U.S. housing crisis is the result of policy choices—not inevitability.
3. Shelter must be treated as infrastructure, not as commodity.

7. Action List

- Enact a federal housing guarantee, with sustained investment in public and non-market housing
- Reform exclusionary zoning laws and create incentives for density and affordability
- Fund local and regional public housing authorities to build and maintain permanent housing stock
- Restrict predatory ownership, corporate bulk-buying, and speculative vacancy
- Expand tenant protections, eviction defense, and rental stabilization programs
- Require all federally funded housing to meet accessibility, safety, and equity standards

8. Strategic Rationale

Housing is where democracy begins. It enables every other right—from voting and education to civic engagement and economic opportunity. By treating shelter as infrastructure, the state rebuilds the most elemental foundation of trust. Market-driven systems cannot and will not serve those with greatest need. A public guarantee provides the permanence that private systems deny. It tells citizens: you belong here. And belonging is the soul of democracy.

9. What You Can Do

Support local campaigns for affordable housing, zoning reform, and public construction. Demand your elected officials fund and protect non-market housing. Share your story if you've faced eviction, housing instability, or displacement—it's not personal failure; it's political design. Advocate for eviction moratoriums and tenant protections. Join neighborhood coalitions fighting for housing justice. The more people insist that shelter is a civic right, the harder it becomes to deny.

10. Further Reading

See Matthew Desmond's *Evicted* and Keeanga-Yamahtta Taylor's *Race for Profit* for historical and sociological context. Explore Vienna's housing model through *Red Vienna: Housing for the Many* by Eve Blau. For comparative policy and urban planning frameworks, consult *Homes for All* by the National Low Income Housing Coalition and reports by the OECD on public housing in Europe and Asia.

READER'S GUIDE: A Place to Live—Housing as Democratic Infrastructure

1. The Stakes

Housing is not just a human need—it is the platform on which all rights are built. Without shelter, a person cannot vote, enroll their children in school, serve on a jury, or receive public services. Yet in the United States, shelter has been surrendered to speculation. This chapter pair shows that housing is the clearest test of whether democracy still serves people or merely protects capital. If the republic cannot guarantee a place to live, it cannot claim to represent all who live there.

2. The Structure

The first chapter (*Shelter and the Soul of a Democracy*) diagnoses the collapse of housing as a public good and traces the social, economic, and democratic consequences of its commodification. The second chapter (*This Time, We Choose to Build for People*) offers the historical roots, political sabotage, and policy architecture behind the crisis—and sets up a full-scale structural remedy. Together, the chapters argue that housing is not just a market failure. It is a moral one. And that failure demands a democratic response.

3. The Collapse

Over decades, public housing was dismantled, protections stripped, and the market allowed to dictate who gets shelter and where. Wall Street and corporate landlords seized on the vacuum, transforming homes into revenue streams. Policies rewarded speculation, punished renters, and eroded local control. Evictions surged.

Affordability vanished. Displacement became normalized. This collapse did not happen all at once—and it was no accident. It was engineered, legislated, and defended by those who profit from exclusion.

4. The Remedy

Housing must be treated as democratic infrastructure—permanent, public, and protected. Reform includes:

- A national public housing authority empowered to build, acquire, and maintain millions of non-market homes
- Federal investment to close the 7 million-unit shortfall in affordable housing
- Zoning reform and land use law overhaul to permit density and affordability where exclusion was once codified
- Repeal or redesign of tax subsidies that currently reward speculation (e.g., 1031 exchanges, mortgage interest deductions)
- Tenant protections, eviction defenses, and universal legal representation in housing court
- Public ownership and community land trusts to retain affordability across generations
- Targeted programs for veterans, seniors, Indigenous communities, and the disabled
- Robust enforcement of anti-discrimination, habitability, and fair housing laws

This is not about erasing the private sector—but about creating a parallel system strong enough to guarantee shelter as a civic right.

. . .

5. What Comes Next

Implementation will face resistance from the most powerful interests in real estate and finance. Developers, landlords, and the donor class will fight to protect their privileges. Zoning boards, tax laws, and regulatory capture will not shift overnight. But the chapter is clear: public power must be rebuilt to meet public need. Housing justice will not arrive through charity or market tinkering. It will come through organizing, legislation, and democratic will.

6. Three Things to Remember

1. Housing is the address where your rights begin—and where democracy is anchored.
2. The current system works exactly as designed: for profit, not for people.
3. Shelter must be treated as public infrastructure, not a luxury commodity.

7. Action List

- Create a national housing guarantee funded and enforced by federal law
- Restore federal support for public and social housing construction at scale
- Enact rent control legislation and expand tenant rights nationwide
- Redirect housing tax policy to favor need-based shelter over speculation
- Fund public acquisition of distressed properties for affordable use

- Reform zoning to allow multi-unit and mixed-income development across urban and suburban areas

8. Strategic Rationale

Housing reform is democracy reform. When people are displaced, they are disempowered. When they are unhoused, they are unheard. The current system not only deepens inequality—it erodes civic participation, economic stability, and public trust. A nation that fails to provide shelter cannot sustain liberty. But a nation that invests in shelter as a right lays the foundation for a just, enduring republic.

9. What You Can Do

Support tenant unions, housing justice coalitions, and campaigns for rent control, public housing, and zoning reform. Demand that your city build for people, not profit. Challenge local ordinances that entrench segregation. Attend zoning hearings. Back state and federal candidates who support a housing guarantee. Talk about shelter as a right, not an asset. The more people see housing as democracy infrastructure, the faster the politics begin to shift.

10. Further Reading

See *Evicted* by Matthew Desmond for lived impact, and *Race for Profit* by Keeanga-Yamahtta Taylor for the history of racial exclusion in housing policy. For global models, explore Vienna's public housing system and Finland's Housing First approach. Reports by the National Low Income Housing Coalition and the Joint Center for Housing Studies at Harvard provide critical data on affordability, policy, and displacement.

READER'S GUIDE: **A Home for All — How to Build a Housing System That Lasts**

1. The Stakes

Housing is not a luxury. It is the condition for democracy itself. Without a home, a person cannot vote, register for services, or participate in civic life. This chapter reframes housing as democratic infrastructure—a guarantee that must be delivered with the same permanence and scale as roads, schools, or power grids. The stakes are not just economic or humanitarian. They are constitutional. If people cannot live securely, they cannot live freely.

2. The Structure

This is a paired reform chapter that follows a six-part structure: Build, Preserve, Guarantee, Reclaim, Protect, and Belong. Each section addresses a core failure of the current housing market—and offers a public alternative. The chapter builds from principles to policies, outlining a federal housing system that includes construction benchmarks, legal mandates, enforcement structures, and cultural change. The result is not a stopgap, but a new public institution built to last.

3. The Collapse

America's housing system has failed. Rent is unaffordable. Public housing is decaying. Homelessness is rising. And speculative finance has overtaken public need. Local zoning laws block new supply. Private developers extract profit without accountability. Meanwhile, short-term subsidies mask long-term decay. The collapse is not accidental. It is the logical outcome of a system designed to serve wealth, not people—and to treat shelter as a commodity, not a right.

. . .

4. **The Remedy**

A federal, permanent housing system with enforceable mandates:

- Build 100 million homes over 20 years—publicly funded, owned, and maintained
- Preserve and restore existing units with long-term affordability and tenant protections
- Enact a federal Housing Guarantee Act establishing shelter as a legal right
- Reclaim housing from speculative markets through land trusts and resale covenants
- Protect residents through eviction defense, legal aid, and anti-discrimination enforcement
- Ensure integration into communities—transport, schools, clinics, and planning rights

5. **What Comes Next**

Implementation will require federal legislation with binding timelines and indexed funding. State and local governments may help—but not obstruct. Zoning overrides, land transfers, and labor planning must begin immediately. And public trust must be earned through transparency and results. This is a 20-year project—but the first five will determine its survival. The only path forward is bold, coordinated, and permanent. Anything less ensures failure.

6. **Three Things to Remember**

1. Housing is not a market privilege—it is a civic right
2. Shelter enables democracy; without it, people are erased
3. The only way to end housing injustice is to build a system that cannot be undone

7. Action List

- Pass the Housing Guarantee Act and tie funding to enforceable benchmarks
- Launch a federal housing trust funded by estate taxes, vacancy fees, and speculation taxes
- Remove local zoning barriers to affordable and public housing development
- Create national benchmarks and annual reporting on construction, maintenance, and equity
- Invest in public-sector construction crews, apprenticeship pipelines, and land acquisition
- Protect new housing stock from privatization through law and design

8. Strategic Rationale

Housing is upstream of every democratic right. Without it, participation collapses. The private market cannot meet this need—because its incentives oppose affordability and permanence. This chapter offers a structural alternative: a federal housing system that delivers scale, equity, and durability. It must be shielded from sabotage, funded by law, and defended by public culture. Shelter is not seasonal policy. It is a constitutional function of democracy.

. . .

9. What You Can Do

Support local initiatives for public housing, land trusts, and tenant protections. Challenge exclusionary zoning in your city or state. Pressure your representatives to back federal housing legislation with teeth. Talk about housing not as charity or cost, but as essential infrastructure. Organize with others to defend existing public housing and demand new investment. The system will only be built if it is publicly desired—and politically non-negotiable.

10. Further Reading

Read *Evicted* by Matthew Desmond for a ground-level view of housing injustice. See *The Color of Law* by Richard Rothstein for the legal history of segregation. For a case study in speculative failure, explore *Golden Gates* by Conor Dougherty. For forward-thinking policy and design, consult the work of Shelterforce Magazine and the National Housing Law Project. And for fiscal insight, review *The Public Wealth of Cities* by Dag Detter and Stefan Fölster.

READER'S GUIDE: **The Floor Beneath Every Life**

1. The Stakes

This chapter makes a foundational claim: that democracy cannot function without economic stability. It is not enough to vote. To participate fully, people must be housed, fed, supported, and able to recover from loss. Without a reliable floor beneath every life, liberty becomes conditional and consent becomes coercion. This is not just about poverty. It is about power—and whether a nation serves its people or disciplines them through hardship.

2. The Structure

This paired reform chapter addresses five interlocking guarantees: food, wages, unemployment, retirement, and veterans' care. It opens by framing the constitutional and historical basis for these public obligations, traces their deliberate dismantling, and contrasts U.S. failures with global successes. The second half offers specific, structural solutions—rooted in law, justice, and design—to restore a functioning floor beneath every American life.

3. The Collapse

Economic stability in America did not simply erode. It was stripped away by ideology, cruelty, and neglect. Food aid was stigmatized. Wages stagnated. Union power was crushed. Unemployment insurance became a maze of dysfunction. And Social Security, though still popular, was left vulnerable to sabotage. The result was not merely economic strain—it was systemic instability. When survival is a gamble, democracy becomes a fiction.

. . .

4. The Remedy

A restored foundation built on five guarantees:

- **Food:** Universal free school meals, expanded and simplified SNAP, and public grocery support in food deserts
- **Wages:** A raised and indexed federal minimum wage, criminalization of wage theft, support for sectoral bargaining, and enforceable union rights
- **Unemployment:** Universal, portable benefits for all workers, with fair payment, supportive services, and dignity by design
- **Retirement:** Social Security reform to phase out the earnings cap, strengthen survivor benefits, and recognize unpaid caregiving
- **Veterans' Care:** Full modernization and guaranteed funding for the VA, with extended respect and support for all public service roles

5. What Comes Next

Each of these reforms must be enacted not as isolated improvements but as structural guarantees. That means permanent funding, legal mandates, and automatic protections insulated from sabotage. We already have the knowledge and international examples. What remains is the will. These reforms will face resistance, but the cost of inaction is higher: a nation that cannot protect its own cannot survive intact.

6. Three Things to Remember

1. Economic survival is not charity—it is the precondition of self-government
2. Poverty is not caused by laziness—it is produced by policy
3. The right to recover is as vital as the right to speak, vote, or work

7. Action List

- Pass legislation to guarantee universal school meals, expand SNAP, and eliminate lunch debt
- Raise and index the federal minimum wage and criminalize wage theft
- Redesign unemployment insurance to be universal, portable, and humane
- Reform Social Security to reflect modern longevity, inequality, and unpaid labor
- Fully fund and modernize the VA and expand care guarantees for all national service roles
- Reframe public discourse: these are not benefits—they are constitutional functions

8. Strategic Rationale

A society that forces people to earn survival through suffering will eventually collapse. These reforms do not merely protect the vulnerable. They stabilize the entire system. Economic security is democratic infrastructure. Without it, all other freedoms erode. With it, the nation is equipped to withstand crisis, restore trust, and cultivate participation. The floor must be rebuilt not as a patch—but as a permanent platform for liberty.

9. What You Can Do

Support local food access programs, minimum wage campaigns, and labor rights coalitions. Challenge rhetoric that equates poverty with failure. Share your story—and others'—to counter false narratives about dependency. Pressure lawmakers to protect Social Security and reform unemployment insurance. Support veterans not just with applause, but with advocacy. Help rebuild the cultural consensus that survival is a public right, not a private reward.

10. Further Reading

See *The Deficit Myth* by Stephanie Kelton for economic frameworks that support social guarantees. Read *Evicted* by Matthew Desmond and *Nickel and Dimed* by Barbara Ehrenreich for firsthand accounts of hardship under current policy. For global comparisons, consult *The Nordic Theory of Everything* by Anu Partanen. To understand labor rights and union erosion, read *Beaten Down, Worked Up* by Steven Greenhouse.

READER'S GUIDE: **The Floor We Build Together**

1. The Stakes

This chapter delivers a powerful argument: that food, wages, and unemployment support are not charity, but national infrastructure. Without them, democracy becomes fragile, reactive, and unworthy of trust. In their absence, despair spreads, participation shrinks, and freedom erodes. These are not marginal policies. They are the foundation on which every other right depends. To rebuild that foundation is not generosity. It is justice made real.

2. The Structure

This paired reform chapter advances three core guarantees: food, fair wages, and unemployment security. It moves from current failures to clear solutions—grounded in precedent, international examples, and administrative reforms. The final sections address implementation, funding, and resistance—showing that none of these reforms are radical, untested, or unaffordable. What they require is not invention, but courage, coordination, and commitment.

3. The Collapse

Hunger persists not because of famine, but because of stigma and obstruction. Wages stagnate while corporations profit from public subsidies. Unemployment systems are punitive by design—fragmented, outdated, and cruel. Together, these failures are not isolated policy errors. They are the structural outcome of a political culture that treats survival as a reward for compliance rather than a condition of democracy. The result is instability, shame, and widespread loss of trust.

. . .

4. The Remedy

A new floor built through three national guarantees:

- **Food:** Universal school meals, expanded SNAP and WIC, automated enrollment, and publicly funded food infrastructure to eliminate hunger and shame
- **Wages:** Raise and index the federal minimum wage, abolish subminimum exceptions, empower local wage setting, and block federal funds to low-wage employers
- **Unemployment:** A unified federal system with national benefit floors, wraparound support, gig worker inclusion, and dignity-focused design
- **Enforcement:** Shift control of nutrition programs to federal platforms, empower the Department of Labor with audit authority, and centralize UI under Treasury with IRS integration
- **Funding:** Restore progressive taxation, close loopholes, redirect fossil fuel subsidies, and implement new wealth-based surcharges to finance lasting public stability

5. What Comes Next

Reform begins immediately. Year One legislation sets triggers, launches enrollment, and begins wage and UI transitions. By Year Three, the national unemployment system replaces state patchworks, food aid is universally administered, and wage benchmarks are indexed. A new public commission tracks compliance and ensures resilience. These guarantees are not stopgaps. They are permanent systems—binding by law, sustained by funding, and defended by public demand.

6. Three Things to Remember

1. Hunger, poverty wages, and unemployment cruelty are policy choices—not inevitabilities
2. Food, wages, and economic support are not charity—they are infrastructure
3. A resilient democracy begins with a dignified floor that no one can fall through

7. Action List

- Pass national legislation for universal meals, automated SNAP, and food infrastructure investments
- Raise the federal minimum wage with built-in indexing and remove all subminimum wage categories
- Replace the current UI patchwork with a centralized federal system, linked to Social Security and IRS records
- Restore progressive tax rates and close tax loopholes to fund public guarantees permanently
- Support the creation of an independent Economic Dignity Oversight Commission to monitor compliance and equity

8. Strategic Rationale

A nation that cannot feed, pay, or support its people is a nation unfit to govern. These reforms meet the federal duty to promote the general welfare and restore democratic legitimacy through visible, functional systems. They reduce chaos, prevent collapse, and equip people to thrive. A republic that invests in survival builds trust, resilience, and civic strength. Without these guarantees, liberty is a lie. With them, democracy has a future.

9. What You Can Do

Organize for local wage reform. Support campaigns for school meal expansion. Join efforts to federalize unemployment and protect gig workers. Challenge narratives that equate hardship with failure. Advocate for fair taxation—not as punishment, but as democratic investment. Talk about food and wages as rights, not privileges. Help others see that these reforms do not erode responsibility —they make it possible. A floor is not the end of freedom. It is where freedom begins.

10. Further Reading

Read *Scarcity* by Sendhil Mullainathan and Eldar Shafir for insights on the cognitive toll of poverty. See *The Working Poor* by David K. Shipler and *Broke in America* by Joanne Samuel Goldblum for accounts of economic precarity. For global comparisons, consult OECD's *Employment Outlook* and UNICEF's reports on school nutrition. On wage policy and enforcement, read *Beaten Down, Worked Up* by Steven Greenhouse and *The War on Normal People* by Andrew Yang.

READER'S GUIDE: **Security in the Long Run**

1. The Stakes

This chapter reclaims Social Security not just as a program, but as a promise. It confronts the growing mismatch between the original structure and modern economic life. Without bold reform, the system will drift—still operational, but increasingly misaligned, unfair, and unsustainable. Retirement, once a shared civic guarantee, risks becoming another source of division and distrust. The stakes are not insolvency. They are legitimacy, equity, and the future of shared security in a just democracy.

2. The Structure

This paired reform chapter begins by diagnosing how Social Security, though intact, has become distorted—delivering the most to those who need it least. It details the historic and political erosion of fairness, and then lays out a two-pillar reform agenda: recalibrating public benefits based on need, and creating portable, worker-owned retirement accounts. Together, these reforms restore alignment between Social Security's mission and today's working realities—grounded in equity, sustainability, and dignity.

3. The Collapse

Social Security still functions—but it no longer functions fairly. The wealthy receive the largest checks and live the longest. Caregivers, low-wage workers, and those with interrupted careers often receive the least. Meanwhile, the administrative capacity of the system has been starved, its trust fund threatened, and reform proposals blocked or distorted. What has collapsed is not solvency, but justice. The result is growing resentment and a widening gulf between the program's purpose and its outcomes.

4. The Remedy

A two-pillar system to modernize and equalize retirement security:

- Shift Social Security benefits gradually from income-based to needs-based for new retirees, phasing in over ten years beginning in 2030
- Lift the payroll tax cap so all income contributes equally to the trust fund
- Recognize unpaid caregiving, part-time work, and interrupted careers through adjusted benefit formulas
- Fully restore survivor and disability protections, and modernize the Social Security Administration for speed, clarity, and trust
- Launch portable, regulated retirement accounts for all workers, with rising contributions, employer matching, and public oversight
- Fund these reforms through progressive tax reform and redirecting regressive subsidies—ensuring a sustainable, equitable safety net

5. What Comes Next

Implementation begins in 2030, with public benefits transitioning over a decade and portable retirement accounts growing alongside. The first reforms focus on equity and modernization; later phases build resilience and wealth. These are not replacements for the public system, but reinforcements. As more Americans build real savings, Social Security can focus on protection—delivering enough for all, while enabling more to arrive with more. The future of retirement must be both fair and durable.

6. Three Things to Remember

1. Social Security is not failing—but it is falling out of alignment with the world it serves
2. Wealthy retirees do not need maximum checks; vulnerable workers need real support
3. Retirement must become a system of protection and ownership—not luck and inertia

7. Action List

- Pass legislation to lift the payroll tax cap and phase in needs-based benefit formulas for new retirees
- Restore SSA funding to eliminate delays and expand disability and survivor access
- Recognize unpaid labor—especially caregiving—as contributory work
- Establish regulated, portable retirement accounts for all workers with rising contributions
- Reform federal tax policy to finance retirement justice through equity, not austerity
- Block all efforts to privatize or weaken Social Security under the guise of solvency

8. Strategic Rationale

The current system favors longevity, wealth, and continuous work—conditions few vulnerable Americans can meet. Without structural reform, Social Security becomes another symbol of unfairness. But if redesigned with purpose, it can restore trust, expand ownership, and guarantee that retirement is not a reward for privilege, but a foundation for dignity. This chapter offers a plan to realign a legacy system with modern life, proving that security is not an illusion—but a function of democracy done right.

9. What You Can Do

Speak out against efforts to raise the retirement age or privatize benefits. Support candidates and coalitions that back tax fairness and structural reform. Organize within your workplace to demand retirement plans that supplement—not replace—Social Security. Share stories of caregivers, gig workers, and low-wage retirees who are too often invisible in the national debate. Help make clear that retirement is not the end of participation—it is the test of whether the system worked.

10. Further Reading

For history and insight, read *The Triumph of Injustice* by Emmanuel Saez and Gabriel Zucman and *Retirement Heist* by Ellen E. Schultz. For the case against privatization, see *Social Security Works!* by Nancy Altman and Eric Kingson. On international comparisons, consult OECD's *Pensions at a Glance*. To understand wealth inequality and savings disparities, read *The Hidden Cost of Being African American* by Thomas M. Shapiro.

READER'S GUIDE: **A Promise Not Yet Kept**

1. The Stakes

This chapter calls the nation to account for the broken promises made to its veterans. It exposes the contradiction at the heart of American patriotism: public praise without public care. At stake is not only the well-being of those who served, but the credibility of the republic itself. A democracy that sends people into danger must offer more than slogans when they return. If care is not guaranteed, then honor is hollow—and the nation's moral compact is breached.

2. The Structure

This paired reform chapter begins with historical context and political betrayal—from the GI Bill's successes to decades of neglect and defunding. It then outlines a comprehensive agenda: integrating veteran care into universal systems, guaranteeing housing and income security, modernizing the VA, fully funding mental and elder care, and ending political exploitation. Comparative international models reinforce the point: the U.S. has no excuse for continued failure. The chapter closes with a call to rebuild trust through obligation, not performance.

3. The Collapse

Veterans in the U.S. face long wait times, mental health neglect, housing instability, and bureaucratic indifference. The Department of Veterans Affairs is underfunded and overburdened. Successive Republican administrations, especially under Trump, praised troops while slashing services. The result is not a system of gratitude, but a gauntlet of delays and denials. Veterans experience record suicide rates, unresolved trauma, and political exploitation. The promise of care has become a symbol of dysfunction.

4. The Remedy

A renewed national contract for veteran care:

- Integrate veterans into the broader universal health system with lifetime access and priority care
- Guarantee permanent, supportive housing for all veterans, with on-site services and medical access
- Provide secure income through disability benefits, civilian job pathways, and expedited unemployment access
- Fully fund and modernize the VA, with reopened field offices, digital systems, and accountability tied to dignity metrics
- Destigmatize and expand mental health and elder care with barrier-free access, home-based services, and specialized support
- Protect veterans from political misuse and restore the apolitical mission of care through legal enforcement and oversight
- Fund all reforms through tax equity, redirecting a small portion of defense spending to fulfill our moral debt

5. What Comes Next

These reforms must be enacted not as isolated improvements, but as a complete transformation. Implementation begins with full VA funding, universal health integration, and new housing development. Federal hiring reforms, income supports, and digital modernization must follow. Caregivers must be formally recognized and supported. New oversight structures must ensure the veteran system works—not as performance, but as promise kept. The goal is not generosity. It is repayment—timely, full, and real.

6. Three Things to Remember

1. Veteran care is not charity—it is a contract
2. Political praise without public systems is betrayal
3. Trust is built through action, not applause

7. Action List

- Pass legislation to integrate veteran care into national health, housing, and income systems
- Restore full VA funding and expand rural, mental, and elder care access
- Build and staff dedicated veteran housing with wraparound services
- Create permanent legal protections against the political weaponization of veterans
- Fund all obligations through closing tax loopholes, capping war profits, and redirecting defense spending
- Establish an independent Veteran Care Accountability Authority with full investigative powers

8. Strategic Rationale

America's treatment of its veterans reflects its seriousness as a democracy. Broken care systems erode morale, widen distrust, and dishonor service. Other democracies have proven that effective veteran care is achievable, integrated, and fair. The U.S. has greater resources—it lacks only the political will. These reforms restore integrity to a national obligation. If the republic is to be trusted by those who defend it, it must keep the promise it made: to care, for life.

9. What You Can Do

Support organizations that advocate for veteran care—not just charity. Challenge candidates and officials who oppose VA funding or exploit veterans for political gain. Push for integration of care into broader health, housing, and income systems. Volunteer in legal aid, job training, or mental health initiatives for veterans. Most importantly, speak about veterans not as symbols, but as citizens—people who have earned more than performance. They have earned systems that work.

10. Further Reading

Read *Thank You for Your Service* by David Finkel and *Wounding Warriors* by Daniel Gade and Daniel Huang for insight into the physical and bureaucratic toll of military service. See *The Forever War* by Dexter Filkins for the broader political context. For comparative systems, review OECD's *Integrating Veterans into Civilian Life* and RAND's studies on veteran health care access and mental health integration. For a systems-level blueprint, consult reports from the Veterans Legal Services Clinic at Yale Law School.

READER'S GUIDE: **The Architecture of Care**

1. **The Stakes**

At stake is the ability of families to raise children without being punished economically, professionally, or emotionally. The United States has allowed its support structures to rot, treating child care as a private burden rather than a public obligation. This is not just a crisis of convenience—it is a collapse of moral priority. When families must choose between safety and income, presence and survival, the entire purpose of democratic government is undermined. A society that fails to support those raising the next generation is not merely unprepared. It is unjust.

2. **The Structure**

This chapter reframes care as essential infrastructure, not personal struggle. It begins by exposing the financial squeeze on modern families and tracing the policy abandonment that led here —from the dismantling of WWII-era care systems to Nixon's 1971 veto of national child care. It then lays out six pillars of reform: access, workforce dignity, built-in infrastructure, guaranteed paid leave, workplace flexibility, and public delivery. International comparisons highlight America's failures and alternatives. The chapter closes with a funding roadmap, moral argument, and call to treat care as foundational to freedom.

3. **The Collapse**

America's care crisis is not accidental—it is structural and sustained. As wages stagnated and costs surged, families were told to work harder, not supported more. Care was privatized, stigmatized, and neglected. Millions now live in child care deserts, where care is unaffordable or unavailable. Workers are underpaid and burned out. Parents—especially mothers—are forced out of the workforce. Attempts to create a national system were vetoed or defunded. The result is an economy that punishes caregiving, a nation that dishonors its future, and a system collapsing once again.

4. The Remedy

A care system rooted in infrastructure, not improvisation:

- Guarantee universal access to high-quality early childhood care in every community
- Pay care workers professional wages with benefits, training, and career advancement
- Embed care centers in schools, housing, health hubs, and transit corridors
- Pass national paid family leave for birth, adoption, caregiving, and medical need
- Ensure workplace flexibility through predictable scheduling and care-aligned policies
- Deliver care through public and nonprofit partners, not for-profit chains
- Fund reforms through repealed tax cuts, closed loopholes, and public-private partnerships

5. What Comes Next

Rebuilding the architecture of care begins now—with wage increases, preschool expansion, and infrastructure investment. Federal policy must shift from patchwork tax credits to stable grants. States can lead, but national coordination is essential. These reforms are not a luxury—they are the new foundation for economic survival and democratic dignity. A society that invests in care does not just help parents. It liberates potential, unlocks equity, and prepares itself to endure.

6. Three Things to Remember

1. Care is not a private problem—it is public infrastructure
2. Child care workers are essential professionals, not expendable labor
3. The cost of inaction is higher than the cost of reform

7. Action List

- Fund and expand universal child care and pre-K systems at the state and federal level
- Raise wages and benefits for care workers to professional standards
- Pass national paid family and medical leave through federal legislation
- Require employers to provide scheduling flexibility and remote/hybrid options
- Build care infrastructure into all public development and transit planning
- Redirect corporate tax breaks toward care system construction and access grants

8. Strategic Rationale

Care is the hidden infrastructure on which everything else

depends. Without it, families collapse, economies stall, and gender inequity worsens. Treating care as private sustains inequality and suppresses opportunity. But public investment creates cascading benefits—economic, social, and democratic. Other nations have proven this. America can catch up. The goal is not to replicate one model but to meet one obligation: to make care a right, not a privilege, and to ensure that no parent or provider must sacrifice survival to support the next generation.

9. What You Can Do

Vote for candidates who champion universal care and paid leave. Join or support coalitions advocating for child care infrastructure and labor rights. Pressure local officials to include care in zoning, school planning, and transit development. Speak up in your workplace for schedule transparency and caregiving support. Amplify the voices of child care workers and push back against narratives that frame care as indulgence. Every time you treat care as essential —not secondary—you help rebuild the future.

10. Further Reading

See *Raising America* by Ann Hulbert for a historical look at child-rearing debates. *The Fifth Trimester* by Lauren Smith Brody explores the unpaid cost of caregiving after childbirth. For comparative policy models, consult *Cribsheet* by Emily Oster and OECD's *Starting Strong* reports. *Essential Labor* by Angela Garbes offers a powerful blend of memoir and manifesto on caregiving. For economic framing, review *The Care Economy* by Heather Boushey and related reports from the National Women's Law Center.

READER'S GUIDE: **Fair Taxation and Wealth Reform**

1. The Stakes

Without a fair tax system, democracy cannot survive. The chapter makes clear that the current tax structure in the United States is not broken by accident—it is functioning as designed: to serve the rich, starve the public, and dismantle any resistance to oligarchy. When taxation becomes a tool of extraction rather than contribution, it drains not only national revenue but the moral foundation of shared prosperity. If this system continues, it will collapse under the weight of inequality, debt, and declining legitimacy. The chapter warns that taxation is not just about funding government—it is about whether we believe in a society at all.

2. The Structure

The chapter begins with a direct diagnosis: the tax system is working perfectly for the powerful. It then outlines the comprehensive economic agenda embedded in Republican tax and deregulation policy—an eighteen-point blueprint for plutocratic consolidation. Next, it explores the four main levers of economic hollowing—wage suppression, offshoring, price inflation, and automation—demonstrating how each drives collapse. Historical parallels and international comparisons show how societies fall when wealth becomes immune and labor becomes disposable. The final third moves to solutions: restoring progressive taxation, funding the public good, and using tax policy not to punish wealth but to preserve the republic.

3. The Collapse

This chapter offers one of the book's clearest explanations of structural collapse. The economy is failing not because of external forces but because its incentives now reward profit without contribution, automation without compensation, and debt without limit. Americans are trapped between low wages, high prices, and vanishing services. The wealthy shield themselves from consequence while the public is told to borrow, hustle, and hope. Republican tax cuts and deregulation are not economic strategy—they are social demolition. The chapter's most damning claim is also its simplest: a tax code that exempts the rich is not a policy failure—it is a form of national self-erasure.

4. The Remedy

- End the preferential treatment of capital gains and tax them like wages.
- Enforce corporate taxation through a public minimum and global profit accountability.
- Fund and modernize the IRS to pursue high-income tax evasion and offshore abuse.
- Restore progressive tax brackets so top earners contribute proportionally to national needs.
- Redirect public revenue to universal services: health care, housing, education, and care.
- Prohibit tax shelters, close loopholes, and expose corporate filings to public review.
- Reverse deregulation that allows wealth extraction without civic obligation.
- Redefine taxation as democratic infrastructure—not punishment, but participation.

5. What Comes Next

The chapter sets the stage for economic restoration not through austerity, but through fairness. Future reforms will build on the funding principles established here: those who profit from America must pay to sustain it. The next chapters will show how that funding empowers democratic stability, environmental resilience, and lasting public good. No meaningful reform—from child care to clean energy—can succeed unless the wealthy and corporations are made to contribute. The collapse was engineered through tax code. The recovery begins in the same place.

6. Three Things to Remember

1. No tax system is neutral. It either reinforces democracy or accelerates collapse.
2. When wealth becomes immune and labor becomes disposable, societies fall.
3. Fair taxation is not radical. It is how America once built a middle class, and how it can again.

7. Action List

- Repeal Trump-era tax cuts for corporations and the ultra-wealthy.
- Restore top marginal rates and close capital gains loopholes.
- Fund the IRS to pursue high-dollar fraud and enforce equity.
- Institute a corporate minimum tax and expose public filings.

- End tax incentives for offshoring and penalize abusive shelters.
- Use public revenue for universal services, not elite subsidies.

8. Strategic Rationale

Fair taxation is the most direct and achievable way to reverse the economic hollowing of the United States. It underpins every other democratic reform by providing stable, moral, and adequate public funding. Without it, even the best policies will collapse under austerity or corporate sabotage. Restoring tax justice is also strategically persuasive—it is not punitive, but pragmatic. It aligns prosperity with participation and wealth with responsibility. Rebuilding national trust requires proving that no one is above contributing. That begins here.

9. What You Can Do

Support progressive taxation measures at the local, state, and federal level—especially initiatives to tax capital like income and to expose corporate filings. Join campaigns that push for IRS modernization and transparency. Educate others about the role of tax policy in inequality, not just public budgeting. Refuse the myth that taxing the rich harms growth. Help reframe the conversation: taxation is what makes society possible. Without it, we are not a nation. We are a market with laws—and one that is rapidly failing.

10. Further Reading

For deeper insight, explore *Capital in the Twenty-First Century* by

Thomas Piketty, *The Triumph of Injustice* by Emmanuel Saez and Gabriel Zucman, and *Winner-Take-All Politics* by Jacob Hacker and Paul Pierson. Articles from the Institute on Taxation and Economic Policy (ITEP), the Roosevelt Institute, and the Economic Policy Institute offer ongoing data and analysis.

READER'S GUIDE: **Restore the Power to Tax**

1. **The Stakes**

A government that cannot fund itself cannot govern. The American tax system no longer serves its constitutional purpose. It is cluttered with ideological distortions, corporate giveaways, and wealth-friendly loopholes that sabotage fiscal integrity. This is not just mismanagement—it is deliberate erosion of public trust, financial sustainability, and democratic fairness. Without restoring the power to tax clearly and fairly, every other reform is at risk.

2. **The Structure**

This chapter begins by recalling the original purpose of taxation: to fund government. It traces the evolution from pure revenue to behavioral manipulation, categorizing legitimate uses and exposing harmful distortions. It then details the sabotage embedded in recent Republican tax policy, culminating in a proposal to separate taxation from subsidies. Four core benefits are outlined, followed by broader democratic and moral implications. The tone is constitutional, economic, and ethical.

3. **The Collapse**

The modern U.S. tax code is no longer a tool of governance—it is a weapon of sabotage. Tax policy now funds the wealthy, punishes the poor, and conceals giveaways behind misleading names. Programs that once reduced poverty or supported innovation have been overwhelmed by regressive cuts, performative credits, and ideological poison pills. The result is not only budgetary chaos, but structural injustice: a tax system that deepens inequality, corrodes democracy, and undermines belief in government itself.

. . .

4. The Remedy

- Restore taxation to its constitutional purpose: raising revenue
- Separate taxation from spending incentives and ideological subsidies
- Eliminate gimmicks, distortions, and hidden carveouts
- Simplify the code with fewer brackets, a standard deduction, and transparent rates
- Link revenue directly to national spending, with public accountability
- Require all subsidies to pass as open, standalone spending bills
- End the strategic use of deficits to justify cuts to public services

5. What Comes Next

This reform changes not just how taxes are written—but what they mean. It breaks the toxic feedback loop between tax distortion and political sabotage. By restoring clarity, honesty, and purpose to the tax code, it clears a path to honest budgeting and democratic trust. The goal is not just balance sheets, but civic legitimacy. No government can endure without both.

6. Three Things to Remember

1. Taxes were meant to fund government—not to manipulate society or reward allies

2. The current system enables inequality, cynicism, and sabotage
3. Restoring clarity and honesty in taxation is a prerequisite for democratic trust

7. Action List

- Remove all non-revenue provisions from tax bills
- Establish rules that separate taxes from subsidies or policy favors
- Mandate transparency in tax rates and eliminate opaque loopholes
- Require public debate and funding sources for any tax-exempt program
- Link taxation levels explicitly to government spending decisions
- Use tax policy to promote fiscal honesty, not ideological warfare

8. Strategic Rationale

When taxation loses its purpose, democracy loses its compass. Every distortion of the tax code undermines economic stability and public legitimacy. By restoring the original purpose of taxation—to fund the needs of the nation—this reform clarifies the role of government, reestablishes fiscal responsibility, and limits the abuse of power. It is a structural reset that enables every other reform to succeed.

. . .

9. **What You Can Do**

Learn how the current tax system operates—and how it conceals inequity. Advocate for separating tax and spending policy. Call out hidden subsidies, unfunded credits, and ideological gimmicks in tax bills. Support candidates who demand fiscal clarity and reject performative tax cuts. Talk to your community about why honest taxation matters. It's not about punishment or generosity—it's how we share the cost of freedom.

10 FURTHER READING

For context on tax history and structure, read *Taxes in America* by Leonard E. Burman and Joel Slemrod, *The Hidden Wealth of Nations* by Gabriel Zucman, and *Fiscal Therapy* by William G. Gale. For moral arguments and democratic framing, see Elizabeth Warren's essays on wealth and tax justice and legal commentaries on Article I taxation powers.

Reader's Guide: The Nation That Lasts

1. The Stakes

No democracy can survive if its people are abandoned. This chapter argues that care is not a luxury, a handout, or an ideology—it is the foundation of democratic legitimacy. Without universal health care, housing, food, wages, and support for families, a republic becomes performative: voting exists, but participation does not. In a country where survival depends on charity, luck, or exploitation, the social contract is already broken. This is not a theoretical warning. It is a material one. Debt, eviction, hunger, illness, and despair are now endemic in the United States—and they are symptoms of collapse. What begins as neglect becomes injustice. What begins as injustice becomes revolt. The chapter makes this truth undeniable.

2. The Structure

The chapter opens with a historical indictment: societies that abandon their people fall. It defines the U.S. government's long failure to care for its citizens as a moral betrayal and a political collapse. It then lays out the reforms required to restore public dignity—universal health care, living wages, housing access, child care, and food security—arguing that these are not optional, but essential. The middle third uses international comparisons to show what care looks like when it works—and why taxation is not punishment but reciprocity. The final section moves from critique to covenant, reminding us that the Constitution begins with the general welfare, and that redemption must begin with its fulfillment.

. . .

3. The Collapse

The chapter shows how the United States has drifted from a republic of shared investment into an economy of individual struggle. Safety nets have become riddled with conditions and exclusions. Vital services are unaffordable, inaccessible, or privatized. Public systems no longer serve the people—they serve profit. This is not an accident. It is the result of a decades-long political project to dismantle collective provision and turn democracy into a marketplace. The chapter makes clear that such a nation is not free. It is fragile. And if care remains concentrated among the rich while the rest are left to fend for themselves, collapse is not only likely—it is already underway.

4. The Remedy

- Guarantee universal health care through a public system accessible to all.
- Provide affordable, dignified housing as a baseline right and public investment.
- Ensure living wages and unemployment protection as democratic infrastructure.
- Establish publicly funded child care and family support systems.
- Create national food access programs to end hunger permanently.
- Reform taxation to fund these services through fair and progressive revenue.
- Treat care not as charity, but as civic infrastructure—designed, delivered, and accountable.

5. What Comes Next

The chapter transitions from care to structure—arguing that public dignity requires not only compassionate policy, but functional design. What follows are detailed reform chapters that address education, justice, inclusion, and democratic preparedness. But without care, those reforms will falter. The next steps build upon what this chapter reclaims: that democracy is not just the right to participate in government—it is the experience of being protected, valued, and included by it. From here, the project expands to make that experience permanent.

6. Three Things to Remember

1. Democracies fall when they stop caring for their people.
2. Public care is not generosity—it is how freedom becomes real.
3. No reform is sustainable without fair funding, and no funding is fair without progressive taxation.

7. Action List

- Support universal public systems for health care, housing, food, and family support.
- Demand living wages and robust unemployment insurance at local and federal levels.
- Back progressive tax reforms to fund public care without corporate capture.
- Join campaigns that link economic dignity with democratic stability.

- Reject austerity narratives and reframe care as a national investment.

8. Strategic Rationale

This chapter reframes care as the precondition of democracy—not its reward. Without a society where people can survive, participate, and thrive, all other democratic reforms become abstract. Care is not about benevolence. It is about design. It is how a people knows they are not forgotten—and how they gain the strength to participate. As political instability rises, the restoration of care becomes not only a moral imperative, but a strategic one. A cared-for nation resists collapse. A neglected one invites it.

9. What You Can Do

Organize, vote, and speak for care-based policies. Challenge narratives that treat public programs as wasteful or unearned. Share real stories about the impact of housing, health care, and wage insecurity—and how public systems can provide stability. Volunteer with mutual aid networks while advocating for permanent government action. Support leaders who champion structural reform, not temporary aid. The fight for democracy begins with making sure people can live.

10. Further Reading

To understand the foundational role of care in democracy, read *The Deficit Myth* by Stephanie Kelton, *Evicted* by Matthew Desmond, *The Spirit Level* by Richard Wilkinson and Kate Pickett, and *The Care Manifesto* by The Care Collective. Articles from the Brookings Institution, New America, and the Center for Budget and Policy Priorities also explore care-centered policy in depth.

READER'S GUIDE: PART II. A NATION THAT EDUCATES AND ELEVATES

―――― ✦ ――――

Reader's Guide: A Nation That Educates and Elevates

1. The Stakes

Without a functioning system of public education and dignified labor, democracy cannot survive. When citizens are denied the chance to learn, question, and participate meaningfully in economic life, the result is not just stagnation but subjugation. A society built on debt, exhaustion, and propaganda loses its ability to self-govern. The stakes are nothing less than civic capacity, democratic resilience, and the moral fabric of the nation itself.

2. The Structure

The chapter opens by framing education and labor as twin

pillars of democratic survival, then traces a historical arc of public investment and civic purpose. It details the collapse of that covenant through sabotage, privatization, and authoritarian design—culminating in Trump's second-term policies and the One Big Beautiful Bill. It closes with a tripartite reform agenda—public education, college access, and workforce dignity—while connecting to early learning and lifelong renewal.

3. The Collapse

America's education and labor systems have been deliberately undermined. Public schools were defunded and politicized; higher education became a debt trap; labor protections were stripped away. The result is a population trained to endure, not empowered to participate. Under Trump, these trends hardened into structure. The OBBB codified dependence and disempowerment into law—ensuring inequality not by accident, but by design.

4. The Remedy

- Fully fund and protect public K–12 education, including teacher pay, curricular integrity, and access equity
- Restore higher education as a public good by reducing costs and delivering broad student debt relief
- Strengthen technical, vocational, and trade education as dignified, equal pathways
- Ensure labor rights: fair pay, benefits, union protections, and safe conditions—especially for gig and contract workers
- Build inclusive lifelong learning systems through apprenticeships, workforce centers, and digital skill access

- Protect education from political interference, censorship, and ideological control

5. What Comes Next

This chapter lays the groundwork for reforms that continue across the book. Early childhood education is addressed in the child care section; economic security and labor protections are deepened in later chapters on wages and unemployment. The ongoing task is to weave these reforms into a complete system—where every stage of life includes access to education, skill, dignity, and democratic contribution. Renewal depends on integration, not fragmentation.

6. Three Things to Remember

1. Democracy requires education that teaches truth, not obedience
2. Public education and labor dignity are structural defenses against authoritarianism
3. No learning system is just if its destination is debt, exhaustion, or instability

7. Action List

- Repeal censorship and surveillance laws targeting educators and curricula
- Pass national student debt relief and tuition support for public higher education

- Fund and integrate trade, vocational, and community college programs nationwide
- Enact federal labor laws guaranteeing wage floors, benefits, and union rights for all workers
- Support early and adult learning through expanded funding and universal access programs
- Block efforts to eliminate the Department of Education or defund public institutions

8. Strategic Rationale

These reforms restore the foundation of self-rule. A people who cannot think critically, learn freely, or work with dignity cannot sustain a democracy. By investing in education and labor not as market functions but as civic infrastructure, we secure the conditions under which liberty, equality, and shared responsibility become possible again. The point is not charity or efficiency—it is survival by solidarity.

9. What You Can Do

Support public educators under attack. Show up at school board meetings, speak against curriculum bans, and defend teachers who teach truth. Vote for candidates who support debt relief, labor protections, and public funding for education at all levels. Volunteer or donate to local literacy, job training, or apprenticeship programs. Talk about education not as an individual burden, but a public promise—and help others see it that way too.

10. Further Reading

See *Democracy and Education* by John Dewey, *The Shame of the*

Nation by Jonathan Kozol, and *College Unbound* by Jeffrey J. Selingo. For labor, read *Beaten Down, Worked Up* by Steven Greenhouse and *No Shortcuts* by Jane McAlevey. Key articles appear in *The Nation*, *The American Prospect*, and *The Chronicle of Higher Education* on censorship, labor dignity, and the collapse of civic education.

READER'S GUIDE: **The Collapse of Public Education**

1. The Stakes

Public education is the foundation of democratic life. When it fails, the republic falters. What's at stake is not only access to opportunity, but the entire system of civic formation, national cohesion, and public trust. The destruction of public education threatens the very idea that every child—regardless of wealth, race, or ZIP code—deserves the chance to think, contribute, and belong in a functioning democracy.

2. The Structure

This chapter opens with historical grounding in the foundational role of public education, then moves through key expansions from Reconstruction to the postwar era. It traces a four-decade collapse driven by funding cuts, market logic, disinformation, and ideological attack—culminating in Trump's second term and the passage of the One Big Beautiful Bill. It closes with a clear indictment: the system was not simply neglected. It was deliberately sabotaged.

3. The Collapse

The American public education system has been dismantled through design. From Reagan to Trump, funding was slashed, teachers discredited, public schools vilified, and private interests empowered. Racial integration was undermined through property-based inequality. Standardized testing replaced support. Censorship, book bans, and surveillance became tools of control. The final blow was the OBBB—codifying abandonment as law, and turning schools from engines of opportunity into sites of submission.

. . .

4. The Remedy

- Restore public education as a national priority, rooted in equity, truth, and democratic purpose
- Fund schools based on student need, not local wealth or politics
- End censorship laws and protect academic freedom at all levels
- Reverse policies that incentivize privatization, vouchers, and segregation by ZIP code
- Support and protect teachers with fair pay, professional respect, and classroom autonomy
- Ensure universal access to early childhood education and affordable higher education
- Disband ideological review boards and reinstate Title IX and civil rights protections
- Rebuild trust by reinvesting in schools as democratic, not partisan, institutions

5. What Comes Next

This chapter names the betrayal. The next chapter begins the work of reconstruction—across public schools, universities, job training programs, and labor systems. Later chapters will expand on how economic fairness, family policy, and disinformation reform all depend on a public educated to think critically, live securely, and engage in shared purpose. What comes next is not only rebuilding systems, but renewing belief in what they are for.

. . .

6. Three Things to Remember

1. The collapse of public education was planned, funded, and passed into law
2. Schools did not fail America—America abandoned its schools
3. Education must be reclaimed as a public good, not a partisan battleground

7. Action List

- Repeal the One Big Beautiful Bill and reinstate funding and protections at every level
- Restore Title IX, special education, and multilingual student support programs
- Pass legislation banning political censorship of curricula and teacher speech
- Establish federal minimum funding standards to equalize opportunity across ZIP codes
- End federal and state programs that divert funds to private or for-profit schools
- Ensure teachers have collective bargaining rights, fair pay, and protection from harassment
- Launch a national trust-building initiative between schools, communities, and democracy

8. Strategic Rationale

No democracy can survive without an educated, empowered, and united public. The collapse of education fractures civic understanding, accelerates inequality, and weakens resistance to authoritarianism. Rebuilding public education is not a cultural issue—it is a structural necessity. Without it, democratic government becomes hollow, and public trust disappears. Repairing the system is not nostalgia. It is survival.

9. What You Can Do

Speak up for your local schools. Defend libraries, teachers, and school boards under attack. Push back against book bans and surveillance laws. Vote for candidates who support public investment, academic freedom, and equitable access to education. Attend town halls and board meetings—not just as parents, but as citizens. If you can, donate to public school foundations, literacy programs, or legal defense funds for educators. Reclaim the language of public good.

10. Further Reading

See *The Schools We Need* by E.D. Hirsch Jr., *Savage Inequalities* by Jonathan Kozol, and *Schoolhouse Burning* by Derek W. Black. For the policy history of education collapse, see *A Nation at Risk* (1983), *The Death and Life of the Great American School System* by Diane Ravitch, and investigative journalism in *ProPublica*, *The Washington Post*, and *The New York Times* on school privatization, censorship, and the impact of the OBBB.

Reader's Guide: **The Restoration of Public Education**

1. The Stakes

Without trusted teachers and functional schools, democracy crumbles. The classroom is where citizens are shaped—where young people learn to think, question, listen, and believe in their future. The assault on teachers and the abandonment of schools isn't just a political trend—it's a structural unraveling of civic life. If we fail to protect the educators who build our public, we will lose not only our schools but our republic.

2. The Structure

The chapter opens with a cultural reckoning—how we lost reverence for teachers and replaced it with mandates and suspicion. It then reframes the education crisis as structural, not personal, and proposes reforms that rebuild teaching as a profession worth pursuing. It presents funding equity, a National Teaching Pathway, return-to-service options, curriculum restoration, and democratic trust as the core pillars. It closes with moral urgency and institutional resolve.

3. The Collapse

Public education collapsed not from disinterest, but from design—through underfunding, politicization, and fear. Teachers are silenced, overburdened, and driven out. Students are tested into conformity. The profession has become unsustainable. The result is a generation of children taught less to question and more to comply. We have lost teachers, trust, and shared truth. No reform is complete unless it repairs that loss.

. . .

4. The Remedy

- Replace property-tax funding with equity-based federal and state formulas
- Create a National Teaching Pathway with salary guarantees, housing support, and long-term benefits
- Offer return-to-service bridges for caregivers, elders, and experienced educators
- Recruit short-term professionals to teach civics, science, and the arts through national programs
- Develop a national bilingual teaching corps and provide early English language support
- Restore curriculum freedom and repeal censorship and surveillance laws
- Redesign success metrics to reflect creativity, courage, and civic contribution
- Support teacher leadership through fellowships, sabbaticals, and mentoring pathways
- Rebuild cultural respect through national campaigns and storytelling
- Protect teachers from targeted harassment, disinformation, and ideological purges

5. What Comes Next

This chapter's focus is the teacher and the system that supports them—but its implications run deeper. Future chapters address curriculum transparency, online safety, early education, and workforce development. What comes next is broader than a profession—it is the restoration of a society that trusts, funds, and learns from those who teach. And it begins by recognizing that education reform is not a fix for schools alone. It is a path to democratic renewal.

6. Three Things to Remember

1. Teachers are not failing—systems are failing teachers
2. Public education must be rebuilt as a profession, not a test site
3. Protecting schools means protecting democracy itself

7. Action List

- Enact national legislation to equalize school funding across states and districts
- Launch a federally supported National Teaching Pathway and bilingual teaching initiative
- Repeal censorship laws and restore teacher protections at the state and federal levels
- Redefine success metrics away from standardized tests toward civic and creative benchmarks
- Support return-to-service pathways for former educators and caregivers
- Fund national storytelling and media campaigns that re-center teachers in public life
- Block efforts to outsource or privatize public education under the guise of "choice"

8. Strategic Rationale

These reforms recognize teachers as the civic infrastructure of democracy. A system that values memory-keepers, truth-tellers, and builders of possibility cannot be easily controlled or dismantled. When public education is strong, equitable, and trusted, it becomes a living defense against authoritarianism and a daily practice of freedom. Structural change—not sentiment—is what will protect it from collapse again.

9. What You Can Do

Publicly support teachers when they are attacked. Call your representatives about censorship laws, return-to-service programs, or national fellowships. Donate to local education foundations, reentry grants, or public awareness campaigns. Elevate stories of educators who made a difference in your life. When possible, volunteer time or resources to schools in your community—and treat teaching not as a fallback, but as the front line of democracy.

10. Further Reading

See *Teachers Have It Easy* by Daniel Moulthrop, Dave Eggers, and Ninive Clements Calegari; *The Teacher Wars* by Dana Goldstein; and *Freedom Writers Diary* by Erin Gruwell. For policy design, read *We Need Teachers* by Jack Schneider and articles from *The Learning Policy Institute*, *Education Week*, and *The Atlantic* on return pathways, bilingual instruction, and civic renewal through education.

Reader's Guide: The System That Took Their Future

1. The Stakes
When higher education becomes a barrier instead of a bridge, democracy falters. Students are trapped in a system where debt is required and opportunity is uncertain. The promise of education has been replaced by credentialism, market sorting, and institutional self-preservation. What's at stake is not only access to knowledge and careers, but trust in a system that once claimed to offer fairness, mobility, and hope.

2. The Structure
The chapter opens with the democratic rationale for higher education, then traces its evolution—from land-grant ideals and the G.I. Bill to the current credential economy. It critiques skyrocketing costs, employer overreach, and institutional bloat. It reveals how bipartisan neglect, employer dependence on degrees, and right-wing attacks on access have created a system of coercion disguised as merit. The chapter closes with a moral indictment and a call to abandon what no longer works.

3. The Collapse
College has become a distorted, unsustainable system. Public funding has declined, tuition has exploded, and student debt has reached historic highs. Employers demand degrees regardless of relevance, while universities expand for revenue rather than purpose. Alternative paths are stigmatized. The result is a generation burdened by debt, alienated from institutions, and no longer convinced that college leads to security. The bridge has collapsed—and millions are stranded on both sides.

. . .

4. The Remedy

- Restore public funding to reduce tuition at community colleges and public universities
- Enact broad student debt relief, especially for low- and middle-income borrowers
- Reinstate regulations on for-profit and predatory institutions
- End degree inflation in job postings for roles that do not require college credentials
- Expand and elevate non-college pathways: apprenticeships, public service, and skilled trades
- Create incentives for employers to prioritize skill and experience over paper qualifications
- Redesign university priorities around teaching, research, and public service—not branding or expansion
- Ensure federal oversight to prevent tuition exploitation and protect academic integrity

5. What Comes Next

This chapter focuses on college—but the next chapters expand the vision. We explore adult education, workforce dignity, and systems that offer second chances, not just first credentials. What comes next is not the abandonment of higher learning, but its realignment with public purpose. The future lies in multiple, respected paths to adulthood and contribution—not in a single, costly pipeline that rewards exclusion.

. . .

6. Three Things to Remember

1. College has become a gatekeeper, not a guarantor
2. Debt-financed education is not freedom—it is coercion
3. Reform must shift from prestige to purpose

7. Action List

- Increase federal and state investment in public colleges to reduce tuition and fees
- Pass legislation for comprehensive student loan forgiveness and fair repayment systems
- Enforce regulations on for-profit institutions and protect students from exploitation
- Launch a national credential reform initiative to reduce unnecessary degree requirements
- Fund and promote skilled trades, union apprenticeships, and public service pathways
- Align higher education metrics with mission—teaching, equity, and service—not enrollment or profit

8. Strategic Rationale

Higher education should serve the public good, not private debt markets or brand empires. These reforms restore balance by reducing coercion, increasing accessibility, and rewarding contribution. When college becomes one valid option among many—and when none of those options require lifelong debt—we return to a system that empowers, rather than traps. Structural change will preserve excellence while eliminating gatekeeping.

. . .

9. What You Can Do

Support student debt relief measures and speak out against unnecessary credential requirements in hiring. Challenge local and state officials who defund public colleges or stigmatize alternative paths. Donate to scholarship funds, public university initiatives, or local trade programs. Talk openly about your own experience—whether in college, a trade, or elsewhere—to help normalize multiple forms of success. Refuse to equate degrees with worth.

10. Further Reading

See *Lower Ed* by Tressie McMillan Cottom, *The Merit Myth* by Anthony Carnevale, and *The College Trap* by Dan Currell. Articles in *The Chronicle of Higher Education*, *The Atlantic*, and *ProPublica* offer current reporting on debt, credential inflation, and university governance. For employer reform, see reports from the Burning Glass Institute and Brookings Institution on degree requirements and workforce policy.

Reader's Guide: Dignity Without Debt

1. The Stakes

A democracy cannot thrive if success depends on a single, debt-laden path. When honest work is stigmatized, skilled careers are undervalued, and public funding flows only toward elite institutions, we undermine our workforce, our economy, and our civic foundation. The stakes are generational: a society where contribution is only honored through credentials becomes one that wastes its people—and betrays its promise.

2. The Structure

This chapter begins with a moral reckoning of the student debt crisis and the myth of college as the only path. It charts the consequences for individuals and the nation, then proposes a new model: multiple dignified, funded, and visible pathways to work, learning, and contribution. It lays out principles for public investment, cultural change, debt reform, and employer responsibility—concluding with a powerful redefinition of worth.

3. The Collapse

Debt has become the price of adulthood. College is treated as mandatory, even when it doesn't serve the student, the economy, or the job. Non-college careers are hidden, underfunded, and dismissed. Meanwhile, employers over-rely on credentials, and federal policy rewards exclusion over inclusion. The result is a bottlenecked workforce, a disillusioned generation, and a nation that mistakes branding for contribution.

. . .

4. The Remedy

- Build strong, well-paid, and secure non-college pathways across key industries
- Fund national training corps, union apprenticeships, and career-aligned community college programs
- Offer federal wage subsidies and benefits for certified trades and public service fields
- Restore visibility and respect for alternative careers through media, curriculum, and public recognition
- Reform student debt: cap interest, forgive balances beyond principal, and end lifetime repayment traps
- Phase out federal loans by directly funding public education and training systems
- Eliminate unnecessary degree requirements in hiring practices across sectors
- Invest public funds only in public-serving institutions—not elite private colleges with vast endowments
- Adopt international models that blend academic and vocational learning without stigma

5. What Comes Next

This chapter addresses the systems outside college—but future chapters explore how public employment, labor law, and tax reform reinforce or erode these gains. What comes next is a culture of recognition: where all contributions are honored, debt is no longer a rite of passage, and national identity includes every form of honest work. It begins with choice. It continues with respect. It ends with freedom.

. . .

6. Three Things to Remember

1. Not all education must come from a university to be valuable
2. Public funding should build public futures—not private fortunes or lifelong debt
3. Dignity comes from contribution—not credentials

7. Action List

- Pass national legislation to fund alternative career training and apprenticeship programs
- Reform federal repayment laws to cap interest and limit long-term debt burdens
- Launch public storytelling and scholarship programs that elevate trade and service careers
- End federal aid to private institutions that hoard endowments or restrict access
- Issue executive orders removing degree requirements for federal jobs where unnecessary
- Redirect funding from loan programs to direct subsidies for community colleges and workforce training

8. Strategic Rationale

Freedom without options is not freedom. These reforms open new paths, reduce debt dependence, and restore balance to a distorted labor market. When public systems support many ways to contribute, they increase resilience, reduce inequality, and reflect the true diversity of human skill. These changes strengthen democracy—not by lowering expectations, but by broadening who can meet them.

9. What You Can Do

Support candidates and policies that promote student debt reform, trade programs, and wage equity across sectors. Share your own path to contribution—especially if it differs from the college narrative. Encourage young people to explore all options, not just one. Recognize and celebrate the skilled labor and care work all around you. Challenge hiring practices that rely on credentials over ability. Be part of the cultural shift that redefines what success looks like.

10. Further Reading

See *The Years That Matter Most* by Paul Tough, *Debt-Free U* by Zac Bissonnette, and *Shop Class as Soulcraft* by Matthew B. Crawford. Reports from Georgetown's Center on Education and the Workforce, Brookings, and the OECD offer models of vocational excellence and global comparisons. For international pathways, explore Germany's dual-track system and Australia's TAFE programs.

READER'S GUIDE: The Collapse of Worker Power

1. The Stakes

When labor rights collapse, democracy erodes. Without workplace power, workers become disposable—stripped not only of wages and protections, but of agency, dignity, and trust in democratic systems. The stakes are civic and structural: an economy built on exploitation, a society ruled by concentrated wealth, and a workforce that fears punishment more than it believes in progress.

2. The Structure

The chapter opens with a moral and constitutional framing of labor rights, then traces the long arc of U.S. labor history—from judicial hostility and violent suppression to New Deal gains and postwar rollbacks. It details how conservative forces systematically dismantled worker protections, culminating in Trump-era attacks and the One Big Beautiful Bill. It closes by exposing the global alternatives and the civic collapse caused by worker disempowerment.

3. The Collapse

Labor power in America was not lost by accident—it was dismantled by design. Courts, legislatures, and corporations worked together to suppress organizing, weaken enforcement, and protect employers from accountability. From Taft-Hartley to Trump's anti-union policies to the OBBB, the system now favors capital at every turn. The result: stagnant wages, misclassified workers, algorithmic surveillance, and a workforce with no margin for dissent.

4. The Remedy

- Repeal the OBBB and restore state-level authority to strengthen labor rights
- Enact card-check recognition and speed up union election timelines
- Redefine "employee" to close gig economy loopholes and end forced misclassification
- Raise the federal minimum wage and index it to inflation
- Fund proactive enforcement at OSHA, NLRB, and wage theft units
- Expand portable benefits, paid family leave, and scheduling protections nationwide
- Ban forced arbitration and restore collective bargaining rights for public and federal workers
- Promote industry-wide bargaining models and worker board representation
- Ensure algorithmic transparency and workplace data rights
- Invest in worker education, leadership development, and organizing infrastructure

5. What Comes Next

This chapter exposes the roots of economic inequality and civic decay. The next explores how to rebuild—not just with laws, but with new systems of support, solidarity, and dignity. Later reforms will integrate housing, healthcare, and public employment to ensure that labor power is not isolated. What comes next is the restoration of worker voice—not as nostalgia, but as democratic necessity.

6. Three Things to Remember

1. The collapse of labor power was engineered—not accidental
2. Weak labor rights lead directly to civic disillusion and authoritarian appeal
3. Restoring worker power is essential to restoring democracy

7. Action List

- Repeal Taft-Hartley provisions and ban right-to-work laws
- Pass national legislation to expand OSHA, NLRB, and DOL enforcement budgets
- Implement card-check recognition and protect union organizers from retaliation
- Require gig platforms and contractors to classify workers correctly and provide benefits
- Enforce algorithmic accountability and data rights in the workplace
- Introduce industry-wide bargaining mechanisms and worker board representation

8. Strategic Rationale

Labor rights are not just workplace issues—they are power structures. When workers can organize, they check corporate excess, rebuild community, and anchor democratic participation. These reforms restore balance between capital and labor, shift the burden of risk off the individual, and rebuild solidarity in an economy that currently rewards fragmentation. Structural worker power is the foundation of structural democracy.

9. What You Can Do

Support union drives in your community. Shop from unionized businesses. Pressure lawmakers to raise the minimum wage and protect organizing rights. Challenge forced arbitration clauses in your workplace. Speak publicly against gig misclassification and wage theft. Fund or volunteer with workers' centers, labor alliances, or legal aid for exploited workers. Help rebuild the habits of solidarity that hold democracy together.

10. Further Reading

See *Beaten Down, Worked Up* by Steven Greenhouse, *The Big Squeeze* by Steven Greenhouse, and *State of the Union* by Nelson Lichtenstein. Reports from the Economic Policy Institute, National Employment Law Project, and the Century Foundation provide legal and policy context. For global models, consult ILO publications and EU labor rights overviews.

READER'S GUIDE: **Full Employment and National Contribution**

1. The Stakes
When people are denied the opportunity to contribute, they are denied purpose, agency, and belonging. In a democracy, that denial becomes destabilizing—economically, socially, and politically. This chapter reclaims the right to contribute as a public guarantee, not a market accident. Full employment is not just an economic goal. It is the fulfillment of democracy's promise: that everyone has a role to play in building the future.

2. The Structure
The chapter opens with a powerful contrast between today's gig-based, unstable job market and the public purpose of dignified work. It imagines a country built by empowered labor, then lays out a national plan to match willing workers with public needs. Each section builds toward a vision of a permanent infrastructure for public employment, training, and contribution—funded proportionally, executed professionally, and grounded in democratic values.

3. The Collapse
The current labor market is not merely failing—it is functioning exactly as designed: to reduce costs, discard workers, and maximize profits. Public institutions have accepted this, allowing chronic underemployment, gig precarity, and skill waste to persist. The result is a system that excludes millions from meaningful work, even as national needs go unmet. What we've called "the labor market" has become an engine of waste—of talent, of dignity, and of democracy itself.

. . .

4. The Remedy

- Establish a guaranteed public employment option for all willing workers
- Rebuild the Department of Labor as a matchmaker of labor to national need
- Expand and unify training pipelines across civilian and military systems
- Ensure fair pay, full benefits, and strong performance standards for public jobs
- Deploy workers to unmet public needs: care, infrastructure, climate, education
- Hold public programs to high accountability and efficiency standards
- Fund the system through proportionally tiered taxes on income, not profit
- Offer employment as a covenant of contribution—not a punishment or prize
- Use public employment to raise private-sector standards and drive equity

5. What Comes Next

The next chapters explore how this employment backbone connects to deeper national needs—housing, education, care, and digital infrastructure. Together, they create a society where no one is discarded and no talent is wasted. Full contribution is the moral and practical foundation for every other reform: a functioning democracy must put its people to use in the service of the common good.

. . .

6. Three Things to Remember

1. The job market as it exists is not natural—it is a policy choice
2. Public employment can meet needs markets ignore—without replacing them
3. Matching willing workers with public purpose is a democratic obligation

7. Action List

- Enact legislation creating a national employment guarantee with opt-in access
- Reform tax policy to fund public employment based on income and ability to pay
- Modernize and integrate national training pipelines from school to service
- Create permanent roles in housing, care, climate, and public works sectors
- Establish accountability standards for all public job placements
- Use the public sector as a model employer to raise workplace norms
- Ensure displaced or underutilized workers are retrained, not abandoned

8. Strategic Rationale

This plan restores labor as a pillar of democracy. It ends the cycle of exclusion and instead creates a regenerative loop of training, employment, service, and contribution. It gives people dignity, gives government capacity, and gives the nation resilience. Public employment does not undermine the private sector—it sets a floor that lifts the whole economy. At its heart, this is not about efficiency. It is about shared purpose, visible fairness, and lasting strength.

9. What You Can Do

Talk openly about the value of public work. Defend the dignity of those who build roads, care for the elderly, or teach children. Pressure your representatives to fund and expand employment programs. Vote for candidates who understand that job guarantees are not giveaways—they are investments in the future. Support training centers, public apprenticeships, and worker-led cooperatives. Be ready to advocate for a society where every willing hand has something real to build.

10. Further Reading

Key works include *The Case for a Job Guarantee* by Pavlina Tcherneva, *When Work Disappears* by William Julius Wilson, and *America's Forgotten Working Class* by Joan C. Williams. Also see New Deal histories, Brookings Institution studies on public job programs, and policy proposals from the Roosevelt Institute and Center on Budget and Policy Priorities.

Reader's Guide: **What We Choose to Build Together**

1. The Stakes

If we abandon the connection between education, labor, and democratic capacity, we risk creating a society of compliance, exhaustion, and silence. Without honest schooling and dignified work, people lose not only opportunity but also voice. When that happens, democracy shrinks—and authoritarian control fills the void.

2. The Structure

This summary chapter weaves together the education and labor reforms that preceded it, showing their common foundation in democratic purpose. It names the collapse of schools, debt-laden colleges, and exploitative work as a single betrayal—and then presents the unified alternative: systems built to prepare, empower, and include. It ends with moral clarity and collective resolve.

3. The Collapse

Public education has been politicized and gutted, college has become financially punishing, and labor protections have been stripped. These shifts were not accidental. They emerged from a broader abandonment of democratic aims in favor of economic control. The result is alienation, inequality, and lost civic power.

4. The Remedy

- Restore public education as a universal, equitable, and censorship-free system

- Fund both college and non-college paths as public goods
- Remove predatory lending and privatized profit from postsecondary systems
- Guarantee dignified labor rights, wages, and protections for all workers
- Affirm contribution, learning, and honest work as core to self-government

5. What Comes Next

The next challenge is to build public belief. The infrastructure of learning and labor can be restored—but its purpose must also be reclaimed. Schools must become civic sanctuaries, work must become a site of shared investment, and education must reopen futures, not close them off. That transformation is cultural as well as political.

6. Three Things to Remember

1. Democracy depends on people who believe they matter
2. Labor and education are not costs—they are the republic's foundation
3. Systems of exhaustion and silence serve authoritarian rule

7. Action List

- Fund K–12 education fully and equitably in all states

- Enact federal protections against political interference in school curricula
- Create debt-free public pathways for college, apprenticeships, and training
- End exploitative for-profit education models
- Establish a national job guarantee and strengthen collective bargaining rights
- Legislate fair wages, portable benefits, and just working conditions across all sectors

8. Strategic Rationale

When people are equipped to learn, work, and lead, they cannot be easily ruled. The ability to think, question, earn, and contribute makes democracy function—and protects it from collapse. These reforms are not idealistic extras; they are the tools of collective power and enduring freedom.

9. What You Can Do

Support candidates who champion public education and labor rights. Join or organize within unions, school boards, and civic associations. Challenge narratives that treat work as punishment or education as indoctrination. Talk to others about the connection between daily dignity and democratic possibility—and help restore that link.

10. Further Reading

Read *The Teacher Wars* by Dana Goldstein, *The New Jim Crow* by Michelle Alexander, *Bullshit Jobs* by David Graeber, and *The Sum of*

Us by Heather McGhee. For essays, see "Debt and the American Dream" by Astra Taylor and "The Abandonment of Public Goods" by Keeanga-Yamahtta Taylor.

READER'S GUIDE: PART III. A NATION THAT IS SAFE, JUST, AND FREE

---◆---

Reader's Guide: Part III. A Nation That Is Safe, Just, and Free

1. The Stakes

If justice becomes a weapon and safety becomes a privilege, democracy cannot survive. A nation that protects the powerful while punishing the vulnerable breeds fear, not freedom. When policing becomes domination, when courts become partisan, and when safety is promised only to some, the rule of law collapses—and public trust with it.

2. The Structure

This chapter begins by distinguishing true safety from authoritarian control. It traces how American institutions were corrupted by fear, inequality, and profit—through both policy and design. It builds across domains—policing, gun law, surveillance, courts, cybersecurity, and incarceration—then culminates in a unified reform agenda grounded in equity, restraint, and democratic accountability.

3. The Collapse

What collapsed was the integrity of American justice. From the rise of mass incarceration to Trump's second-term abuses—pardons for insurrectionists, attacks on protesters, repeal of cybersecurity standards, and dismantling of police oversight—systems meant to ensure safety became tools of punishment, profit, and political control.

4. The Remedy

- Restore the purpose of policing through federal standards, independent accountability, and de-escalation
- Reinstate common-sense gun laws: background checks, assault weapon bans, and safe storage mandates
- Rebuild cybersecurity and infrastructure protections to defend elections and public systems
- Ban foreign interference: end shadow lobbying, foreign political donations, and digital propaganda
- Reform the criminal justice system: eliminate cash bail, shrink prisons, restore clemency and restorative justice
- Repeal Trump-era immunity expansions, protest criminalization laws, and anti-transparency measures
- Reinvest in violence prevention, public defenders, and community safety infrastructure

. . .

5. What Comes Next

Future chapters expand the principles outlined here: restoring civil rights enforcement, rebuilding public trust in government, and eliminating systemic impunity. The reforms laid out in this chapter are a hinge point—where survival shifts into renewal. What comes next is institutionalization: making these guarantees durable, equal, and permanent.

6. Three Things to Remember

1. Public safety is not the absence of crime—it is the presence of justice
2. A nation cannot be safe if it is unjust, unaccountable, or armed against its own people
3. Every reform must rebuild trust—not through fear, but through equity, service, and restraint

7. Action List

- Repeal federal and state laws granting broad immunity to law enforcement
- Establish binding national standards for police conduct and use of force
- Restore DOJ civil rights oversight and expand pattern-and-practice investigations
- Pass national gun safety legislation, including universal background checks

- Reinstate funding for red flag laws, community-based violence intervention, and public health-based safety programs
- Reverse 2025 budget cuts to cybersecurity and election protection
- Ban foreign influence in political financing and digital manipulation
- Reform federal sentencing laws, reduce prison populations, and end private prison contracts
- Restore clemency authority and fund restorative justice initiatives in federal courts

8. Strategic Rationale

These reforms do not merely fix policy—they restore legitimacy. Safety rooted in fear breeds authoritarianism; safety rooted in justice rebuilds democracy. Each reform counters a deliberate sabotage of public trust. Together, they bind power to law, law to equity, and equity to the people. This is how democracy survives—and how it lasts.

9. What You Can Do

Support candidates and coalitions committed to police reform, justice equity, and gun safety. Volunteer with organizations fighting mass incarceration and protecting civil liberties. Testify at local government meetings. Advocate for independent police oversight and transparency in your city. Organize against policies that criminalize protest or enable unchecked surveillance. Speak, act, and vote for systems that serve and protect all people—without fear or favor.

. . .

10. Further Reading

The New Jim Crow by Michelle Alexander; *Punishment Without Crime* by Alexandra Natapoff; *Rise of the Warrior Cop* by Radley Balko; *Gunfight* by Adam Winkler; *Digital Disconnect* by Robert McChesney; Brennan Center for Justice reports on policing, protest rights, and election security.

Reader's Guide: To Serve and Protect

1. The Stakes

When public safety becomes a tool of repression, democracy fails. Policing that protects only the powerful, punishes the vulnerable, or silences dissent is not safety—it is control. The test of democracy is whether the law serves the people or merely rules over them. A republic cannot endure when the governed live in fear of those sworn to protect them.

2. The Structure

The chapter begins by reaffirming the democratic purpose of policing and the gap between that ideal and American reality. It traces the collapse of legitimacy—from historical injustice to modern abuses of power under Trump's second term. It then outlines a comprehensive path forward: national standards, civilian oversight, rebalanced roles, and structural reforms that rebuild both safety and trust.

3. The Collapse

Policing in America collapsed under the weight of impunity, inequality, and political abuse. From qualified immunity to militarized tactics, from criminalizing protest to defunding oversight, the system has been designed to protect itself—not the people. Trump's second term made this collapse national policy, codifying surveillance, force, and silence as the new definition of public safety.

4. The Remedy

- Establish national policing standards: de-escalation, duty to intervene, constitutional training
- Abolish qualified immunity and strengthen legal accountability for misconduct
- Tie federal funding to transparency, equity, and community-based outcomes
- Empower civilian oversight boards with subpoena power and disciplinary authority
- Prohibit rehire of officers fired for cause across jurisdictions
- Expand non-police crisis response teams for mental health, housing, and addiction
- Redirect funding from militarization to training, prevention, and community trust
- Create a Public Safety Innovation Fund to research and scale non-carceral models
- Appoint and confirm judges committed to accountability and equal protection

5. What Comes Next

This chapter lays the groundwork for restoring equal justice—not just in policing, but across the justice system. Future chapters address incarceration, courts, civil rights, and surveillance. Each builds on this premise: safety without justice is tyranny, and reform is not an attack on order—it is a defense of the Constitution and the people it serves.

6. Three Things to Remember

1. The badge does not exist above the Constitution—it exists to uphold it
2. Real safety comes from dignity, opportunity, and care—not domination or fear
3. Reform is not anti-police—it is how democracy reclaims control from impunity

7. Action List

- Pass federal legislation ending qualified immunity and requiring national standards
- Repeal state laws that criminalize protest or shield police from discipline
- Fund community-based public safety programs and civilian response models
- Require public reporting on stops, arrests, force, and complaints by all departments
- Ban no-knock warrants, chokeholds, and the use of military equipment in schools
- Appoint oversight-minded federal judges and watchdogs to DOJ civil rights posts
- Amend state laws that allow rehiring of fired officers without full review
- Enact legal bans on retaliatory punishment of police whistleblowers
- Create federal grants tied to reduction in harm, not increase in arrests

8. Strategic Rationale

Policing is the front line of government. If it is unjust, democracy is hollow. These reforms reclaim public safety for the people—by ensuring that those entrusted with power are trained, constrained, and held accountable. Reform is not surrender. It is sovereignty. A democracy polices with the people, not against them.

9. What You Can Do

Join local efforts to establish police oversight, reduce school policing, and expand non-criminal crisis response. Advocate for federal accountability legislation. Volunteer with civil rights organizations and legal defense funds. Support leaders committed to transparency and justice. Push your city or county to track and publish public safety data. Speak against fear-based policies that trade freedom for control. Real safety begins with real voices—yours among them.

10. Further Reading

Policing the Black Man, ed. Angela J. Davis; *The End of Policing* by Alex Vitale; *Locking Up Our Own* by James Forman Jr.; Vera Institute reports on community alternatives; Campaign Zero's policy frameworks.

READER'S GUIDE: **Justice That Heals**

1. The Stakes

When policing breaks trust, the result is not just injustice—it is fear, escalation, and cycles of harm. A democracy cannot sustain legitimacy if its agents of safety are experienced as sources of threat. If we fail to fix policing, we will continue to lose lives, erode public trust, and sabotage our own ideals of justice, restraint, and liberty for all.

2. The Structure

This chapter begins with the broken promise of protection and the misplaced burden placed on police. It exposes the dangers of scope, fear, and militarization before offering a full reconstruction of the policing role. Each paragraph advances a solution—narrowing duties, redefining response, raising standards, rebuilding trust, and honoring both community safety and officer dignity.

3. The Collapse

American policing has become a force of overreach, reacting to every crisis while lacking the training and boundaries to respond well. Untrained enforcement in mental health, addiction, and social tension creates unnecessary conflict and danger. Militarization, low training standards, fragmented oversight, and burnout make trust and safety impossible—for both civilians and officers.

4. The Remedy

- Redefine emergency response with a new non-police number (e.g., 987) for social and mental health crises
- Demilitarize departments and end the Pentagon pipeline for military gear
- Require national peace officer licensure with civil rights, trauma, and de-escalation training
- Ban chokeholds, no-knock warrants, and undocumented detentions
- Mandate body cameras and create independent civilian oversight boards
- Reassign community safety tasks (e.g., traffic enforcement) to non-police systems
- Establish long-term community policing teams and neighborhood presence
- Create a national Justice Corps of unarmed first responders
- Increase police pay and wellness support while raising expectations
- Reform training culture from combat readiness to peace readiness

5. What Comes Next

Restoring public trust will take time. Even the best reforms will face cultural resistance, political attacks, and operational challenges. What comes next is long-term accountability, constant re-evaluation, and commitment to justice over expedience. The next chapter expands this vision beyond policing—toward a justice system built not to punish, but to heal.

6. Three Things to Remember

1. Safety comes from skill and service, not fear or domination
2. Reform means narrowing the role, not abandoning it
3. Real trust requires structural change, not cosmetic shifts

7. Action List

- Pass federal legislation for national officer certification and ongoing training
- End military surplus transfers to local police departments
- Establish and fund 987 response systems with civilian crisis teams
- Create binding use-of-force standards enforceable nationwide
- Fund state or regional civilian oversight bodies with investigative authority
- Provide grants for community-based public safety infrastructure
- Tie federal funding to compliance with transparency and restraint standards

8. Strategic Rationale

A democratic society cannot rely on fear-based enforcement. Public trust must be built structurally, not assumed. When we reduce the role of policing to what it can do well—and reassign the rest—we create a safer, more just system that honors constitutional rights and community dignity. Reform is not softness. It is precision.

. . .

9. What You Can Do

Join or support local efforts for police oversight and crisis response reform. Attend city council meetings. Advocate for co-response programs and unarmed mental health teams. Support candidates who prioritize community safety and civil rights. If you're a professional in law, health, or social services, explore roles in the future Justice Corps.

10. Further Reading

See *The End of Policing* by Alex S. Vitale, *Policing the Black Man* edited by Angela J. Davis, and *Tangled Up in Blue* by Rosa Brooks. For systemic alternatives, read *We Keep Us Safe* by Zach Norris and recent articles from the Brennan Center for Justice and the Marshall Project.

READER'S GUIDE: The Weaponization of a Nation

1. The Stakes

Gun violence is not a cultural tragedy. It is a policy failure. The mass deaths of children, the terror of schools and churches, and the normalization of weapons in public life are not the price of freedom —they are the cost of political corruption. A functioning democracy cannot survive when the machinery of death is protected more fiercely than the lives of its people.

2. The Structure

This chapter begins with the original purpose of the Second Amendment, traces its distortion through political movements, Supreme Court rulings, and legislative betrayals, and ends with a damning portrait of a country addicted to violence for profit. The final paragraphs confront global comparisons, cultural disfigurement, and the future we lose if this continues.

3. The Collapse

What was once a safeguard against federal overreach has become a weapon of political and commercial abuse. The gun industry profits from death, the courts have enshrined a fraudulent reading of the Constitution, and Congress is complicit. Children are buried. Survivors become activists. Fear is normalized. And the violence continues—not by accident, but by design.

4. The Remedy

- Repeal PLCAA and allow civil lawsuits against negligent gun manufacturers and dealers
- Ban civilian access to assault-style weapons and high-capacity magazines
- Create a national gun licensing, registration, and insurance system
- Enact mandatory safe storage laws and require trigger locks
- Require background checks for all gun purchases, including private and online sales
- Fund gun buyback programs at the federal, state, and municipal level
- Restore and expand research funding into gun violence as a public health issue
- Prohibit open carry and expand red flag laws with due process protections
- Ban gun sales to those with histories of domestic violence, stalking, or extremist affiliation
- Require national reporting of lost, stolen, or trafficked firearms

5. What Comes Next

There will be fierce resistance. The industry will sue. Extremists will threaten. But lives will be saved. Each reform reduces risk. Each regulation slows the cycle. The next chapter will show how justice reform, police reform, and gun reform must advance together—toward a public safety model rooted in service, not domination.

6. Three Things to Remember

1. The Second Amendment was written for militias—not unregulated individual arsenals
2. Gun violence is preventable; other nations have proven this
3. Profiteers and politicians have built and protected this crisis—for money and power

7. Action List

- Repeal or amend PLCAA to permit legal accountability for the gun industry
- Pass a new federal assault weapons ban with sunset-proof enforcement
- Enact universal background checks and close the private sale loophole
- Fund community-based violence interruption programs
- Create a national firearms registry with insurance and renewal requirements
- Ban political contributions from gun manufacturers and their affiliates

8. Strategic Rationale

Gun violence corrodes every public space—from schools to stores, buses to ballot boxes. It breeds fear, silences protest, and fuels authoritarianism. Disarming this crisis is not about confiscation. It is about restoration: of peace, of trust, of constitutional balance. No reform matters if people are too afraid to gather, speak, vote, or live freely.

. . .

9. What You Can Do

Support grassroots gun reform groups, especially those led by survivors. Pressure your state legislature to adopt licensing, safe storage, and red flag laws. Demand your federal representatives act to repeal PLCAA and restore an assault weapons ban. Vote for candidates who put children before corporations. Join vigils, rallies, and survivor campaigns to keep the pressure visible and personal.

10. Further Reading

See *Gunfight* by Adam Winkler, *The Second Amendment: A Biography* by Michael Waldman, and *Enough* by Gabrielle Giffords. For data and reform advocacy, consult Everytown for Gun Safety, the Giffords Law Center, and the Johns Hopkins Center for Gun Violence Solutions.

Reader's Guide: **A Future Without Fear**

1. The Stakes

No modern democracy tolerates unchecked violence from within. A nation that regulates cars, elevators, and pharmaceuticals must also regulate machines designed to kill. The current system is not freedom—it is failure. Licensing, registration, and insurance for every gun are not radical measures. They are the bare minimum of a society that values life more than profit, and justice more than fear.

2. The Structure

The chapter begins with a simple analogy: we regulate every dangerous device except guns. It then lays out a comprehensive, rights-respecting framework: licensing by weapon type, registration linked to ballistic data, mandatory insurance with victim compensation, national buybacks, international responsibility, and educational reform. It ends by reclaiming safety, civic duty, and life without fear.

3. The Collapse

Gun violence continues because the system is designed to protect industry, not the public. Manufacturers are shielded, owners are unaccountable, and no national standards exist. While children drill for death in schools, the industry faces no liability and no obligation to change. This reform makes explicit what should have been obvious all along: responsibility must be real.

4. The Remedy

- Require licensing for every gun owner, with practical and written tests
- Register all firearms to legal owners, linked to ballistic and transaction records
- Mandate liability insurance, with variable premiums and a national compensation fund
- Repeal PLCAA and allow victims to sue manufacturers and dealers for negligence
- Launch a two-year amnesty and subsidized compliance transition
- Fund federal buybacks and safe surrender options for unregistered weapons
- Impose national standards for weapon safety, childproofing, and theft prevention
- Regulate advertising and restrict glorification of violence or political manipulation
- Ban international exports to unauthorized actors and close the "sporting use" loophole
- Integrate de-escalation and gun safety into school curricula and community programs

5. What Comes Next

The following chapters will address justice reform, police restraint, and broader questions of national belonging. But this chapter marks a turning point. No lasting safety, dignity, or democracy is possible when death is easy, consequence is rare, and violence is profitable. The next step is not to fear the future—but to build one worthy of trust.

6. Three Things to Remember

1. Guns remain almost entirely unregulated compared to other dangerous technologies
2. Responsibility does not mean confiscation—it means standards, proof, and care
3. Real reform starts with structure: licensing, registration, insurance, and oversight

7. Action List

- Pass national gun licensing and registration laws with tiered training requirements
- Repeal PLCAA and restore civil liability for gun industry negligence
- Create a national gun harm insurance fund supported by industry and excise taxes
- Ban high-risk advertising and cap political donations from gun manufacturers
- Close export loopholes and restrict U.S. weapons sales to vetted government buyers

8. Strategic Rationale

The United States leads the world in gun violence because it leads in gun deregulation. That is not cultural inevitability. It is policy design. Every country that has restructured its laws has seen violence drop. Licensing, insurance, and accountability are not threats to liberty—they are the tools that ensure it survives in a world where fear is no longer the governing force.

. . .

9. What You Can Do

Support political candidates who back full-spectrum gun reform, not just background checks. Attend town halls and demand state compliance with licensing, insurance, and storage laws. Join organizations pushing for PLCAA repeal and weapon safety innovation. Participate in buyback campaigns. And make clear that this issue is not about partisan identity—it is about whether a nation chooses to protect life or enable death.

10. Further Reading

Recommended: *Gunfight* by Adam Winkler, *Loaded* by Roxane Dunbar-Ortiz, and *Bleeding Out* by Thomas Abt. For data and policy models, consult Everytown, Giffords Law Center, and the Johns Hopkins Center for Gun Violence Solutions. International comparisons: Australia's 1996 reforms and Japan's licensing structure.

READER'S GUIDE: Cybersecurity and Infrastructure Protection

1. The Stakes

When invisible systems fail, lives are disrupted without warning. Power grids crash. Hospitals lose patient data. Votes disappear or are doubted. If infrastructure collapses—whether from attack, neglect, or decay—trust in democracy collapses with it. A government that cannot keep its systems working cannot keep its promises. And when failure becomes normal, fear replaces confidence. A republic cannot function on panic and improvisation. It must guarantee reliability, even when no one is looking.

2. The Structure

This chapter begins by reframing democracy not as a set of visible rituals, but as a foundation of functioning, often unnoticed systems. It then examines real-world cyber and infrastructure failures—foreign attacks, aging software, and privatized neglect—before exploring why these risks persist. The chapter builds from observation to indictment, ending with a call for public responsibility, federal standards, and a national strategy rooted in protection, not patchwork.

3. The Collapse

Critical systems in the United States—power grids, election platforms, hospitals, and pipelines—have become vulnerable to failure and attack. Many are privately owned, poorly regulated, and run on outdated software. Hackers succeed. Cities are held hostage. Yet no unified defense exists. Deregulation, decentralization, and profit motives have left the country exposed. When breaches occur, there is little accountability. Instead, the public absorbs the risk—and the damage.

4. The Remedy

- Establish national cybersecurity and infrastructure protection standards
- Mandate baseline federal security for all critical systems —public and private
- Create a national audit cycle with emergency funding for upgrades
- Enforce penalties for noncompliance and negligent vulnerabilities
- Implement real-time threat tracking and breach response coordination
- Integrate cybersecurity into national defense frameworks
- Require paper backups and physical redundancies in voting systems
- Centralize accountability without eroding local implementation
- Treat protection as a public duty, not a private burden

5. What Comes Next

Even with stronger protections, the threat landscape will evolve. Breaches will still occur. The test will be how we respond—not whether failure happens, but how often, how severely, and how recoverable. What remains is to establish resilience as national infrastructure policy: not just reacting to the last failure, but preparing for the next one. The next chapters continue this work—

strengthening democratic stability through truth, transparency, and leadership that does not exploit collapse but prevents it.

6. Three Things to Remember

- Democracy relies on systems you don't see—until they fail.
- Sabotage is profitable when standards are weak and oversight is missing.
- Protection is not a partisan issue. It is the silent foundation of trust.

7. Action List

- Pass federal legislation mandating security standards for all critical infrastructure
- Establish and fund a National Infrastructure Protection Agency
- Require cybersecurity compliance audits for private contractors managing public systems
- Mandate paper backups for all election equipment
- Penalize companies and agencies that fail to secure essential systems
- Coordinate state and federal response protocols to breaches and attacks
- Fund training, drills, and emergency simulation programs nationwide
- Create public reporting and transparency dashboards for system integrity

· · ·

8. Strategic Rationale

Without secure infrastructure, democracy fails from within. Systems must be reliable enough to disappear into the background—so that people can live, vote, and work without fear of collapse. A national strategy must make resilience the default and coordination the norm. This is not only about defending against hackers—it is about preventing decay, ensuring continuity, and rejecting the myth that government cannot function. We either defend our systems—or lose them.

9. What You Can Do

Advocate for federal standards by contacting your representatives. Support state legislation requiring paper ballot backups. Vote for local officials who prioritize infrastructure modernization. Attend town halls on local utilities, school IT, or public health networks to ask about cybersecurity protections. Report phishing scams and suspicious activity. Encourage public transparency around system failures—demand answers when they occur. Public pressure, when focused, can shift the balance from patchwork to prevention.

10. Further Reading

Read *Sandworm* by Andy Greenberg for a look at state-sponsored cyberwarfare, *This Is How They Tell Me the World Ends* by Nicole Perlroth for a history of the cyber arms race, and *Click Here to Kill Everybody* by Bruce Schneier for accessible proposals on digital security in a connected world. For policy work, see reports by the Center for Strategic and International Studies and the Aspen Institute's Cybersecurity Group.

Reader's Guide: **The Cybersecurity Redemption Plan**

1. **The Stakes**

If the U.S. fails to secure its digital infrastructure, the consequences will not be limited to data loss or inconvenience. Lives are at stake—from hospital outages to water contamination, from corrupted voter rolls to grounded air traffic. The collapse of digital trust would erode not only safety, but democracy itself. Every breach weakens public confidence. And once belief in the reliability of systems is lost, it may never return.

2. **The Structure**

The chapter opens by exposing the myth of secure, privately managed systems. It then recounts repeated failures in key infrastructure, followed by comparisons to successful international models. It calls for urgent U.S. action grounded in public accountability and national coordination, before concluding with a powerful call to rebuild both infrastructure and the public trust it sustains.

3. **The Collapse**

Private management of public systems has proven inadequate. Hospitals, schools, pipelines, and power grids have suffered repeated breaches. No mandatory standards exist. Companies self-police, conceal failures, and treat cybersecurity as a cost issue. The federal government lacks the authority and structure to enforce national protection. Catastrophe is no longer a question of if—but when.

4. **The Remedy**

- Establish a centralized, civilian-led national cybersecurity authority

- Create mandatory breach audits, threat testing, and enforcement powers
- Launch a full national inventory of digital infrastructure vulnerabilities
- Fund paper backups, secure communications, and stress tests
- Require breach disclosure with penalties for concealment
- Mandate transparency from any private entity managing public systems
- Build a civilian cybersecurity corps through service pipelines and retraining
- Form a Cyber Defense Compact with international allies for coordination

5. What Comes Next

Even with strong systems in place, vigilance cannot lapse. Threats will evolve. What comes next is a commitment to permanence—ensuring infrastructure security is not reactive or partisan, but embedded into national governance. Future chapters explore the broader challenge of rebuilding civic trust and truth itself in the digital age.

6. Three Things to Remember

1. The U.S. is the only major democracy without mandatory cybersecurity enforcement
2. Private profit models have repeatedly failed to secure public systems
3. The greatest breach may not be technical—it may be the collapse of belief

. . .

7. **Action List**

- Create a permanent federal cybersecurity authority with audit and enforcement powers
- Pass breach disclosure laws for all critical infrastructure sectors
- Fund local cybersecurity teams and national training programs
- Require all infrastructure vendors to meet public standards and allow inspection
- Mandate paper fallbacks and resilience plans for voting, health, and emergency systems
- Establish international cybersecurity partnerships for shared threat response

8. **Strategic Rationale**

Democracy depends on systems the public can trust—health records, courts, ballots, communication. If those systems are vulnerable, so is the republic. Only national coordination, civilian oversight, and enforced standards can defend public infrastructure from escalating threats. This is not regulation; it is the foundation of democratic legitimacy in the digital age.

9. **What You Can Do**

Support candidates who advocate for civilian cybersecurity leadership and mandatory infrastructure protections. Demand transparency from utilities, hospitals, and local governments about breach readiness. Ask your school district, city, or county what cyber plans exist—and what's missing. Advocate for digital literacy, ethical hacking education, and paper backups for essential services in your community.

10. Further Reading

See *This Is How They Tell Me the World Ends* by Nicole Perlroth for a gripping account of global cyber vulnerabilities. Read *Sandworm* by Andy Greenberg on Russia's attacks on Ukraine and the implications for Western infrastructure. For policy insight, consult reports by the Center for Strategic and International Studies and the Aspen Institute's Cybersecurity Group.

READER'S GUIDE: Defending Democracy from Foreign Interference

1. The Stakes

When foreign interference infiltrates a democracy, the damage goes beyond stolen data or votes—it shatters public trust. Citizens no longer know what is real, who to believe, or whether their voices matter. The result is paralysis, cynicism, and surrender. If the United States fails to protect its information environment and electoral systems, it risks becoming a country that still holds elections—but no longer believes in them.

2. The Structure

The chapter begins by tracing the erosion of democratic legitimacy through foreign influence campaigns, beginning with Russia's 2016 operation. It then outlines the failure of both political parties to adequately respond, the convergence of foreign and domestic threats under Trump, and the rise of authoritarian tactics worldwide. The final sections describe the inadequacy of current defenses and propose concrete reforms to safeguard truth, elections, and public belief.

3. The Collapse

U.S. democracy was infiltrated by foreign actors using digital tools to manipulate voters, sow division, and weaken belief in fair elections. The government failed to respond with urgency or unity. Agencies were politicized. Platforms backed away from protections. And a sitting President not only benefited from the sabotage—he invited and amplified it. The result is a democracy still vulnerable, still fragmented, and still unprepared for what comes next.

. . .

4. The Remedy

- Establish a national Democracy Defense Agency
- Mandate transparency on platforms: funding sources, foreign origins, coordinated activity
- Require real-time takedowns of foreign-controlled political assets
- Fully fund secure election systems: paper ballots, audits, local capacity
- Penalize domestic use of foreign-sourced material in campaigns
- Impose consequences on platforms that allow known interference
- Support independent journalism and restrict foreign ownership of news outlets
- Teach information literacy in schools and adult education
- Ban unverifiable voting machines and standardize audit procedures

5. What Comes Next

Even the best defenses will not stop all future interference. The next frontier is cultural resilience: building a democratic culture that prizes truth, resists manipulation, and refuses to reward those who use foreign lies for domestic gain. This includes deep civic education, media reform, and the creation of shared norms that treat democracy not as background noise—but as a treasure that must be defended daily.

. . .

6. Three Things to Remember

1. Foreign interference does not always steal votes—it steals belief.
2. Domestic actors now echo and amplify foreign sabotage.
3. Protecting democracy means defending truth, not just ballots.

7. Action List

- Pass legislation to establish a nonpartisan Democracy Defense Agency
- Require disclosure and moderation of foreign-funded or inauthentic political content
- Penalize campaigns that accept or use foreign assistance
- Fund cybersecurity and auditing in every voting jurisdiction
- Ban unverifiable digital-only voting systems
- Regulate social media political advertising during elections
- Block foreign ownership of U.S. political media platforms
- Expand and fund civics and media literacy education

8. Strategic Rationale

A democracy cannot function without a shared belief in its legitimacy. By hardening both technical infrastructure and public understanding, the United States can prevent hostile actors from collapsing its institutions through digital manipulation. These reforms create resilience—against foreign interference, domestic opportunism, and the slow erosion of trust that destroys a republic from within.

9. What You Can Do

Call for platform transparency and demand that your representatives support strong anti-interference legislation. Share verified information. Support independent media. Learn how to spot manipulation and teach others. If you volunteer during elections, advocate for better cybersecurity and clear audit trails. And when misinformation spreads—online or in conversation—don't stay silent. Correct it. The defense of democracy begins with you.

10. Further Reading

Read *The Road to Unfreedom* by Timothy Snyder, *LikeWar* by P.W. Singer and Emerson Brooking, *Information Wars* by Richard Stengel, and *Active Measures* by Thomas Rid. For investigative reporting, see articles from ProPublica, The Atlantic, and Just Security on digital interference and electoral sabotage. These works detail both the threats and the tools to resist them.

Reader's Guide: The Defense We Still Need

1. The Stakes

Democracy cannot function without trust—in votes, in truth, in the legitimacy of outcomes. Foreign interference attacks that trust at its foundation. What once required spies and violence can now be achieved with memes and deepfakes. If America fails to defend its elections and its information environment, democracy may remain in form but die in function. The threat is not hypothetical. It has already happened—and it is still happening now.

2. The Structure

The chapter opens with a constitutional framing of the right to self-rule, followed by the historical record of Russian interference in 2016 and the lack of unified response. It then tracks the deepening sabotage under Trump, the collapse of platform integrity, and the rise of foreign-aligned digital propaganda. The chapter closes with nine major areas of reform—from federal election security to a Democracy Defense Agency—and a moral call to defend truth as infrastructure.

3. The Collapse

Russian operatives successfully disrupted the 2016 election through cyberattacks, propaganda, and racial division. Trump and his allies denied it, benefited from it, and eventually invited it again. Disinformation defenses were dismantled. Platforms sold out truth for profit. Domestic actors echoed foreign lies. The agencies that once guarded democracy were weakened from within. Today, interference is not an external threat—it is an internal partnership.

. . .

4. The Remedy

- Create a national, independent Democracy Defense Agency
- Require transparency: origin labels, funding disclosure, and bot takedowns
- Fully fund secure elections with paper ballots and national audit standards
- Ban unverifiable digital-only voting systems
- Penalize domestic actors who use or solicit foreign interference
- Enforce election misinformation policies on platforms with real penalties
- Support a free, verified, and independent press; limit foreign ownership
- Mandate information literacy in schools and public education
- Restrict platforms from hosting political disinformation without consequence

5. What Comes Next

New technologies—from deepfakes to AI-fueled propaganda—will make interference easier, faster, and harder to detect. The only path forward is comprehensive defense: technical, institutional, educational, and cultural. This chapter lays out a roadmap for building public resilience, regulatory backbone, and a new democratic infrastructure that values clarity over chaos and integrity over engagement.

6. Three Things to Remember

1. Foreign interference now comes through platforms, not planes.
2. Domestic actors amplify foreign lies—and profit from the chaos.
3. Democracy requires more than ballots—it requires a defended public mind.

7. Action List

- Pass legislation establishing a Democracy Defense Agency
- Fund election security: paper ballots, audits, and staff training
- Require transparency and labeling for all political content on major platforms
- Ban unverifiable voting machines and regulate high-risk periods
- Enforce legal penalties for candidates or campaigns that use foreign-sourced materials
- Require social media platforms to moderate and remove known disinformation
- Support and protect independent, truth-based journalism
- Implement mandatory media literacy curricula nationwide

8. Strategic Rationale

Foreign sabotage exploits American division, indifference, and deregulation. But it can only succeed when we let it. By establishing clear defenses—technical, institutional, and civic—we make the cost of interference too high to be worthwhile. These reforms do not restrict liberty. They defend it, by protecting the conditions under which democracy remains real. The stronger our defenses, the more resilient our republic becomes.

9. What You Can Do

Support platform accountability and demand real penalties for disinformation. Call your representatives to fund federal election defenses and transparency mandates. Share verified sources. Educate others on spotting propaganda. Back journalism that informs rather than inflames. Vote for leaders who tell the truth—even when it's hard. And when lies spread—especially from within—stand up. The defense of democracy begins not with law, but with conscience.

10. Further Reading

Recommended: *The Road to Unfreedom* by Timothy Snyder, *Active Measures* by Thomas Rid, *LikeWar* by P.W. Singer and Emerson Brooking, and *Network Propaganda* by Yochai Benkler. For real-time research and digital threat monitoring, follow the Atlantic Council's Digital Forensic Research Lab, Just Security, and the Stanford Internet Observatory. These offer critical insight into foreign manipulation, platform accountability, and democratic defense.

READER'S GUIDE: **The Collapse of Criminal Justice**

1. The Stakes

A democracy that jails the poor, profits from pain, and punishes by design cannot call itself just. The American criminal justice system has become a machinery of exclusion—targeting race, poverty, and vulnerability while shielding wealth and power. What began as a constitutional promise of liberty and equal protection has mutated into a system that treats harm as failure, cages as treatment, and obedience as the price of freedom. Without transformation, justice becomes a performance, and punishment becomes our national creed.

2. The Structure

The chapter opens with a constitutional contrast: promised liberty versus lived injustice. It traces how post-slavery punishment became a tool of labor and control, then walks through modern failures—cash bail, racial disparities, and pretrial detention. Historic parallels with Victorian England deepen the critique. It then exposes the bipartisan escalation of incarceration from Nixon to Trump, revealing five systemic distortions. The chapter closes with Trump's direct cruelty, the profit motives behind mass incarceration, and a final indictment: this is not justice, but domination in disguise.

3. The Collapse

Justice in America was never neutral. From the 13th Amendment's exception clause to the war on drugs, incarceration has been used to control, exploit, and silence. Pretrial detention jails the poor. Prosecutors target the vulnerable. Corporations profit from confinement. And Trump has used the system not to uphold law, but to reward allies and threaten dissent. Every promise of justice—speedy trial, equal protection, public safety—has been twisted into tools of fear and profit. This is not a broken system. It is one working exactly as designed.

4. The Remedy

- Abolish cash bail and guarantee the right to a speedy trial
- End for-profit prisons, prison labor exploitation, and corporate contracts tied to incarceration
- Eliminate mandatory minimums and three-strikes laws
- Fund public defenders at parity with prosecutors
- Expand alternatives to incarceration: drug courts, mental health treatment, restorative justice
- Reform prosecutorial discretion and require racial impact audits
- Create national standards for sentencing, parole, and compassionate release
- Dismantle federal incentives that reward high incarceration rates
- Prohibit law enforcement donations from bail, prison, and telecom industries

5. What Comes Next

Justice must be rebuilt—not as punishment, but as prevention, restoration, and fairness. This chapter lays bare the failures, the distortions, and the profiteering that created mass incarceration. The next chapter proposes a full transformation: rebuilding safety from the ground up, ending punishment-for-profit, and making dignity a requirement of law. To reclaim legitimacy, America must finally treat justice as a public good—not a private enterprise, not a fear campaign, and not a political weapon.

6. Three Things to Remember

1. American justice punishes poverty while protecting privilege.
2. Incarceration has become both a business and a political tool.
3. Real safety comes from dignity, not domination.

7. Action List

- Pass legislation to abolish cash bail and limit pretrial detention
- Defund and phase out all private prison contracts at the federal and state level
- Restore federal oversight of prosecutorial and police conduct
- Invest in public defense, mental health courts, and community-based alternatives
- Require racial impact statements for all criminal justice legislation
- Create independent commissions to review wrongful convictions and extreme sentencing
- Enact laws to block donations from industries that profit from incarceration

8. Strategic Rationale

Punishment has been mistaken for safety. But mass incarceration has delivered neither. It has devastated families, drained public funds, and entrenched inequality. The real sources of harm—poverty, trauma, neglect—are not solved by cages. Reform is not about leniency. It is about effectiveness, fairness, and decency. America's credibility depends on the ability to deliver justice that protects the public and honors human dignity. Without it, fear will rule—and freedom will die.

9. What You Can Do

Support bail reform efforts and public defenders in your state. Vote for prosecutors and judges who prioritize equity and alternatives to incarceration. Challenge corporate donations to lawmakers from prison and bail industries. Learn how local jails and prisons are funded. Back candidates who treat criminal justice as a human rights issue—not a soundbite. Talk openly about harm, healing, and what real justice should look like. A better system will not build itself. It needs you.

10. Further Reading

Recommended: *The New Jim Crow* by Michelle Alexander, *Locked In* by John Pfaff, *Are Prisons Obsolete?* by Angela Davis, and *Punishment Without Crime* by Alexandra Natapoff. For policy research and reform campaigns, follow the Vera Institute of Justice, Equal Justice Initiative, and The Sentencing Project. These organizations offer data, analysis, and pathways to real accountability and repair.

Reader's Guide: Justice That Restores

1. The Stakes

Justice is the foundation of democratic legitimacy. Yet in America, it has been contorted into retribution, exclusion, and profit. Our current system punishes rather than repairs, isolates rather than restores. It undermines safety, corrodes dignity, and perpetuates harm. The reform chapter insists on a reversal—not just of tactics, but of purpose. Justice must no longer mean cages and cruelty. It must mean responsibility, healing, reentry, and renewal. If we fail to build a justice system worthy of the name, democracy itself will remain stained and unstable.

2. The Structure

The chapter opens with a moral reset: punishment has failed, and restoration must become our aim. It moves from constitutional principle to structural critique, showing how wealth, race, and suffering are used as tools of control. It outlines 12 reform pillars—from bail and sentencing to parole, restorative justice, and reentry. It weaves international models into its argument, demonstrating that safety is built through care, not fear. The final paragraphs affirm that justice must be measured by how many lives we help rebuild—not how many people we destroy.

3. The Collapse

A system built on incarceration cannot claim justice. Pretrial detention punishes poverty. Mandatory minimums erase human context. Private prisons turn suffering into profit. Homelessness, addiction, and mental illness are treated not with care, but with confinement. Probation is a trap. Parole is a threat. And the wealthy walk free while the vulnerable fall. The current system does not prevent harm—it perpetuates it. As long as justice is defined by fear and control, the cycle will continue.

4. The Remedy

- Replace cash bail with risk-based assessment and supervision
- Eliminate mandatory minimums and restore judicial discretion
- End private prisons and predatory prison economics
- Invest in alternatives to incarceration: diversion, treatment, stabilization
- Rebuild probation and parole as support systems, not traps
- Normalize restorative justice, especially for youth and first-time cases
- Expand automatic expungement of nonviolent records
- Fund robust reentry: housing, ID, therapy, jobs, mentorship
- Restore voting rights to all who have served their sentence
- Apply accountability to white-collar and institutional crime
- Adopt best practices from Germany, Norway, New Zealand, Portugal, and the Netherlands
- Redefine safety as prevention, care, and community repair—not just punishment

5. What Comes Next

This chapter marks a shift—from punishment to prevention, from cruelty to care. It proposes a system that still holds people accountable, but refuses to define them by their worst moment. The next steps are clear: rewrite sentencing laws, remove profit incentives, invest in mental health and housing, and make reentry real. Most of all, the work ahead demands a renewed belief—that people can return, rebuild, and belong. Justice, in this vision, is not abandoned. It is reclaimed.

6. Three Things to Remember

1. Safety is created through care, not cages
2. Accountability without cruelty is both possible and essential
3. Justice must restore people, not discard them

7. Action List

- Repeal cash bail and mandatory minimum sentencing laws
- Defund and ban for-profit prisons and exploitative prison contracts
- Expand community-based treatment and diversion programs
- Pass laws to restore voting rights and erase nonviolent records
- Require every jurisdiction to offer restorative justice alternatives

- Fund reentry programs with housing, jobs, and ID access as standard
- Enforce equal accountability for white-collar and institutional crimes
- Study and adopt international best practices in rehabilitation and recidivism prevention

8. Strategic Rationale

Mass incarceration is not just ineffective—it is corrosive. It drains resources, destabilizes families, and undermines democracy. True safety is not reactive. It is preventative, inclusive, and humane. When justice is restorative, communities are stronger, recidivism declines, and dignity is preserved. These reforms aren't naïve. They're proven, cost-effective, and moral. The system we have was built by policy. It can be rebuilt by policy too—if we remember that its purpose is not vengeance, but repair.

9. What You Can Do

Advocate for bail reform and restorative justice in your state. Volunteer with reentry programs or support second-chance hiring in your community. Help returning citizens access housing, work, and mental health services. Push your representatives to end mandatory minimums and restore judicial discretion. Speak openly about the difference between accountability and cruelty. The more we normalize care, the more we can demand it. A just system is not inevitable—it is built by people who choose it.

10. Further Reading

Key works include *Until We Reckon* by Danielle Sered, *The Little*

Book of Restorative Justice by Howard Zehr, and *Just Mercy* by Bryan Stevenson. For real-world models, study reports from the Vera Institute of Justice, the Equal Justice Initiative, and the Justice Lab at Columbia University. Explore international examples in the work of Penal Reform International and comparative criminal justice studies. These sources show what works—and what must change.

Reader's Guide: **A Justice That Holds**

1. The Stakes

Safety is not something we command. It is something we build. It emerges from systems that hold—not just courts and prisons, but housing, health care, digital security, and public trust. This chapter reframes public safety not as a product of fear or force, but as the outcome of fairness, opportunity, and restraint. It insists that real justice is not a show of dominance, but a culture of repair. If we want to live in a country where safety is real and equal, we must dismantle the structures that profit from fear and build new ones that protect dignity, belonging, and truth.

2. The Structure

The chapter opens with the definition of safety as a system, not a slogan. It links together all prior reforms—guns, policing, courts, digital systems, and disinformation—as parts of one structure that must hold. It diagnoses despair as the root of much harm and identifies justice systems as the place where every social failure converges. It critiques profit-driven punishment and false ideas of order. It proposes a new narrative of repair, one grounded in care, prevention, and inclusion. The conclusion is both moral and structural: if justice is to hold, it must do so with truth, accountability, and design—not fear.

3. The Collapse

America's current safety infrastructure is brittle and selective. It isolates public safety from the social systems that sustain it, then calls for more punishment when those systems fail. Police are overburdened, courts are overloaded, and prisons are used to disappear the vulnerable. Fear is sold as safety, cruelty as justice. The result is not order, but instability. Wealth shields some from consequence while others are trapped in permanent suspicion. This is not justice. It is erosion.

4. The Remedy

- Redefine public safety as a structural goal, not a policing tactic
- Link justice reforms to systems of care, housing, education, and health
- Train and equip police to de-escalate, not dominate
- Require licensing, registration, and insurance for gun ownership
- Remove profit motives from prisons, policing, surveillance, and punishment
- Treat addiction, poverty, and illness with support—not force
- Build resilient civic infrastructure: water, power, transit, digital networks
- Enforce accountability for the powerful, not just the vulnerable
- Center stories of prevention, healing, and restoration in public discourse
- Rebuild public trust through truth, transparency, and structural fairness

5. What Comes Next

Justice must stop collapsing under pressure. Each reform in this book is part of that repair: criminal justice, policing, gun laws, cyber protections, democratic safeguards. But the work is not just legislative. It is cultural. It demands we replace fear with care, remove despair at its roots, and restore faith in belonging. A just nation is not built on firepower or vengeance. It is built on the systems that hold when tested—and the courage to build them before the next collapse.

6. Three Things to Remember

1. Safety is not force—it is structure
2. Despair is not criminal—it is a policy failure
3. Justice must hold everyone—or it holds no one

7. Action List

- Pass national gun safety legislation rooted in accountability, not fear
- Fund community-based mental health, housing, and addiction services
- Repeal policies that profit from incarceration or surveillance
- Support truth-based digital governance and protect elections
- Require accountability and training standards for law enforcement
- Advocate for public investment in civic and cyber infrastructure
- Shift public safety narratives from threat to trust and prevention

. . .

8. Strategic Rationale

A nation that protects only through punishment is not safe—it is brittle. Real safety is built through structural strength: truth, access, care, and dignity. These are not vague ideals; they are proven pillars of resilient, low-violence societies around the world. The United States must stop selling safety as spectacle and start building it as infrastructure. This agenda links every reform together in one architectural goal: to create systems that hold. When safety is defined this way, justice becomes not an exception, but the norm.

9. What You Can Do

Challenge narratives that equate justice with cruelty or safety with surveillance. Support local and national reforms that invest in care-based alternatives. Push for police accountability, truth in media, and humane reintegration of those returning from prison. Defend the infrastructure that keeps communities whole—from clean water to accurate voting systems. Speak up for fairness, especially when it is unpopular. The more people believe safety is possible without cruelty, the more possible it becomes.

10. Further Reading

For broader context and policy depth, explore *The End of Policing* by Alex S. Vitale, *We Do This 'Til We Free Us* by Mariame Kaba, and *What Doesn't Kill Us Makes Us* by Stephanie Foo. Institutional reports from the Brennan Center, the ACLU, and the Council on Criminal Justice provide strong evidence-based blueprints. For restorative justice, look to the work of Common Justice, and for democratic infrastructure, consult the Center for Humane Technology and the National Task Force on Election Crises.

READER'S GUIDE: PART IV. READER'S GUIDE: A NATION THAT BELONGS TO EVERYONE

Reader's Guide: A Nation That Belongs to Everyone

1. The Stakes

Belonging is not sentiment. It is structure. And in the United States, that structure is crumbling. The systems that once promised safety, truth, and shared inheritance—immigration, information, and the environment—have been dismantled, monetized, and turned against the public. This chapter makes the case that belonging must be restored not as metaphor but as mandate. A democracy cannot survive if people are denied entry, misled by lies, or poisoned by neglect. Reclaiming the foundations of shared citizenship is not idealism. It is survival.

. . .

2. The Structure

The chapter opens with America's legacy as a nation of arrivals and expands the definition of belonging across three arenas: immigration, digital space, and public land. It tracks the turn from welcome to exclusion, from digital equality to manipulation, and from shared stewardship to corporate extraction. Each collapse is traced not only to systemic drift but to deliberate sabotage—accelerated and institutionalized under Trump's leadership. The chapter closes by naming the true pattern: a structural theft of the commons and a coordinated attack on democratic belonging. The call is clear: restore, reclaim, and rebuild—before it's too late.

3. The Collapse

America's immigration system has become a pipeline of cruelty. Its digital spaces have been handed over to propagandists and profiteers. Its public lands and environmental protections have been hollowed out by deregulation, delay, and corruption. What unites these domains is not just exclusion but extraction. At every turn, public resources—people, truth, land—have been captured and sold. Belonging has been redefined as privilege. And the very tools meant to protect the public have been turned into weapons of denial.

4. The Remedy

- Restore humane, lawful, and inclusive immigration processes
- Remove profit motives from detention, deportation, and border enforcement
- Guarantee legal protection for asylum, naturalization, and family unity

- Enforce transparency, accountability, and legal responsibility for online platforms
- Require algorithmic auditing and public-interest governance of digital systems
- Ban political targeting, manipulation, and paid disinformation campaigns
- Re-establish federal leadership in environmental and public land protection
- End subsidies for extraction and enforce polluter accountability
- Reclaim public space and restore it as infrastructure of belonging

5. What Comes Next

The reforms proposed in the next three chapters are not isolated policies. They are a coordinated answer to coordinated theft. We do not restore belonging by gesture or nostalgia. We do it by rebuilding the institutions that uphold truth, protect life, and welcome difference. A republic cannot survive without shared ground—literal and figurative. Immigration, information, and land are where this battle is being fought. And if we win it, we restore the right to exist, to know, and to belong.

6. Three Things to Remember

1. Belonging is not charity—it is citizenship
2. Public trust, truth, and land are being stolen for profit
3. Reclaiming them is patriotic, not radical

7. Action List

- Advocate for lawful, humane, and accessible immigration reform
- Pressure lawmakers to regulate digital platforms in the public interest
- Support climate legislation that prioritizes protection over profit
- Challenge narratives that criminalize migration or delegitimize truth
- Protect Indigenous rights and restore oversight of public lands
- Fight for environmental justice and against disinformation
- Organize in defense of the commons—digital, legal, and natural

8. Strategic Rationale

A nation that denies belonging cannot sustain democracy. That denial takes many forms: legal exclusion, disinformation, pollution, privatization. But all share the same aim—concentrated power. Restoring democratic belonging means reclaiming the systems, spaces, and stories that allow people to live with safety, dignity, and voice. These reforms are not about returning to a mythical past. They are about honoring a constitutional future—where all persons are protected, informed, and included.

9. What You Can Do

Support immigrant rights organizations, environmental watchdogs, and tech accountability coalitions. Share verified information.

Report disinformation. Contact your representatives. Vote for candidates who defend the commons, not corporations. Push local governments to protect green space and digital access. Make your voice heard in defense of public truth and public trust. And speak with moral clarity: this country is not theirs to hoard. It is ours to reclaim.

10. Further Reading

For deeper understanding, read *This Land Is Our Land* by Suketu Mehta, *Algorithms of Oppression* by Safiya Noble, and *The Ministry for the Future* by Kim Stanley Robinson. Explore reports from the Center for American Progress, the Brennan Center for Justice, and the Electronic Frontier Foundation. For action, look to organizations like the National Immigration Law Center, Earthjustice, and Accountable Tech.

READER'S GUIDE: **Immigration and Citizenship**

1. The Stakes

When immigration policy abandons fairness, it is not only newcomers who suffer—it is the rule of law itself. Constitutional protections extend to all persons, not just citizens. When due process is denied, suspicion replaces justice. When cruelty is institutionalized, democratic legitimacy erodes. A nation built by immigrants cannot survive the betrayal of its own legal and moral foundation without losing part of its identity, its coherence, and its soul.

2. The Structure

The chapter begins with the constitutional principles that apply to all people under U.S. jurisdiction, then traces the long arc of American immigration—from its exclusionary origins to fragile moments of hope. It exposes the intentional destruction of that hope under Trump's two presidencies, especially through bureaucratic sabotage and profit-driven cruelty. The chapter closes with a demand for lawful restoration grounded not in sentiment, but in justice and constitutional duty.

3. The Collapse

America's immigration system failed through decades of neglect, but under Trump, cruelty became policy. Legal processes were obstructed, asylum gutted, and detention privatized for profit. In his second term, bureaucracy conceals the harm—hearings delayed, applications denied, families separated. Courts are politicized. Naturalization is chilled. And the system rewards cruelty while silencing protest. This is not policy failure. It is a deliberate machinery of exclusion.

4. The Remedy

- Establish one immigration agency with unified oversight and public accountability
- Restore due process and judicial independence in immigration courts
- Eliminate arbitrary quotas and backlogs
- Make naturalization timely, accessible, and fair
- End private detention and surveillance profiteering
- Reverse second-term citizenship restrictions that undermine voting rights
- Separate immigration policy from political influence
- Recognize immigrants as part of the nation, not a threat to it

5. What Comes Next

The harm continues—and hardens. Cruelty has shifted from spectacle to silence, from overt bans to buried delays. The next chapter must do more than respond. It must rebuild. That means redesigning institutions, not just restraining abuse. It means removing financial incentives for harm and restoring the visibility, fairness, and moral clarity that democracy demands. We must remember: this is not a fringe issue. It is a constitutional test.

6. Three Things to Remember

1. Immigration policy is not a gift—it is a legal obligation grounded in constitutional rights
2. Trump turned bureaucratic cruelty into a political and financial machine
3. What is enforced now is not law, but exclusion, suspicion, and erasure

7. Action List

- Repeal or reverse second-term administrative changes that block naturalization
- Dissolve overlapping agencies and establish a single accountable immigration authority
- Prohibit profit-driven detention and surveillance contracting
- Restore asylum protections and judicial independence
- Provide permanent status for longtime residents under Temporary Protected Status
- Mandate due process standards and fair hearing procedures across all immigration courts
- Remove politically motivated performance metrics for immigration judges
- Prohibit voter suppression laws that misuse immigration data

8. Strategic Rationale

A democracy must define itself by how it treats the vulnerable. When immigration policy becomes a tool of cruelty and profit, it hollows out the institutions it touches—courts, enforcement, citizenship. Restoring lawful, humane, and independent immigration systems is not only about the border. It is about national integrity, civic inclusion, and the survival of pluralism as a democratic ideal.

9. What You Can Do

Join or support legal aid organizations that help immigrants navigate the system. Share accurate information to counter disinformation campaigns. Pressure local, state, and national officials to protect immigrants from federal overreach. Vote for candidates who defend due process and oppose profit-driven enforcement. If you're part of an institution—school, union, church—organize to create sanctuary policies or sponsorship programs for at-risk individuals.

10. Further Reading

Separated by Jacob Soboroff and *The Line Becomes a River* by Francisco Cantú offer urgent firsthand accounts of immigration enforcement's human toll. J.J. Mulligan Sepúlveda's *No Human Is Illegal* explores the moral and legal dimensions of citizenship and identity. Articles like "The Business of Detention" (The Marshall Project) and "Trump's Second-Term Immigration Plans" (Just Security) reveal the systemic cruelty and ongoing transformation of U.S. immigration policy into a profit engine.

READER'S GUIDE: **Immigration and Citizenship**

1. The Stakes

Immigration is not a marginal issue—it is a test of whether the United States remains a nation of law, dignity, and inclusion. If we deny lawful process to those who seek it, we forfeit our constitutional integrity. If we exploit immigrant labor while denying status and safety, we abandon moral legitimacy. A democracy cannot survive the contradiction of exclusion by design. The question is no longer whether immigrants belong—it is whether we are ready to build a system worthy of them, and of ourselves.

2. The Structure

The chapter begins by asserting the constitutional basis for immigrant protections and then outlines the moral, legal, and historical role of immigration in building America. It exposes the cruelty baked into current systems and explains why clarity and fairness must replace fear and delay. The solution is not open borders but open law—one transparent agency, clear timelines, dignified procedures, and strict accountability for employers who profit from abuse. The final paragraphs frame immigration as the test, not the exception, of democracy.

3. The Collapse

Decades of dysfunction enabled cruelty, but Trump made it the business model. Detention became profit. Courts became barriers. Legal immigration was sabotaged by delay, denial, and politicized enforcement. Employers exploited fear. Protesters were surveilled. And constitutional guarantees were replaced by bureaucratic evasion. Immigration under Trump's second term hardened into a silent machinery of exclusion—one where the appearance of law concealed the erosion of justice.

4. The Remedy

- Establish a single, accountable Immigration and Citizenship Agency
- End profit-driven detention and deportation contracting
- Enforce statutory timelines for asylum, work permits, and naturalization
- Guarantee automatic work authorization while cases are pending
- Create a legal pathway to citizenship for longtime undocumented residents
- Remove arbitrary country caps and increase visa availability
- Transfer workplace enforcement to the Department of Labor and prosecute abusers
- Prioritize border professionalism and restore asylum protections
- Expand integration through language access, civics education, and an Immigrant Service Corps
- Make citizenship timely, accessible, and a public priority

5. What Comes Next

The politics of fear will not vanish on their own. They must be replaced—by moral clarity, legal consistency, and visible success. This reform is not a gift. It is a return to the rule of law and democratic coherence. If we claim to be a nation of laws, we must apply them fairly. If we claim to welcome those who contribute, we must offer them a path to belong. No democracy survives by abandoning the people it depends on. And no future is safe if built on hypocrisy.

6. Three Things to Remember

1. Immigration is not the exception to democracy—it is the test of it
2. Bureaucratic cruelty is not policy failure—it is the business model
3. A lawful system must be clear, consistent, accountable, and rooted in dignity

7. Action List

- Dissolve overlapping immigration agencies and create a single accountable authority
- Repeal caps and delays that discriminate by country of origin
- Codify legal status and a citizenship path for DACA and mixed-status families
- Require statutory processing deadlines and public case tracking
- Penalize employers who exploit undocumented labor and shield workers from deportation
- Shift workplace enforcement to the Department of Labor
- Expand access to legal counsel and interpretation in immigration proceedings
- End private detention and reallocate funding toward humane infrastructure

- Build integration pathways through public service and language access
- Restore asylum rights and invest in trauma-informed border personnel

8. Strategic Rationale

Immigration is not a disruption to national identity—it is a reaffirmation of it. For two centuries, it has built the labor force, enriched the culture, and renewed the idea of America as a place where freedom and contribution lead to belonging. Reform is not about generosity. It is about constitutional duty and democratic survival. To restore the republic, we must restore the systems that define who can join it, who is protected by it, and what kind of nation we choose to be.

9. What You Can Do

Support immigrant advocacy and legal defense funds. Volunteer translation, housing, or transport for local immigrants facing court dates or application hurdles. Demand your representatives back legal clarity and constitutional protections—not performative cruelty. Expose companies that exploit immigrant labor. Share stories that humanize and protect. Join efforts to end private detention and to restore timely, fair, and lawful access to citizenship. Democracy must be built by everyone—or it will be denied to many.

10. Further Reading

Dear America: Notes of an Undocumented Citizen by Jose Antonio Vargas offers a powerful personal account of living in the United States without legal status. *The Far Away Brothers* by Lauren

Markham documents the lives of unaccompanied minors navigating a broken asylum system. Reports from the Migration Policy Institute and articles from the Marshall Project and Just Security provide ongoing analysis of the immigration landscape, reforms, and legal battles.

READER'S GUIDE: **The Collapse of Online Safety and Trust**

1. The Stakes

The digital world is no longer optional. It is where we learn, work, vote, parent, protest, and grieve. But it is not safe. In the United States, digital life is governed by algorithms, not laws—by profit, not public duty. Truth is drowned out by lies designed for reach. Children are preyed on. Immigrants, veterans, and parents are targeted with tailored disinformation. And those who depend on digital tools are blamed when the system fails them. This is not the future. It is the present. And if we do not govern it now, every other democratic reform will fall apart in a sea of fear, confusion, and unreality.

2. The Structure

This chapter opens by reframing the internet as a lived environment, not a neutral tool. It proceeds through escalating examples of digital abandonment—emotional, civic, medical, and democratic. Each section reveals how platforms, protected by legal immunity and driven by profit, incentivize manipulation over safety and lies over truth. The chapter then identifies the political beneficiaries of this chaos, especially the Republican Party and Trump's second-term assault on oversight and reality. It ends with a moral and civic call to design trustworthy digital infrastructure—because no reform can hold if the public cannot find or trust the truth.

3. The Collapse

Safety, trust, and truth have been abandoned online. Not by accident, but by design. The current digital system prioritizes engagement over accuracy, manipulation over transparency, and profit over protection. Platforms mine outrage. Algorithms fragment reality. Political actors exploit chaos. And government abdicates its duty to protect. The result is a captured, dangerous, and unequal information environment—one that punishes the trusting, endangers the vulnerable, and makes democracy impossible to sustain.

4. The Remedy

- Revoke blanket platform immunity when algorithms amplify harm
- Require full transparency for digital ads, targeting practices, and political funding
- Establish a public digital safety agency to audit, enforce, and protect public standards
- Fund independent disinformation research with guaranteed access to platform data
- Mandate algorithmic transparency, user control tools, and opt-out options
- Prohibit surveillance advertising targeting children and medically vulnerable users
- Enforce safety audits for platforms used in schools, healthcare, and civic services
- Penalize digital fraud, harassment, and doxxing with enforceable civil and criminal remedies
- Require public reporting of content removals, appeals, and moderation outcomes
- Overturn state-level protections for propaganda, political deepfakes, and platform negligence

5. What Comes Next

Until we build trustworthy digital infrastructure, democracy remains at risk. Every reform—on health, labor, housing, or justice—depends on public understanding and civic clarity. But when truth is distorted, lies monetized, and platforms protected from consequence, no policy can gain stable ground. The next chapter outlines a public framework for digital accountability, platform transparency, and algorithmic governance—without censorship, without control, and without delay.

6. Three Things to Remember

1. The digital world is not optional—it is the infrastructure of modern life
2. Disinformation is not accidental—it is profitable, targeted, and politically defended
3. Truth, safety, and belonging must be designed—not assumed

7. Action List

- Revoke platform immunity when harm is algorithmically amplified
- Mandate public transparency for digital ads, targeting, and funding
- Fund independent disinformation research and restore access to platform data
- Create a public digital safety agency to monitor, audit, and enforce standards
- Require algorithmic disclosure and opt-out tools for users

- Penalize digital fraud, doxxing, and harassment with civil remedies and enforcement
- End state-level laws that punish moderation and shield propaganda
- Require platforms to publish content removal metrics and appeals processes
- Prohibit surveillance advertising for children and medically vulnerable groups
- Enforce safety audits for platforms used in schools, hospitals, and public services

8. Strategic Rationale

A democracy that lives online must govern online space. Otherwise, it surrenders its citizens to digital ecosystems designed to deceive, exploit, and divide. This is not a fight over speech, but over structure. Regulation does not mean censorship—it means the public, not profit, sets the rules. Just as clean water laws don't control what people drink, but ensure it won't poison them, platform standards must ensure safety, truth, and reliability in the digital world we now all inhabit.

9. What You Can Do

Support nonprofit digital watchdogs and investigative journalists. Share verified resources and debunk disinformation within your own circles. Call on your representatives to support platform transparency, algorithmic audits, and disinformation research. Refuse to share content you can't verify—especially if it provokes fear or rage. Advocate for your school boards, libraries, and workplaces to adopt safer platform tools. Digital safety is not just a tech issue—it is the new battleground for democracy, dignity, and belonging.

10. Further Reading

Antisocial by Andrew Marantz explores how online extremists exploit free speech frameworks to radicalize and recruit. *The Chaos Machine* by Max Fisher investigates the role of algorithms in manipulating human behavior and accelerating polarization. Ongoing reporting by *The Markup* and research from the *Center for Countering Digital Hate* provide timely insights into how platforms are weaponized—and how they can be held accountable.

READER'S GUIDE: **The Restoration of Online Safety and Trust**

1. The Stakes

If digital systems remain unsafe and ungoverned, every part of modern life—education, healthcare, elections, parenting—will continue to be distorted by fear, manipulation, and inequality. Children will be harmed. Voters will be misled. Marginalized communities will face targeted abuse. The very fabric of trust, belonging, and democratic participation will fray, leaving society vulnerable to exploitation by those who benefit most from chaos and deceit.

2. The Structure

The chapter begins by reframing the internet as a lived environment, not a neutral tool. It then builds a layered case for reform, moving from access and safety to algorithmic governance, legal accountability, advertising regulation, child protection, and First Amendment grounding. International examples bolster plausibility, while the conclusion reinforces urgency: digital reform is essential to every other democratic repair.

3. The Collapse

Digital life has outpaced law, ethics, and public oversight. Platforms profit from outrage, lie amplification, and targeted exploitation, while evading accountability under outdated legal shields. Vulnerable groups bear the greatest harm, especially children, low-income users, and non-English speakers. The internet has become an unsafe, unequal place—one where profit outweighs protection, and disinformation overwhelms truth.

. . .

4. The Remedy

- Redefine the internet as a governed environment, not a neutral service
- Guarantee universal broadband access and community connectivity
- Ensure algorithmic transparency and user control over content sorting
- Prohibit monetization and amplification of known falsehoods
- Update legal frameworks: hold platforms accountable for what they promote
- Require child-safe design and ban exploitative tracking
- Extend truth-in-advertising standards to all digital ads
- Mandate platform audits, risk mitigation, and ad traceability
- Protect speech while regulating systemic harm—distinguishing ideas from infrastructure

5. What Comes Next

The work of reform is only beginning. Future challenges include refining liability standards, strengthening data rights, and securing protections across evolving platforms like AI, VR, and immersive spaces. Continued resistance from tech giants and disinformation-driven political factions will demand strategic perseverance. But without these changes, no other reform can fully succeed.

6. Three Things to Remember

1. The internet is no longer optional—it is where people live
2. Unsafe digital systems undermine every other public good
3. Reform does not silence speech—it protects people and the truth

7. Action List

- Pass national broadband equity and access legislation
- Amend Section 230 to reflect platform amplification responsibility
- Enact child safety laws for digital platforms and content
- Create transparency requirements for algorithmic systems
- Extend FTC advertising rules to all digital ads and platforms
- Establish independent oversight bodies for platform audits
- Fund and protect disinformation research and public digital literacy
- Align U.S. law with international best practices like the Digital Services Act

8. Strategic Rationale

Digital reform secures the informational foundation of democracy. It restores conditions under which free speech, civic trust, and fair participation can exist. Without structural rules for access, safety, and accountability, every other democratic institution—elections, courts, journalism, education—remains exposed to distortion, corrosion, or collapse from within a poisoned digital environment.

9. What You Can Do

Contact your representatives to demand comprehensive digital safety legislation, including broadband access and Section 230 reform. Support organizations promoting algorithmic accountability and media literacy. Report harmful content and fraudulent ads. Advocate for your local school to teach online safety and critical media skills. Help others navigate digital systems fairly and safely—especially children, elders, and non-native English speakers.

10. Further Reading

For deeper context, see *Surveillance Capitalism* by Shoshana Zuboff, *The Chaos Machine* by Max Fisher, *Antisocial* by Andrew Marantz, and *Weapons of Math Destruction* by Cathy O'Neil. Key articles include "The Internet Is Broken" by Emily Bell (The Atlantic) and reports from the Center for Humane Technology and Mozilla Foundation on algorithmic bias and platform transparency.

Reader's Guide: **Environmental Injustice and a Broken Climate Policy**

1. The Stakes

If the United States continues to subsidize collapse while calling it balance, the cost will be measured not only in floods and fires—but in public trust, lost lives, and democratic decay. A system that protects polluters and abandons the vulnerable cannot claim to be just. Without reform, climate injustice will deepen inequality, dismantle public health, and expose the most fragile parts of the country to compounding devastation.

2. The Structure

The chapter opens with a constitutional reframing: environmental collapse as a betrayal of core civic promises. It then traces America's former leadership in environmental law, followed by the rise of fossil dominance, environmental racism, and the bipartisan failure to act. Trump's first and second terms receive detailed attention, as do Congressional, state, and judicial sabotage. The conclusion delivers a sweeping but personal reckoning—climate collapse as lived harm, not distant theory.

3. The Collapse

What began as bipartisan environmental progress has been reversed by a fossil-fueled system that rewards profit, evades responsibility, and defers the cost to the public. Laws have been dismantled. Agencies defunded. Communities sacrificed. Trump's return has accelerated the destruction—but it began before him and extends beyond him. The collapse is not accidental. It is designed.

. . .

4. The Remedy

- Repeal fossil fuel subsidies and redirect funding to clean energy
- Restore and strengthen the EPA, NEPA, and the Council on Environmental Quality
- Rejoin and comply with the Paris Agreement with binding legislative commitment
- Enforce environmental justice protections for frontline and Indigenous communities
- Expand disaster preparedness funding and climate resilience infrastructure
- Require climate risk disclosures for corporations and insurers
- End federal leasing for oil, gas, and coal on public lands
- Create legal liability for climate misinformation and pollution harms
- Protect national parks and sacred sites from extractive development
- Fund local transitions to clean energy, prioritizing jobs and affordability

5. What Comes Next

The transition away from fossil rule will not be smooth, but it is necessary—and already overdue. Future work must include legal pathways for redress, expanded international cooperation, and irreversible protections against corporate sabotage. Most of all, it must re-center public purpose in environmental policy, affirming that survival and justice—not delay and deregulation—define a functioning democracy.

. . .

6. Three Things to Remember

1. Environmental collapse is constitutional collapse—it threatens rights and representation
2. Fossil dominance is not accidental—it is protected by law, subsidy, and silence
3. Justice requires accountability: for pollution, policy sabotage, and public betrayal

7. Action List

- Repeal oil and gas subsidies through federal budget and tax reform
- Pass national climate justice legislation with enforcement power
- Restore NEPA and environmental review requirements stripped under Trump
- Protect sacred, tribal, and public lands from extractive leases
- Support litigation against polluters and disinformation networks
- Expand FEMA, DOE, and local climate resilience programs
- Fund frontline communities and ensure equitable access to clean energy
- Require financial institutions to disclose climate-related risks and investments

8. Strategic Rationale

Climate justice is not a separate issue—it underlies housing, health, infrastructure, and democracy itself. A society cannot claim legitimacy while protecting polluters over people. Restoring environmental law is not about regulation for its own sake. It is about defending life, equality, and national stability. Reform must break the legal and financial hold fossil industries have on the public future—and build a system designed for sustainability, not sabotage.

9. What You Can Do

Demand that your representatives end fossil fuel subsidies, strengthen environmental protections, and fund climate adaptation in vulnerable communities. Support local climate justice organizations and Indigenous land defenders. Vote in state and local elections that shape land use, zoning, and energy policy. Learn which banks and insurers fund fossil expansion—and move your money accordingly. Speak up when your parks, water, and future are treated as expendable.

10. Further Reading

See *This Changes Everything* by Naomi Klein, *After Geoengineering* by Holly Jean Buck, and *Losing Earth* by Nathaniel Rich. Articles like "Pollution Is Colonialism" by Max Liboiron and "The Climate Gap" by Rachel Morello-Frosch deepen the justice frame. For public data and accountability tools, explore reports by the Environmental Integrity Project and the U.S. Climate Vulnerability Index.

READER'S GUIDE: **A Nation That Belongs to Everyone**

1. The Stakes

Climate collapse is not simply environmental—it is civic. Belonging, mobility, and public access are being eroded by a fossil economy that still dominates transportation, land use, and tax policy. The future will not be decided by ideology but by infrastructure—who moves, who breathes clean air, and who is included in public life. This chapter lays out a path not only for ending fossil dependence, but for restoring public purpose to public space.

2. The Structure

The chapter opens with a redefinition of climate justice as civic justice—replacing exclusion with access. It moves from tax reform to transportation, detailing a nationwide public transit plan, clean last-mile delivery, and a new class of transit officers. It then turns to public land restoration, access, and equity—including car-free visitation to national parks and community-based EV sharing. The chapter closes with a moral and structural reframing of climate work as a civic transition rooted in justice.

3. The Collapse

The current fossil economy forces individuals to subsidize their own harm. Through tax law, transit inaccessibility, and privatized land use, millions are excluded from clean air, affordable mobility, and public space. Belonging is conditional on car ownership, fossil fuel consumption, and distance from extraction zones. These are policy choices—not inevitabilities. And they can be undone.

. . .

4. The Remedy

- End all fossil fuel subsidies and restore progressive tax rates
- Direct fossil windfall taxes to national clean infrastructure investments
- Build public transit in all U.S. cities over 900,000 residents
- Cap transit fares at $0.50 per ride or $10 per week
- Train a national workforce through public colleges and union apprenticeships
- Create a new class of non-police transit officers for safety and support
- Expand public electric delivery of groceries, medicine, and essentials
- Ban future fossil leases without full ecological restoration and bonding
- Permanently bar repeat violators from new public land leases
- Fund conservation and ecotourism jobs in formerly extractive regions
- Provide rural counties payments-in-lieu-of-extraction for preservation
- Create a National Parks Transit Program with internal electric mobility
- Build ADA-accessible routes and car-free options for park access
- Launch community-based EV share and rental networks for special needs
- Make public mobility optional, affordable, and dignified for all

5. What Comes Next

A just transition cannot rely on emissions targets alone. It must prioritize the experience of those who live within the system being replaced. Public investments in transit, access, and land stewardship must be measured not just by carbon reduced, but by freedom restored—especially for those historically excluded. As new infrastructure is built, the public must be visible, present, and protected—not priced out or left behind.

6. Three Things to Remember

1. Climate justice requires infrastructure justice—mobility, access, and repair
2. Public land and public movement must be reclaimed from fossil dominance
3. The path to belonging is built—not imagined—and it must be open to all

7. Action List

- Repeal all fossil fuel subsidies and pass fossil windfall taxation
- Fund and build public transit in major cities with capped fares
- Expand ADA, senior, and low-income access to national parks and forests
- Launch publicly owned electric delivery and EV share programs
- Restore public land damaged by past extractive leases using bonded funds

- Prohibit new leases to companies with restoration violations
- Invest in rural preservation and ecotourism to replace extractive income
- Build infrastructure that centers mobility, dignity, and safety for all

8. Strategic Rationale

Ending fossil dominance means ending forced participation in unjust systems. A society that traps people into car ownership, denies transit access, and locks up public land behind paywalls and emissions is not free. These reforms rewire the civic economy—restoring autonomy through transit, restoration through public investment, and belonging through shared space. They do not punish drivers or exclude rural Americans—they provide alternatives to dependence, isolation, and exclusion. That is how we reclaim democracy in the climate era.

9. What You Can Do

Support ballot initiatives, bond measures, and local referenda that expand clean transit, fund park access, and prohibit new fossil leases. Advocate for inclusive transit design and national funding for public transportation infrastructure. Donate to groups defending tribal lands, challenging extractive leases, or improving ADA park access. If possible, use and support car-share, rail, and clean delivery systems. Push for tax equity and public redirection of fossil wealth toward climate justice.

10. Further Reading

See *The Ministry for the Future* by Kim Stanley Robinson and *Green New Deal and Beyond* by Stan Cox. Transportation equity is explored in *Right of Way* by Angie Schmitt and climate access in *A Planet to Win* by Aronoff, Battistoni, Cohen, and Riofrancos. For public lands and justice, explore *The Land Was Ours* by Andrew W. Kahrl and reporting from Grist and High Country News on park access, transit equity, and fossil lease reform.

READER'S GUIDE: **The Belonging We Build**

1. The Stakes

When a nation excludes, surveils, or pollutes entire communities, it fractures the promise of democracy itself. This chapter reveals how belonging—real belonging—is not symbolic, but structural. What's at stake is the lived ability of every person to participate, thrive, and be protected. If we fail to build systems that affirm personhood, truth, and shared space, we do not merely divide the country—we dismantle it.

2. The Structure

This chapter completes the fourth section of the book by linking three critical domains—immigration, digital governance, and environmental justice—into a unified argument about structural inclusion. It begins with the legal failures of immigration policy, moves through the collapse of digital safety, and ends with the privatization of public lands and environmental harm. Each domain is analyzed for its systemic betrayals, then reconstructed with specific reforms that together define what modern belonging requires.

3. The Collapse

Immigration policy has become punishment. The digital sphere has become a weapon. The environment has become collateral. These collapses are not accidental—they result from decades of political sabotage, corporate influence, and systemic neglect. People are excluded through unjust deportation and blocked naturalization, manipulated by algorithms, exploited for profit, and displaced by environmental degradation. Each form of harm disproportionately affects the vulnerable, and each undermines the foundation of democratic life.

4. The Remedy

- Create a single, constitutional immigration agency
- Guarantee due process and timely naturalization for immigrants
- Unify immigration systems under rule of law, not fear
- Establish universal broadband access
- Impose algorithmic transparency and liability for digital harm
- Protect children and users from surveillance and manipulation
- Ensure accountability for platform-driven deceit
- Invest in affordable public transit and clean transportation
- Restore and protect national parks, trails, and shared lands
- Tax windfall profits and reclaim fossil fuel subsidies to fund transition
- Reframe public space as essential to democracy and access

5. What Comes Next

The fight for belonging does not end with access. It extends into enforcement, accountability, and lived experience. The systems proposed must be defended against rollback and strengthened to withstand political manipulation. The next chapters move from public belonging to strategic reinstitution—ensuring these reforms are not temporary, but enduring. Belonging, once built, must be protected.

6. Three Things to Remember

1. Belonging is not sentiment—it is structure, access, and dignity
2. Exclusion today is legal, digital, and environmental, not just rhetorical
3. We do not restore democracy unless all people can safely live, move, and speak within it

7. Action List

- Legislate a unified federal immigration agency grounded in constitutional law
- Overhaul digital governance with enforced transparency and harm liability
- Enact child safety protections and platform accountability laws
- Invest in universal broadband as public infrastructure
- Redirect fossil fuel subsidies toward clean energy and transit
- Impose windfall and pollution taxes to fund public space and mobility
- Protect and expand access to national parks, forests, and waterways

8. Strategic Rationale

These reforms confront the systems that define who belongs in America. By rebuilding immigration, digital space, and shared land as inclusive public functions, we reinforce democracy's legitimacy and resilience. They protect against domination by powerful interests and ensure that access to safety, voice, and mobility cannot be hoarded. Structural belonging is not charity—it is constitutional integrity.

9. What You Can Do

Support immigrant justice organizations working on legal representation, advocate for platform transparency laws at the state level, and join local environmental or transit coalitions expanding public space. Share your voice in public comment processes, contact elected officials about funding clean infrastructure, and educate others about the connection between access, justice, and democracy. Reclaiming belonging starts close to home.

10. Further Reading

See *Separated* by Jacob Soboroff for the human cost of immigration cruelty, *The Age of Surveillance Capitalism* by Shoshana Zuboff for the privatization of digital life, and *This Land* by Christopher Ketcham for the capture of public space. Additional insight can be found in *Algorithms of Oppression* by Safiya Umoja Noble and reports by the Center for American Progress on digital and environmental justice.

READER'S GUIDE: PART V. A NATION THAT PREPARES FOR THE FUTURE

―――― ✦ ――――

Reader's Guide: Part V: A Nation That Prepares for the Future

1. The Stakes

Democracy cannot survive if it treats the future as inevitable or ungovernable. The technologies reshaping our lives—AI, surveillance, algorithmic systems—are not neutral. They carry values, shape choices, and create risks that law and culture must confront. This chapter warns that if we do not assert moral control over technology, we risk surrendering truth, privacy, civic agency, and even democratic self-rule. The future is not a passive destination. It is a test of whether we still believe in shaping a world where self-government is possible, where people—not platforms—decide what kind of society we live in.

· · ·

2. The Structure

The chapter opens with a warning against fatalism: that the future is a force beyond our control. It then uses cultural touchstones—Orwell, *The Terminator*, *WarGames*—to trace how fictional fears have become real threats. It details the collapse of public readiness and institutional capacity, and argues that preparation must begin with digital governance and civic renewal. The final paragraphs reassert agency, calling for ethical design, public training, and deliberate invention of a democratic future. It closes with a powerful moral statement: we may not control invention, but we can shape what we allow and who we become.

3. The Collapse

The chapter names the collapse of democratic capacity in the face of rapid technological change. Truth is fragmented, privacy is sold, and surveillance is normalized. Regulation lags far behind invention. AI systems already make critical decisions with minimal oversight or ethical constraint. Meanwhile, the public is unprepared: children lack civic grounding, elders are digitally excluded, and institutions are overwhelmed. Fiction warned us—but in reality, we outsourced the danger to markets and platforms that reward division, distraction, and predictive control. The result is a slow-motion surrender of democratic sovereignty to unaccountable systems.

4. The Remedy

- Reject the myth that the future is inevitable or ungovernable
- Govern digital systems with laws rooted in rights, not profits

- Regulate artificial intelligence with enforceable ethical constraints
- Reclaim data privacy as a democratic right
- Close the gap between technological power and civic understanding
- Train the public—especially youth—in civic, moral, and digital literacy
- Reinvigorate public service and civic engagement as a generational mission
- Center public purpose in innovation and infrastructure
- Restore democratic control over truth, knowledge, and accountability

5. What Comes Next

The next chapters develop the two core solutions named here: digital governance and public service renewal. We will examine how to ensure technology serves democracy, not replaces it—and how to rebuild a civic culture capable of shaping the world to come. These reforms are not abstract ideals. They are urgent, concrete tools for defending truth, privacy, and self-government in the digital age. Our final goal is not to resist the future, but to govern it—ethically, deliberately, and together.

6. Three Things to Remember

1. Technological change is not neutral—it reflects and reinforces values
2. Democracy collapses when truth, privacy, and public purpose are lost

3. Preparing the future means training people to think, serve, and govern

7. Action List

- Pass enforceable legislation regulating AI, data ownership, and surveillance
- Establish a federal digital rights framework for transparency and accountability
- Fund civic and digital literacy in all public education systems
- Create paid public service pathways for youth and transitional workers
- Require ethical oversight in all federally funded tech development
- Launch public campaigns that restore the idea of democracy as a shared moral project

8. Strategic Rationale

A democracy that cannot govern its tools will be governed by them. Every authoritarian movement in history has sought to control communication, truth, and public attention. In the digital age, that power comes not only from the state, but from corporations and systems that shape behavior invisibly. Without laws, ethics, and civic readiness, democracy becomes hollow—even if elections continue. These reforms are essential because they restore public agency and make democracy durable in the face of rapid change. They are not about resisting technology, but about reclaiming control over what kind of world it builds.

. . .

9. What You Can Do

Support organizations that fight for data privacy, AI accountability, and platform transparency. Encourage your schools, libraries, and community centers to teach civic and digital literacy. Raise awareness in your networks about how algorithmic systems affect everything from hiring to healthcare. Volunteer for civic education initiatives, mentor young leaders, or join local advisory boards where public input is needed. The battle for the future is not abstract—it's personal, cultural, and winnable. What matters is whether enough of us choose to act.

10. Further Reading

Books such as *The Age of Surveillance Capitalism* by Shoshana Zuboff and *Tools and Weapons* by Brad Smith and Carol Ann Browne offer deep insight into the risks of unchecked technology. Articles like "The Coming AI Regulation Wars" from *The Atlantic* and "Algorithmic Justice" from the Electronic Frontier Foundation provide urgent context. For fiction that foretold this struggle, revisit *1984*, *The Terminator*, and *WarGames*—each a lens on the warning signs we ignored.

READER'S GUIDE: **Digital Maturity and Democratic Survival**

1. The Stakes

This chapter issues a stark warning: democracy cannot survive in a world where truth is unstable, privacy is nonexistent, and technological power is ungoverned. When algorithms determine what we see, say, and believe—and when those systems are opaque, manipulative, and unchecked—democracy becomes a performance, not a practice. The collapse is not a hypothetical future; it is already unfolding across every sector of public life. If we do not act to reassert human and democratic control over technology, we risk surrendering not just our choices, but our ability to choose at all.

2. The Structure

The chapter opens by naming the invisible threat posed by unregulated digital systems and contrasts constitutional ideals with current failures. It reviews America's historical lag in regulating technology, then details how AI, algorithms, and data exploitation undermine truth, privacy, equity, and safety. Case studies from health care, hiring, and law enforcement illustrate the harm. Fictional warnings—Orwell, Terminator, WarGames—are revisited as real-world analogies. The chapter closes by indicting Republican complicity and warning that without public understanding, reform is meaningless.

3. The Collapse

The erosion of truth and privacy is not the result of rogue actors —it is the outcome of systems designed to monetize attention, exploit data, and manipulate emotion. From deepfakes to algorithmic discrimination, technology is shaping decisions without oversight or recourse. Public institutions are overwhelmed, families are unprotected, and no consensus on reality can be reached. With AI increasingly used to hire, arrest, diagnose, and persuade, democracy becomes a casualty of opacity. And when leaders refuse to regulate or deliberately sabotage guardrails, collapse accelerates.

4. The Remedy

- Protect digital rights as civic rights—privacy, consent, transparency, and autonomy.
- Treat data as a public good, not private property— require clear regulation and consent.
- Regulate algorithmic systems used in hiring, policing, health, and finance.
- Require explainability, fairness audits, and appeal mechanisms for AI decisions.
- Ban targeted advertising to children and enforce protections against online harms.
- Restore net neutrality and fund independent oversight bodies for tech governance.
- Invest in digital literacy and civic education from childhood to adulthood.
- Mandate platform accountability for algorithmic amplification of disinformation.
- Ensure that public infrastructure—not just private firms —guides digital access and innovation.

5. What Comes Next

Later chapters build from this warning toward reform, beginning with a full blueprint for restoring democratic control over digital systems. The coming agenda includes transparency laws, civic technology initiatives, safeguards for truth and privacy, and new public options for communication infrastructure. This foundation is essential: without digital maturity, democratic survival cannot be sustained. The future we build must be governed by principles we choose—before it is governed by systems we no longer understand.

6. Three Things to Remember

1. Democracy cannot survive without control over the systems that govern truth, privacy, and attention.
2. The harms of unregulated technology are present now—not future threats, but current realities.
3. Without civic understanding, no technical reform will be enough to preserve freedom.

7. Action List

- Pass legislation requiring transparency, consent, and limits on data collection and sale.
- Establish independent oversight for all algorithmic systems used in public life.
- Ban algorithmic targeting of children and enforce age-appropriate protections online.
- Fund civic education programs that include digital ethics and resilience.
- Restore net neutrality and ensure broadband access as a public right.

- Require AI and algorithmic systems to undergo regular fairness audits and bias correction.
- Support journalism and fact-based media to counter disinformation.
- Create national standards for digital literacy in schools and public institutions.

8. Strategic Rationale

A democracy cannot function if citizens are manipulated, truth is fragmented, and power is invisible. Technology must serve the public, not exploit it. Governance of digital systems is now as essential as governance of elections, courts, or finance. Our capacity to understand, shape, and regulate digital life determines whether we remain a self-governing people—or become users of platforms we no longer control. Strategic reform now will prevent existential crisis later.

9. What You Can Do

Advocate for digital privacy laws in your state. Support public-interest tech coalitions. Refuse platforms that violate privacy or promote harm. Vote for candidates who understand and prioritize digital reform. Teach others how to recognize manipulation and protect their data. If you're an educator, parent, or student, push for digital literacy programs in your local school system. And always ask the most urgent question: who built this, and who benefits from your belief?

10. Further Reading

Recommended works include *The Age of Surveillance Capitalism* by Shoshana Zuboff, *Weapons of Math Destruction* by Cathy O'Neil, *Terms of Disservice* by Dipayan Ghosh, and the Mozilla Foundation's reports on algorithmic bias and transparency. Articles from the Center for Humane Technology, Brookings Institution, and Just Security also provide critical insight into platform governance, AI accountability, and democratic resilience in the digital age.

Reader's Guide: **Taking Back the Future**

1. The Stakes

This chapter delivers a comprehensive strategy for restoring democratic authority over digital systems before they permanently destabilize public life. It builds directly on the prior warning by proposing structural and civic reforms to reclaim truth, privacy, and cognitive sovereignty. From platform licensing to algorithm oversight and public digital infrastructure, it outlines how to govern the tools that govern us. Without such action, disinformation spreads unchecked, attention is commodified, and civic reasoning erodes. If the collapse of digital governance continues, every other reform collapses with it. But if we act now, we can still shape a future in which democracy endures.

2. The Structure

The chapter opens with a call to reject fatalism and assert democratic control. It separates digital platforms by purpose and proposes licensing based on content type, then introduces transparency laws, veracity settings, and AI auditability. Midway, it proposes a national council for algorithmic oversight and outlines citizen rights to data ownership and appeal. The second half focuses on structural reforms: platform compensation for journalism, public alternatives to corporate tools, and civic/digital literacy programs. It concludes with global examples of what has already been done—and a warning that without cognitive self-rule, every other democratic structure becomes unstable.

3. The Collapse

The chapter frames the collapse not as future dystopia, but

present disorder. Platforms shape perception, AI systems make public decisions, and truth is no longer a shared baseline. Private companies manipulate reality while avoiding scrutiny, and citizens lack both the tools and rights to defend themselves. Children are tracked, voters profiled, families targeted—and democracy becomes an illusion. If digital systems are not reined in by law, equity, and education, we risk a permanent loss of civic agency. The collapse is not just technological. It is constitutional, cultural, and existential.

4. The Remedy

- License platforms by content type: news, opinion, entertainment, propaganda.
- Require a "news license" for platforms distributing factual content—enforce verification, accuracy, and public accountability.
- Create veracity settings and ratings in all major search engines and AI tools.
- Build visible toggles to sort content by truth, source reliability, and citation confidence.
- Regulate all high-risk AI applications in law enforcement, health, education, and housing.
- Establish a National AI and Algorithmic Governance Council with oversight authority.
- Enforce explainability, auditability, and appeal rights in automated systems.
- Require social platforms to compensate journalism, modeled after Australia and Canada.
- Invest in public alternatives to search, learning, and communication tools.
- Protect personal data as private property; enforce consent, transparency, and restriction rights.

- Implement civic and digital literacy education across all schools, workplaces, and public institutions.

5. What Comes Next

Chapters that follow continue the agenda for democratic renewal by reinforcing the importance of civic strength, public belonging, and structural resilience. The fight for truth and digital sovereignty is foundational—without it, justice, elections, and equity cannot function. Having secured a roadmap for governing digital power, we next turn to how democratic culture can be preserved in the face of new challenges—from disinformation to civic fragmentation—and how people, not platforms, can remain at the center of public life.

6. Three Things to Remember

1. The future is not inevitable—it is shaped by those who govern the tools that govern us.
2. Licensing, transparency, and digital literacy are not censorship—they are democracy's survival tools.
3. No other reform will endure if we lose control over the systems that shape truth and trust.

7. Action List

- Pass legislation that licenses platforms by content function and enforces factual accountability for news.

- Implement national veracity settings in search engines and AI tools.
- Require AI audits, transparency reports, and citizen appeals in all automated decision systems.
- Establish an independent national council to regulate algorithmic and AI systems.
- Fund public digital infrastructure and open-source alternatives to major private platforms.
- Require compensation to journalism outlets when platforms re-host or monetize news content.
- Enforce privacy rights: require consent, allow deletion, and ban resale of personal data.
- Mandate digital and civic literacy education across all levels of schooling and public engagement.

8. Strategic Rationale

Digital systems are now the cognitive infrastructure of democracy. If left to private actors, they will optimize for profit—not truth, equity, or civic health. Without rules, education, and public alternatives, people lose agency, and institutions lose legitimacy. These reforms are not speculative. They are modeled on proven international frameworks and rooted in democratic principles. Strategic reform of digital governance does not restrain progress—it ensures it serves the people. We cannot legislate reality, but we can ensure that digital reality does not replace democracy.

9. What You Can Do

Speak up for platform accountability. Share stories of digital manipulation or AI harm with journalists, watchdog groups, or your representatives. Support local digital literacy initiatives and public libraries that teach media skills. Refuse platforms that profit from disinformation or violate consent. Ask your school board to incorporate digital ethics into civics education. Push for laws in your state that protect privacy and restrict exploitative data use. And help others—especially elders and youth—understand how digital systems work, so that civic power does not fade in silence.

10. Further Reading

Explore *The Black Box Society* by Frank Pasquale, *Reclaiming the Internet* by the Mozilla Foundation, and the OECD's AI Principles and implementation guidelines. See case studies from Finland's national curriculum in digital literacy, Australia's News Media Bargaining Code, the European Union's GDPR and AI Act, and Canada's Online News Act. For civic literacy, consult the Center for Civic Education and MediaWise's training for teens and adults. Leading edge research continues at Data & Society, the AI Now Institute, and the Berkman Klein Center at Harvard.

READER'S GUIDE: **Public Service and Civic Reengagement**

1. The Stakes

This chapter argues that democracy cannot survive without citizens who know how to participate and believe their participation matters. The collapse of civic life is not accidental—it is engineered, and it benefits those who seek power without accountability. Rebuilding civic capacity is not a sentimental task but a democratic necessity. This means restoring public service, civic education, and access to digital participation tools. Without a public that can think critically, act together, and feel they belong, no other reform will hold. If democracy is to endure, we must rebuild the habits and structures that make self-government possible.

2. The Structure

The chapter begins by grounding civic participation in constitutional commitments and historical precedent. It chronicles the collapse of civic capacity through defunding, digitization without access, and ideological attack. The middle presents key remedies: digital literacy, modern civic education, critical thinking, and revived national service. These proposals are framed not as add-ons, but as foundational infrastructure. The second half identifies deliberate sabotage by political actors—especially under Trump—and explains how disengagement benefits elites. The final sections call for investment in participation as a structural democratic repair, and emphasize that public service and civic belonging are not optional. They are what make everything else work.

3. The Collapse

Civic participation has withered through neglect, defunding, politicization, and digital exclusion. People no longer know their rights, how to participate, or why it matters. Service programs have been gutted. Civics classes have vanished. Digital systems now gatekeep access to basic functions, locking out the disconnected and undertrained. Critical thinking has been drowned in outrage and misinformation. These collapses are not just accidental—they are strategic, accelerated by political actors who gain from ignorance and disengagement. The result is a population unprepared to govern, vulnerable to manipulation, and increasingly fragmented from each other and from democratic life.

4. The Remedy

- Restore and expand national service programs like AmeriCorps, Peace Corps, and CCC.
- Modernize civic education: teach rights, responsibilities, tools of engagement, and digital navigation.
- Make computer literacy a core civic skill; ensure broadband, hardware, and training in all schools.
- Implement digital civics: teach how to track legislation, contact officials, organize, and protest.
- Teach critical thinking from middle school onward: bias detection, source verification, reflection.
- Fund libraries, community centers, and local forums for civic practice and participation.
- Protect teachers, librarians, and service workers from ideological attack and censorship.
- Create incentives for service: tuition credits, stipends, national honors, and pathways to leadership.
- Require all digital platforms used for public services to meet accessibility and usability standards.

- Treat civic capacity as national infrastructure: fund, evaluate, and continually renew it.

5. What Comes Next

Following this chapter, the agenda turns to how public trust is rebuilt—through shared belonging, fair access, and democratic renewal. Civic reengagement is the bridge between institutional reform and public resilience. Without it, even the best-designed systems will fail through neglect or sabotage. What comes next is a plan to protect and expand the cultural foundations of democracy—so that no citizen is left behind, no truth is left undefended, and no future is shaped without the people's voice.

6. Three Things to Remember

1. Democracy cannot survive without citizens who know their rights and how to use them.
2. Civic participation must be taught, supported, and rewarded—not left to chance.
3. National service and digital literacy are as essential to democracy as voting and free speech.

7. Action List

- Pass legislation to expand and fund modern service programs for all youth.
- Require digital civics and critical thinking as part of every school curriculum.

- Guarantee broadband access and computer training in all public schools and libraries.
- Protect civic educators from censorship, intimidation, and political interference.
- Provide public grants for local civic hubs: libraries, centers, community media.
- Set federal standards for digital usability in government services.
- Fund nonpartisan civic education campaigns through public media and partnerships.
- Create national service incentives: college aid, housing support, health benefits.
- Track and report annually on civic capacity metrics: trust, turnout, participation.

8. Strategic Rationale

No institution in a democracy can endure if the people lose the will or the skill to participate. The erosion of civic capacity benefits those who seek power without oversight and systems without accountability. Reviving civic engagement is not a feel-good initiative—it is a structural repair. We invest in public service, civic education, and participatory access for the same reason we build bridges or hospitals: because the nation does not function without them. This strategy equips every person with the means to belong, contribute, and hold power to account. It is democracy's survival plan.

9. What You Can Do

Volunteer for or donate to local civic education efforts or digital literacy programs. Advocate for the restoration of civics in your local school system. Contact representatives to support service legislation and public investment in participation. Start or join local groups that meet to discuss policy, organize action, or train new voters. Help elders and youth navigate public digital systems. Resist cynicism by modeling engagement. Teach others how to write to a senator, read a bill, or attend a town hall. Democracy is not something we inherit. It is something we practice.

10. Further Reading

See *Why We're Polarized* by Ezra Klein and *The Civic Mission of Schools* report by CIRCLE. Explore the work of organizations like iCivics, Facing History and Ourselves, and the National Conference on Citizenship. For digital tools, review CivicSwitch, Vote411, and BallotReady. Case studies include Finland's integrated digital curriculum, Germany's civic education mandates, and South Korea's service incentives. For structural analysis, consult the Aspen Institute's *Civic Life of the Nation* and Pew Research Center's *Trust and Democracy* series.

READER'S GUIDE: **Rebuilding Civic Power — How Public Service and Modern Civic Education Can Secure Democracy's Future**

1. **The Stakes**

If civic trust continues to erode, democracy will become hollow—its laws unenforced, its elections distrusted, and its people disempowered. Without shared service or common civic understanding, public life fractures into faction, fear, and apathy. Democracy's survival depends not only on institutions but on the capacity of ordinary people to participate, discern truth, and act together. In the absence of those skills and that spirit, no legal system or election mechanism can save a republic from collapse. Civic disengagement is not a passive problem—it is a national vulnerability.

2. **The Structure**

The chapter opens with a call to rebuild civic power as a structural necessity, not a sentimental ideal. It proposes three core pillars: a modern, inclusive public service corps; universal civic and digital education; and the cultural restoration of service as a respected national value. Each pillar is developed with concrete proposals and justification, followed by policy infrastructure, protections against politicization, and implementation mechanisms at every level of government. The chapter closes with urgency and resolve, declaring civic reengagement the foundation of democratic durability.

3. **The Collapse**

Civic participation in the U.S. has been undermined by disinvestment, fragmentation, and contempt for public institutions. Programs like AmeriCorps and Teach for America were defunded or politicized. Civic education eroded under testing regimes and culture wars. Service became undervalued, and digital skills—essential for public engagement—remained inaccessible to many. As civic tools disappeared, so did civic identity. The result is a public that often feels powerless, unprepared, or suspicious of its own democracy. That civic void is easily filled by disinformation, division, and despair.

4. The Remedy

- Establish a modern public service corps, open to all ages and backgrounds, with meaningful benefits and national visibility
- Provide stipends, career pathways, tuition forgiveness, housing support, and health coverage for service participants
- Focus service work on climate, disaster relief, education, elder care, infrastructure, and community technology
- Create a universal civic education curriculum, including lawmaking, local government, rights, and participation skills
- Incorporate modern digital civics: system navigation, disinformation awareness, and digital safety
- Guarantee broadband, devices, and tech support in every school and community learning center
- Expand AmeriCorps, Peace Corps, and launch a new Digital Service Corps
- Ensure low-barrier, inclusive access for immigrants, returning citizens, foster care alumni, and underserved groups
- Restore libraries, post offices, and schools as hubs of civic learning and service recruitment

- Protect civic programs from partisan distortion, unstable funding, and ideological influence

5. What Comes Next

Implementation must be both expansive and protected. The next phase is mobilizing political will, securing permanent funding, and insulating civic programs from polarization and misuse. Civic infrastructure must be maintained as national infrastructure, with accountability mechanisms and broad access. The long-term goal is a country where shared service and civic knowledge are as normal as voting—and where democracy is renewed not only through reform but through daily participation. Chapters ahead continue this vision of democratic durability through belonging, truth, and future readiness.

6. Three Things to Remember

1. Democracy requires more than elections—it needs educated, empowered people
2. Public service builds trust, unity, and practical repair at every level
3. Civic reengagement is the foundation that makes all other reforms possible

7. Action List

- Fund and launch a national public service corps modeled on proven programs

- Require and support universal civic education in all public schools
- Provide stable, nonpartisan funding to AmeriCorps, Peace Corps, and new civic initiatives
- Equip every school and library with broadband and digital access
- Integrate digital literacy and system navigation into adult education
- Expand eligibility for civic service to all residents regardless of background
- Designate post offices, schools, and community centers as civic learning hubs
- Legislate protections against ideological manipulation of civic programs

8. Strategic Rationale

Civic strength is national strength. A republic cannot endure without a public that can govern itself. Shared service and universal civic education reduce polarization, increase public accountability, and equip people to solve problems together. These reforms restore what democracy needs most: trust, truth, and the ability to act. They also prepare a rising generation with transferable skills, rebuild democratic norms, and inoculate the country against authoritarian drift. Civic reengagement is not an accessory—it is the scaffolding that holds the democratic structure upright.

9. What You Can Do

Support local civic education efforts by volunteering, advocating for curriculum updates, or attending school board meetings. Promote and participate in service projects—whether through

AmeriCorps, disaster relief, mutual aid, or community programs. Help young people apply for service opportunities or connect elders to mentorship programs. Contact legislators about funding public service and broadband access. Teach digital literacy in libraries or community centers. And model civic engagement—by voting, organizing, learning, and reminding others that the strength of our republic depends on its people.

10. Further Reading

See *The Upswing* by Robert Putnam and Shaylyn Romney Garrett for historical context on civic decline and renewal; *Civic Sermons* by Eric Liu for examples of public service as democratic faith in action; and *Our Kids* by Robert D. Putnam for insights into opportunity gaps and community connection. Also relevant is Danielle Allen's *Our Declaration*, which blends civic education with political philosophy, and the Knight Foundation's report *Beyond the Ballot*, which explores civic engagement in a digital age.

Reader's Guide: **The Future We Choose**

1. The Stakes

This chapter closes the fifth section of *American Redemption* by asserting that the survival of democracy in the digital age depends not on technology itself but on whether the public is prepared to use, govern, and shape it wisely. It warns that disinformation, disengagement, and platform chaos are not side effects but existential threats. The stakes are not theoretical: without digital literacy, civic renewal, and restored trust in public power, every other reform will collapse. This chapter reframes the future not as fate but as a political project—one that must be claimed, built, and protected if it is to serve democracy rather than destroy it.

2. The Structure

The chapter opens by dismantling the myth of technological inevitability and arguing instead for moral and civic authorship. It then recounts the erosion of public power in digital systems and the resulting collapse of trust. Citing both fictional and real-world examples, it identifies the dangers of an uninformed public in an AI-dominated information environment. The argument builds to a clear call: to prepare for the future not passively but through civic investment. The chapter names public service, civic education, and digital governance as essential to resilience, ending with both a warning and a charge.

3. The Collapse

The digital world—once celebrated as democratizing—is now distorted by invisible algorithms, surveillance capitalism, and disinformation at scale. Platforms amplify lies, isolate users, and reward fear. AI can mimic reality, manipulate voters, and erode trust faster than truth can recover. Meanwhile, the public is unequipped to navigate the information environment. Disconnection and confusion deepen apathy and polarization. As technology outpaces governance, democracy loses its grip not because of external conquest but from internal collapse—caused by a citizenry denied the tools to understand, respond, or resist.

4. The Remedy

- Build a future-oriented civic infrastructure rooted in education, service, and trust.
- Regulate digital platforms to protect users and uphold truth, not suppress dissent.
- Ensure universal digital literacy and civic fluency, beginning in schools.
- Fund, protect, and normalize national public service across generations.
- Expand support for libraries, journalism, and public knowledge institutions.
- Develop public technology systems governed by law, not profit.
- Reclaim cultural and political narratives from those who profit from chaos.
- Insulate civic and service programs from politicization and partisan capture.

5. What Comes Next

The chapters that follow will shift from defining problems and offering reforms to preparing for personal and collective readiness.

Where this section focused on how to shape the future at scale, the next section of the book—beginning with Phase I: Defense—equips individuals and communities for survival, resistance, and democratic renewal. Readers will now be invited to act directly and deliberately, not just by supporting policy change but by becoming stewards of democracy in their own lives, neighborhoods, and networks.

6. Three Things to Remember

1. The future is not predetermined—it is something we build, protect, and choose.
2. No democracy can survive if people cannot tell truth from lies or use the systems that govern them.
3. Civic service, education, and digital literacy are not luxuries—they are the new infrastructure of freedom.

7. Action List

- Enact and enforce digital platform regulations that protect truth and public safety.
- Provide universal access to modern, nonpartisan civic education in schools.
- Establish a new Digital Service Corps to support ethical tech development.
- Expand national service programs with meaningful stipends and career support.
- Fund digital literacy programs in libraries, job centers, and community colleges.

- Protect public-interest journalism and prevent media consolidation.
- Insulate service and education programs from ideological censorship.
- Incentivize state and local partnerships to support federal civic initiatives.

8. Strategic Rationale

Without a civically fluent and digitally capable public, every other reform proposed in this book is vulnerable to sabotage, apathy, or collapse. The digital environment mediates nearly all aspects of modern democracy—elections, education, employment, and protest alike. Preparing for the future means designing systems that restore agency, fight confusion, and ensure that power answers to people. Rebuilding truth, trust, and public power is not idealism—it is survival strategy. It is how we inoculate the republic against authoritarian decay.

9. What You Can Do

Join or support civic service programs in your state. Demand civic education in local schools. Take a digital literacy course or help a community group offer one. Subscribe to and share public-interest journalism. Write to your representatives about tech accountability and AI regulation. Host a discussion group about the future of democracy. Contribute to library funding initiatives. Speak out when civic education or public service is mocked or defunded. Every act that strengthens public capacity is an act of democratic defense.

. . .

10. Further Reading

See *Surveillance Capitalism* by Shoshana Zuboff for an in-depth look at the power of tech platforms, *Democracy in the Age of AI* by Nathan Gardels and Nicolas Berggruen for a global policy perspective, and *Digital Minimalism* by Cal Newport for strategies to reclaim agency. The Aspen Institute's "Commission on Information Disorder" report outlines actionable reforms, while *The People vs. Tech* by Jamie Bartlett explores how digital systems threaten democratic norms. All are accessible online or through major libraries.

READER'S GUIDE: AMERICAN REDEMPTION

Reader's Guide: American Redemption

1. The Stakes

This chapter closes the trilogy with a sobering truth: American democracy is not lost—but it is on the edge of collapse. The stakes are generational. If we fail to resist authoritarian capture now, the next generation will inherit not a republic, but its ruins. Every reform named in this book depends on one outcome: whether a self-governing people still exist—and are willing to act. This is not theory. It is survival. The choice between tyranny and rebirth must be made now.

2. The Structure

The chapter opens with a warning: that democracy does not end with a single leader but with a pattern of erosion. It traces that pattern across decades, detailing the design and acceleration of democratic collapse. It names the inflection points. Then it pivots: to what remains possible, to what must be built, and to what timeline is still available. It ends with a direct commission to the reader—naming the work ahead, the urgency of leadership, and the final window of opportunity.

3. The Collapse

American democracy has not been defeated by invasion, but by design. From voter suppression to judicial capture, media corruption to economic sabotage, the systems that once supported self-government have been repurposed to serve minority rule. What failed was not just policy, but the moral and structural core of the republic. Institutions now serve power, not people. The appearance of democracy remains—but the substance is gone unless restored by collective action.

4. The Remedy

- Reclaim the moral clarity that democracy is not inevitable—and act accordingly
- Name and undo the structural designs of minority rule and authoritarian entrenchment
- Resist immediate harms through coordinated defense at every level of government
- Elect a pro-democracy Congress in 2026 and reclaim the White House in 2028
- Restore a full legislative agenda by 2032 to rebuild the foundation of democratic life

- Remove or replace officials—Democratic or Republican—who fail to defend the republic
- Reimagine leadership as service, and elevate those who live that principle
- Refuse nostalgia and rebuild from what was good and what was never just
- Treat housing, child care, digital safety, and fair taxation as core democratic infrastructure
- Recognize that redemption is not restoration alone—but a long act of becoming

5. What Comes Next

This is the final chapter—but not the end of the work. What comes next is the test of everything written here. Will we act in time? Will we rise beyond exhaustion, denial, or despair? The future is unwritten—but the clock is not. The next page belongs to all of us. What we do now will determine whether future generations inherit a republic—or wonder how we lost one.

6. Three Things to Remember

1. Democracy does not collapse all at once—it is dismantled by design
2. Redemption is not purity—it is refusal to surrender
3. The future is not written—but it is ours to write, starting now

7. Action List

- Build, fund, and support pro-democracy coalitions at every electoral level
- Remove from office any official—regardless of party—who enables authoritarian power
- Create and share public education campaigns about the stakes of 2026–2040
- Elevate local leadership committed to justice, truth, and democratic service
- Fight gerrymandering, court capture, and voter suppression with coordinated legal and political strategy
- Center care, dignity, and equality in every reform—housing, health, work, education
- Demand institutional accountability from courts, agencies, and media
- Prepare for and resist authoritarian policy through nonviolent, organized, strategic defense

8. Strategic Rationale

Nothing else in this book matters if we do not act on it. The structural repairs are real—but they require power to enact, and people to defend. Redemption is not a return to 1950 or 1990. It is a forward act: of undoing what is unjust, rebuilding what was destroyed, and creating what has never existed. Every other democracy that fell thought it had more time. We must not make that mistake.

9. What You Can Do

Start now. Talk to people who don't know what's at stake. Support local elections. Volunteer in key districts. Join a movement. Run for office if you can. Give if you cannot. Reject fatalism. Share the truth. Keep learning. Hold the line. Restore what you can. And never forget: your actions, now, are not small. They are the test of democracy itself.

10. Further Reading

To understand the broader arc of democratic collapse and resistance, see *How Democracies Die* by Levitsky and Ziblatt and *On Tyranny* by Timothy Snyder. For an American lens, read *The Fifth Risk* by Michael Lewis and *Twilight of Democracy* by Anne Applebaum. For strategy and action, follow reports from Protect Democracy, Democracy Docket, and the Brennan Center for Justice.

READER'S GUIDE: AMERICAN REINSTITUTION

R eader's Guide: American Reinstitution

1. The Stakes

A democracy cannot survive on adrenaline. The American people did the impossible: they defended the republic through crisis. But the end of emergency does not mean the end of danger. Without reinstitution—without deliberate anchoring of reforms, values, laws, and civic norms—every gain remains fragile. Emergency powers must be wound down. Structural protections must be codified. And a culture of truth, accountability, and public duty must be restored. This is the final task of a surviving republic: not simply to rebuild what was lost, but to ensure it cannot be lost again. The stakes are existential. Either we anchor democracy now—or watch it unravel once more.

2. The Structure

This chapter is structured as a constitutional reckoning after survival. It opens with a moral framing: emergency cannot become the norm. It then presents four sections. First, emergency powers that must be rescinded or rebalanced. Second, permanent reforms that must be locked into law. Third, civic and cultural norms that cannot be legislated but are essential to democratic durability. And fourth, a redefinition of public leadership rooted in service, not ambition. The conclusion returns to the six constitutional promises, declaring this work not only as restoration, but as a generational covenant to preserve democracy's future.

3. The Collapse

America entered an era of constitutional breakdown that lasted decades. What followed—the rise of minority rule, court capture, executive overreach, disinformation, and legal paralysis—nearly dismantled the republic. Restoration was only possible through extraordinary emergency action: expanding courts, overriding state suppression, asserting federal control, and suspending traditional norms. These acts were not partisan overreach; they were survival. But survival alone is insufficient. A democracy cannot permanently function in a state of exception. The longer emergency measures remain in place, the greater the risk that they, too, will become tools of abuse. That is the collapse reinstitution must now prevent.

4. The Remedy

- Sunset or rebalance all emergency measures, including court expansion and filibuster suspension

- Codify permanent reforms: term limits, ethics rules, campaign finance, and voting rights
- Rebuild civic norms through education, truth-telling, and cultural memory
- Create constitutional firewalls around DOJ, FBI, elections, and emergency powers
- Clarify Second Amendment limits and enforce firearm responsibility
- End gerrymandering and restore proportional, fair elections
- Disqualify insurrectionists under Section 3 of the 14th Amendment
- Redefine political leadership as civic duty—enforce term limits, ban lobbying and stock trading
- Replace corporate-controlled platforms with public digital infrastructure
- Require full tax, financial, and conflict disclosures for public officials

5. What Comes Next

Every era leaves a legacy. Ours must be reinstitution: the full embedding of structural democracy. That means dismantling what was built in crisis, but keeping what sustains the republic. It means translating moral awakening into law, and law into civic habit. Cultural norms must be taught anew. Leadership must be redefined for a generation unafraid to serve and step aside. This is not about returning to a past. It is about anchoring a future no demagogue can again endanger. What comes next is the final turn—from emergency to equilibrium, from resistance to permanence, from redemption to endurance.

. . .

6. Three Things to Remember

1. Emergency is not a destination—it is a bridge to equilibrium
2. No reform lasts unless it is codified, taught, and expected
3. Democracy survives only when we anchor it with intention

7. Action List

- Repeal or limit temporary emergency powers used during the Restoration phase
- Pass constitutional amendments to safeguard elections, ethics, and campaign finance
- Enact a national Voting Rights Act 2.0 with automatic registration and equal access
- Implement term limits and public funding for Congress and the Court
- Establish and fund national civic education for all ages
- Prohibit lobbying, stock trading, and donor capture among elected officials
- Create a National Museum of the American Collapse and Restoration
- Legislate a public digital infrastructure for elections and information
- Restrict future use of "national emergency" powers by statute
- Institutionalize disqualification procedures for insurrection and lying under oath

8. Strategic Rationale

This is the capstone to the American Redemption trilogy. The Restoration chapter showed what needed to be done. Reinstitution shows what must endure. It finalizes the work of democratic renewal—not by idealizing the past, but by designing forward. Every reform is both shield and foundation. Every reversal of emergency powers is a signal: the republic does not need constant adrenaline to survive. What it needs is memory, law, and leadership. If this phase fails, all others will be undone. If it holds, democracy gains not just a new chapter—but a fighting chance at another 250 years.

9. What You Can Do

Support and campaign for candidates who publicly commit to codifying permanent reforms and winding down emergency powers. Share the idea of reinstitution with civic groups, school boards, veterans' organizations, and community forums. Encourage local schools and libraries to teach democratic structure, civic norms, and the Restoration era as part of U.S. history. Reach out to media outlets and elected officials demanding action on ethics, term limits, and digital accountability. And above all, live the civic values described in this chapter—truth, restraint, memory, service—as if they were yours to protect. Because they are.

10. Further Reading

For historical context and democratic design, see *The Fifth Risk* by Michael Lewis and *How Democracies Die* by Steven Levitsky and Daniel Ziblatt. For civic renewal and ethical leadership, consult Danielle Allen's *Our Declaration* and David Blight's *American Oracle*. On memory and reinstitution, Timothy Snyder's *On Tyranny* and Anne Applebaum's *Twilight of Democracy* are indispensable. Finally, for legal frameworks and democratic durability, examine Lawrence Lessig's *They Don't Represent Us* and the Brennan Center's published series on constitutional reform and electoral integrity.

AFTERWORD: THE REDEMPTION ARCHITECTURE

"I am planting a tree under whose shade I do not expect to sit."
— Greek Proverb

Every generation has its moonshot.

When President John F. Kennedy declared that the United States would go to the moon—not because it was easy, but because it was hard—he summoned the full force of government, science, labor, education, and imagination. It wasn't a single act. It was a unified endeavor. Thousands of engineers, welders, physicists, machinists, mathematicians, and teachers worked toward the same goal. Not every part of the system worked perfectly—but enough worked together, and in the same direction—to land a human being on the moon. What mattered was not that every piece was flawless—but that every piece knew its purpose.

That is what we ask of this generation: not perfection, but alignment. Not certainty, but clarity of aim. Our task is no less audacious. To build a democracy that delivers—not in theory or sentiment, but in lived and measurable ways—on the Constitution's six promises:

safety, liberty, justice, equality, voice, and belonging. That is our North Star. And like the moon landing, it will not come from one bill, one leader, or one party. It will come from a system that understands its purpose and aims its tools in the same direction.

To succeed, we may need to reimagine the tools themselves. Some departments will need to change. Missions will need to be clarified. Where agencies overlap or compete, we must choose collaboration over turf. Homeland Security cannot be a holding tank for every threat we refuse to define. Immigration cannot be split between three cabinets. Public transportation cannot live apart from affordable housing. The Department of Labor must not be siloed from education, nor education from democracy. Reorganizing does not mean starting over. It means recognizing that a government built to preserve privilege will not—cannot—deliver justice. Structure follows purpose—and if the purpose is freedom that lasts, then our institutions must reflect that aim.

But no structure works without people. This blueprint cannot build itself. It must be carried out by millions of people who choose service, who train for it, who accept imperfect tools and still go to work every day to make them better. They will not be famous. They will not go viral. But they will build the future. We will need new teachers, case workers, transit planners, digital defenders, court reporters, and counselors. We will need cabinet secretaries who see themselves as stewards, not celebrities. We will need thousands of quiet heroes—and millions of determined citizens—working toward something larger than themselves. That is the only way this lasts.

No plan is flawless. This one is surely not. But it is possible. It is principled. It is ready to be taken up and tested and made better by those who follow. And if it works—if it delivers, and delivers, and delivers—it will be because enough people understood the moment they lived in and chose to build something worthy of it.

We've begun the work. Now we pass it to you—deliberately, and with hope.

— Jim Vincent, August 2025

EPILOGUE: THE CIRCLE WE COMPLETE

"The future is not a gift. It is an achievement."
— Robert F. Kennedy

We began in survival.

American Renewal was written in the shadow of collapse—the second Trump presidency, the dismantling of democratic guardrails, the erosion of public trust. It was not a platform. It was a lifeline. A call to hold. A plan to endure. A vow to refuse surrender—while there was still something left to save.

Then came the work of recovery. *American Restoration* laid out the blueprint for what must follow defense: to rebuild what was broken, restore what was stolen, and redeem the promises that democracy had made but failed to keep. It was not idealism. It was repair.

But repair alone is not enough.

American Redemption answered the deeper question: What does it mean to be a free people, governed by shared purpose, with no one left out or left behind? These were not reforms for convenience or efficiency. They were reforms for belonging. They were a reckoning with the country we became—and a declaration of the country we still could be.

And now we arrive at reinstitution. The final turning of the arc. Not back to what was—but forward to what lasts. What can endure not four years, but four generations. Not only because we designed it better, but because we remembered who we are.

This book is not the end of the work. It is the moment of handing over. We have written down everything we know—about power, about harm, about hope. We have mapped what collapsed, why it mattered, and how it can be rebuilt. But none of it will live unless it lives in you.

This is your country. Your inheritance. Your possibility. Your unfinished sentence.

History will not remember most of us by name. But it will remember whether the arc we stood on bent toward cruelty or courage. Whether we flinched—or held. Whether we waited for permission—or began.

We do not know who will pick up this book in ten years or fifty. But if you do, and if your hands are steady and your heart still burns, know this: we wrote it for you.

Because we believed you would come.

Because we believed that—even after everything—someone would still care enough to continue.

And if you are that person, then nothing is lost.

Not yet.

Not ever.

APPENDIX A: AMERICAN REDEMPTION – FIXING WHAT NO LONGER WORKS

These reforms were not written as policy preferences. They were built as tests of democratic function. Each one identifies a systemic failure that regulation could not fix—and then proposes a structural alternative designed to last. The result is not a wishlist, but a new foundation for a democratic state—where public power is used to solve shared problems, and where fairness is not a slogan, but a system you can count on.

Each reform in *American Redemption* follows a shared arc. First, it exposes the failure of regulation—not because oversight is useless, but because it is often reversible, captured, or too slow to meet the scale of collapse. Second, it names how the dominant for-profit system betrayed public trust—by treating citizens as customers, workers as costs, and democracy as an obstacle to extraction. And finally, it offers a public alternative strong enough to compete, stabilize, and reset the field—not by force, but by proof. Each is designed to work—not through control, but through credibility.

Together, they reflect a single insight: *you cannot fix captured systems by regulating them better—you must build something better.* These reforms aim to replace systems that extract with systems that protect. Each one is a standalone response. And taken together, they form an interdependent structure of democratic restoration—a republic that serves the people, and is built to last.

Reform Summaries by Domain

I. A Nation That Cares for Its Own

Universal Health Care

The U.S. health care system is the most expensive in the world—and among the least fair. Regulation has tried to patch gaps through mandates, subsidies, and insurance expansions, but the underlying model remains fractured and extractive. For-profit insurers deny care to maximize margin; hospital chains consolidate and inflate prices. The proposed reform does not eliminate private care—but it creates a robust, universal public option: guaranteed, portable, and free at the point of service for all essential care. Built correctly, it will outcompete private offerings on simplicity, trust, and transparency—reshaping incentives across the entire sector. It anchors every other reform by eliminating medical debt, restoring trust, and treating health as a right, not a reward.

II. A Nation That Educates and Elevates

Dignity Without Debt

Higher education in America has been restructured around debt. Regulation has tried to manage tuition spikes and predatory lending, but the student loan economy now traps generations in long-term economic instability. This reform addresses the crisis from two ends: (1) making public colleges tuition-free or debt-minimal, and (2) elevating non-college pathways—technical, civic, and community-based learning—as equally valid forms of contribution. The goal is not simply access, but fairness: no one should be penalized for seeking education, nor privileged for affording it. This reform helps reset labor, civic trust, and economic mobility by ending a system that punishes aspiration.

III. A Nation That Is Safe, Just, and Free

To Serve and Protect

American policing has grown too broad, too violent, and too unaccountable to meet the standard of democratic public safety. Regulation has failed—because it cannot address the core design flaw: that policing is often the first response to problems it cannot solve. This reform narrows the role of armed officers, redirects resources to trained responders for mental health, domestic calls, and community mediation, and builds oversight into every layer of the system. Safety is redefined—not as control, but as competence. The goal is not to abolish police, but to redesign public safety from the ground up—centered in restraint, trust, and service.

IV. A Nation That Belongs to Everyone

Immigration and Citizenship

The immigration system in the United States has collapsed under decades of cruelty, contradiction, and congressional inaction. Reform efforts have failed because they have tried to regulate dysfunction without redesigning the process itself. This reform proposes a full reorganization: restoring lawful, timely, and humane pathways to entry, permanent residency, and citizenship. It ends exploitative bottlenecks, enforces due process, and honors both border order and human dignity. Democracy begins with who belongs. This reform ensures that belonging is a function of law—not race, fear, or power.

V. A Nation That Prepares for the Future

Digital Maturity and Democratic Survival

Digital systems now mediate nearly every aspect of civic life—from voting and employment to education and public discourse. But they operate without consistent regulation, public design, or civic obligation. Algorithms profit from division; platforms optimize for attention, not truth. This reform sets clear national standards for data privacy, online integrity, and algorithmic transparency—alongside a publicly governed digital service infrastructure that provides trusted civic access, especially in marginalized communities. A democracy cannot survive if its digital environment is hostile to truth, privacy, or participation. This reform defines the rules—and builds the tools—for a democratic digital future.

Closing Integration

The strength of these reforms is not just in their moral clarity or structural soundness—but in how they support each other. Universal health care eases pressure on wages and retirement. Labor protections make education more equitable. Fair taxation funds public infrastructure without distortion. A lawful immigration system supports family, economy, and trust. Digital regulation defends truth and participation across every sector.

THIS IS NOT A CHECKLIST. It is a civic architecture. A system of interdependent reforms that—together—create the conditions under which democracy can be real, felt, and permanent. They cannot all pass at once. But they must all be part of the frame. Because the goal is not just to win power. It is to build a country that keeps its word.

ALSO BY JIM VINCENT

American Renewal: A Manifesto for Resistance, a Blueprint for Restoration, and a Vision for Redemption

Vincent Press, 2025   ISBN: 978-1-7641693-0-1

American Renewal (Extended Edition): Now with Reader's Guides

Vincent Press, 2025   ISBN: 978-1-7641693-1-8

American Restoration: Rebuilding the Foundations of Democracy

Vincent Press, 2025   ISBN: 978-1-7641693-2-5

American Restoration (Extended Edition): Now with Reader's Guides

Vincent Press, 2025   ISBN: 978-1-7641693-3-2

American Redemption: A Government of the People, by the People, for the People

Vincent Press, 2025   ISBN: 978-1-7641693-4-9

American Redemption (Extended Edition): Now with Reader's Guides

Vincent Press, 2025   ISBN: 978-1-7641693-5-6

Essays on Tyranny: Resisting Trump's Attack on Democracy

Vincent Press, 2025   ISBN: 978-1-7641693-6-3

The Quiet Habit of Giving: The Quiet Practices That Make Love Last

Vincent Press, 2025   ISBN: 978-1-7641693-7-0

Every Day: Turning Betrayal into Recovery

Vincent Press, 2025   ISBN: 978-1-7641693-8-7

ABOUT THE AUTHOR

Jim Vincent is a U.S. citizen, born and raised in the United States, where he lived for fifty years. He now resides in Australia, with children and grandchildren still living in the country he calls home. His writing reflects both an unbreakable connection to the American experiment, and a deep concern for its survival.

As an American living overseas, Vincent brings a perspective shaped by two advantages: distance from the tribal divisions that dominate U.S. politics, and the lived experience of another functioning democracy. From that vantage point, he sees more clearly what has been lost in the United States—and what remains possible.

He is the founder of *Jim Vincent US*, an independent publication focused on resisting authoritarianism and rebuilding democratic power. His *American Renewal* trilogy—comprising *American Renewal*,

American Restoration, and *American Redemption*—offers not just a warning, but a blueprint. It is a body of work grounded in history, strategy, and moral clarity. He writes not for applause, but for action—because the republic must be reclaimed, not remembered.

He can be reached at https://jimvincentus.substack.com

COLOPHON

American Redemption is the third and final volume of the *American Renewal* trilogy, following *American Renewal* and *American Restoration*. Together, these books chart a path from democratic survival to democratic permanence—from resistance, to repair, to reinstitution. Across the trilogy, thirty-six reforms are proposed as foundational requirements of a just and enduring republic. This is not the end of our responsibility. But it is the completed blueprint for those who choose to carry the work forward.

www.ingramcontent.com/pod-product-compliance
Lightning Source LLC
Chambersburg PA
CBHW061205070526
44583CB00025B/3117